The Long Night of the Watchman

Other Works of Interest from St. Augustine's Press

James V. Schall, S.J., *The Regensburg Lecture*

James V. Schall, S.J., *Modern Age*

James V. Schall, S.J., *The Classical Moment*

James V. Schall, S.J., *The Sum Total of Human Happiness*

James V. Schall, S.J., *Remembering Belloc*

Marc D. Guerra, ed., *Jerusalem, Athens, and Rome:*
Essays in Honor of James V. Schall, S.J.

Karol Wojtyła, [Pope John Paul II], *Man in the*
Field of Responsibility

Ernest Fortin, A.A., *Christianity and Philosophical Culture*
in the Fifth Century

Servais Pinckaers, O.P., Morality: *The Catholic View*

Rémi Brague, *On the God of the Christians*
(and on one or two others)

Josef Pieper and Heinz Raskop, *What Catholics Believe*

Josef Pieper, *Happiness and Contemplation*

Josef Pieper, *The Christian Idea of Man*

Gabriel Marcel, *Man against Mass Society*

Dietrich von Hildebrand, *The Heart*

Robert Hugh Benson, *Lord of the World*

Peter Kreeft, *The Philosophy of Jesus*

Peter Kreeft, *Jesus-Shock,*

H.S. Gerdil, *The Anti-Emile:*
Reflections on the Theory and Practice of Education
against the Principles of Rousseau

George William Rutler, *Principalities and Powers:*
Spiritual Combat 1942–1943

The Long Night of the Watchman
Essays by Václav Benda, 1977–1989

Edited by F. Flagg Taylor IV

Translated by Barbara Day

ST. AUGUSTINE'S PRESS
South Bend, Indiana

Manufactured in the United States of America.

2 3 4 5 6   27 26 25 24 23 22

Library of Congress Cataloging in Publication Data: 2017938396

ISBN 9781587314780

The paper used in this publication meets the minimum requirements of the American National Standard for Information Sciences - Permanence of Paper for Printed Materials, ANSI Z39.48-1984.

St. Augustine's Press
www.staugustine.net

Acknowledgments

Many people and institutions have been essential to the publication of this book. The translation was made possible by funds from two sources: the Dean of the Faculty's Office at Skidmore College and Pavel Bratinka and other friends and associates of Václav Benda. My travel to the Czech Republic has been supported by Faculty Development Grants from Skidmore College, the H. B. Earhart Foundation and the Judith Johnson Carrico '65 Fund. I am very grateful for the generosity of all of these individuals and institutions. My initial interest in the Czech Republic was generated by a trip funded by my wonderful mother!

I thank the Benda family and Erik Lukavský at Fra, the publisher of the Czech volume on which this translation is based, for permission to use these texts for Barbara Day's English translation. Paul Wilson generously granted permission to use his translations of chapters 11 and 19, and František Janouch, the publisher and editor of the volume *A Besieged Culture* granted permission to use the translation of chapter 30. Many thanks to Ondřej Němec for his permission to use his photograph for the cover of the book and to my student Maddy Morency for her cover design.

It has been a true pleasure working with Barbara Day on this book. She is a tireless and exacting translator. Barbara and I also want to extend many thanks on this score to Pavel Bratinka. Pavel read the entire manuscript and checked the translation against the Czech version. It is always a great benefit to be able to rely on a native speaker and he saved us from more than a few errors. Pavel has been extraordinarily patient with my numerous email inquiries about translation problems and various references which most English speakers would miss. My editorial notes also owe much to his wisdom and generosity. I would also like to thank Marketa Goetz-Stankiewicz for her insights on both the Czech language and the world of Czech dissent.

Adam Hradilek of the Institute for the Study of Totalitarian Regimes arranged my first meeting with the Bendas back in 2011. He and Barbara Day have both been crucial in assisting me with introductions to various people in the dissident community. It was at that first meeting that Kamila Bendová showed me the Czech edition of her late husband's writings.

Getting to know Kamila and her son Patrik has truly been one of the great privileges of my life. They have been unfailingly generous in spending time with me during my visits to Prague. The hours together discussing their family's life under Communism have been extraordinarily fruitful and meaningful. I cannot express how grateful I am for their willingness to discuss their experiences. Kamila's courage and selflessness are something to behold.

Table of Contents

Introduction

The names of Aleksandr Solzhenitsyn and Václav Havel are now familiar to many with an interest in the rise and fall of totalitarian regimes in the twentieth century. Each figure has multiple biographies written about him and many of their writings have been translated into English. Yet the fight for freedom, especially in the case of the former Czechoslovakia, was waged by many individuals who were quite thoughtful about the nature of their totalitarian enemy and how their battle could and should be fought and won. Václav Benda (1946–1999), a close friend and ally of Havel's, is one such figure and his writings deserve a wide audience.

Benda was one of the central figures in the Czech dissident movement of the 1970s and 1980s. He was twice a spokesman for Charter 77 and a founding member of VONS (the Czech acronym for The Committee to Defend the Unjustly Persecuted). Benda was also a leader of one of the three primary subgroups within the broader Charter 77 community. There was an avowedly leftist contingent, made up mostly of ex-Communists (many purged as the party was "normalized" in the aftermath of the Prague Spring in 1968) and socialists of various stripes.[1] Then there was a secular, intellectual and artistic contingent who usually had not been involved with the party or politics more generally—this was the milieu from which Havel emerged. Finally, there was a religious group, some of them Catholic and some Protestant. Members of this third group seldom had any connection to the Communist Party and some—such as Benda—had more conservative views than many of their fellow Chartists. Throughout Charter 77's

---

1   "Normalization" was the term used by the Communist Party of Czechoslovakia to describe the process of purging the reformist and unreliable elements from within the Party and reasserting its totalitarian control in the aftermath of the Soviet invasion of August 1968.

existence there was a kind of tacit agreement that the three spokespersons should be representatives of these three groups.[2]

Benda began studying philosophy and Czech literature at the Philosophical Faculty of Charles University in Prague in 1964. In January 1968 he was elected by his fellow students as the chairman of a new independent organization called the Academic Council of Students. After a brutal crackdown on a student demonstration in late October 1967 near Strahov, this organization called for the resignation of the Minister of the Interior. They also worked hard to encourage the rehabilitation of renowned professors like Václav Černy and Jan Patočka who had been expelled from the university. After the Soviet invasion in August 1968, the Philosophical Faculty was "normalized." Only faculty members who approved of the "fraternal assistance" of their Soviet comrades were allowed to retain their positions. In September 1969 Benda left the Philosophical Faculty to join the Natural Science Faculty where it was also possible to study philosophy. However, three days after his arrival all teaching stopped. Six months later this department would become an institute for the study of Marxism-Leninism and its faculty would also be required to sign a statement approving of the Soviet invasion. Benda again moved, this time to the faculty of Mathematics where he studied computer science. His wife Kamila, whom he had married in 1967, took her degree in Mathematics in 1969. Kamila would find employment at the Institute of Mathematics at the Czech Academy of Sciences and Václav, while continuing his studies, supplemented their income by doing translations from German to Czech. Václav took his degree from the Faculty of Mathematics in 1975 and would find his way to employment at the Research Institute for Computers in the winter of 1976. And here is where the writings collected in the present volume begin. In "A Small Lesson in Democracy" (the first essay collected in this volume), Benda recounts his dismissal from this Institute as a result of his signing Charter 77.[3]

2   On Charter 77 readers should consult the many works of Gordon H. Skilling, Jonathan Bolton's *Worlds of Dissent: Charter 77, The Plastic People of the Universe, and Czech Culture Under Communism* (Boston: Harvard University Press, 2012), and Michael Zantovsky's *Havel: A Life* (New York: Grove Press, 2015).
3   Any biographical and personal details contained in this introduction are derived from my interviews with Kamila Bendová, her son Patrik Benda (editor

Law and Publicity

The Declaration of Charter 77 was released on January 1, 1977 and it had 243 initial signatories. It declared that it had "no rules, permanent bodies, or formal membership." Instead, it described itself as a "loose, informal and open association of people of various shades of opinions, faiths and professions." What united this informal group was a "will to strive individually and collectively for the respecting of civil and human rights." The Charter seized on what was initially dismissed as a pointless and symbolic gesture by many in the West. The gesture was part of the Helsinki Accords of 1975, the negotiations conducted for and the agreement resulting from the Conference on Security and Cooperation in Europe. These negotiations were aimed at reducing Cold War tensions. One plank of the final agreement meant that signatories would formally recognize the borders and territorial arrangements in place since World War II. Thus it seemed to legitimize the Soviet domination of its Warsaw Pact satellites. In exchange, the West required that these countries sign on to international covenants on a range of political, civil, and economic rights—covenants that virtually nobody in the West expected the Communist regimes to abide by. But these two international covenants actually became part of the Czechoslovak legal code in October 1976. Charter 77 declared that Czechoslovak citizens were entitled to these rights and it was also the state's duty to ensure that such rights were secured and respected for its people.

The Charter announced that the state must live by its own laws. The Declaration pointed to a number of areas where freedoms such as public expression and religious confession were not secured but directly infringed by the state. Charter 77 thus carefully avoided casting itself as any kind of political opposition. It took advantage of a statutory right of Czechoslovak law—the right of petition—and announced its intention to use that right to continue to point out when and how the political authorities failed in their legal duties. Thus the Charter encouraged Czechoslovak

of the Czech volume on which this translation is based), and Pavel Bratinka, a close friend of the Benda family. Readers may wish to consult one of my interviews with Mr. Bratinka: "Hope and Change, Czech Style," *The American Interest* (January/February 2012), pp. 84–91.

citizens to take the law seriously and to use whatever possible legal appeals they could to their own advantage.

Despite the fact that Charter 77 was technically legal under Czechoslovak law, the regime refused to acknowledge this fact. It undertook a particularly vicious media campaign in the late winter and spring of 1977 without ever publishing even the smallest part of the declaration. Signatories and sympathizers were ridiculed and smeared in public—some imprisoned—and the broader population was incentivized to join in the condemnation. Needless to say, signatories had no means publicly to refute these smears. This culminated in a disgraceful event at the National Theatre in the spring when prominent cultural figures signed the "Anti-Charter" (without any familiarity with a single word of the declaration) on national television and urged others to join them. Václav Benda signed the Charter during this counter-offensive by the regime. The viciousness of the response actually convinced Benda that the Charter was something worth supporting—anything that upset the regime that much demanded his involvement. The decision to sign was very much a family decision. Benda had been married to his wife Kamila for a decade and they already had five children. Even though they knew there would likely be consequences for their family—the termination of Benda's employment and reduced educational opportunities for their children—they also wanted to live according to their beliefs. The decision ended up bringing their family closer together. The regime certainly raised the costs of having any connection to the Charter movement. In rushing to the defense of those persecuted by the regime, the dissidents would discover another key element of their strategy: publicity.

This part of the story begins with a party—a "ball" to be more precise, the Railway Workers' Ball which was held at the end of January 1978. As Benda put it at the time, "It's bad for your health to meet only at funerals and in front of court buildings" (13). So many Chartists hit upon the idea of attending the ball and having a pleasant winter night out for a change. Tickets and clothing were purchased for the event. The StB (secret police), however, got wind of this plan and stationed themselves at the door and throughout the event. Some Chartists were simply refused entry and got their money back. Others, however, were roughed up by the police and arrested. Three people were detained: Havel, Pavel Landovsky, and Jaroslav

Kukal. A committee was formed to protest the unjust imprisonment of these three men and a letter was circulated to publicize their fate as widely as possible. In about six weeks, the three men were released. In this case, the publicity and the resulting pressure seemed to have the desired effect! This was the precedent for the formation of a supplementary organization to Charter 77, known by its Czech acronym VONS, the Committee to Defend the Unjustly Persecuted. The Committee issued its declaration on April 27, 1978, to publicize and come to the aid of people unjustly persecuted by the political authorities. The seventeen signatories all included their addresses on the declaration. As Kamila Bendová put it to me, "One can't do politics anonymously!"[4] VONS members were extremely attentive to the law. They attended the criminal trials of victims of state persecution whenever possible and provided aid to families of political prisoners. Information was passed to organizations like Amnesty International and Voice of America. No longer was it possible, as it had been in the 1950s, to make somebody disappear without a trace. There was a veto rule within the group—a single vote not to accept someone's case would require refusing the appeal. And VONS also required the agreement of the family of the person being persecuted before they would act. Some people felt they would be better off if VONS did not make a fuss on their behalf. One must emphasize just how labor-intensive all of this work was. It involved the incessant typing and retyping of documents, attending trials, circulating petitions and documents, and smuggling information out of the country—all under the watchful eyes of the StB. Anyone could bring a case to the attention of VONS members. And soon word got out that there were three Prague addresses where one could always go for help—the Benda flat on Charles Square being one. While her husband Václav was in prison for four years from 1979–1983 for his VONS activities, Kamila continued this policy of their flat as one of these welcoming addresses—one ought to keep in mind that she worked full time and had five children. I asked her about this—her children must have gotten quite used to having strange people in their flat—she noted sometimes as many as ten per day! When Václav was in prison, she arranged it so that Tuesdays and Fridays

---

4   Interview with the editor, January 2014, Prague. Mrs. Bendová was not herself
     one of the seventeen signatories.

were widely known as the "visiting days" in the Prague community. But people used to tell her, "Oh, you've got visiting days on Tuesday, I won't come then, they'll be too many people, I'll come the next day!"[5]

Resuscitating the Body Politic

As Benda notes in the "The Parallel Polis" (chapter 19 of this volume and the essay and concept with which his name is most associated), there was a major flaw in the Charter's strategy. On one hand, nobody in the Charter—across the broad political spectrum of its members—expected the totalitarian system to reform in any concrete or meaningful way. And further, Benda argued that anything that looked like moderation on the part of the regime was more apparent than real. Repressions could wax and wane for a number of reasons. One reason for a decrease in repression, he argued, was the "requirement for the existence of exceptions" (29). It was always useful for the regime to have some examples where they had not resorted to persecution of opponents. More importantly was the "rule that there are no fixed rules: the uncertainty of persecution raises the feeling of threat and chiefly evokes various suspicions, jealousies and tensions—why him and not me or why me and not him" (29–30)? So both fundamental reform and moderation were extremely unlikely—any hopes along these lines were futile. On the other hand, the Charter's strategy was predicated on taking the regime's word as to its good intentions with respect to its laws. The Charter reminded the regime that its tyrannical behavior did not comport with Czechoslovak laws which themselves pointed to transcendent principles of justice. It short, the Charter treated the regime as if it were an ordinary tyranny. Of course Benda and others well knew that there was nothing ordinary about Communism. As Benda describes the relevant distinction:

> The history of mankind is varied and accompanied by laws wise
> and unwise, better and worse, just and unjust, written and cus-
> tomary. However, there was always something which stood
> above people, which appeared to be disinterested and which

5   Interview with the editor, June 2013, Prague.

was portrayed with a bandage round its eyes, some sort of guarantee for the last against the first. Admittedly, more than one monarch or member of the nobility disregarded the laws, obeyed only their own will and rampaged in their own way: the point, however, was that it was plain to them, their witnesses and their victims that they were breaking the law and willfully standing over and above the law. In short, there was some kind of world order, albeit not the most perfect; possible revolts were also a part of it, in fact they underlined its meaning, they did not make it impossible to distinguish good and evil, to call things by their real names. It wasn't until now that They thought up the current diabolical law, that in its very text justifies *carte blanche* in advance anything the authorities could think to be beneficial, and no less *carte blanche* declares anything that would contravene the current intentions of the authorities to be a crime. (23–24)

Now, beyond this strategic difficulty which the Charter faced, it also had to face the reality of the battlefield after the initial clash upon the Charter's release. The regime's nasty anti-Charter campaign in the winter and spring of 1977 had succeeded, to a large extent, in isolating this informal movement from much of the population. In the spring of 1978 the leaders of the Charter community decided there was a need to meet in order to develop a long-term strategy to ensure the movement could endure. Benda, "with the zeal of a newcomer," complied with the instructions to write something for the group to consider. He argued that the way forward for the Charter was to ensure that the sense of moral commitment inspired by the Charter could find concrete expression in people's everyday lives. Benda argued that any positive program could neither act as a political opposition in hopes of reforming the political system nor attack the system directly with a view to its destruction. Benda proposed rather to ignore the regime's official structures and promote the development of parallel structures in areas such as the economy, education, and culture. Only in such alternative social structures could true human community be discovered and nurtured.

This strategy was necessary, in Benda's view, due to the peculiar and unprecedented nature of totalitarian tyranny. As Benda noted, "Whereas regimes in some traditional West European democracies and the worst Latin American dictatorships are the embodiment of the same concept of 'politics' (qualitatively certainly very different), in a totalitarian state the word 'politics' represents only a sequence of sounds whose meaning is, as a whole and in its singularities, nontransferable to any previous human experience with this concept" (193). Benda's parallel polis was derived from his understanding of totalitarianism's method of imposing unity on its populace. Here he was in agreement with the Polish philosopher Leszek Kolakowski who used the formula perfect integration through perfect fragmentation.[6] Benda saw that the Communist regime either sought to infiltrate and coopt independent social structures for its own purposes, or to de-legitimate and destroy them. It sought to maintain a populace of isolated individuals without any habits of or desires for association. For Benda, the "decisive modus operandi of Czechoslovak totalitarianism is the atomization of society, the mutual isolation of the individuals, and the destruction of all bonds and verities which might enable them to relate to some sort of higher whole and meaning and thus determine their behavior in spheres beyond pure self-preservation and selfishness" (267). Benda, on more than one occasion in this volume, extended Churchill's iron curtain metaphor and argued such curtains were lowered not only between East and West, but between the countries of the Warsaw Pact, between regions, between social classes, between local communities, between various social groups, between members of a family, and even within individuals and their "inner selves"!

Benda argued that some of these activities and social structures had already been in existence for many years. "Samizdat" or self-publishing had existed even in the 1950s, but really started to assert itself as a regular social force in the beginning of the 1970s with publishing ventures directed by Ludvik Vaculík and Václav Havel. And the phenomenon known as the "Second Culture" included a vibrant underground music scene as well as cultural journalism covering literature, theater, music and film. So Benda wanted to support and encourage activities that were already in existence

---

6   See Kolakowski, "The Marxist Roots of Stalinism," in F. Flagg Taylor IV, ed., *The Great Lie: Classic and Recent Appraisals of Ideology and Totalitarianism* (Wilmington, DE: ISI Books, 2011), p. 162.

as well as secure the space for new endeavors such as underground educational seminars. Thus in the parallel polis the specter of "dissent" would always become embodied in a concrete activity rooted in the real longings of people. People who might have had neither the desire nor steadfastness to become entangled in a battle with the Party and its apparatus might well simply want to play the music of their choice or study theology. Benda argued that totalitarianism was bound to always be subject to "strange dialectic." Its aspirations would always be emphatically total—it would seek to control everything, to stamp out every last vestige of free thought and action, yet practically the regime was bound to fail. People would, by nature, continue to secure spheres of freedom (however small or seemingly insignificant they might seem). Yet Benda argued that this "natural resistance might never be enough." As he put it in a subsequent reflection (chapter 19 of this volume) on his seminal essay from 1978:

> There is, however, a fundamental difference between the natural resistance of life to totalitarianism and the deliberate expansion of the space in which the parallel polis can exist. The former is a cluster of flowers that has grown in a place accidentally sheltered from the killing winds of totalitarianism and easily destroyed when those winds change direction. The latter is a trench whose elimination depends strictly on a calculated move by the state power to destroy it. Given the time and means available, only a certain number of trenches can be eliminated. If, at the same time, the parallel polis is able to produce more such trenches than it loses, a situation arises that is mortally dangerous for the regime: it is a blow at the very heart of its power—that is, the possibility of intervening anywhere, without limitation. The mission of the parallel polis is constantly to conquer new territory, to make its parallelness constantly more substantial and more present. (233)

The concept of the parallel polis was also quite important as the 1980s wore on. Benda was constantly looking to build these structures and seeking allies anywhere he could find them. As we see in his letter to Roger Scruton, he insisted on exploring alliances with the peace movements of

Western Europe, even if their understanding of socialism and its problems was quite different from his. And he was very much in favor of the student-led movements and demonstrations of the late 1980s.

Truth and Charity

Benda's witness against the totalitarian menace was unmistakably Christian. His Roman Catholic faith guided his thoughts and deeds throughout the late 1970s and 1980s. He was under no illusions that a believing Christian of any kind, or a Roman Catholic in particular, could carve out a space for peaceful coexistence with the Communist regime while truly living according to his faith. Benda argued that "Totalitarian power is not atheist for a random historical reason, for example, because there was a moment when it petrified as 'scientific worldview' some contemporary erroneous theory; it is atheist because it must be so logically" 191). Benda was always frustrated with those who liked to invoke Matthew 22:20–21 to suggest that the Christian could just "render unto Caesar" what was necessary and then turn to God. In the context of Communism, what was demanded by Caesar was precisely "everything indivisibly"—and the regime would brook no compromise here. "Totalitarian power destroys both body and soul, knowing neither exception nor pardon; it is not (like other historical governments), a mere inducement to sin and a test of human freedom, but rather a denial of this freedom and a reign of death" (196).

While Benda in no way underestimated the destruction the regime wreaked on the Catholic Church in his native land and was remarkably honest about its weakened state, he did not think the situation was by any means hopeless. He took the measure of the destruction in a number of essays here, most especially in "Catholicism and Politics." He noted the de facto destruction of the religious orders, the imprisonment of vast numbers of bishops, priests, and Catholic lay persons, the emigration of tens of thousands of Catholics, the refusal to allow for the appointment of new bishops and priests, the use of the state clerical organization Pacem in Terris to control priests, and the state control and infiltration of the seminary in Litoměřice, Slovakia. The Church paid a high price for all of this brutal, extensive, and systematic repression. Benda characterized the most troubling effect of all of this as a kind of privatization of faith—

one might pray in one's home and attend mass on Sunday (which itself entailed problems as the regime paid close attention to who attended religious services), but that would be the extent of one's care of the soul. He told the story of a Catholic woman who refused to sign a protest petition on behalf of a group of believers because she thought the action needlessly provocative of the authorities. The woman had argued that even in the 1950s it was possible to make some contributions to one's faith—especially if one avoided unnecessarily provocative displays. So, for example, she had sent parcels of rolls or buns to interned priests. While not wanting to discount the courage and significance of such an action, Benda called this manner of living one's faith "a retreat into the ghetto, a voluntary relinquishing of openness and of universal shared responsibility" (68). In part this sort of mentality was directly related to the Church's subjection to decades of terror and persecution. The Church had succumbed to a kind of isolationism, always on the defensive and convinced that a retreat into a "pure spirituality" might allow it to remain untainted by the corrupt surrounding environment.

For Benda however, such a posture was both a moral and theological failing and a strategic mistake. Let's look at the moral failing first. The Christian faith, as Benda understood it, had a deeply civic dimension. Czech Catholicism, he argued, had emphasized prayer and humility—goods to be sure—but perhaps such emphasis had come with the exclusion of the charity and witness which also demanded a place in the life of the Church. In his view, Czech Catholicism suffered "from a lack of truth (which means moving away from Christ) and from its inability to carry out the second part of the first and most important commandment—that is, love for one's neighbor, and hence a thirst for justice and responsibility in a world which was good when God created it and entrusted it to man" (263). Living a truly Christian life, especially in the midst of the challenge of totalitarian evil, entailed not only caring for the salvation of one's own soul, but most importantly a concrete commitment to the care of others. Christians needed to recover their openness, their willingness to bear direct witness to the sufferings of their fellow citizens.

For Benda this was the great challenge that had to be faced precisely because the totalitarian system's perpetuation depended on the retreat from charity. And here we can begin to glimpse the strategic error in this embrace of a pure spirituality. Not only did this retreat mean ceding unnecessary ground to the totalitarian enemy, it also stemmed from a profound misunderstanding of the changing face of the enemy. Here Benda drew a distinction—common among some other Czech thinkers and writers like Havel—between the communism of the 1950s and the version on offer during the "normalization" period of the 1970s and 1980s.[7] During the former period the regime looked like "Lucifer, the most sublime of the angels of God." Benda's elaboration of this distinction is worth quoting at length:

> At that time it was essentially a Manichean struggle between the principles of good and evil, when through its loudness the lie substituted for truth, when through its logic appearance substituted for reality, and when the easiness of the way to the Fall substituted for historical salvation. In this time ... he stood fast who took counsel with his own soul and remained in Truth. However, the Communism of the last decade is more like the Nietzschean "spirit of gravity": apathetic, gloomy, devouring. Power stands against truth, nothingness against reality, the immobility of the cycle "from anniversary to anniversary" against history. In this time, which is oppressive rather than cruel, he who consults *only* his own soul and believes that Truth—the Truth which became incarnate in a specific place and at a specific time and lived among men and suffered for them—is a mere *position* on which it is sufficient to *persist*, does not stand fast. (69)

The ideological evil had moved from being a kind of militant invasive species which seized the body politic from the outside to a bacteriological weapon shot into the veins of each individual citizen. Benda argued that the peculiar evil of communism in its later stage was that it had become "a restrictive weight that every citizen already carries on himself or herself,

---

7   See, for example, Havel's essays "The Power of the Powerless" and "Stories and Totalitarianism." They can be found in *Open Letters: Selected Writings, 1965–1990*, Paul Wilson, ed. (New York: Vintage, 1991).

and *within himself or herself*" (69). One couldn't define oneself against nothingness—the only choice was "throwing off one's bonds and opening oneself to something new and unknown" (69). He thought the new and unknown in this context of Christianity was a radical openness to the claims of others—love of one's neighbor. This would be the adventure which Christians must be willing to undertake with any and all citizens willing to join them. It would run directly counter to the "mass flight into privacy" characteristic of the time and thus secure a place as a social force to be reckoned with.

Conservative Radical or Radical Conservative

Benda called himself a conservative radical or a radical conservative. He understood the totalitarian phenomenon to have its roots in the modern philosophic and scientific project to master nature and render the individual free from limits and conditions outside of his control. One can find his reflections on these themes in many of these essays, but in particular see "Concerning Responsibility in Politics and for Politics." The "blinding light" of the many benefits of the technological change had hidden the darker effects of such transformations. The free West for Benda was subject to many of the same debilitating forces as the unfree East (though he was always careful not to draw a moral equivalence between the two sides in the Cold War—he characterized the difference as analogous to the difference between a diseased organ and a malignant tumor). One can say that he took the full measure of the breadth and depth of the moral and political crisis of the West which saw its apogee in totalitarian regimes. While the totalitarian state and its incessant "planning" and coercive social engineering rendered individual responsibility inoperative, Benda thought the liberal idea of the "minimal state" the other side of this coin. As he wrote in his letter to Roger Scruton, "I see a grave danger for freedom in boundless and formally absolutized Liberalism, both in the sense of freedom being threatened by disintegrative tendencies and of it being impossible truly to pursue it without the existence of a background determined by a firm order" (118). While the state should certainly respect the private sphere and not in any way seek to formally implement a system of public virtue, it ought not simply stand aside from questions of morality and insist only on procedural fairness. Free human beings must embrace the responsibility of making a case for some understanding of the public good. They must bring such an understanding into the public square for evaluation and challenge. Democratic forms, for Benda, were good insofar as they fostered this sense of political responsibility. Without this confidence in and respect for politics in an Aristotelian sense, democratic forms would become empty vessels for whatever the "will of the people" might find choice-worthy at a given moment.

Benda seemed to advocate for an ethical posture which combines humility with a joyful embrace of one's political and communal responsibilities. He certainly did not want to be seen as advocating for some sentimental return to a better age, though he argued that the cultural and spiritual goods of Western civilization in general and the Czech heritage in particular had been seriously undervalued. As he put it, "What does matter is the humility which brings a change of thinking and returns meaning to past deeds, rather than their desperate and suicidal negation, or attempt to throw the guilt on someone else … The only thing that really needs to be radically set aside is man's overweening pride in himself and in his reason. In the name of this pride, two immeasurably valuable things, man and reason, were degraded to a mere means of achieving sort of questionable higher aims and violated to the very edge of destruction" (216).

Though I have tried to communicate some of Benda's principal themes and concerns as a dissident, I am afraid that I have made the work of a dissident sound too abstract and intellectual. Today it is easy to forget that the regime had real agents with faces—people whose very reason for being would become bound up with making Václav Benda's life and work as difficult and miserable as possible. The everyday challenges of this kind of life emerge in many of the shorter essays from the first and third parts of the book. We get a sense of what "protective supervision" must have felt like in "One Year After Orwell," and we hear about a punishment inflicted on young Martin Benda in "Why Hesitate Over a Final Solution?" Benda sketches many important, yet little known, events like the massive pilgrimage to and mass at Velehrad in the summer of 1985 and the pilgrimage to honor St. Agnes in March 1988. One ought to be attentive to the tone of these writings in all their variety: it is by turns sarcastic, angry, strident, humble, grateful, hopeful, and even joyful. Benda never seemed to succumb to despair. He and his family were subject to constant surveillance and harassment. There were house searches that sometimes lasted for ten or more hours, frequent interrogations, and their friends were often asked to serve as informants (some refused, some agreed, and others emigrated). And from 1979 to 1983 Benda served a prison sentence as a result of his involvement in VONS. Kamila and the children had been allowed to visit him four times each year for one hour per visit. She successfully smuggled the Eucharist to him at great risk. Kamila wrote him hundreds upon hundreds of letters during his imprisonment. She continued the work of VONS and the Charter in his absence. Yet Benda and his family never wavered. Indeed, on the day of his release from prison in 1983, Benda returned home to a party in his honor. Almost immediately a petition was thrust into his hands protesting something. His wife Kamila told him that he ought to promptly resume his position as spokesman of Charter 77 so the regime would understand that the imprisonment had no effect on him! The solidarity and commitment of his friends and most especially his family made it possible for him to persist in his battle with totalitarianism.

Even in the midst of these myriad persecutions, Benda was grateful for the givenness of things. "Fortunately the world around us is real," he wrote, "the children get up, get dressed and have their breakfast, go to school. The family really does exist, it is together or divided, has its joys and woes, its friends and interests" (10). "They" merely appeared from time to time as phantoms, playing on fears and the sense of isolation. "We should continue to surround their totalitarianism with our reality. For to assert itself, totalitarianism needs complete emptiness, nothingness" (256). The family read samizdat editions of Tolkien's works and even watched the film *High Noon*. The children took the confrontation with the regime as a kind of adventure. Václav Benda died in 1999 so I never had the privilege of meeting and talking with him. But I believe he understood perfectly how his life and work was made possible by his family. In his essay "The Family and the Totalitarian State" he argued that the family ought to secure three fundamental gifts for its members:

> The first gift illustrated here is the fruitful fellowship of love,
> in which we are bound together with our neighbour without
> pardon by virtue simply of our closeness; not on the basis of

merit, rights and entitlements, but by virtue of mutual need and
its affectionate reciprocation ... The second gift is freedom,
given to us so absolutely that even as finite and, in the course
of the conditions of the world, seemingly rooted beings, we
are able to make permanent, eternal decisions; every marriage
promise that is kept, every fidelity in defiance of adversity, is a
radical defiance of our finitude, something that elevates us—
and with us all created corporeally—higher than the angels. The
third and final gift demonstrated in family fellowship is the dignity and unique role of the individual. In practically all other
social roles we are replaceable and can be relieved of them,
whether rightly or wrongly. However, such a cold calculation
of justice does not reign between husband and wife, between
children and parents, but rather the law of love. (243–44)

Fellowship, freedom, and the dignity of the individual. These are also
the gifts that Benda thought any politics worthy of the name should foster
and protect.

A Note on the Contents

The contents of this volume follow the Czech edition exactly. The three
sections of the contents reflect three different kinds of texts. The first section, "Reflections," is comprised of shorter essays usually prompted by a
specific event or action. The second section, "Essays and Inquiries," is
comprised of longer pieces often of a more analytical and philosophical
character. And finally, the last section, "Reports and Defenses," is made up
of shorter documents often written for a specific purpose and sometimes
related to the regular work of Charter 77 or VONS. The pieces are
arranged chronologically within each section. It is worth noting that this
thematic arrangement obscures somewhat the evolution in Benda's thinking. Read chronologically, one can see Benda's movement toward a strategy
of gradually building a concrete opposition that might be capable of moving into power should the system collapse.

Part I:
Reflections

1

A Small Lesson in Democracy

Prehistory

Among the measures associated with my signing of Charter 77 was a meeting called by the relevant section of the Revolutionary Trades Union Movement (ROH)[1] on July 8, 1977. A resolution was adopted virtually unanimously (with one abstention—mine) which states *inter alia* that those present did not agree with what I had done, but definitely did not think it appropriate to expel me from ROH and on the contrary planned to devote greater care to me in the future. However, the works' committee (ZV) of ROH did not accept the section's attitude and proposed to the general conference that my membership should be cancelled for having committed a gross violation of the ROH statutes by signing Charter 77. I was duly invited to the conference and, as a guest, requested permission to speak, which was eventually granted by Chairman Ramba with the admonition that it was unnecessary for me to say anything. (The conference was held on August 9, 1977; 101 out of 119 authorized delegates were present representing around 1050 employees of the Research Institute for Computers [VÚMS]. The record below is as faithful as possible a reproduction of what I said, drawn up shortly after the conference.) I said the following:

---

1   ROH (Revoluční odborové hnutí, 1945–1990) was the nation-wide umbrella organization governing all union labor. The "relevant section" would have been the union branch at Benda's workplace, The Research Institute for Computers, while the "works committee" would have been a small group of representatives at this branch. (Ed.)

Defense

"I believe that in the course of making your decision you should be guided above all by the ROH statutes, for whose alleged violation I'm to be expelled. I have three comments to make on this:

First. The statutes explicitly impose on a member of ROH an obligation to help with the consolidation of Socialist legality. That was exactly what I did by signing Charter 77; my intention was to help with the introduction and wider application of specific laws. There can of course be different opinions as to how far the result corresponded to my intention, and it is clearly a matter for debate. Nevertheless, I think that it is difficult to consider an attempt to fulfill a duty laid down by the statutes as a gross violation of the statutes.

Secondly. According to the statutes, a member of ROH has the right to express and defend his opinions as long as there has been no resolution against them by the supreme bodies. At the time I signed the Charter, no such resolution existed.

Thirdly and lastly. As you know, the proposal of the committee is in conflict with the standpoint of the section. But the members of the section know me personally and the members of the committee and most of the rest of you do not. Additionally, most of you don't know what the Charter says. If you are guided by the opinion of the supreme bodies, these bodies, according to the statutes, have the authority to expel me themselves, of their own competence. However, if you as delegates of the conference are to decide, you should be more familiar with the matter. If you wish, I can read Charter 77 to you; I don't however want to bore you and take up your time. Nevertheless, I think it's difficult for you to make a responsible decision and to assess the legitimacy of my argument without a better knowledge of my person and the matter for which I'm being expelled. Thank you."

Repercussions

Chairman Ramba replied with a sharp invective: "Whether I thought I would be allowed to propagate opinions here which had been generally condemned, etc., etc." After that the director of the institute spoke, his speech consisting partly of an enumeration of those with whom it was necessary to talk seriously, and partly of an enumeration of the benefits to the institute of being in a good political position and the disadvantages which would ensue if its reputation were to be damaged. When eventually the vote took place, thirty-three delegates spoke out for my expulsion, seven against (among them all six representatives from my allotted workplace) and sixty-one delegates abstained. So the proposal for me to be banned was not passed, and the conference came to an end in some slight confusion.

The next day I was summoned to a sitting of the works' committee (with the rare privilege of being able to use the taxi service at my employer's expense). Here I was informed that the institute's proposal for the immediate termination of my employment according to §53 para. 1 b, c of the Labor Code (gross violation of working discipline, threatening the security of the state) was being discussed. When I asked about the reasons for my dismissal, the director read the relevant paragraph of the Labor Code; when I asked again, he informed me that the reason for terminating my employment was my speech to the ROH conference. After my brief protest, the committee had (in the absence of any representative from my workplace) unanimously approved the immediate termination of my employment. Then I was escorted (in the director's car) to my workplace (under strict surveillance, so I couldn't speak or say goodbye to any of my colleagues) and finally expelled from the institute.

Into the next round

When the same day I presented my membership card to the works' committee asking about my transfer, the chairman took it from me saying that a decision would be made about my further membership on Tuesday, September 13. I admired his prophetic powers on Monday, September 12, when it was announced that—on the basis of spontaneous requests from many sections—the works' committee was going to convoke an extraordinary conference concerning my expulsion on Tuesday, September 13. The operations of the institute came to a complete standstill for two days, and discussions about my case ran continuously at every level. Among other threats and promises, further signatories of Charter 77 in the institute were used as hostages. Their fate was inexorably bound to the outcome of the new conference. Moreover, to ensure the right result, at least some delegates were not elected but named from on high (which I can prove, thanks to the solidarity of some colleagues).

By virtue of my membership in the works' committee I tried to take part in the negotiations at my own (former) workplace; I was however evicted on the grounds that this was not a union meeting but a working meeting. On the other hand, I had the opportunity for a longer heart-to-heart with the director of the institute. He regretted my inadequate sense of responsibility with regard to my five small children, and contrasted this with the sleepless nights he spent on their behalf. He went on to say he suspected that my good mood issued from a hidden income from abroad. Thinking about the undesirable state of my family finances, I wanted to make a sharp protest, then however the hidden treasures laid up in heaven occurred to me ... Since I had some doubts as to whether the director would consider heaven to be a domestic or foreign institution, I confined myself to a restrained reply and devoted myself to a longer conversation on educational matters. Then we moved to technical matters, and I pointed out that the work newly assigned (as punishment) would absorb all my time and energy, and that it was up to the institute leadership if they wanted to make a professional dissident of me. The director was very taken aback by the last statement, and in further conversation he repeatedly made me an offer that through the Regional Committee of the Czechoslovak Communist Party he could ensure me skilled employment in another institute. The offer was—very discreetly—linked with the condition that at the forthcoming ROH conference I would renounce my words. After that we parted amicably.

The next day the extraordinary ROH conference took place, the only item on the agenda being the issue of my membership. After some longish speeches by delegates of the leadership I was allowed to speak, roughly as follows:

"At the forum of the last conference I successfully defended myself against the charge that I had violated the statutes of ROH. I don't intend to repeat my defense today, for in the meantime the works' committee committed so many and such gross violations of the statutes that it is the members of the committee who should be expelled from ROH for factional activity, since apart from anything else they rejected the standpoint of the supreme body—the conference—and intrigued against it. I don't however have any illusions about the result of the voting, I know what pressure you have all been subjected to. I only want to point out that it no longer concerns just my case: from solidarity with the delegates of the previous conference and with regard to your own self-respect, in being expected to submit to the unprecedented force of this authority, you should think again about how to vote. Thank you."

Chairman Ramba then asked the delegates whether any pressure had been put on them. No answer. The president then assured me: "You see, no pressure has been put on anyone," and proposed they move on to the vote. At that one of the deputies spoke up and in a sepulchral voice delivered a self-criticism for his vote at the last conference. Even so, all the delegates and guests kept a straight face. With this single delay the Conference then accepted the proposal for my expulsion from the ROH (the single defiant delegate was, in the meantime, shifted to another workplace as a punishment; of the nine delegates from my workplace, three turned up shortly before the voting, having finally learned how to vote).

P.S. The State Security (StB)[2] authorities and the leadership representatives of the institute, who had worked hand in glove in dealing with my Charter 77 signature, were for the most part willing to recognize the legitimacy of my conclusions, but reproached me for not having turned to the appropriate places with my critical attitudes—for example, to the social organizations and the people's council. As is clear from what went before, I did try to do so and I am therefore allowing myself to present to the aforementioned authorities the outcome of my attempt to obtain their kind consideration.

October 10, 1977

---

2   The Státní bezpečnost (State Security) or StB was the plain-clothes security force in Czechoslovakia, responsible for monitoring any and all activity by citizens which the Communist party determined to be contrary to the interests of the state. (Ed.)

2
From My Personnel File

In about an hour's time I have to finish work and set out for my employment—or the other way round. I was born a year after World War II, I'm
a white man, a Roman Catholic, of no political affiliation, of impeccable
character. In August 1968 my wife and I, fully aware of the "unforeseeable
consequences," decided not to use our valid passports and to stay in
Czechoslovakia.[1] In 1977—after I signed Charter 77—we several times refused the offer of free tickets to emigrate to Austria. We are cheerful and
contented in our life; I consider it to be extremely unreasonable, once
you've shown some eccentric willingness to throw yourselves to the lions,
to complain that their teeth are not very clean. In saying this, I want to
make it quite clear that I'm not defending either the lions or their use as an
argument in civil life.

From the age of eighteen I've pursued the following professions (for
the most part not from choice): philosophy student, assistant lecturer in
philosophy, schoolteacher, hydro-biologist, unemployed (on benefits),
mathematics student, mathematician on the railways, programmer, and
stoker. My temporary professions have included: laborer in a brewery and
on a building site, cowherd, assistant arts editor, linguist, translator, teacher
of logic, and computer expert. All these for the most part involuntary
changes were not caused by any troublesome oppositional involvement of
mine but rather from the fact that I was not willing to be sufficiently

---

1   On August 21, 1968 the Soviet Union, along with the militaries of other War-
    saw Pact nations, invaded and occupied Czechoslovakia in response to what
    became known as the Prague Spring. Many Czechs considered emigration
    after this brutal crackdown. (Ed.)

politically engaged in implementing the directives then handed down from above.

Maybe I'm culpably patient. I took it in silence when a stroke of the pen put a virtual end to all my literary activity (and for a time a formal end too) and devoted myself to philosophy. I took it in silence when membership in the Communist Party became a necessary condition for employment as a philosopher, and switched to mathematics. I took it in silence when, as a Christian, I could not be a mathematics editor nor even obtain an academic title (and here I mention only those limitations I experienced personally), and devoted myself fully to computer programming. It was eventually the perfidy of the ruling power that shook my confidence, the perfidy which in all its absoluteness resolved to vent its wrath against culture, not on known and recognized representatives, but on a peace-loving group of weak and destitute young musicians.[2] We do, after all, have a commandment binding us to defend widows and orphans against tyrants. It was only thanks to the ferocious and indiscriminate attacks on Charter 77, attacks in which the power tried to involve every citizen, that I finally decided to join this civic activity—since we have more commandments that forbid us to bear false witness against our neighbor. Let your "yea" be yea, and your "nay," nay.

So for the time being I work in a boiler-room during the day and the rest of the time I try to divide between sleep, family, civic activity, mathematics, and philosophy. Thanks to our family's patriarchal regime, my wife desists from public declarations and has so far been able to keep her position as a mathematician. Thanks to the same regime, I can be absolutely certain (and have verified it experimentally) that in the event of my imprisonment everything that can be done for me will be done, and more beside.

For our four older children—five-year-old Marta, three-year-old Patrik and the schoolboys, nine-year-old Marek and seven-year-old Martin—the occasional visits from the police are a welcome adventure.

---

2   This is a reference to the Czech rock band called The Plastic People of the Universe. The trial related to this band, which included one of the musicians and the band's artistic director and took place in the fall of 1976, was part of the impetus for the formation of Charter 77. (Ed.)

Over the last year they have enriched their repertoire by two new games: "playing at Charter" and "playing at unemployed." Our (current) "Benjamin,"[3] year-old Filip, is best at being an alarm clock—nevertheless, he already sits on his potty, runs around, prattles away and generally destroys the furnishings.

The dispute with authority I've entered—and in this country that means we've all entered it, the whole of my family to the third generation and all those friends who are not quick enough to denounce me in public—will be long, exhausting and, by all human standards, hopeless. Whenever I use phrases like "for the time being" and "so far," all I'm saying is that it could get worse. Not even surrender or desertion offers any hope (and in that I can't fail to see the intervention of Providence); the power against which we stand is marked by two qualities—it prefers to strangle in solitude and darkness, and it never forgets or forgives. If I could quote the as yet most serious victim of the struggle, Professor Patočka, who died in the Lord (though almost in the offices of the secret police): "It is not a battle but a war. And just as victory in battle does not mean victory in the war, so defeat in battle does not mean defeat in the war."[4] It is a strange war (and please understand that I can only with difficulty work my way into the mentality of the victim or the martyr—I am much more suited to the guise of a tank division, urban guerrilla or, in the old-fashioned way, simply to raise a crusaders' flag and march on the capital). It is a war waged exclusively in words—and at the same time the authorities have ten printing houses at their disposal for each of our typewriters.

Moreover, we're thrown back many centuries: to before the invention of the car, the telephone, printing, the postal service and so on. We spend several hours running around town to arrange something which in the twentieth century should be sorted out by two short phone calls. We spend hours and hours repeating and transcribing facts which could be summed up in one newspaper column. We keep to the law, we operate legally and

3 "Benjamin" refers to a family's youngest son. Benjamin was the name of Jacob's last and thirteenth child as recounted in the book of Genesis. (Ed.)
4 Jan Patočka (1907–1977), student of Husserl and Heidegger, was a prominent and influential Czech philosopher. He was one of the first three spokesmen of Charter 77. Already ill, he died on March 13, 1977 after repeated and lengthy interrogations by the StB. (Ed.)

publicly. The state power denies the law, it cracks down on us illegally and conspiratorially. It is a war of nerves; and don't they just relish it and start screaming when one of us resists the tenth absurd and unlawful procedure, when one of us hurls back an insult to the hundredth received, or when in exhaustion, once in a while, one finds relief from the constant pressure by getting drunk.

Fortunately the world around us is real; the children get up, get dressed and have their breakfast, go to school. The family really does exist, it is together or divided, has its joys and woes, its friends and interests. Whereas they, those others, are only phantoms who from time to time emerge from the mists with a sloppily donned human mask, meticulously concealing their acts and chiefly their names. They try to wrap their spider's web around us, exploiting the fact that everyone is afraid of them. A phone call or a short interview is enough (no, they will never put anything in writing!). Your rights are no longer valid, your claims will not be examined, your documents and contracts will be cancelled, they will throw you out of your employment and your school and you will not be accepted anywhere else, they will deny you medical care (all this has already happened). One cannot not obey an order; but one can fail to understand it properly, let it disappear in the blind alleys of bureaucracy or at least balance its execution by hidden manifestations of good will—the Czechs have considerable experience in that. And we are fortunately—despite what the media tell you—protected by a firm shield of general sympathy. Of the many hundreds of people I spoke to last year (I do not of course count official "conversations") only *three* spoke against Charter 77—and one of those came to me later to say that he had now read it and couldn't understand what was wrong with it.

We came across only one serious objection: yes, we were right, but we were mad, we had no hope in this contest of a dwarf against a bunch of giants, we were stepping voluntarily into the jaws of the lion and the fiery furnace, a sensible person does not lose his head so pointlessly. Incidentally, some unexpected failures of power during the year signally reduced the number of those who raised this objection.

Nevertheless, I should explain in conclusion whether I act as I do only because we have such commandments, or whether I can promise some concrete results from my actions. I consider (it's a strictly personal point of view!) all the injustices, illegalities and social evils to be so bound up with the whole system that I have little hope in any substantial improvement. I see my particular task as being something different. The system of two truths (far outstripping that of the 1950s and in a sense even Orwell's "doublethink") has been brought to perfection in contemporary Czechoslovakia. On the outside everyone is committed to agreement, optimism and periodic rejoicing; behind closed doors everyone (middle Party cadres and StB officers not excepted) expresses themselves negatively, pessimistically and with deep skepticism. Believing in Communism has become just as dangerous as speaking one's mind about it—all those fanatics have gradually been eliminated.

This system is deeply immoral, for it not only produces suffering but also takes away its name (and consequently meaning). This system is unusually stable (so stable, it excludes history). It nominally promotes a carrot and stick policy as the government's means to an ideological basis which guarantees it a safe identity of power and doctrine (maybe the election of Caligula's horse as senator is a primitive and naïve prototype). However, this system faces one mortal danger—it is founded on the idea that everyone recognizes the carrot and stick as an argument (and it is truly a *weighty* argument). The simple exclamation "the king has no clothes" can lead to uncontrollable and unexpected results and can fundamentally change the state of things. Naturally, in a kingdom administered by a bogus tailor, in the middle of a throng of royal guards and courtiers—all of whom are of course naked too—only a fool or a child can insist on something as such. Well, I am convinced that to be a fool or a child is not only the way to enter the Kingdom of Heaven (unless you become as these little children, you will not enter; for the wisdom of this world is foolishness with God) but, under the given circumstances, our only earthly political hope.

January 1978

3
They Did Not Pass!

From now on I will use the designation Chartist: it is succinct and striking with a rich historical context and I like it better than the term "signatories," behind which I always hear diplomatic protocol and High Contracting Parties. Complicated circumlocutions such as "a free association of citizens who have decided to promote the application of Czechoslovak law actively and to draw attention to its abuses etc." are on the one hand impractical and on the other do not sufficiently capture the present reality. It turns out that civic initiative automatically guarantees passage—as we see from the following story—to a completely new category of citizens or almost-citizens who will end up with a note about *Sonderbehandlung*[1] in goodness knows how many documents and languages; let us hope that the appropriate rubric will be incorporated into the usual personnel questionnaires without unnecessary bureaucratic procrastination.

So: some Chartists decided that they would attend a public ball, as it happened, the Railway Workers' Ball. This is the ball season, Lent has not yet begun, so why not take a well-earned break, after the mostly innocent and varied work of the past year. After all, the laws themselves are not in any way a subject for humor and moreover, it's been demonstrated that attempts to keep them can cause much more unpleasantness than any kind of obliging criminal misconduct. It is bad for your mental health to meet only at funerals and in front of court buildings, and besides, it can provide opportunities for your fellow citizens to gape at you with morbid relish.

The Chartists bought tickets and began planning what to wear for the ball. Someone— and we know who—(probably) opened a new file,

---

1   In Nazi terminology this expression meant execution without judgement. (Ed.)

"operation ball," and (certainly) sent out anonymous letters. Wistful and poetic letters, explaining that participation in the ball was a desecration of the dignified legacy of Professor Patočka.[2] The letters unfortunately misfired. The syllogism:

Some philosophers are morose old fogeys.
Professor Patočka was a philosopher.
Therefore Professor Patočka was a morose old fogey,

was considered suspect thousands of years ago. Moreover, many of the addressees already knew Professor Patočka and did not need either a letter or an introduction to formal logic to make an assessment. So inevitably it came to the closing act—the attempt to attend the ball.

So we have the Chartists, in the roles of enthusiastic almost-debutants (high-school graduation had been the first and last ball for a good many of them); a whole "anti-Chartist" bunch of StB in the roles of organizers and observers; and a uniformed emergency squad in the role of a battle-ready swarm patrolling the surroundings, its nervous buzzing suitably underscoring the whole atmosphere. One has to allow that the gentlemen of the StB had dutifully studied their albums of our (illegally taken) photographs—the whole action ran absolutely precisely and without any sort of identity checks. Come to that, even if some innocent railway worker or guest at a local café had suffered, everything was in order and his innocence only apparent, because by today's rules he would certainly be a potential Chartist.

The most fortunate Chartists were given their money back at the entrance (two hours before the ball was due to start the StB had declared the empty halls to be overcrowded), expelled from the building and ordered to disperse (we were among them, and escaped unharmed, apart from a slight scuffle over the tickets and the loss of part of my wife's ball outfit). The less fortunate were given, instead of their money back, a couple of blows and kicks, and instead of merely shaking a leg on the dance floor were forced to seek hospital treatment or domestic first aid (Pavel Kohout was something of an exception among them, the women and girls were a

2   See ch. 2, note 4.

far more popular target for the martial arts).[3] Finally, the least fortunate were treated like the preceding group but were also detained, and will possibly be accused of the criminal attrition of police truncheons and boots (in this category I identified only Otka Bednářová, Vašek Havel and Pavel Landovský as almost hopelessly damned, but there were many others, unfortunately unknown to me).[4]

And so concluded the Chartists' ball—without even having begun. I want to end this text with a reflection directed to the Minister of the Interior who allegedly said of himself that he is not a security officer but a Party employee seconded to the Interior and upholding the interest of the Party. Minister: Under these circumstances I consider it superfluous to point out details such as the unlawful and outright criminal procedure by the organs of your Ministry— you and your organs certainly have more important worries. For the time being I will concern myself only with matters closer to you, the strategies and tactics of power. More or less incidentally I would like to draw your attention to the deep frustration of most of the members of your forces (the above-mentioned brutality with regard to women is only one of its manifestations) and to the need for serious psychological and sociological research into the causes of this phenomenon and into ways of eliminating it. Maybe you will retort that this frustration actually sharpens up your boys—but I would say (cynologists, forgive me, please) that this argument may apply to dogs but certainly not to people. Mentally unstable and deformed members of the security forces are not only a danger to society but not very effective either, and at the same time present a permanent threat to their employer. Now, however, to a specific matter: let us imagine a game of chess between the Chartists and your Ministry (forgive us if we try to play according to the rules, whereas you constantly break them). The material and positional

3   Pavel Kohout (b. 1928) is a prominent Czech playwright and novelist. He was involved in the formation of Charter 77 and forced into exile in 1979. (Ed.)

4   Otka Bednářová (b. 1927) was a radio and television reporter prior to 1968 and Charter 77 signatory. She was also a founding member of VONS and was tried and imprisoned along with Benda in 1979. Vašek is the familiar version of Václav. Pavel Landovský (1936–2014) was a prominent Czech actor and playwright and Charter 77 signatory. (Ed.)

advantage on your side is overwhelming. Our only chance is to put into effect strategies so surprising and unforeseeable as to lead you into a situation of informational collapse (originally the invention of the Russian school of chess, I warmly recommend that your operational employees make a study of this). Fortunately (thanks to incorrect moves made during the opening) you drove so many shrewd people to join the Chartists that we can certainly think up surprising moves faster than you can work out directives for appropriate operations, and so you are always playing under time pressure. From time to time you try to solve things by sweeping the chess pieces under the table, and then you lose further valuable minutes replacing them. Today's action was a typical example of banging your fist on the chessboard. Your people behaved at the ball as though they were under orders to liquidate an armed rebellion by dangerous prisoners. The successful filling of the plan to frustrate provocative anti-socialist actions is a part of your activities. You also protected the poor railway workers from the danger of the Chartist plague (what if some dashing railway girl lost her head so much in the whirl of the waltz that she was willing to sign something?!). You saved them from having to meet and chat with us—here however I must slowly pass to the liability account to give us enough time to think about serious matters. The authorized guardians of law and order committed wanton and criminal acts, yet again confirming our conviction that a civic effort to enforce the law is urgently necessary. Moreover, they committed these acts publicly and thus damaged the good name of the Republic abroad (I am sure they will try to put the blame on their victims again). However, I consider the most serious case against you is that you mortally offended all the Chartist ladies; you deprived them of a long-anticipated and much-desired social occasion. Maybe today you'll laugh and scornfully flap your hand. I may be wrong in my estimate of the ladies' reaction, but if I'm right you'll soon bitterly regret every underestimation. Women are usually a passive and restraining element in civic and political life. They can, however, under certain circumstances deviate from their usual role; and that is when governments fall, states are shaken and history sets out on very unpredictable paths.

You have (maybe in miniature) created such circumstances with today's intervention. You have imprudently activated a player whose power and behavior are largely unknown to you. That decidedly makes the next phase of the game an extremely interesting one.

January 28–29, 1978

4
Why Hesitate over a Final Solution?

It was clearly a mistake from the very start and a simple misunderstanding, but I still think that I bear only a minor share of the blame. For several decades (with minor intervals) they have been trying to eradicate the professional cultivation of any sort of oppositional political activity in this country—taking the appropriate professionals with it, as far as possible. Since "oppositional" is an extraordinarily flexible category, politics has become a very unhealthy profession. Which has caused it to become a bit stale over time. This is the only reason it could have turned out that the interest of a few citizens in human rights and other rights guaranteed by the state (and their interest in whether everything really does function as fairly as we are told it does) was assumed to be a primary, even disloyal political activity. We did from time to time try to clarify that our interest had nothing to do with ministerial chairs nor support for the machinations of international reaction, but with citizens Pavel Veselý and Jiří Nejezdil who had been locked up, the former because he sang a little song and the latter because he wrote a furious letter to the authorities. Or perhaps František Vzpurný, who was sacked because he didn't want to write a furious letter to the authorities. Our explanation went unheard and in time we had—one way or another—to reconcile ourselves with the fact that we had been assigned the role of political opponents. Nevertheless, as amateurs—moreover involuntary ones—we have the right to certain mistakes and naiveté.

I confess that until lately I was living in such a basic, almost culpable error. When I was officially warned that by signing Charter 77—which called for compliance with the laws of the state—I had ranked myself among the enemies of the state, I considered it an expression of an order-loving leadership's resentment towards every activity, albeit a sympathetic one. I was sacked from my job, interrogated, and finally imprisoned for several days. The secret police disconnected my telephone, checked my mail, and in the course of a house search turned my apartment upside down, stealing this and that. I saw in this some sort of game, in which the brainpower and chiefly muscle power of the StB apparatus had to be exercised to be fit for the real tasks to come. When my friends were arrested instead of the louts who had stopped us from going dancing, and when other friends were dragged in handcuffs from the hospitable embrace of the police to unknown forests and beaten up, I was willing to understand that a game is a game, and that in the heat of the game the loser tends to cheat from time to time. Even when someone in power requested the health records for me, my wife and our five small children, I was in my notorious naiveté persuaded that, to improve the economic indicators, the secret police had decided (as additional production on the side) to devote themselves to the fight against mumps.

Mea culpa, mea maxima culpa. I am grateful to the fortunate coincidence of an otherwise insignificant event for my eyes being opened at last. About two months ago the newspapers announced an audition for boys aged 8 to 10 for the lead role in a film. Because it was being held in our local cinema, Vyšehrad, I sent my two eldest sons for their amusement and instruction. Out of three hundred children they eventually chose my second-born son, eight-year-old Martin. Everything took place in a proper manner; he passed the camera and costume tests and then a swimming course, the school had no objection, and filming was due to start in mid-July. A few days beforehand the chief personnel officer from Barrandov Film Studios rang to say that there had been an order "from above" forbidding Martin Benda to act in the film *Zlatí úhoři* [*Golden Eels*]. I dried my wife's tears and those of Martin (purchasing ice-cream cake for the purpose) and hardened my heart, for the Lord God said, woe on him, who shall offend one of these little ones, and that it would be better for him if a millstone were hung around his neck and he were cast into the sea.[1]

At the same time I realized that I'd been mistaken and that this wasn't a game at all, because what sort of game can an eight-year-old and the state play together? I realized that we are mortally dangerous to the state not by what we do, but by our very existence, and that its behavior is just a series

---

1   Matthew 18:6; Luke 17:2. (Ed.)

of desperate attempts at self-preservation. Well then, as a conscious and active citizen I challenge the responsible organs: enough of such half-measures. Bullying and harassment are making us ever more stubborn. Not even yellow stars would solve anything, as we are all of the same race and one cannot rule out a mass influx of madmen willing to share the same humiliation. There is only one satisfactory and definitive solution: to root us out. Come to that, small children are as expendable as rabbits and the disposal of their remains is relatively simple. All you have to do is make a decision and shake off undue respect with regard to the law—it is no use hesitating, since time never solves anything. From the purely practical point of view I recommend a global approach, because neglected citizens could become dangerous.

June 19, 1978

5
Year One after Orwell

My friend Jirka Gruntorád returned from prison exactly a week before Christmas Eve.[1] He spent four years in there, partly because he didn't want to stop being my friend but officially for copying out poems and recording songs; maybe he was the last to have Jaroslav Seifert mentioned in his sentence, since Seifert's poetry is now published officially.[2] But then, he is the first political prisoner in whose case they remembered preventive supervision: they immediately gave him the maximum, three years. They strenuously corrected him in a correctional educational institution, even beat him: and he, the dear boy, complained. For having the gall to complain they added another fourteen months in jail—apparently he had caused the injury himself, with the intention of casting suspicion on his honest guard.

But we live in an epoch of humane government. Jirka was able to return to his profession as a workman, they only moved him from being a bricklayer to a stoker: come to that, in weather like this, stokers are very necessary, in the end he was running in circles between three boiler rooms. The conditions of the preventive supervision placed on him were not a lot stricter than normal for the most hardened criminals; he was even able to spend New Year's Eve with us. The day after Epiphany the court released

1   Jiří Gruntorád, Charter 77 signatory, was sentenced on July 7, 1981 to four years in prison and three years of preventive supervision for subversive activities (distributing non-official literary texts, among other charges). He is now the executive director of Libri Prohibiti, an archive of samizdat material in Prague. (Ed.)
2   Jaroslav Seifert (1901–1986) was a prominent Czech poet and signatory of Charter 77. He was awarded the Nobel Prize for literature in 1984—which was why his poetry could be published officially in 1985. (Ed.)

him from the additional fourteen months prison: it seems it couldn't be ruled out that he might not have been just a tiny bit beaten up.

However, this humane government, maybe more mindful of its good intentions and good name than of the law, does have its executors, endowed with considerable power: this judicial judgment clearly caused their cup of patience to overflow. On Friday, the eleventh day of the first year after Orwell, the heavens over my friend darkened. At noon he was given an hour's notice to leave his job, where the previous evening he had still been considered indispensable; for several days a hundred or so tenants cowered in blankets over gas stoves— that however, was a mere bagatelle from the point of view of the higher interest. In the afternoon he was given new conditions of preventive supervision, this time as sharp as a north wind across the broad steppe.

He has to report to the police twice daily. He is not allowed to leave Prague 2; right in front of his windows is the Nusle bridge, which tempts one out for a stroll—it's hard to say exactly where the borders between the Prague districts run, but by the time he gets to the far end of the bridge Jirka will undoubtedly be a hardened criminal. He's not allowed to leave his flat at all at night and during the day only when the police have approved the aim and purpose of his walk in advance. Restaurants in the immediate vicinity are banned completely, and he needs to obtain permission in advance to make other visits. Jirka was always one for reading rather than haunting pubs, so this ostentatiously illegal provision appears somewhat superfluous: the StB officers have clearly added it in the hope of calming the conscience of their uniformed colleagues—the unprecedented strictness of the preventive supervision becomes more understandable if it signals that the subterfuges of a dangerous boozer and troublemaker have to be checked. Plus all those other restrictions which normally belong to preventive supervision. I'm just repeating to you what I was told: if you find it a little illogical and overdone, it's not me you have to persuade but the relevant authorities.

The injustice is so multi-layered that it is tedious to try and decipher and organize the tangle. Jirka was unjustly sentenced and was with still less justice (if one can talk about degrees of injustice) placed under preventive supervision. The law is already bad from the start; moreover, in Jirka's case most of the measures rely partly on its willful interpretation, partly on its direct violation. And justice cannot be reached. House arrest with all that implies, as the police may enter your flat at any time—that has been announced already. If they want, they can deprive you of your employment—and then put you in prison because you can't show where your income comes from.[3] If they want they can forbid you to do your shopping and let you die of hunger. If they want they can prevent you defending yourself against anything at all, because you won't be allowed to visit a lawyer or take a letter of complaint to the post office. Naturally, all of that already existed; a number of us—some for years on end—have been subject to similar bullying. We could at least protest, even if we came up against a wall of indifference, delays and false interpretations of the law. It was our natural right to try to fool the police and avoid their supervision— though we had to count on the appropriate measure of revenge. What is new is that now all these shameful provisions are given free passage—sanctioned by a law which currently provides stiff penalties for any kind of passive or active defense. We are impotent and condemned to impotence.

It thus seems that the naïve question of justice or injustice, truth or untruth, should have been forgotten long ago, and that it's better to ask what They can do. The answer that best suggests itself is absolutely everything— and that we should therefore weep over our efforts. At first glance there is nothing truer than that there can be little doubt about our impotence and their absolute power. They have it all: legislators, interpreters and executors of the law. The history of mankind is varied and accompanied by laws wise and unwise, better and worse, just and unjust, written and customary. However, there was always something which stood above people, which appeared to be disinterested and which was portrayed with a bandage round its eyes, some sort of guarantee for the last against the first. Admittedly, more than one monarch or member of the nobility disregarded the laws, obeyed only their own will and rampaged in their own way: the point, however, was that it was plain to them, their witnesses and their victims that they were breaking the law and willfully standing over and above the law. In short, there was some kind of world order, albeit not the most perfect; possible revolts were

3 Czechoslovakia, like other Communist countries, had laws prohibiting "parasatism." According to article 203 of the criminal code, if you were without employment, you could be convicted of being a burden to the state. (Ed.)

also a part of it, in fact they underlined its meaning, they did not make it impossible to distinguish good and evil, to call things by their real names. It wasn't until now that They thought up the current diabolical law, that in its very text justifies *carte blanche* in advance anything the authorities could think to be beneficial, and no less *carte blanche* declares anything that would contravene the current intentions of the authorities to be a crime. In the Nuremberg trials or the Eichmann trial, the accused were still able to claim they were only carrying out orders, had to carry them out—they were thus trying to set one law against another, though the weaker against the more powerful. Now the murderers of a priest[4] plead—not without pride—that they have fulfilled the intentions of the power and destroyed its adversary according to their best convictions: it is a very logical and legally backed defense, since an action which is not dangerous to the interests of society (interests which are already in the constitutions carefully identified with the interests of the power) cannot, according to the new laws, qualify as a crime even if it fulfills the requirements of ten capital crimes simultaneously. Something however is wrong; the law is silent and looks as though it is willing to sacrifice its devoted servants. It has nothing in common with the events of recent decades when the revolution devoured its servants with relish and en masse: that was always justified as jealousy, their guilt was defined as disloyalty, never as too much zeal. Whereas here it seems that original meanings suddenly shine through the newspeak and downgrade that unshakeable totalitarianism to a mere house of cards, built moreover for a refreshing breeze.

It would be stupid to cultivate optimism on the account of one's neighbors, but even in our country one can observe remarkable instances. Jirka Gruntorád is, in spite of all the bullying, cheerful and resolute, his friends are on the increase, and his worst misdemeanor is a justified indignation when matters can no longer be equated with common sense. Whereas They walk with their heads hanging, They are afraid of each other, scared of the

4   Benda here refers to Jerzy Popiełuszko, a well-known Polish Roman Catholic priest linked with Solidarity. In October 1984 members of the Polish secret police abducted him and beat him to death. This murder had an unforeseen consequence: its masterminds, mostly officials of the Ministry of the Interior, were investigated and sentenced to years of imprisonment. Popiełuszko was recognized as a martyr and beatified by the Church in 2010. (Ed.)

future, of anything at all. I would not want to provide Jirka and many others with cheap comfort or make light of their situations (I have after all no illusions about that fact that I could be caught again between these mill wheels), but what is raised against them looks more like revenge and impotent fury over defeat than any really effective political activity. They have no future ahead of them—and they know it. That does not, however, make them any less dangerous and it would be a bad idea to underestimate them. Their worst problem is that they are almost boundless in the damage they can do, but do not have it in their power to succeed in anything or in any way; such ontological status is sterile from the start, and in time wearisome. Jirka's policeman promised to ensure him re-employment—but returned very downcast. They can deprive anyone of work, imprison them, disrupt their life, see that their names are wiped out of literature, science or the memory of the nation and God knows what else. They can also infiltrate their agents wherever they wish. However, I am often tempted to wager that this allegedly omnipotent security apparatus is not capable—even if it wanted to a thousand times over and if it was in any way advantageous for them—of returning one single person to their position, cancelling just one refuse dump, arranging the building of just one house for people, or doing anything beneficial. My principles do not allow me to take up the wager, but if I did I would assuredly win.

They can do anything, but surprisingly it does them no good. We have to withstand everything, but each manful endurance strengthens the position of what I would—maybe immodestly—call justice, freedom, truth or good, which in itself undoubtedly has an element of hope.

January 17, 1985

6

On Politically Motivated Repressions

I would like to express my opinion on two problems which have recently caused some attention, discussion and varied misunderstandings. First, whether one can observe any reduction or mitigation of politically motivated repressions of all kinds. Secondly, whether repressions have in recent years focused predominantly on Roman Catholic (or generally Christian) activists and whether Charter 77 is on the other hand relatively tolerated— and if so, why. I maintain in advance that the two problems are linked and should be dealt with together.

For the nearly ten-year existence of Charter 77—which concurs almost exactly with the existence of publicly articulated "civil unrest" in normalized Real Socialism[1]—varied forms of repression have been and still are alternated many times over; from defamatory campaigns in the press through administrative measures of every kind (literally beginning with birth and ending with the grave) up to massive police repression (interrogations, house searches, several days' detention, guards, frequently bordering on house arrest—as well as downright dark, terrorist acts) and judicial repression (attempts to fabricate "proxy" criminal delinquency, motivated for the most part by purely political reasons, are still repeated, although not too successfully). The targets of these attacks also change: for example, in the case of Charter 77, efforts to isolate it from society through the far-reaching intimidation of all potential sympathizers (from relatives and friends of individual signatories to their

1　This phrase or its variants ("actually existing" or "really existing") came to prominence during the Brezhnev era, after the crushing of the Prague Spring in August of 1968, to combat the notion that there could be multiple models of Socialism. (Ed.)

neighbors and work colleagues) alternated with efforts to crush and anaesthetize it by gradually "trimming the edges" (that is, the imprisonment and persecution of less well-known signatories) and with efforts to destroy it by one firm blow, at the price of imprisoning the best-known activists who were theoretically considered to be "untouchable." None of these methods have met with unqualified success, and so we have to be aware that the state power will return to them in a different order—always assuming they don't think up something completely new (preventive supervision and the cruel method of its application with regard to political opponents is one such "pleasing" novelty which in itself upsets any belief in the reduction of repression). I think it is absolutely clear that the aim (the destruction of anything independent of the state power) remains exactly the same, and that the only consideration guiding the choice of appropriate repressive means is their degree of effectiveness; that one cannot report any sort of reduction or thaw, that it would be foolish to rely on it, and that at least from the operative point of view it is more important to expect the opposite. If I'm to be quite precise, I should add that the rule I mentioned about the essentially unchanging surface of repressions does include two important exceptions—although there is no guarantee that these waves will not return. In 1980–81 the police behaved exceptionally brutally, and resorted broadly to acts of direct terror; similar events have occurred with us, and still do, yet they are on the whole non-typical and their high frequency in those years was clearly connected with the extreme nervousness of the state authorities in neighboring Poland. Finally, it seems that the international impact of several large show trials (for example, VONS [Committee for the Defense of the Unjustly Prosecuted]) has jeopardized not only Czechoslovak but also Soviet interests abroad to such an extent that from roughly 1980 our authorities have been unable to organize any large (from the point of view of the number of defendants, of the seriousness of the accusations and of the anticipated international reaction) political trial without the agreement of Big Brother. However, not so well known are the individual trials and trials of groups of lesser-known, predominantly young people; moreover, just about every year numerous groups of people are taken into custody without any of them being put on trial (1981: predominantly journalists and writers in connection with the "French truck"; [2] 1983: members of the Order of St Francis; 1984: again the Franciscans; 1985: two groups of activists in religious and secular samizdat).

Another question—especially connected with the second problem—is whether, at least for a specific period of time, the forms and intentions of individual repressions can be explained completely "rationally." It is quite well known that some people had to endure relatively long punishments, others were imprisoned several times for short periods without being brought to court or for ridiculous infringements, and yet others avoided a similar fate for the time being; in the case of one person, house searches may be repeated almost annually; another is regularly interrogated and followed; and someone else again is apparently left in peace for years on end; one person is consistently hounded out of unskilled jobs while another is allowed to remain in a relatively responsible position; with one person the police behave with maximum correctness while another is systematically abused and humiliated, or worse; someone is allowed to travel abroad, someone else prevented from visiting the neighboring town; one family's children are allowed to attend relatively "elite" schools without problems, while others are denied any kind of higher education, and so on—often without it being possible to find any connection between this different treatment and their activity, political tendency, public profile or type of handicap. The first reason is the *requirement for the existence of exceptions*: whenever we complain about some form of persecution to international organizations or whenever we protest to the public here or abroad, the authorities always need at least a few examples to hand where they can show they did *not* resort to such procedures against political opponents. A second and I think more serious reason is the *rule that there are no fixed rules*: the uncertainty of persecution raises the feeling of threat and chiefly evokes various suspicions, jealousies and tensions—why him and not me, what is he guilty of, or what am I doubting or exaggerating, how has one person maybe paid off the police and how has this or that group adapted

2   The "French truck" refers to the attempt, on April 27, 1981, by two Frenchmen to smuggle into Czechoslovakia books for use in underground seminars and books from Czech émigré publishing houses abroad. The attempt was thwarted by the border police and the seizure also led to a rash of reprisals against dissidents in Prague. (Ed.)

politically? There is only one effective way to face these tactics: to be absolutely in solidarity with the victims of repressions and at all costs not to try to understand the strange logic of police thinking. Let the following part of my reflection be read with this in mind.

It is extremely important to record the indisputable facts, albeit only indirectly documented in numbers (the authorities carefully keep the alarming results of their research secret): the number of practicing Roman Catholics in Czechoslovakia has grown sharply in recent decades; the Church has asserted its position in matters of religious freedom, no longer limited to mere freedom of worship but understood as the freedom of a full religious life to which a measure of civic freedom belongs; the number of individuals and groups who *as Christians* devote themselves one way or another to behavior relating to the life of society is increasing. The state power is deeply disturbed by these demonstrations, and understandably allocates to Catholics a considerably larger share of the appropriate "bread of repression." (Insofar as judicial repression against larger groups of persons over the last three years is concerned, it has been confined exclusively to the Roman Catholic environment and to non-conforming youth.)

This part of the story is clear—there are no doubts as far as these facts are concerned. However, some interpretations of these facts and the political construction built on them are more uncertain: that the state power is here turning against the real enemy while tolerating Charter 77 as a potential ally (for example, in relation to the peace movement in the West) as apparently it has shown a shift to the left over the last three years;[3] that the

---

3   Allow me two notes in the margin. The first is purely personal: in 1984 I was spokesman for the Charter and was sharply criticised for having caused the Charter to shift "to the right," apparently directly into the embrace of the integral Catholics—now I learn that it was "to the left," apparently directly into the embrace of the Communist rulers! Living society differs from the ideological monster in that it cannot avoid certain shifts—but maybe the gentlemen could kindly decide what I actually did cause. The second concerns the inadequacy of historical enlightenment: it is a notorious fact that regimes of a similar kind are much more unforgiving towards "heretics" than towards adherents of completely different principles. (Over the last 15 years the harshest political punishments have been suffered by the independent Socialist Rudolf Battěk, the reform Communist Jaroslav Šabata, and the Trotskyite Petr Uhl.) (VB)

focus of the struggle has been transferred from the civic to the religious field; and that the defense of human rights, the fight for the law to be kept and for its improvement has lost its meaning (from this some deduce that Charter 77 has been written off, others sound the alarm that the Catholics present the threat of a new totalitarianism).

I prefer however to keep my feet on the ground and only draw attention to some other circumstances of political repressions—maybe that will at the same time throw into doubt the far-reaching conclusions I mentioned, which I consider to be unreasonable and tendentious. Our awareness of repressions is extremely fragmentary and incomplete, which necessarily distorts the whole picture. It is understandably much less likely that the public will get to know about an isolated group of young people sentenced in an outlying region for alleged extortion in the context of performing their music than about persecutions in the relatively well-organized and connected Roman Catholic environment. But more is involved. For example, the Jehovah's Witnesses (who incidentally have also grown considerably) are superbly well-organized, but virtually refuse any sort of contacts outside the context of their sect; the repressions against them plainly continue unabated, but we are only exceptionally able to provide information about them. Finally, while on the one hand Catholics do not complain about ordinary police arbitrariness (hundreds and thousands of interrogations and other bullying thus go by unnoticed), on the other they show their own timidity whenever ordinary criminality, especially economic, is in play. We know of several large trials with priests and laypersons (often sentences of many years) and of some in preparation; much about them remains unclear; we are unable to distinguish real criminality (for declared faith is no guarantee of honesty) from cases of those who acted formally against the law but without any personal advantage and in the conviction of a higher justice, and from victims of a police and judicial conspiracy of people persecuted exclusively for their religious activity (there are clear signs that all three categories are represented).

Still more important than the possible distortion is the question, *what* are these Catholics prosecuted for? I would venture the hypothesis that various persecutions for successful pastoral duties, for participation in divine service, for marriage in church, for family prayer circles and similar "offences" are not diminishing but nevertheless take place far more selectively—not that the state has come to terms with the existence of Christian citizens, but that at present it has other, more serious, worries with them. In an effort to bring division into the Church, it has even begun to flirt with those whom it thinks would be satisfied with a limited freedom of worship. In recent years judicial and police repression against the Roman Catholic environment has concerned almost exclusively activities which either have a civic dimension or in which this dimension prevails; the enforcement of the right to promulgate one's faith and to proclaim it publicly, to file various petitions and submissions, to cultural activity, to independent education, to activity by the male religious orders (whose legal existence the state does not recognize) and eventually (and chiefly) to the dissemination of information with the help of literature and journals (mostly but not exclusively religious), whether produced by samizdat or acquired from abroad.

Just a few notes in conclusion. Christians have a major share in programmatically nondenominational activities such as Charter 77 and VONS. If in recent times religious activists suffering persecution have not as a rule been signatories of Charter 77, it goes to show that cooperation between individual independent groups has become operationally more efficient and successfully replaced the former "personal union."[4] From the outside (since it is better to keep quiet about some matters for the time being) it is clear that it is thanks above all to the Charter and VONS that news about repressions reaches the public. However, it is happening with increasing frequency that the distribution of the materials of these civic initiatives and cooperation with them are being included among the "criminal acts" of religious activists.

April 6, 1986

---

4   Benda is suggesting that by 1986 it was no longer the case that more or less the same figures were involved in all of the various "dissident" activities. A division of labor developed which enhanced the efficiency of the movement. (Ed.)

7

The Church Militant

In Africa they caught a lion. They bound him, gave him nothing to eat and after a week let him into the arena. The lion sees a huge crowd of people, hears their roar and sees some emaciated wretches in front of him. He thinks sadly to himself: "So it's all over for me. They've thrown me to the mercy of the Christians ..."

Traditional French Joke

At the end of last year, the Bohemian and Moravian bishops—including the late Bishop Vrana of Olomouc, decidedly not of blessed memory, but may much be forgiven him for this last deed at least[1]—announced the Decade of the Spiritual Renewal of the Nation,[2] each year of which is dedicated to a Czech saint and to one of the themes from the Ten Commandments. The culmination of the decade, inspired by the Polish example of thirty years ago,[3] is to be the celebrations for the millennium of St. Adalbert in 1997. The first year, 1988, is dedicated to the Blessed Agnes (who is to be canonized during the year) and in her spirit to the defence of life, that is, a life in service.

One of the many events already undertaken or planned for this year—quiet and meditative or spectacular, working or celebratory—was the na-

---

1   Josef Vrana (1905–1987) was a notorious collaborationist bishop who headed the state-sponsored clerical association *Pacem in Terris* (1971–1989) which was dedicated to controlling the Catholic clergy in Czechoslovakia. (Ed.)
2   See chapter 22, in this volume. (Ed.)
3   The Polish example is the celebration conceived of and organized by Cardinal Stefan Wyszyński. Poland celebrated its millennium of Christianity in 1966, marking the baptism of Poland's first prince, Mieszko I. (Ed.)

tional pilgrimage in honor of the Blessed Agnes of Bohemia and in support of her canonization. Its culmination was a pontifical mass, celebrated the first Sunday after the Feast of Agnes by the Czech Primate Cardinal František Tomášek in St. Vitus's Cathedral. For reasons that are not entirely clear, the pilgrimage evoked an exceptionally hostile reaction from the state power. The details have already been and will be thoroughly recorded; I will content myself here with setting out the overall impression this reaction made on me: that is, one of nervousness and simple disproportion. For such an innocent occasion as divine service with prayer shared by a large number of people, the totalitarian apparatus was mobilized to a degree we can compare only with the turbulent times of twenty or forty years ago. The transport system in the whole republic was disrupted for at least two days, a large part of the armed forces put on full combat alert, and so forth. We can overlook the fact that this cost a great deal of money which came out of our own pockets. In one sense the state power achieved its aim; 8,000 to 10,000 pilgrims participated in the ceremonies and the whole number of those who reached Prague Castle, albeit with a delay, did not amount to more than 12,000 to 15,000 of an estimated 50,000 to 60,000. There remains the question as to whether the state power achieved anything by its "success." I would say absolutely not; it woke up the foreign press to what was going on, and was at the same time too feeble to terrorize the believers. We can and will repeat similar ceremonies for the simple reason that Christians are called to honor the holy day. In the course of its disproportionate actions the regime may very easily find itself in the situation of the shepherd in the fable who cries "Wolf, wolf" so many times that in face of a real threat he calls for help in vain. Moreover, the newspaper *Rudé právo*,[4] in its anti-Church articles, provided us with a list of people who could be seen as a sort of "emergency staff" of the Roman Catholic opposition for the whole of the Czechoslovak Republic. Certain corrections will be necessary; nevertheless, the very thought is wonderful. I emphasize that I do not consider us to be an "opposition" because the disintegration and evil we are forced to face is not a manifestation of any "position" but rather nihilism and the denial of values. Similarly, our Catholicism is not the

4   *Rudé právo* was the newspaper of the Communist Party of Czechoslovakia. (Ed.)

declaration of some sort of exclusive confession but rather universal in the original sense of the word, in which Catholics, Protestants and atheists are bound not to serve a lie and to be true brothers.

I am not venturing to assess the spiritual context of the pilgrimage. I will limit myself to some marginalia which represent departures from the original program of the pilgrimage and which I believe can contribute to illuminating its spirit. Cardinal Tomášek diverged from the set program three times: when he began his sermon with a prayer for those who could not take part in the mass (certainly thinking of those currently interned or otherwise disabled); when he quoted the papal blessing for the Feast Day of the Blessed Agnes and the Decade of National Spiritual Renewal; and when he three times blessed the crowd from the balcony of his palace (which the authorities had forbidden him and which he had categorically ruled out several days before the pilgrimage).

The participants in the mass and the subsequent demonstration also diverged at least three times from the anticipated framework. The first time was when, instead of the newly-composed hymn to the Blessed Agnes, they sang the Old Czech *Jezu Kriste, štědrý kněže* [Jesus Christ, generous priest], a well-known Hussite chorale to whose definitive form it is said Jan Hus himself contributed—maybe our Protestant brothers will correctly understand that this apparent coincidence was no mere accident. The second time was when the crowd in front of the Archbishop's palace sang— and this has not been usual on similar occasions of the faith—the Czechoslovak national anthem, thus underlining the national character of the Decade and maybe even making the first step towards eliminating the mutual distrust between Catholicism and being Czech which, however artificially nourished, has its unavoidable historical rationale. The third was at the very end, when the participants in the demonstration, holding hands, spread round the periphery of the square during the singing of the hymn *Po lásce poznáte nás, křesťany* [You will know us, Christians, by our love], exposed themselves to the lenses of the police cameras and eventually knelt on the not-too-clean March pavement to share prayer under the Cardinal Father. This gesture (by no means non-binding: at least one case is already documented of someone being sacked for participation in the pilgrimage) speaks clearly: here you have us, we are exposing ourselves to you, we are quiet, peaceful and humble, we are not rebelling, we render to Caesar what is Caesar's but do not let him take our souls and our faith—then we are prepared to accept the Cross of Christ.

I did not take part in these events in person and strictly speaking not even in spirit, as I was interned in Ruzyně Prison and at the incriminating time was being interrogated by representatives of the StB. I talked to many participants and listened to a recording of the whole event. In the final instance, however, I invoke Christ's words: blessed are they who have not seen and yet believe.[5]

Written after the conclusion:

On March 25, the day of the Annunciation to Our Lady, a demonstration took place in Bratislava for the renewal of religious rights and civil rights in general and for the installation of loyal bishops in the episcopal thrones. Preventive measures were similar to those in the case of the Prague pilgrimage. However, in this case a planned and unusually brutal attack was made on the peacefully praying crowds, estimated at roughly 15,000 persons. An exceptionally wide range of oppressive means was employed: cars were driven into the crowd, truncheons were used, water cannon, dogs, tear gas. Many people were slightly injured and 150–200 participants, among them ten Western correspondents, were held for several hours. Slovakia is enraged, society in the West and in the East indignant, and Primate Tomášek declares in the name of Bohemian and Moravian Catholics that this demonstration of force and hatred challenges us to a yet more valiant struggle for religious rights and freedoms.

March 14, 1988

---

5   John 20:29. (Ed.)

8

Three Important Memoranda from the Czech Primate

Cardinal Tomášek, Archbishop of Prague and currently the only properly functioning Roman Catholic bishop in the Czechoslovak Republic, in recent weeks published three extraordinarily important texts which go beyond the framework of internal Church issues and directly touch the whole social situation in Czechoslovakia.

The first was the Easter message to the clergy and believers of all Christian churches and to all people of goodwill in our land. The message is above all a call to unity, a unity marked not by triumphalism but by a humble confession of the historical faults of the Roman Catholic Church. With express reference to the ecumenical speeches of Cardinal Beran at the Second Vatican Council he calls on all Christians and all people of goodwill in general that they, remaining faithful by their traditional and specific spiritual experience, commit themselves in mutual respect to the Decade of Spiritual Renewal of the Nation. The official representatives of the Protestant churches accepted this message with some misgivings; however it was read out during divine service in many congregations and in whole presbyteries and is considered to be an exceptionally important step towards ecumenical cooperation.

The Cardinal's next two letters, symbolically dated April 23, 1988 (the Feast of St. Adalbert) are connected with each other. The first is addressed to Prime Minister Lubomír Štrougal. It is a reminder of the petition of more than half a million Roman Catholics for the restoration of religious freedoms,[1] and refers to the cruel persecution and silencing of Christians

1   This was a thirty-one point petition written and circulated by the Catholic lay-activist and Charter 77 signatory Augustin Navrátil (1928–2003). The petition

and the Church in the last forty years and the attack on a peaceful manifestation of Christians in Bratislava. It emphasizes that "Catholics are aware of their rights, they will go on asking for them and are resolved to make sacrifices." Nevertheless, by requesting a change in the attitude of the state to the Church and by requesting a separation of the state from the Church as the most appropriate legal adjustment of relationships, they are not taking the path of confrontation but the path of dialogue which they offer to the state and for which it is high time. Dialogue however presupposes "mutual respect between partners and a sincere intent to reach a serious agreement." It certainly cannot include people who command trust neither from the Holy See nor from the believers of the Church at home, such as, for example, the members of the clerical association *Pacem in Terris*, banned by the Church.[2] On the contrary, in his letter the Cardinal announces an important step directed against the attempt by the state to isolate the hierarchical Church representatives and not to allow—that is, to criminalize—any sort of organized share by laypeople and the rank-and-file clergy in the life of the Church and in the responsibilities for it; if the dialogue is to have a real future then—with reference to the fact that the state has the freedom to accredit its experts and officials—it will also accredit a group of experts from the ranks of the priests and laypeople which will examine the issue of the relationship of the state and the Church and which in the name of the Church at home can share in negotiations with the state in the future.

The third letter from the Cardinal is addressed to all Roman Catholic believers in Czechoslovakia, especially to the signatories of the 31-point petition for religious rights and freedoms. The Cardinal thanks all the signatories to the petition, including the non-Catholics and non-Christians who supported it. He notes that in recent decades virtually all true

called for religious freedom and separation of church and state. It began circulating in December 1987 and continued to attract signatures for the next two years. (Ed.)

2   On *Pacem in Terris*, see ch.7, note 1. On March 8, 1982 Czech and Slovak bishops made their first visit as an episcopate to Pope John Paul II. On that same day the Vatican issued a decree which prohibited priests from participating in any political organizations. Though the document did not mention *Pacem in Terris* by name, the references to "peace" and "ideology" made it clear that this association was now banned by the Vatican (Ed.)

Christians had to bear witness to Christ through multiple privations and sufferings, often even the loss of liberty or of life. He expresses special thanks to those who continue non-publicly in activity which is banned by the state power and which is at the same time an indivisible part of the true Christian life. In this connection he emphasizes that there is only one Church of Christ and that its division into an "official" and a "secret" Church is pure fiction and slander.

In his letter the Cardinal appeals to the responsibility of the laypeople for the Church and to their duty to defend it against injustice. He calls here for a step which is fully consistent with Christian social teaching but which is so radical that it was described by sympathizers from the ranks of non-believers as a Catholic version of "Two Thousand Words."[3] According to the Cardinal, it is not enough to apply for one's rights with regard to secular powers and to demand them, but rather to assume them, in the sense that under the rule of law everything that is not expressly forbidden is allowed. The Cardinal calls for us as Christians not to fear carrying this out. If I understand his message correctly, it is a call for the active implementation of Christian values and for passive resistance to all the totalitarian demands of the Communist state. Apparently I am not so far wrong, for the Cardinal's letter ends with the solemn pronouncement that no one should remain undefended and that everyone who is unjustly persecuted in connection with the faith or with the Church can count on the Cardinal's protection and on "the help of competent professionals.

Note: On May 20, 1988, Deputy Prime Minister of the Czechoslovak Socialist Republic Martin Lúčan, in a speech to the "newly-appointed bishops (apart from Antonín Liška, who is hospitalized) and a group of priests—members of *Pacem in Terris*—in the name of the government refused the offer of a dialogue between the state and the Church, sharply attacked Cardinal Tomášek, and called his letter to Prime Minister Štrougal

3   "Two Thousand Words" was a manifesto published on June 27, 1968 in several Prague newspapers. It was written by Czech author Ludvík Vaculík, with a few dozen other prominent signatories, and it called for increasing the pace of the Prague Spring reforms. It attracted hundreds of thousands more signatures in the days following its publication. (Ed.)

"an abuse of the interests of believers and the Church for political purposes" which "leads to coercion." Lúčan further rationalizes the negative standpoint towards the Cardinal's offer of dialogue by saying that "in conflict with ethical principles, without even waiting for an answer, the letter was provided to the Western media as the basis for new attacks." To that I'll observe that the Cardinal Primate has been waiting in vain for years for answers to all sorts of proposals and submissions which the government of the Czechoslovak Socialist Republic has simply ignored in conflict with the letter of valid laws—it was only with this letter, published in media independent of the will of the Czechoslovak state, that the government representatives were forced to make this prompt, albeit externally negative, reaction.

May 21, 1988

9

A Call from Bratislava

The basic facts about the premature "Good Friday" in Bratislava, be they not very precise and something of an underestimation, i.e., the facts about the generally peaceful Bratislava demonstration by Catholics and its brutal "pacification" by police units, were published in the media worldwide, even ours (naturally, in a very special version). I talked for a long time to David Blow, a BBC correspondent who was hit by a truncheon during the demonstration, then detained and, when he showed the policeman his press accreditation, punched again. I nevertheless got the impression that what made a bigger impression on him than this unfriendly treatment was the fact that, as an involuntary guest in a police car, he was present at the attacks on the participants in the demonstration. He regarded the policemen's natural, human, professional and sporting enjoyment at having knocked down yet another granny as completely inappropriate and as a manifestation of sadism, and thought he had fallen into the hands of madmen. (This, of course, is as seen through the distorted lens of a namby-pamby Western reporter.) I would, however, rather stress that the brutal police attack on a crowd singing the national anthem and praying with rosaries is a manifestation of the decline of state power and its lack of confidence in itself. The crowd should first have been provoked to shouting anti-state slogans and throwing stones at the police. That would have justified a spirited intervention—at least in Western public opinion, accustomed to violent demonstrations and for the most part very tired of them. However, a state which has to bring out water cannons and other measures against lighted candles and rosaries is clearly alarmingly insecure. A state which finds it necessary to turn on its own symbols—in this case the national anthem—so to speak denies its own purpose, and declares itself to be violence pure and simple. At the very least it surrenders the privilege of the power entrusted to it by

God, whereby Christians are bound to respect those requirements which are not in conflict with other laws of God. Cardinal Tomášek was therefore right when he solemnly pronounced in the cathedral that the Bratislava demonstration is not a political matter but rather a witness of faith which has to be published again and again and which is the duty of all true Christians. I end this part of my reflection with an almost anecdotal, but nevertheless well-documented story. Before the Prague pilgrimage in honor of the Blessed Agnes an inspection of members of the StB was held, at which they all received a rosary and a two-crown or five-crown piece for the collection. We thank the government for this exceptional, albeit modest, contribution; in connection with the rosary, we hope that at least in one case it might rest not only in the pocket but also in the heart of the recipient.

The question now is, what next? What next, after a Catholic petition for basic human rights and freedoms, signed by more than half a million Czechoslovak citizens?[1] What next, after the Bratislava demonstration and the brutal attack on it? The mood in Catholic and non-Catholic circles, especially in Slovakia, is indignant and belligerent. Even my friend Ladislav Hejdánek, in the past always skeptical as regarding our possibilities, all at once writes in *Lidové noviny* that there are only two social forces in Czechoslovakia, the Communists and the Catholics, that their future development will depend on how they balance each other, and that all the other groups have only a marginal importance and must adapt themselves.[2] I think that is imprecise; the Communists have all the power but have long since ceased to be a social force, whereas the Catholics are maybe today a social force but their power options are almost nil. I consider even that to be unjust: the Catholics in Czechoslovakia have learned sufficiently from their historical mistakes and faults (they declared that clearly for example in the Easter ecumenical call by the Czech primate Cardinal Tomášek, whose authority today among Roman Catholics throughout Czechoslovakia is vast and

1 See ch. 8, note 1 (Ed.)
2 Ladislav Hejdánek (b. 1927) is a philosopher and Protestant theologian. He was a Charter 77 signatory and also served as a spokesman from September 1977 to February 1978 and from June 1979 to January 1980. *Lidové noviny* was a monthly journal published in samizdat—today it is a daily newspaper published in Prague. See "Potřebujeme majestát," *Lidové noviny* vol. I, no. 4 (April 1988), p. 3. (Ed.)

unassailable) and do not want to be a force which would adapt or subjugate anyone—not even in the name of temporary unity of action in the fight against evil. We want to be an equal partner among equal partners and to join up freely with those of whose good intentions we are convinced—nothing more, but nothing less.

The question "what next" was not answered. The present totalitarian power is in a sense tragically impotent; it has lost the ability to solve any sort of burning problem, whether economic, ecological or social. Almost all that remains in harmony with its instinct for power for the sake of power is the effectiveness of its repressive apparatus. I'm considered a radical and a follower of extreme solutions. However, it's from this position that I deem it necessary to stake the whole of my good reputation on this affirmation: in the next few months an open confrontation with power would mean defeat, maybe bloodletting and certainly the frustration of the results of many years of efforts, a step back, maybe even more; such a confrontation would immeasurably strengthen the totalitarian power for it would at last be able to ascribe an incontestable success to its account, be it only for the military and police. The hour when confrontation is necessary will certainly come; woe to him who fails to recognize it, but three times woe to him who wants willfully to speed it up. Meanwhile we must arm ourselves with the virtue of Christian patience, which has served us so well in recent years; we have to put continual pressure on the totalitarian power, at least *de facto*, maybe outside the unjust law and in defiance of it, to expand the space of religious and civil liberties, but to leave the contest "who whom"[3] to the future and under no circumstances to be provoked into it. In this regard the Bratislava demonstrators can be an example of the Christian attitude and political acumen. They could have chosen to be defiant in a way which would have provoked street battles. Wisely and catholically they decided on passive but consistent resistance. In this way they won an important battle. The war however continues and the totalitarian power in it has all the options to maneuver, but hardly any hope of success.

May 1988

---

3   The Bolshevik slogan connoting the struggle for power. (Ed.)

10

The People's Party: Problems and Hopes

Recently, the hot potato of the "leading role" of the Communist Party and its anchorage in the constitution has been tossed around in various ways, not so much as to get injured, but for it not to cause too much public exasperation. In the end, the real power evidently decided to emphasize the leading position of what is known as the National Front,[1] naturally including the role, guaranteed by the appropriate law, of the Communist Party. In that way the totalitarian power of the Only True Party remains untouched, and only the scenery has to be rearranged a little. In this regard the maneuvers of what are known as the non-Communist Parties and their media have to be judged extremely skeptically, since the tactical camouflage operation of the Communist Party, to which the other parties capitulated unconditionally for decades, currently requires them to pretend they are at least autonomous subjects of political life. At the same time, however, the intention does in itself hold a moment of hope, since the prevailing power cannot seriously consider taking direct repressive interventions against allegedly autonomous partners in the National Front.

For some years an internal tension has been intensifying in the Czechoslovak People's Party, in its membership and (in some fields) influence the most significant of all the formally non-Communist Parties (it has nearly 50,000 members, whereas the Socialist Party has around 14,000 and

---

1   The National Front was a coalition of political parties born in the immediate aftermath of World War II—the coalition was dominated by the socialist parties. After the coup by the Communist Party in February 1948, the National Front really existed in name only—the government was dominated by the Communist Party. (Ed.)

the two Slovak non-Communist parties around 1,000 each).[2] This was openly demonstrated a year ago, when Dr. Sacher, director of the Central Party School, wrote a critical open letter to the leadership of the party, for which he was to be relieved of all his functions and his membership in the party. The case triggered a struggle in the People's Party, in the course of which its presidium and central committee have become virtually incapable of resolutions, and at least three of the seven regional organizations of the People's Party rebelled—Prague, South Moravia (which represents a third of the membership) and South Bohemia. The logical issue of these processes and of the situation in the People's Party is the collection of signatures asking the convening of the congress to be brought forward (to June 1990 instead of March 1991 as set by the leadership). The number of signatures is already approaching the threshold of one-third of the membership required by the statutes. A no less logical issue was the creation of an opposition platform within the People's Party, announced at the countrywide gathering on October 14, 1989 by 73 delegates from almost the whole of the Czechoslovak Socialist Republic under the name "revival current." This calls for a return to the traditions of the party, including its Christian nature. It also asks for the resignation without delay of those functionaries who compromised themselves irremediably in the past. It has to be explained in this connection that some leading functionaries of the People's Party are not only political agents of the Communist Party of Czechoslovakia but actual police agents—most recently demonstrated in the attempt to solve the internal struggle with the help of the StB.

With the creation of an opposition platform in the People's Party a historically unprecedented event occurred—that is, a joint sitting of the committee of the People's Party with the committee of the Communist Party. It seems that the People's Party luminaries were not granted the right to unlimited repression on this occasion; the next day the Central Committee of the Czechoslovak People's Party passed an essentially toothless resolution which criticizes as formally unsuitable the way in which the revival current was established, and leaves the question of further

---

2   The Czechoslovak People's Party was a Catholic party and a member of the National Front. Today it is known as the Christian and Democratic Union-Czech People's Party (KDU-ČSL). (Ed.)

development in the party essentially open. It would be premature to label the recent events a tactical success; however, they definitely offer a new opportunity; for the revival current, for the People's Party and in the end for the whole of society. It will be extremely difficult to capitalize on this chance; it is however vitally important for us all.

November 1989

Part II:
Essays and Inquiries

11

The Parallel Polis[1]

Charter 77 has at least two remarkable achievements to its credit: it has gathered together a broad spectrum of political opinion and civic attitudes; and it has managed to remain legal. It has paid for these achievements by finding itself, from the outset, in a rather schizophrenic situation. On the one hand, despite deep differences in the principles behind their criticism and even deeper ones in their notions about how change might be brought about, everyone takes a very dim view of the present political system and how it works. On the other hand, we behave as though we had failed to notice that the claims the regime makes about its own good intentions, and the laws that appear to limit its totality, are merely propagandistic camouflage. This tactic of taking the authorities at their word is, in itself, a shrewd ploy. Nevertheless, with all due respect to shrewdness, such an approach cannot bridge the gap between the positions mentioned above.

Charter 77 managed, at least temporarily and quite effectively, to eliminate this schism by stressing moral and ethical attitudes over political ones. Today this solution no longer works, and the original dilemma has returned in an even more pressing form. The reasons for this are roughly the following:

1 The death of Professor Patočka, who was unquestionably the *spiritus movens* of this solution.[2]
2 The regime has finally realized that its virulent campaign has transformed a political problem into a moral one and that it has thus unwittingly accepted our choice of weapons. From that moment on

1   Translation by Paul Wilson.
2   See ch. 2, note 4. (Ed.)

the official media have fallen silent on the subject of the Charter, and the regime has limited itself to acts of strangulation in the dark. The official term for it is "whittling away at the edges."

3   The moral attitude was postulated abstractly, without raising any concrete issues or aims. An abstract moral stance, however, is merely a gesture; it may be terribly effective at the time, but it cannot be sustained for more than a few weeks or months. Proof of this phenomenon is familiar to the Charter signatories: the ecstatic sensation of liberation caused by the signing of the Charter gradually gave way to disillusionment and deep skepticism.

Without underestimating the importance of the first two points, I feel that the third is decisive, and sufficient in itself to create a problem. I am therefore suggesting a strategy that should gradually lead us out of the blind alley we are in today. This strategy can be summarized in two phrases: what unifies and drives us must continue to be a sense of *moral commitment and mission*; and this drive should be given a place and a perspective in the creation of a *parallel polis*.

The moral justification of a citizen's right and duty to participate in the affairs of a community (affairs that are "political" in the broadest sense of the word) is beyond all doubt. This was the source of the Charter's public mandate, and at first, it was enough to overcome the differences of opinion within the Charter. It was a guarantee of unity, tolerance, cooperation and, to a certain extent, persistence. Moreover this moral stance is so closely associated with the Charter in the eyes of the public and most of the signatories that any other formula could legitimately lay claim to continuity only with great difficulty. I am not asking, therefore, *whether* we should proceed from a moral basis, but *how* to make that aspect inspiring and mobilizing once more, and *how* to ensure that its influence will persist. I am asking what *kind* of specific efforts or "positive" program can derive its energy from that morality in the future.

A citizen may certainly see there is a moral commitment involved in challenging an evil political power and trying to destroy it. Nevertheless, in the circumstances, such a commitment is suicidal, and cannot hope for public support in any rational ethical system. Likewise, a citizen may feel morally obliged to size up the situation realistically and try to bring about at least partial improvements through compromise and reform. But given the ethics of the present regime, we cannot expect that the moral motivations of such behavior will generally be appreciated, or be in any way morally appealing.

There is a third way of ameliorating conditions in the community. Most structures that are connected, in one way or another, with the life of the community (i.e., to political life) are either inadequate or harmful. I suggest that we join forces in creating, slowly but surely, parallel structures that are capable, to a limited degree at least, of supplementing the generally beneficial and necessary functions that are missing in the existing structures, and where possible, to use those existing structures, to humanize them.

This plan will satisfy both the "reformists" and the "radicals." It need not lead to a direct conflict with the regime, yet it harbors no illusions that "cosmetic changes" can make any difference. Moreover it leaves open the key question of the system's viability. Even if such structures were only partially successful, they would bring pressure to bear on the official structures, which would either collapse (if you accept the view of the radicals) or regenerate themselves in a useful way (if you accept the reformist position).

Both wings will object because this plan reeks of the movement to "enlighten the masses" and it is politically naïve. Yet here we all are in the Charter, and the Charter is undeniably a naïve act, politically speaking, as are all attempts to base one's actions on morality. In any case my suggestion comes directly from the present form of Charter 77, which grew out of actions taken to defend parallel structures that already existed (the Second Culture[3]) and which devotes much of its efforts to "humanizing" existing official structures (like the legislative system) by reinterpreting their meaning. Official politicians should recall that it was they, in the end, who

---

3   The term "second culture" refers to the musical and artistic "underground" or the alternative cultural currents in Czechoslovakia. The movement became more self-conscious in the early 1970s, partly due to the writings of the poet Ivan Martin Jirous (1944–2011). See in particular his "Report on the Third Czech Musical Revival" which was circulated in samizdat in February 1975. It is available in English in Martin Mahovec, ed., *Views from the Inside: Czech Underground Literature and Culture, 1948–1989* (Praha: Ústav české literatury a literární vědy, 2006), pp. 7–31.

brought the community to its present state and that the decent thing to do would be to rethink either their political beliefs or their notion of what is and what is not politically naïve. There is no third way.

Perhaps it is beyond our powers to implement this plan. Nevertheless it is realistic in the sense that it has already worked. Here are two examples that are at once remarkable and yet very different. Parallel cultural structures today undeniably exist, and they are a positive phenomenon. In some areas, like literature, and to some extent in popular music and plastic arts, the parallel culture overshadows the lifeless, official culture. A phenomenon just as undeniable (and negative, though more functional and more human) is the parallel economy, based on systematic theft, corruption and "favors." Under the shiny surface of official economics this parallel economy is a factor in most consumer relations, and also in industrial and trade relations as well.

Here, in brief and in no particular order, are the details of my plan:

a) This point is the preamble to all the others. Our legal system is one of the worst in the world, because it exists solely for propagandistic purposes and for that reason is extremely vague and completely lacking in any legal guarantees. At the same time, and for the very same reasons, this allows it to be interpreted in a very liberal way. We must systematically exploit this discrepancy, and we must be prepared at any time for it to be used systematically against us. The transition from a totalitarian to a liberal system would mean a transition from the principle of "whatever is not expressly permitted is forbidden" to the principle of "whatever is not expressly forbidden is permitted." This can be accomplished only by continually testing the limits of what is permitted, and by occupying the newly won positions with great energy.

b) So far, the Second Culture is the most developed and dynamic parallel structure. It should serve as a model for other areas and, at the same time, all available means must be deployed to support its development, especially in neglected areas like literary criticism, cultural journalism, theatre and film.

c) A parallel structure of education and scientific and scholarly life has already established a certain tradition, although in the past two years it has tended to stagnate. I consider the organization of a parallel education system to be of utmost importance, both for personal reasons (I cannot harbor too many illusions about the chances of my children getting an official education) and for more general reasons. The "underground," which is by far the most numerous element in the Charter, has been able to overcome sectarianism and become political; but if this change is to last, we will clearly have to do "educational" work in these circles. I feel that here in particular there is room for us to aim high with a "maximalist" program.

d) In its early stages the Charter was able to create a parallel information network that was functional and prompt and involved at least several tens of thousands of people. The gradual degeneration of that network, which unfortunately occurred faster than could be explained by the waning of the Charter's initial sensational impact, is considered one of the greatest failures of the Charter and one of the most critical symptoms, so far, of a crisis in its development.

The most important materials from Charter 77 were disseminated by direct, internal circulation (i.e., not via foreign radio broadcasts) to an estimated tens of thousands or even, in the case of the original declaration, to several hundred thousand people. Recently the number of those receiving Charter material has shrunk to hundreds, or at best to some thousands of citizens.

The contents and form of the information circulated will obviously be of key significance. The circulation of information must be considered as important as the actual preparation of the material. Everyone who complains today about the lack of information should feel obliged to circulate the information they do receive more effectively.

The informational network so created must be used regularly. Long periods of inactivity are more dangerous than overloading it, because this leads to loss of interest and the stagnation of connections already established.

Close to the sources, effectiveness is more important than politeness. It is essential to pass information on to places where its further dissemination is assured. I would rather see some "prominent" person informed of something second-hand than have the flow of information clogged, thus limiting it to a narrow scope of people.

There is an urgent need to improve the flow of information to groups outside Prague. It is even more urgent for these groups to establish mutual connections and create autonomous information networks of their own. Here, too, the most important factor in deciding who shall be given the information is whether or not that person can type.

In the future, we will have to consider using other means of reproduction besides the typewriter. A thorough analysis of the legal aspects of this problem should be prepared, and the possibilities of using such technologies as photocopying should be explored. At the moment, the tasks facing us in the parallel economy are unimaginable, but though our opportunities are limited, the need to exploit them is urgent. The regime treats the economy as a key means of arbitrarily manipulating citizens and, at the same time, it regulates it as strictly as possible. We therefore have to rely on strictly confidential accounting practices (any other kind would cross the line into illegal activity), and we must develop a wide base for charitable and other support activities. Our community ought to be based on a system of mutual guarantees that are both moral and material. To demonstrate the morality and disinterestedness of our own motives by ostentatiously ignoring material factors, is, in such circumstances, just as naïve and dangerous as informing the state security forces about the details of our lives because we consider what we do to be honest and legal. We must resist this pressure by consistently turning to international solidarity for help, starting with support from individuals and organizations and ending with far more effective forms of scientific and cultural cooperation that would assure our relative independence from official economic structures (i.e., honoraria for works of art or scientific articles, stipends, etc.).

e) The ground must be prepared for the creation and encouragement of parallel political structures. This would include a wide range of activities, from raising people's awareness of their civic responsibilities, to creating the proper conditions for political discussion and the formulation of theoretical points of view. It would also include support for concrete political currents and groupings.

As regards to a parallel foreign policy, my premise is that the internationalism of any problem, though it may stand little chance of success, can do no harm. Some of the parallel structures I have mentioned here, in economics and education, for instance, cannot hope to function, in the beginning at least, without support from abroad. Publicity for our efforts will provide protection against arbitrary actions by the regime and, for the majority of citizens, it is also the main source of information (foreign radio and television).

No less important is mutual cooperation between related trends in other East Bloc communities. In decades past almost every country in the bloc has paid dearly for the lack of such cooperation. At the moment publicity for what we are doing is quite insignificant and our cooperation with parallel movements inside the bloc has always been painfully inadequate. We must immediately create a team to investigate the reasons for such inadequacies and propose specific remedies.

The individual parallel structures will be connected with the Charter in varying degrees. Some will become an integral part of it; others will be midwifed and wet-nursed by the Charter; yet others the Charter will provide with a guarantee of legality. The parallel structures so formed will go beyond the framework of the Charter in various ways and sooner or later they must become autonomous, not only because they don't fit into the Charter's original form and mission, but because were they not to become autonomous, we would be building a ghetto rather than a parallel *polis*.

Even so, the Charter ought not to limit its involvement in such initiatives in any fundamental way, for by doing so, it would shift its focus from civic activity to merely monitoring such activity, and it would thus lose most of its moral energy. For the future, we will have to accept the fact that we will probably find it easier to agree on a common starting point for our efforts than on any external limitations to them. A citizens' initiative like the Charter will inevitably overflow into related initiatives and, because it is a free association, it has no means authoritatively to establish its own limits. The Charter was, is, and will continue to be based on the confidence that individual groups of signatories will responsibly avoid actions unacceptable to other groups, or that would undermine the original unity and solidarity in the Charter.

Charter 77 must continue to fulfill its proper purpose, namely to compile basic documents which draw attention to denial of human rights and suggest ways of correcting the situation. Documents should appear at the very least at two-month intervals. They ought to be addressed not only to the authorities, but also—and above all—to our fellow citizens. They should therefore deal with genuinely urgent problems. They should not be inordinately long and they should be sufficiently comprehensible even for a lay public, avoiding legal or specialist jargon.

If our aim is to combat the general feeling of futility and hopelessness, rather than contributing to it, we must try to learn from our failure to hold a dialogue with the regime. That means going even further. There is nothing to stop us from presenting, in addition to our usual demands for institutional change, proposals for parallel civic activities that would enable improvements to be made in the given state of affairs. If producing documents ceases to be the sole aim and comes to be considered as merely one aspect of a more persistent effort to investigate the causes of our present misery and to suggest ways of rectification, the Charter 77 is really in no danger of degenerating and becoming a mere producer of dry, rustling papers. Such an approach would represent the most natural transition to the plan, here presented, to create a parallel *polis*.

12

Catholicism and Politics:
The Situation Today, its Roots
and Future Possibilities

Although it is not a very praiseworthy custom, I will begin by outlining what this article is not. Above all, it is not a historical study; if I do mention some historical facts, I am completely unqualified to do so, and lay no claim to academic learning. Nor will I try and use the facts as proof of my assertions, but rather just as illustrations to facilitate the understanding of any reader unfamiliar with our circumstances.

This reflection is actually a reaction to a challenge arising from numerous discussions with Czech and sometimes Slovak and Polish friends—discussions for the most part rudimentary and quite awkward. That leads to another qualification: I am cunningly renouncing in advance any sort of final conclusions, whether in breadth or in depth of understanding. I am going to try and express exclusively my own—and I underline the choice of the first person singular—*my own* overall impression in as idiosyncratic, perhaps even one-sided, a form as possible. I want to encourage discussion, not to summarize and conclude it.

Finally, I'm only going to talk about *Czech* Catholicism—simply because I know distressingly little about Slovak conditions. Overall, I have the impression that Slovak Catholicism is much closer to Polish than to Czech; that it has a relatively large base, an unquestioned unity with national tradition, an uninterrupted historical continuity and accordingly a markedly conservative nature, and so on. Perhaps the only difference between the Slovak and Polish churches is that in Slovakia *political* Catholicism was historically connected with the wartime Fascist Slovak state which has become not only a political whip, applied abundantly and indiscriminately, but also a deep trauma with which political Catholicism in Slovakia is still struggling. In my eyes this is an important reason—though not the only one—why, in spite of numerous similarities between the Slovak and the Polish Catholic Church, their political influence and activity are simply not to be compared. Nevertheless, I apologize in advance to my Slovak and Polish friends for the short-sighted picture of their situation, to which I will be referring from time to time in this and other instances.

I would like to add something positive to all the hedging about in this prologue. I am firmly convinced that the churches in East Europe are now in a position to take a decisive lead in bringing the church in general out of its current state of stress and uncertainty. However, this is not the subject of my article, and all I can do here is to acknowledge a joyous claim together with an overwhelming responsibility. At the same time, we have to face a general crisis, not to mention political paralysis. Considerable importance is ascribed to Third World countries in this connection and many even harbor great hopes for them. I agree in the sense that every solution which does not take note of the existence and problems of the Third World, or even does something against it, something that is at the Third World's expense, is condemned to failure in advance. However, I am certainly not expecting some new political path from the Third World, some universal answer—what we see on the political horizon of the Third World (and nothing is lacking, from the best to the worst) are not manifestations of crisis but of chaos; moreover, of chaos without any forces capable of shaping events, because most of the energy of this greater part of mankind will unfortunately, maybe for a long time to come, be consumed by the immediate pursuit of self-preservation. But nor can one speak about a healthy *polis*, about a dynamic political life, in the countries of the Eastern bloc nor even in the traditional democracies of the West; the manifestations of crisis are too clear. With this the comparison ends; beyond this the manifestations involved are simply of a different order, impossible to compare at any reasonable theoretical or practical level— the best analogy that occurs to me is the difference between a diseased organ and a malignant tumor. The Western Left, in the broadest sense of the word, may be correct about critical analyses of political life in their own countries; but insomuch as they do not understand the vast difference between totalitarianism and democracy (and they do *not* understand it and evidently for some fundamental reasons do not even *want* to understand it), I can have no faith in their behavior or their solutions. That is one of many reasons—I will come to some others—why I believe that the nations of the Eastern bloc are truly at this moment best able to formulate the basics of a radically new political order and to offer a way out of the worldwide political crisis.

I have suggested that in terms of the future role of our nations in the renewal of the church and in the renewal of political life, I derive my optimistic and maximalist demand from the same basis. Therefore, insofar as I will turn my thoughts to the future, I will be developing a single theme: the mission of Catholics and Christians in the formulation of this new form of *polis*. For I am convinced that we are *hic et nunc* facing a single problem that can be theoretically formulated as a need for a new theology, a new content to faith, a new philosophy and science, and a new *polis*. In Eastern Europe—relatively unusually in the history of Christianity—the political aspect already has a certain priority in practical terms, in that every expression of faith is automatically considered a politically relevant act (unfortunately, in Czechoslovakia as a rule that's what the police think too).

Shortly after writing the previous paragraph I learned that a representative of the Polish Church, an outstanding theologian of the new type (new in the Gospel sense, which has little in common with the standard polarization of conservative/progressive), the Krakow Archbishop Karol Wojtyła, had been elected Pope. This is a marvelous promise that the hopes expressed above are not mere speculation; and this election gives the right to those who do not share my faith in the imminent violation of the College of Cardinals by the Holy Spirit, to object that I was too pessimistic in evaluating the ability of the church and the world to overcome the present crisis.

When the independent Czechoslovak Republic was established in 1918 the overwhelming majority of the population was—at least formally— Roman Catholic, although the official concept of its statehood came, to a large measure, from the anti-Catholic, reformed tradition (which, though false to the complex religious history of the Czech lands, was also an appropriate punishment for the spiritual, cultural and political sterility of the Czechoslovak Catholic Church at that time). The resulting paradox developed differently in the life of the two parts of the Republic. Slovak Catholicism—more widespread, vital and authentically national—succeeded in retaining its decisive political influence, at the price of denying not only Czechoslovak statehood but unfortunately even democratic traditions. Czech Catholicism, on the other hand, essentially withdrew from politics and from active cooperation in the social environment at all, limiting itself to a lackluster and a rather unsuccessful defense of its traditional position. The only significant exception was in the Catholic-oriented artistic—especially literary—sphere, naturally viewed negatively by official church circles or in the best case with suspicion.

The Communists were able to exploit the historical handicap of Slovak Catholicism and between 1945 and 1948—by a deft combination of political and police methods— completely excluded it from the political stage; nothing could help, not an overwhelming election victory, not the reluctant support of other democratic forces in the Republic, not even left-wing "courtship" by some Catholic politicians.

By contrast, at the time of the Communist coup in 1948, the Catholic Church in the Czech Lands was the only influential and organized power that was uncompromised and uncorrupted by earlier political concessions to the Communists or by defensive cooperation with them. At the same time, it was a politically inexperienced power, unprepared to enter the struggle. The Church's reaction matched the situation: on the one hand, it did not try actively to influence the course of events; on the other, it emphatically refused to sanction the result of the coup, to evaluate the new political conditions "realistically," or to take the first steps in a Communist courtship. Thanks to this somewhat quixotic attitude, the Catholic Church became the first exemplary object of systematic repression. Above all, its organizational and intellectual potential was liquidated. All the bishops were interned or imprisoned. In 1949 the religious Orders were *de facto* dissolved and of 12,000 monks, 8,000 were either imprisoned or interned on average for five years (the representatives of some Orders were not released until the spring of 1968). A considerable number of the secular clergy were either imprisoned or deprived of the possibility of fulfilling their calling. Tens of thousands of Catholic lay people spent long years in prison; and of the leading intellectuals, few, especially writers, avoided punishment. Tens of thousands more Catholics in all the above-mentioned categories avoided a similar fate only by emigrating. Harsh discrimination and administrative sanctions were dealt out to *everyone* who continued courageously to acknowledge their faith.

All things are plain before God, and this entire investment will be remembered and in time yield its reward. However, I have to evaluate here the consequences of the Church's attitude from a limited human, and chiefly political, point of view. For the twenty-year gap between 1948 and 1968 the answer seems clear: crushing repression, the falling-off of the "lukewarm" majority, the limitation of church life to a minimum of ritual manifestations—in my opinion, that is all more than balanced by the high moral credit which the Catholic Church of the time acquired in the eyes of society. In those years the Protestant churches embarked on a path of compromise with the Communist regime which enabled them to preserve a certain—albeit limited—space for church life, and saved them—albeit relatively—from systematic repression. Nevertheless, this period confirms the primacy of truth over pragmatism; the regeneration—often politically motivated to start with—of religious awareness, especially among the young people and intelligentsia, is overwhelmingly focused on the suppressed and devastated Catholic Church. However, development over the last decade (after 1968) considerably complicates this simple evaluation. In the Protestant Church, thanks to its more favorable fate—albeit with the payment of no small libations at who knows what altars—a situation was created where the leadership of these churches react to pressure from the authorities at least with reluctance, and where some simple believers and clergy in one way or another engage themselves in society actively and courageously. The Catholic Church, on the other hand, pays a high price for its previous heroic period and it seems to be squandering the accumulated treasure of suffering and the moral credit derived from it on some sort of "hangover." Those who survived long imprisonment are now old and, with some honorable exceptions, tired and skeptical (though few are literally "broken"). The top church hierarchy is composed partly of such people and partly of those who—voluntarily or under pressure—became puppets or direct agents of the security services; the natural outcome is its utter servility *vis-à-vis* the regime. The policy of awarding and withdrawing state permission to hold the office of a priest (in some periods more than 50 percent of priests lost the right to work as such); of systematically transferring more active priests from parish to parish; of deliberately eliminating—sometimes with the use of psychological and sociological techniques—the better students and teachers from the theological seminaries; etc., etc.; this policy has over the decades wreaked havoc among the clergy. The level of political and cultural isolation is high; at the very least, a significant portion of the lower clergy (although the situation here is incomparably better than in the hierarchy) is "involved" with official power to one extent or another. The most serious thing lacking is effective solidarity between the community of believers and their pastors—it is in fact thanks to such solidarity that many Protestant congregations have in recent times shown themselves able to defend and sometimes even vindicate themselves against various repressions. The timid, official post-Vatican II attempts to involve the laity more widely in the life of the Church were completely suppressed after 1968. At the same time, any unofficial extra-liturgical contacts—whether among believers or between priests and lay people—are administratively liable and, under the Czechoslovak legal code, even criminally liable. I cannot resist mentioning one specific example, far from the most glaring, but interesting in the Czechoslovak-Polish context. It seems that at an Esperanto camp held in Herbortice in August 1977, a Polish and a Czech priest (Fr. Zielonek and Fr. Srna) held Mass in a tent before the wakeup call—with the knowledge of the camp leader J. Šváček and in the presence of several campers. Soon afterwards Fr. Srna had his state permission withdrawn, and now criminal proceedings are being taken against him and against J. Šváček for "obstruction over the supervision of churches and religious organizations" (§178 of the criminal code). They are threatened with up to two years in prison.

What I have indicated in the preceding paragraphs is the result of a general and thorough "decimation of cadres" (albeit the word decimation is a euphemism here)—and so one way or another one has to keep this in mind. However, I consider the psychological impact caused by decades of terror to be the most serious and politically most dangerous result. The overwhelming majority of Czech Catholics are convinced (unfortunately this is for the most part confirmed by their own experience) that by merely attending divine service and privately acknowledging their faith they have expressed so much courage and willingness to suffer for Christ that no one has the right to expect further manifestations of civic courage and commitment from them. Plainly, there is an element of failure in this attitude, of the "Kingdom of God" having been exchanged for a certain accommodation with the world—albeit in the role of second-class citizens, subjects of discrimination. There is also an element of justified mistrust with regard to their former persecutors who have now lost their rights and loudly call for general solidarity—often without giving sufficient guarantee that when they speak of rights they are not thinking of their own lost privileges.[1] Nevertheless, whether we condemn it or apologize for it, this attitude remains a political fact and has to be considered in the future. Moreover, there is a danger that even those who, during everyday encounters with the absurdities and injustices of social life, see the moral intolerability of such an attitude and attempt to break it (and from time to time this happens to every honest believer who has eyes to see and ears to hear), that even they, under the pressure of automated self-censorship, will limit themselves to some "minimal" gesture. To illustrate what I mean, I can give the example of a good and educated Catholic woman who not long ago refused to sign a protest petition of a group of believers as too unreasonable a provocation of the authorities, pointing out that even in the 1950s one could in the end do at least something; that she herself, for example, had, from time to time, dared to send parcels of buns to imprisoned and interned priests. I would not want you to underestimate the long-term courageous dedication of this woman, nor should you put such "bun Catholicism" on a level with "goulash Socialism"; in our country, many people found themselves (and still do sometimes) in prison for years for such good deeds.[2] In the context of an individual's efforts to get close to the Truth (that is, the truth about salvation) and as an example for the

1 Benda refers here to the "reform Communists" who were purged from the Party in 1968 and persecuted thereafter. (Ed.)

2 "Goulash socialism" refers to socialism as practiced in Hungary from the 1960s until 1989. Goulash is a Hungarian dish consisting of a variety of quite disparate ingredients—thus the term connotes an idiosyncratic brand of socialism, in some respects more moderate and livable than the more orthodox versions practiced in the other Warsaw Pact nations. Benda is thus at pains to emphasize that his readers not equate his "bun Catholicism" and the situation in Czechoslovakia with the situation in Hungary. (Ed.)

neighbors, I consider such actions indispensable and worthy of high praise. Only: we are in a situation when the community itself of the universal church, when the *polis* in the widest sense of the word, is threatened to its very foundations, and when everyone confronts the challenge, like it or not: what would you rather save, your own life or the life of this community, of this terribly tortured body of Christ? And face to face with this challenge, "the above-mentioned" action is in and of itself insufficient and, as an example to others, even dangerously misleading. For, as in the case of the overwhelming majority of the nation as it flees from civic life into the sphere of family and friends, this is also a retreat, maybe more honorable, but nevertheless a retreat into the ghetto, a voluntary relinquishing of openness and of universal shared responsibility.

How does this deeply pessimistic evaluation of mine concerning the situation of Czech Catholicism compare with the optimistic outlook—even politically optimistic—announced at the beginning of this article? I do not want to refer automatically to Solzhenitsyn's "treasure of suffering,"[3] though I firmly believe that *every* suffering is meaningful and in the end *somehow* appreciates in value; for such an appreciation does not have to be immediate, nor does it have to be reflected positively in the *political sphere*—and when it comes down to it, this is a political essay. Moreover, my response should not be seen as—at least *prima facie*—deriving from the perspectives given by the new papal election (even though this election does essentially influence the distribution of forces and the dynamic of Czech Catholicism) since I declared my hope before this revolutionary event took place.

If, in the paragraph above, I was deliberately harsh in formulating the challenge today facing Czech Catholics (and maybe even their Slovak, Polish and other brothers), I wanted in this way to underline the harsh and uncompromising conditions under which their hope to be "the salt of the earth" must be realized.[4]

---

3   Though this exact phrase does not seem to occur in Solzhenitsyn's writings, he investigates the importance of suffering in *The Gulag Archipelago*, part iv, chapter 1, "The Ascent." There he speaks of one's eyes being purified by suffering and one's soul being ripened from suffering. See *The Gulag Archipelago*, volume II, Thomas Whitney trans. (New York: Westview Press, 1998), pp. 598, 611. (Ed.)

4   Matthew 5:13. (Ed.)

However, in shifting the meaning of Christ's statement from the spiritual level—from the level of a personal approach to the Kingdom of God—to the political level (I am not afraid to say, to the level of a struggle for political power) I opened the route to a fundamental source of hope; meaning hope in this world too. For the majority of Czech Christians, Communism was and is identified with Satan and the Antichrist—and I am happy to agree with them. The thing is, Satan has a dual historical form; in the 1950s he was more like Lucifer (the bearer of light), the most sublime of the angels of God, the spirit of deception and deceit and eternal volatility. At that time it was essentially a Manichean struggle between the principles of good and evil, when through its loudness the lie substituted for truth, when through its logic appearance substituted for reality, and when the easiness of the way to the Fall substituted for historical salvation. In this time, when an overwhelming majority fell, and many were destroyed as a warning, he stood fast who took counsel with his own soul and remained in Truth. However, the Communism of the last decade is more like the Nietzschean "spirit of gravity"[5]: apathetic, gloomy and devouring. Power stands against truth, nothingness against reality, the immobility of the cycle "from anniversary to anniversary" against history. In this time, which is oppressive rather than cruel, he who consults *only* his own soul and believes that Truth—the Truth which became incarnate in a specific place and at a specific moment and lived among men and suffered for them—is a mere *position* on which it is sufficient to *persist*, does not stand fast.

For as long as evil was aggressive and polemical (albeit it always had a few punches in reserve in case of lack of arguments), one could "fence oneself in" against it and from this established position oppose it—whether through active polemics or passive suffering. If however contemporary political evil is now primarily a restrictive weight that every citizen already carries on himself or herself, and *within himself or herself*, then the only possibility is to shake off that evil, to escape its power and set out on the path to truth. Under such circumstances every real struggle for one's own soul becomes a manifestly political act, and even creatively political, because it is no longer merely "defining oneself" against

5   See Nietzsche's *Thus Spoke Zarathustra*, section 55. (Ed.)

something (there is nothing to define oneself against); but rather throwing off one's bonds and opening oneself to something new and unknown. So it is paradoxically possible, in a society for which mass flight into privacy is characteristic, as is simple indifference with regard to the scenery of official pseudo-politics, to speak of a latent politicization, of the growth of political potential—and Christians could and should become one of the means through which this potential is realized and acquires a visible shape. My preceding pessimistic evaluation of the contemporary state of things derives from the fact that to see this opportunity, to accept it without equivocation and to be willing to wager everything on it, seems to be almost humanly impossible; historical perspectives are hopelessly blocked, the regime is ever more cohesive and more powerful than before, the government of fear still more universal. Yet my optimism derives from the fact that all this is true only *for the moment*, and that the slightest social movement (perhaps just the courage of a few who, in spite everything, will commit themselves to the opportunity) can resurrect life processes whose momentum and consequences no one can foretell. For fear is for the most part fiction, maintaining itself by sheer inertia; the system which has deliberately repudiated fanatical adherents and relies on a mass of acquiescent opportunists, has guaranteed itself *easy* obedience—but not in any way *blind* obedience, because any kind of personal responsibility is too much of a risk for its machinery and so in the end even the regime's terrorist intentions are crushed and peter out in a complicated bureaucratic jungle. Even its cohesiveness and power are questionable, for they are not the functions of a living organism but the mechanical operations of a seriously worn-out machine which can be hopelessly disrupted by the jamming of the smallest of its parts. Christians especially should be clear about the hopelessness of momentary historical perspectives and the stability of terrestrial "Thousand Year Reichs." In this then I see a basic source of hope, and especially hope in the future role of political Catholicism. And if I add in the new papal election, thanks to which traditional Catholic respect for authority, which has operated so unfortunately up to now—especially after the appointment of a collaborationist hierarchy—will acquire completely new dimensions, then in spite of everything this hope appears real to me and its realization will take place in the near future.

To the extent that one can outline what *could* be realized in politics and Catholicism in our land, it should be possible to articulate our own possible contribution towards resolving the crisis of the contemporary world—and especially the crisis in politics. I want to say in advance that I do not know how to do this, and that in any case I cannot—because such a formulation would be a political program, and the change I have in mind is essentially above political programs—or rather, avoids them altogether and deals with life (which is to some extent an emotional claim, but emotion is one of the factors to which that "treasure of suffering" accumulated over recent decades has returned a positive meaning). Nevertheless, it is perhaps possible to give a partial answer; to warn what this change should *not* be and to outline some of the attitudes with which we *do* necessarily have to come to terms.

I will begin with a very simplified scheme of contemporary political stratification in Czechoslovakia. The overwhelming majority of the population is made up of those who are "loyal" to the system. Their agreement is not considered by the regime to be true loyalty but rather a decently rewarded "collective guilt," whose extent and appraisal are indeed graded, and in which however everyone shares—from the lowest worker up to the prime minister. Tactically the system is virtually perfect; almost everyone has some personal interest in maintaining the status quo and almost everyone has some share at least in carrying out the repressive functions of the regime. Strategically, it is a catastrophic system, for two reasons. First, no one (maybe not even the First Secretary of the Communist Party) believes in its future, and so everyone is looking for a way to avoid the responsibilities of his or her position, while at the same time exploiting its benefits as much as possible (and as quickly as possible) with the motto "after us the Flood." Secondly, this system of constant humiliation and forced, active participation in various shameful deeds mostly evokes manipulated feelings of impotence and guilt—and hatred is increasingly its logical outcome (I have found myself in a variety of social environments in recent years, and the extent of this hatred sometimes fills me with horror). If this "loyal" mass wakes from its lethargy (or if something awakens it) then its gaze will be fixed essentially on the past, with a semi-conscious and unclear longing for restoration, and a burning longing to take revenge for its spoiled life and at the same time to wash away its guilt in a bloody rampage (if the regime, perhaps only dimly sensing this, is filled with hysterical fear, not even the opposition thinks of it as a consolation but rather a threat of squandering the future opportunity). That infinitesimal minority of the population which is consciously and *manifestly* politically disloyal can be divided into two categories. The first consists of the "liberals," who focus on the present and try exclusively *hic et nunc* to recognize and legitimate their own attitude; characteristic for them is an emphasis on the moral and existential position, the reform of contemporary mankind, and in some cases "small works,"[6] leading to a change for a better. This is accompanied by skepticism towards changes of political forms and towards radicalism going beyond mere "moral example." The second category includes a whole range of "Socialist" orientations—from Socialists of an uncertain mindset through Social Democrats and Eurocommunists to Trotskyites. Common to them all is a distinctive orientation to the future, linked one way or another with a change (albeit revolutionary rather than reformist) in the present state of affairs. There are advantages and disadvantages to this orientation, with the latter derived from the former: the socialist position is precise and intelligible and thus highly attractive; but it neglects the present, has a voluntarist interpretation of the past, and thus includes the permanent threat that the proclaimed ideal will remain mere theory at the price of cruelly real sacrifices.

Nevertheless, thanks to the sheer elementariness and "nakedness" of the political situation, and to the fact one cannot talk about political life—not to mention an opposition—in Czechoslovakia as one would understand it in European discourse, not to mention that *any* freely conceived initiative *at all* (even the cultivation of postal pigeons) automatically becomes a political act *par excellence* with all the practical consequences for

6   Small works or *drobná práce* is a concept developed by Tomáš Masaryk in his *The Czech Question* in 1895. There Masaryk argued that Czechs had to exercise habits of individual responsibility in all facets of their everyday lives—only through such small works could they develop the resources to become capable of political and cultural independence and thus escape the dominance of the Austro-Hungarian Empire. Later, the idea of small works also became relevant to those seeking a way to escape the dominance of Soviet Communism. (Ed.)

its initiator; thanks to all this, some sort of unity is beginning to bridge the range of differences I have described. Up to now, its most complete and most characteristic expression is the free citizens' initiative Charter 77. The community of Charter 77 signatories (and the much wider circle of those who sympathize with them and one way or another actively support them) includes not only almost all the currents of the "conscious" political opposition but also those who, from a need to maintain free human speech, refused to become "established" at the price of shared guilt and tried to flee from political life (most of the cultural underground which forms one of the largest elements of the Charter belongs to this). It was not until they were in the environment of Charter 77 that they learned the civic alphabet of virtues—i.e., in the true sense of the word political—while at the same time they give the "political" elements of the Charter a genuine lesson in human freedom and in the life in Truth. This unity is a great school for its participants, and in itself represents a novelty from which it should be possible to draw more than one lesson. Meanwhile, outside observers unfortunately find it a riddle they are incapable of solving satisfactorily; the regime explains it by common hatred (which if it weren't just phraseology might contain perhaps at least a partial truth). Western observers dig till they are exhausted, trying to find out which political group and which tactical aspect this unity serves (I can assure them that however exact the answer, it would not bring them a step closer to understanding what it is really about). However, the very source of this unity is also its greatest handicap; it is a unity of necessity, a unity of defense, which in its present form is incapable of achieving any greater success than it has so far. It is a unity whose participants have voluntarily resigned from politics—from politics as *techné*—in the name of the struggle against everything which makes human life unfree and undignified. To the extent to which *techné* is today identified with authority and manipulation, to that extent this resignation is justified and stimulating. But freedom and human dignity are not absolute given facts, but rather gifts which mankind and society must learn to accept in their history, and for which they must also know how to struggle. Therefore in my opinion politics as *techné*—i.e., the art of the struggle for the fate of the *polis*—does not cease to have its justification in the future too—albeit in constant oscillation between that futility and the necessity of Jacob's struggle with the angel.[7] And in this sense the earlier unity of Charter 77 seems provisional and inadequate. In conclusion, I will attempt from the Catholic point of view—or from what I consider the Catholic point of view—to indicate the possibilities open to the new politics and the "more essential" unity. In spite of elements of synthesis, this is not a proposal of some sort of reconciliation or historical compromise, but rather an appeal to those who are willing, in the given conditions and despite all basic disagreement, to cooperate in order to transfer the conflagration to a new, less charted and therefore more interesting field.

However, I must first backtrack a bit. The political stratification I mentioned has a certain analogy in the Christian environment. The Protestants are—thanks among other things to some degree of Puritanism—relatively immune with regard to the usual approach of combining loyalty to the regime and shared guilt with hatred towards the regime. On the other hand, they are often unreservedly willing to accept a moralistic (in my terminology liberal) attitude; or on the contrary, to support the idea of creating a radically new and just society, programed to some formula in advance (an essentially Socialist idea). Incidentally, both attitudes derive from the same moralistic concept of politics; they differ only in whether they put emphasis on the "private" or "public" nature of morality.

It is different in the Roman Catholic environment, where the three attitudes outlined above are shared roughly in the same proportions as in the rest of the population. However, there is an important shift; whichever of these political orientations Catholics incline towards, they almost always keep it at a sufficient distance, and are at the same time almost always capable of fundamentally appreciating the contribution of others with a different orientation. They are "more sinful," or at least more tolerant with regard to sin than Protestants are, and better at understanding the positive meaning of sin in the history of redemption (see *felix culpa*, the "Fortunate Fall" in the canticle of the Easter liturgy). Therefore, where failure is concerned they are capable of adopting not only more tolerant but also more appreciative attitudes, while remaining healthily skeptical with regard to the liberal (that is, Socialist) faith in radical individual (that is, social) reform. At the same time however, they see the problem of salvation primarily in

7   See Genesis 32:22–32. (Ed.)

its social and historical dimensions; they therefore pose the question of shared responsibility and collective guilt even more acutely than the most puritan of Puritans, and are willing to recognize the place and even longing for revenge, modified to a form of atonement and righting of wrongs in historical time. It was Catholicism that formulated the redemptive role of individual "moral" example as dogma, in the worship of the saints. And finally, the coming of the Kingdom of Christ as being conditional on our concrete efforts in preparing its ground and building its foundations in historical time, is becoming ever more clear to Catholics (let me illustrate this by the decision of the Second Vatican Council which replaced the liturgical prayer for the conversion of renegade Jews with a prayer that they remain faithful to their God and mission to be a visible archetype of the history of Redemption).

Thus Catholics are, first, more "involved," more guilty—not only by momentary failure, but also because the Communist regimes find well-tried patterns in the history of the institutional church for their own worst practices; at the same time however, this awareness of guilt also means a more severe, more uncompromising standpoint, clearly distinguishing between "good and evil." Secondly (and I will be expanding this and the following point), Catholics are open to the merits of particular solutions and at the same time maintain a certain immunity with regard to these solutions. Thirdly, they are extremely skeptical with regard to politics in general; at the same time they are aware that at the present time "something like politics" is the only thing that can save us. Indeed, if I had to characterize the standing of the nations of "really existing Socialism"[8] with regard to the rest of the world, I would use the preceding statements unchanged. That includes the offer of a broad and comfortable road to failure; it is enough to deny one's guilt (individual or national) and passively wait for angelic choirs or Western armies to liberate us from the supremacy of the Antichrist.

When in my historical reminiscences I spoke about "political Catholicism," I was deeply aware of the contestability and inner contradiction of such a (common) collocation. But I refrained from avoiding the term in the belief that it would acquire a positive meaning in

8   See ch. 6, note 1. (Ed.)

the light of my perception of the shape of future politics—far removed from politics in today's sense of a self-preserving and punitive struggle for power and at the same time "more political," if we understand by this a commitment to a playful and sacred concern for the matters of the *polis*.

The starting point for this new politics is closely connected with the attitudes I noted above as being symptomatic of the awakening (or reawakening) political awareness of the Catholic population, and with the special nature these attitudes are acquiring, thanks to historical circumstances. For understanding associated with detachment can mean an effort to polish the corners, to accept healthy elements while at the same time rejecting excess. In the worst case this leads to opportunistic compromise; in the better, to an attempt at synthesis, in aggregate not exceeding the current possibility of merged elements. It can however also mean agreeing to what is most radical in sectional concepts, while saying it is still insufficiently radical, because only sectional. Such an attitude is "catholic" in the true sense of the word; its possibility was demonstrated at least in the happy moments of Christian history, and I believe that a chance of such "happy moments" is opening before us again today. It is the same with being skeptical as regards politics, and at the same time finding that all our hopes are one way or another bound up with politics. It can lead to a rejection of politics, linked with a good deal of pessimism or, on the contrary, to strong political commitment at the price of the acceptance of "necessary evils" (victims—how many already?) on the altar of a better future. Indeed, if we accept or if we let ourselves be forced into accepting the currently valid concepts of politics, no other solution remains to us. But we can also postulate and start implementing a completely different, new kind of politics (I tried in my essay "The Parallel Polis" to show that the possibility of such politics is open even in our conditions; the present essay provides a certain idea—albeit partial, and measured to the specific situation—about what should in my opinion, be the starting point and continuation of the new politics). The word new is confusing, for it creates the idea of some sort of lawful and automatically positively evaluated "progress"; nothing could be further from what I think. I see "the only thing that can save us" as being a "return to the sources," to life and politics. This does not of course mean a return to the sources in the sense of nineteenth-century practices, which always meant an arbitrary division between "right" and "wrong" at a random point in history (by which both were usually devalued and misinterpreted), but rather a real path on which everything "good and evil" in the development of politics until now will be re-examined and newly understood—that is, which would make sense of the past in a way that will help to illuminate our problems today. The election of John Paul II shows that such a view of the "new" is not just my naïve personal hope and that it can realistically happen worldwide (and especially for "Catholics" from one point of view and for the "countries of the Eastern bloc" from another). At the very least, at the theological level the election suddenly called into question the generally accepted polarity between conservatives and progressives in the Church and opened a new possibility in which such a division would no longer be meaningful. It is a mere possibility—nevertheless, I believe it will happen, and in its beneficial influence on other spheres of human culture. In the same way I believe that the "new politics" is possible, that it is the only alternative to the Apocalypse, and that our nations in general and their Catholic population in particular have a unique chance to articulate its beginnings. It should be a "bloody serious" politics, binding "up to the neck"; yet it should be (as far as possible) unbloody and (necessarily) playful. It should be politics with commitment (and to set an example, I have taken this commitment on myself, although political activity was the last thing in my life I longed for) but not involving submission (for instance, the state or any other type of organization of society can be a useful factor in limiting evil, but never an instrument for the realization of "paradise on earth"). It should be a politics in which human rights and the rules of parliamentary democracy—and also the privileges and freedoms of the "feudal" world and the requirements of social justice—are a matter of course, because they have already been realized one way or the other, but are not enough. Because the use of an existing model is sometimes necessary for technical reasons, I will—to the substantial displeasure of my left-thinking friends—label my political concept as being conservatively radical. I am very curious as to whether, after reading this essay, they will consider our political disagreement to be a mark of verbal misunderstanding, or of real antagonism. Nevertheless, I am convinced on the basis of many indicators that at the present time there are only two paths open to the Catholics of the Czech Lands: the path of political and therefore Christian failure, and the path—wearisome and thorny—of searching for a new, conservatively radical politics.

January 5, 1979

13

Comments on Some
Frequently Heard Comments

The Jews answered him: "We have a law, and by our law he ought to die, because he claimed to be the Son of God."
—John, 19:7

... some Josef Zvěřina or other, who claims to be a priest.
—*Rudé právo*, September 24, 1983

... for trolls, as you probably know, must be underground before dawn, or they go back to the stuff of the mountains they are made of, and never move again.
—J. R. R. Tolkien, *The Hobbit*

By their fruits ye shall know them. There are those who merely dress as priests—and make no mistake, this requires considerable courage in this time of persecution. And to wear priestly garb outside the church buildings does indeed form a resistance to the orders of the power ruling over a certain part of temporal penalties and temporal possibilities. But there are also some who, neglecting even the measure, even the dignity of their vestments, are in time willing to dress or let themselves be dressed as something else. The will and authority of the Magisterium don't matter to them, understandably even the nicknames reminiscent of canine breeds don't matter to them, nor the duality and mutual irreconcilability of the sources of their titles and benefits.[1] And then there remain the tremendously salty and

---

1   Benda is alluding to membership in the state-sponsored clerical organization

indigestible types, who really do claim to be priests; who, as priests, sacrifice themselves for Our Lord and, after the fashion of Our Lord, sacrifice themselves unto death. These are the priests who thirst after righteousness and do not abandon widows, orphans or prisoners. They do not turn their face away from the wounded and the stripped wretch by the road, and do not lower their gaze, mumbling empty and apologetic words, when the truth is loudly and menacingly abused. They, from folly for Christ again and again, willingly "sew their coat of shame" as *Rudé právo* delicately puts it (this euphemism betrays only a little of what is usually also a coat of nettles and of suffering). In compliance with the wishes of the malignant power, and according to the will of Him who is Lord of times and actions, only a few of these faithful servants are not dead or wiped out of human memory.[2] It is my deepest conviction that one of these is Father Josef Zvěřina, known in the familiar Christian way as Joey by those for whom he has been a help and support.[3] Joey's deeds are sure evidence of many things; it is however written that if faith without deeds is dead, deeds without faith are unfruitful—he, in deep Christian humility, always puts his faith to the test—he is a warrior for faith, not in any way God's pensioner and shrewd purchaser of eternal certainties. We know that only God can judge our heart and our loins; if however there is some sort of secular guide for weighing up true faith, then it is that unfailing trust and cheerfulness, that joy from a well of goodness that radiates from Father Zvěřina over all who have eyes to see—in spite of all the adversities which long ago caused the downfall of others and which for him are just a reason for a gentle smile; in spite of an unbelievably long chain of trials and wrongs; and in spite of

Pacem in Terris, used by the regime to control priests. These priests were nicknamed "Pax Terriers" (like Fox Terriers) by their opponents.(Ed.)

2   Benda here enumerates three categories of priests: first, there are those who perform their liturgical duties but scrupulously avoid conflict with the regime. Second, there are those priests who actively collaborate with the regime—usually members of the clerical assocation Pacem in Terris. Third, there are those priests who are steadfastly true to their calling and vocation. They were brutally repressed by the regime—many were imprisoned while others had their state permission to be priests revoked. (Ed.)

3   Josef Zvěřina (1913–1990) was ordained in Rome in 1937. He was imprisoned from 1952 to 1965 and was an early signatory of Charter 77. (Ed.)

his age—since the occasion for this sincere homage is the fact that according to the calendar and other reliable evidence Josef Zvěřina has reached the age of seventy; but only according to those, as when you meet him, when you are struck by the youthful élan of this priest, man, citizen and scholar, such a thing would never occur to you. A man of true faith, a man who is truly offering himself to others!

However, we want to celebrate the truth here by trying to cast a little light on some lies which pose as truth or disguise themselves, relying on their likelihood and plausibility, as being for the truth. These consist of a group of assertions or slogans which these notes of mine (and they really are only notes or notions, something like the third cock-crow, which does not mean that morning has come, just that it's on the way) will reveal as interconnected. These slogans suggest that Socialist ideas, whether Marxist or of related provenance, are good in essence and just happened to get damaged by some unfortunate practices; and that the ideal of "social equality" in particular is our shared human task, something not to be doubted—one can at most dispute the appropriate means for its attainment. Similar voices can be heard among Christians, and in Christian language, appealing to the Gospel. It is to these that my reservations are addressed, and I will try to articulate them in the language of the Gospel.

First then, let us look at Marxism and Socialist ideas in general. I would go directly to their "purest" and "most authentic" nucleus which supposedly represents the guiding intellectual and moral impulse of the last hundred years. Thanks to the imperatives in which I grew up and studied, I know more than a little about these ideas; nevertheless, I would like to say something at the outset for those who at any price try to defend the indefensible, and for those whom perhaps more favourable circumstances, thanks to this note, might allow to be saved from wandering down vain paths. It is notoriously well-known that human life is short and uncertain, and that a surfeit of information becomes one of the most serious obstacles to the truth. It is therefore extremely useful to acquire one simple criterion: the moment someone promises to realise heaven on earth through our own human powers, the moment they invoke a return[4] to mankind's

---

4   Even logic limps here, because one has to rely on history and its laws; and history is fundamentally where one is going without being able to return. Not

original intact state, there is no need to read further—at best the speaker is a competent fraudster, at worst a fanatical madman. However, revelation and historical reality are in rare concord in showing us that every demand to "change this or that, that's all" or "just get rid of this obstacle or the other, this or that human tare spoiling the harmony of the plan as a whole" so that absolute good will eventually be achieved, always results in hecatombs of dead and in the intolerable enslavement of the survivors without a single step being advanced towards the promised ideal. The second a priori objection is also well grounded in the Gospel: "By their fruits ye shall know them" and "Not everyone who says to Me, 'Lord, Lord,' shall enter the kingdom of heaven."[5] Ever since the ageless fall of the angels and the primeval *peccatum originale*, it has been very well known that it is never man, a being made in God's image, who corrupts good ideas; if evil emerges somewhere, then always only from the seed of a pure spirit and pure ideas to which man in his weakness succumbs again and again. The fruit of human deeds is imperfect, wizened, immature and bitter: however, if it is full of poison, if it brings death and corruption, we can say without fear of being wrong: this poison is the fruit of the spirit, bad thoughts damage (merely weak) people and spark off in them the possibility of doing evil. Ignorance does not sin and evil is not present and incarnate in any creature, for God "saw that it was good"; it is only that the spirit can in its freedom give rise to these malignant things.

Each of these reasons is sufficient in itself for us to shrug our shoulders over this folly and devote our time to prayer instead. One can of course point to numerous specific curses to be found in the very principles of this teaching—a teaching destined to become a major deception, the undoing of many, and a terrible punishment for the accumulated transgressions of man. We can name a few of the curses at random. There is the sin of pride against God and against all creation, crowned at a secular level with the words: "the philosophers have only interpreted the world in

---

even the Redemption as a sovereign act of God implies in any way the recall of the angel with the flaming sword from the gates of Paradise; it rather promises a new empire and the opening of a path to it, full of uncertainty and suffering and service, a path truly historical. (VB)

5   Matthew 7:19–22. (Ed.)

various ways; the point, however, is to change it"[6] (to avoid any misunderstanding—Christ's "change of heart" is precisely the opposite process. In His case the starting point is listening, not destructive government). There is the sin of despair and Nihilism. This sin either denies—through the concept of "alienation"—anyone or anything other; or annihilates—by hard historical determinism and "turning upside-down"—even the sinner himself and his freedom. Then there are the countless sins against the truth when it is made the property of a class, of its revolutionary vanguard and finally only of the "objective" interests of this vanguard expressed by hallmarked oracles. Such "truth" is dead—morally and ontologically indifferent. Following the proven method of the "aping God," these ideas— which as practical guidance are inseparable from their realization—were supplemented by much that originated in the Old Testament and in rabbinical tradition, or in the historical structures of the Roman Catholic Church, in an only slightly changed form; however, the overall aim and purpose is vastly different. And so on. Here, though, we intend to pause a little longer over one Socialist idea—one defended very obstinately as healthy, and introducing much confusion into many Christian minds: the ideal (we admit immediately that we would rather call it a curse) of social equality.

It has to be said to start with that the societies belonging to this so-called Real Socialism have turned social inequality into an issue to a historically unprecedented and unanticipated extent (a secure minimum social security—in the given case contestable at most —characteristic of a closed society has nothing in common with social equality). That is the logical consequence of our reasonings above; however, like all truths that are too obvious, this fact always becomes the theme of doubts and discussions. The second thing that has to be said (and not even the most original theoretical sources of Socialism keep this too much of a secret) is that the possibility of realizing this ideal requires violence; that the price of achieving social equality is the liquidation of political and civil equality, the denial of the dignity of the individual human being and his or her freedom. It represents a return to somewhere deep in pre-Christian times. It is however clear that neither of these statements is sufficient to discredit the ideal itself, at most only the method used and its effectiveness; for does not the striving

6   Karl Marx, *Theses on Feuerbach*, XI. (Ed.)

for social equality remain something permanently binding (and a top priority) for a Christian, is not the lack of it a challenge and at the same time a "bad conscience" *vis-à-vis* not only today's world but any sort of future?

This problem has a number of disparate aspects, and as so much learned and deep has already been written about it, we must be content here with a few odd notes. Poverty is decidedly a gift, one of the greatest, and intended for all; as one of the most important forms of Christ, always present as a treasure both for those who follow their Lord and imitate him—for the poor—and for those others who meet Him in this manner, blessing Him and recognising Him in their most wretched neighbour. Whereas the concept of poverty is morally and ontologically clear, whereas poverty has many times been rightly elevated before the eyes of the world as one of the good paths, the question of property seems much more deceptive and double-edged; it has always been easier to say something reckless about it, and to claim it as the good and only true tidings. Property is certainly something threatening, an obstacle to salvation, especially when someone's potentialities are not up to ownership, or where they have a hard heart; it is with difficulty that the rich man (it is completely peripheral whether it is a single ring that makes a man rich, or whether it needs to be estates worth half the country) enters the kingdom of heaven; a young man grew sorrowful and left the path of Jesus, for he had many riches. Property however is at the same time something good and right, a recognised and undoubted measure of values, even though it should take the form of treasure in heaven; if we leave aside the structure of a large part of Jesus' parables, it is Mosaic Law which, for justice and generosity towards the poor, promises the multiplying of property—as a reward and a thing beneficial before God and man. It is probably possible to see an analogy between property and that "fortunate guilt" without which we would not recognise the glory of the Redeemer, with the sin of our forefathers acquiring the ability to recognise good and evil; it is a stumbling block for many, but at the same time a great and essential school, a school of responsibility and respect for the work of the Lord God and His rule. Since it is essential that we belong to God, Christ came to "His own" to enable us truly to live as creatures made in the image of God, to enable us to be true to our Sonship. That is why it is essential for us too to be the owners of something, so we can learn to develop a caring relationship of affectionate responsibility for what is entrusted to us. Property is, like freedom, an inviolable manifestation of the earnestness of God's love for us—which entails the full possibility of self-condemnation and the abandonment of God. And its responsible management is, however, the unconditional precondition of our salvation—at least in that single and unavoidable form of the history of salvation in which we find ourselves.

Corresponding to this double-edged nature of property is the double imperative the Christian receives through revelation: on the one hand, the urgent call to charity on which salvation depends, to generosity, to sharing with one's brother; and on the other, a categorical ban on "coveting the estate of your neighbour." Any attempt to attain an ideal of social equality based on a lack of respect for this ban necessarily overturns the entire code, and opens up a path on which one precept after another is disavowed with iron logic, and truth turns into a lie—it is then that such property in particular is deprived of the privileges to justify itself by generosity and creative multiplication. Poverty then changes from a hope and a gift to a real curse.

Some additional comment must be added still on this ideal; that is, whether, even in a case in which peaceful and morally harmless paths to its realization are sought, without any dishonesty or ulterior motives (which is however historically extremely rare)—is it Christian or even binding for a Christian to behave in this way and have such an aim? Our Lord said that the poor will always be with us, and sharply refused an offer to turn stones into bread— that is, an offer of the "positive" realization of social equality, of the eradication of poverty without breaking the commandments and violating human freedom. The content of our following Christ and our limits is unequivocally determined by this—the limits beyond which it becomes a delusion, and an arrogant attempt to spoil God's plans. At all times and in all places we should help to eradicate or ameliorate social inequality, to provide charity and to share our goods with our brother (even then each retains their share of the property—and thus also freedom either to multiply it or to squander it), to be untiring in this direction; not only should the left hand not know what the right is doing, we should not remember today what we did yesterday. However, as far as possible no ideals are to be solemnly erected (it is not only good intentions that pave the road to Hell; ideals are usually even more reliable in leading there), in any case, not the ideal of social equality. If for no other reason, then for Christ's holy promise that He will be with us to the end of time—not only in the Eucharist, but in the poor and the suffering whom we will meet always and daily. This means that striving for social equality is not only *not* the duty of Christians, nor a task they have neglected—it is one of the great deceptions repeatedly presented by the father of lies in the mask of the most cunning of animals: after the Tree of Knowledge eat still of the Tree of Life, and you will be as gods because you will be able to improve His creation by your own powers and to redeem yourselves from the curse of the first sin.[7] Ideals are universally respected, and the ideal of social equality claims to be so good and undisputed it definitely becomes a scandal and a stumbling block for many if one tries to deny its very foundation—however, beginning with Christ's Cross, what has not been a scandal in Christianity? It's time we weaned ourselves from the agreeable language of the aggiornamento.[8]

1983

7   Genesis 3:3–5. (Ed.)

8   *Aggiornamento* is an Italian word meaning "a bringing up to date." It became used routinely by participants in the Second Vatican Council to connote a spirit of change and openness to change. (Ed.)

14

The Ethics of Polemics and the Necessary Measure of Tolerance

An Open Letter to the Editors of Rozmluvy

Not long ago, a new review for philosophy and literature, *Rozmluvy* (Discussions) edited by Alexander Tomsky, was launched in London. Excellent news; the contents are sound and well-edited, and judging by the personality of the editor in chief and other members of the editorial board, the venture will have a long and significant life. The copy which reached me—one of several so far available in Czechoslovakia—has its technical flaws; thirty-two pages are missing (consequently one third of the contributions was damaged or wiped out); that is not such good news, and if our domestic samizdat production were concerned, whoever was responsible would have been on the carpet. At least it means that my duty to be fair in evaluating the issue as a whole is diminished. The Christian (Roman Catholic) orientation of the journal is plain at first sight. It seems that within this context it will adopt a relatively right-wing or conservative position; that too is excellent news, as for some years now we have been feeling with some bitterness that this position has been vacant in the spectrum of émigré production—to the detriment of our *common* thought, and of culture as a whole. Dark rumors reached us in advance that its purpose was not merely to provide a service *for* something (good works, for example), but that it was also intended to serve *against* something; specifically, to discredit *Roman Studies*[1]—so precious and indispensable, and in every parameter (including

---

1 The bi-monthly journal *Římská studia* (*Roman Studies*) was published by the Křesťanská akademie v Římě (Christian Academy in Rome), an exile publishing house founded in May 1950. (Ed.)

religious and political "orthodoxy," assuming someone wants to spot a *casus belli*) showing year by year a noticeable improvement in quality. That is not good news at all, especially when Alexander Tomsky's introduction does nothing to overturn relevant suspicions. Nevertheless, aware that the Spirit bloweth where it listeth, and that for the Spirit, overcoming an accidental negative limitation is a mere trifle, I will await the next number of *Rozmluvy* with unmitigated hope and turn to the real impulse for this letter.

Regarding the essay by Rio Preisner,[2] "On what is known as the parallel culture—in Bohemia too,"[3] I observe in advance that it is not only wide-ranging but also quite crucial and important. In general terms, I am actually inclined[4] to share Preisner's fundamental concept of historical parallelism and the strife between the Christian and Gnostic cultures, agreement and negation, *agapé* and *eros*—with all their irreconcilability, with the impossibility or outright *aporia* of their mutual dialogue. It is precisely my agreement and high estimation of Mr. Preisner's well-written text that provokes and perhaps even justifies me in pointing out three impermissible polemical modes of argument, and in trying to determine the boundaries it cannot be ethical (still less as Catholic) to cross. While focusing on Preisner's text, I will also take aim at much else I have been reading recently.

In Medias Res

Rio Preisner makes the 1979 polemical essay by Vilém Hejl[5] "A parallel culture or an autonomous one?"[6] the starting point of his devastating

2   Rio Preisner (1925–2007) was imprisoned in the 1950s, after which he worked as a translator and began to write. After the Soviet invasion in 1968 he emigrated and eventually became a professor of German at Pennsylvania State University. (Ed.)

3   *Rozmluvy* 1, London 1983, pp. 10–44. (Ed.)

4   My inclination is in spite of some of Preisner's over-simplified connections, especially where the Classical period is concerned. (VB)

5   As a youth Vilém Hejl (1934–1989) was banned from higher education and spent some time in prison. He was active in the Prague Spring and a signatory of Charter 77, after which he emigrated and joined Radio Free Europe in Germany. (Ed.)

6   Unfortunately I don't have Hejl's article to hand, which under normal circumstances would be an unforgiveable error on the part of the discussant; how-

analysis of the Czech parallel culture. With respect to Mr. Hejl's opinions, and in all modesty, I am obliged to remind Mr. Preisner that this concept, including all the associated terminology, was first formulated very systematically in my own programmatic reflection "The parallel polis" of May 1978 (Preisner must know of its existence since it was published in the collection *Křesťané a Charta 77* [Christians and Charter 77] which he cites elsewhere). I reserve the right not to identify completely with my opinions of that time; many years have passed, and in any case, the theses were formed in reply to a specific challenge and in a situation that was not very encouraging, and were severely limited by the effort to find a compromise formula. It is however the case that my formulations have provoked a debate lasting several years in the samizdat and exile press. This has an indirect continuation in the excitable polemics about "small works"[7] that spring up from time to time to this very day (Rio Preisner *demonstravit*); I dare say that all of it contributed in no small measure at least to a method of self-awareness and self-definition of domestic parallel activities. Well then, it is part of elementary hermeneutic courtesy (all the more so with an author who in other respects processes everything from the year zero— or from Adam) at least to mention the source, even though he may have chosen to examine an interpretation that suited him better. Apart from avoiding the breaking of the rules of good behavior over this, Preisner could also perhaps have avoided a number of absurdities and contradictions he insists on, or at least reproduces without any signs of critical detachment (I am as a Christian duty-bound to assume that my brother's over-critical behavior is in good faith and without any ulterior motive). To warn us that the parallel culture is an "unclear category which no one has yet tried to define more precisely" is to ignore hundreds and thousands of pages devoted in recent years to the fundamental and terminological clarification of just this category; everyone has the right to question the results of these efforts and to make their own critical evaluation, but to deny the efforts themselves presupposes a deliberate blindness. To equate "parallel culture," "(parallel) literature" and the "semi-legal Padlock

---

ever, the circumstances are demonstrably not normal, so I hope this can be excused. (VB)

7   See ch. 12, note 6. (Ed.)

Edition"[8] is a direct attack on Logos, intrinsic to which is something like a hierarchy of concepts: for example, it is long-standing common sense for the concept "art" to be subsumed under the concept "culture," just as the concept "literature" is subsumed under the concept "art." Similarly, the Padlock Edition is only one (albeit the oldest and most distinguished) of dozens of similar publication initiatives—an empirical fact which every critical judge is bound to know. Logos also expects evidence from us, an answer in the style "yes, yes, no, no." To call Padlock Edition "semi-legal" might seem a trifle "half-hearted" when applied to, for example, the laborer Jiří Gruntorád or the writer Jaromír Šavrd, currently serving long prison sentences for just such publishing activities. I don't know whether "it would be quite impossible to speak about parallel science, for example, alongside this"; the act of "speaking" is a matter of taste, of the right moment, of truth and, last but not least, of the Holy Spirit. Nevertheless, such a thing as parallel science *does* exist, with such an abundance of evidence and insistence that it is almost superfluous for me to invoke the testimony of dozens or hundreds of samizdat periodicals and books oriented to philosophy, theology, history, literary criticism, political science and economics; of many serious specialist and educational seminars, some of them in the second decade of their existence; of relatively active mutual contacts with international members of the professions and so on—to explain that all away as a phantom demonstrates a certain willful blindness, some sort of special preference for auto-phantomization. If it were not for the real existence of parallel science, the existence of this journal could not sufficiently be imagined, nor most of its contents and thus (*cum grano salis*) Mr. Preisner's article. Two marginalia touching on the problem: the first is that if one compares the "parallelism" of science with that of literature, for example, the "parallelism" simply disappears. There is virtually no official counterpart, however tawdry, to, at the very least, philosophy and a substantial part of theology; there have recently been serious indications that "parallelism" is no longer a perquisite of the social sciences and that—under the pressure of the reality of annihilation—it expands as far as to include such unexpected preserves as mathematics or biology,

8   In Czech *Edice Petlice* [Padlock Edition], the first samizdat publishing initiative, begun in 1973 by Ludvík Vaculík. (Ed.)

for example. I could go on with my list, but a conceited feeling that it is somehow "my business" has already led me into almost too much detail.

I would therefore rather turn to a further application of the same mode of argument, this time connected with some very nasty personal insinuations about the Protestant pastor (currently boiler man, what else) Miloš Rejchrt.[9] Over four dense pages, to be incessantly labelled as (I'm choosing only the most risqué, and for economy I'm omitting some adjectives): a "voyeur enchanted by the educative idol of Socialism," a "left-winger," a "day-dreamer," a "Manichean dualist," an "exculpator of the Gulag" and a "socialist absolutist" is unpleasant, not to mention against all requirements of justice and love; and justice and love are the things that nourish us and without which it would have been impossible to survive this fate and to bear witness. Rejchrt has written and done a lot in recent years, including fundamental and far-reaching things, provoking truly inspiring discussion. Out of all this, Preisner has focused his ire on Rejchrt's sharp six-year-old response to an article by the exile Antonín Strnad, criticizing relationships in Charter 77 and especially its cooperation with "ex-Communists"—perhaps such a choice of targets is defensible; however, surely this is not the most appropriate target.[10] My subhead "in media res" is used here very transparently.

There are also what I would call rhetorical (polemical) tactics: for example, Rejchrt deliberately escalates his reasoning, to some extent even rushes it, because he wants the appropriate counter-position to reach its climax as sharply as possible and have a definitive effect. Naturally, if only the first half of such a "turnabout" is cited, the end result is nonsense; even worse, it can be turned it into any kind of sense you want. That is exactly what Preisner does: he conceals Rejchrt's counter-position, omitting references to millions of victims, self-deification, and monstrous abuse.[11]

9   Miloš Rejchrt (b. 1946) is a Protestant pastor and signatory of Charter 77. He served as a spokesman for the Charter from January 1, 1980 to January 13, 1981. (Ed.)

10 Miloš Rejchrt, "Dopis A. Strnadovi," in Vilém Prečan,ed., *Křesťané a Charta 77: Výběr dokumentů a textů* (Cologne and Munich 1980), pp. 239–45. (Ed.)

11 Preisner quotes this passage from Rejchrt: "The social system espoused up to now by Socialists represents probably the most rational method of organizing society, with socialized means of production and a grandiose planning

Such treatment of the text is no longer a mere injustice and a scandal, it disrupts the elementary rules of any polemic and thus spoils the ground for any dialogue. Additionally, if Preisner had not been so carried away by the application of his polemical mode he would certainly have noticed the allegedly incriminating passage (and more problematic places could in fact be found in that letter) is so anti-Gnostic, aimed so much against self-deifying rationalism, that it could successfully be used to support his point and illustrate his own position.

The Facts Must Serve

And if the facts don't serve the purpose, so much worse for the facts; it's not so difficult simply to misunderstand them, or to adapt them a little to serve one's own purposes. Preisner quotes quite extensively, paraphrasing various reflections by Václav Havel, especially where he speaks of the "underground." He is exceptionally benevolent in not awarding bad marks for behavior to the actual author—only what is Preisner doing with Havel's text? When Havel describes the origin of Charter 77, whose earliest beginnings do indeed date from a shared defensive and civic stand in support of imprisoned and persecuted members of the underground (summer 1976), Preisner takes that to mean that the underground is the "spiritual

> of the material and spiritual spheres. As we know, its capabilities are impressive; it not only shows itself able to industrialize a primitive agricultural state in a short space of time, but also manages to build a decent social security system ..." However, he omits what immediately follows: "Thanks to its potential, covering all fields of human life, it is at the same time much more threatened by evil and the abuse of its gigantic power. Almost unnoticed, it is able to liquidate millions of people in internment camps ..., ensure that a certain person cannot find any kind of employment, and effectively prevent any kind of private education. In short, it is made up of greater good and greater evil. The question remains as to whether it is humanly possible to protect the Socialist organized state from abuse to which every human work tends (above all when it idealizes itself and sees itself as an absolute good with a view to which any sort of criticism is a metaphysical crime), whether past experience is not so cautionary that it would not be better to stay with the earlier unsatisfactory types of organization of society which ... are not directly threatened by such monstrous abuse." (Ed.)

background to Charter 77." Out of an awareness of the indivisibility of freedom, on this occasion given very animated expression, out of respect for the human, civic and even artistic rights of others, out of things which unite us *in spite of* our profound differences in opinion and attitude, Preisner immediately makes "a connection from the underground to the political philosophy of Jan Patočka." Havel's attempt to characterize the breadth of it, as presented in *"das Meinungsspektrum der Charta 77"* through the provocative enumeration *"Vom Musik-Underground über Sozialisten bis zu Trozkisten, von verschiedenen Schriftstellern und Einzelgängern bis zu Katholiken und Protestanten"* provides sufficient cause for Preisner to smuggle the underground into the position of "seedbed" and "first cause" of the Czech parallel culture.[12] This is not only an extraordinary abuse of quotations, but also historically nonsense; the underground is only one of many branches[13] of the parallel culture (as I said, literature and music belong here as do the other arts and sciences), branches which until the second half of the 1970s were undoubtedly developing independently and to a large degree in isolation. And so on—it is really easier to cut through the knot of these pseudo-interpretations than to undo it.

The *"causa* Rejchrt" adds another example of "the facts must serve." Miloš Rejchrt is a relatively young Protestant pastor: it is my personal sin that, in place of Christian love and respect, I often have a tendency to demonstrate animosity towards the "lambs" and those around them; however, I proclaim with all seriousness that Rejchrt is one of the most promising and most open spirits, and that he is in most respects far more "Catholic" than a number of my Catholic friends. Now, how does Preisner treat this just man? It is not enough for him to vilify him personally; he

12 To be correct I am leaving Preisner's quotation in the German translation, otherwise on the whole it follows the original. (VB) [The German passages read "the range of views in Charter 77" and "from the musical underground to socialists up to Trotskyites, from various writers to loners up to Catholics and Protestants." (Ed.)]

13 Most probably far from being the earliest, though much hangs on the chosen methodological approach—we could trace the genesis of many "parallelisms" as far as the first diffident beginnings in the 1950s; though indeed, the breadth of Preisner's viewfinder would enable us to go back as far as the First Republic. (VB)

must add to his opinion timeless validity (this of course brings us to pure Gnosticism, Mr. Preisner, against which you otherwise fiercely and rightly campaign—for without the Incarnation there is no forgiveness) and suitable authority, so that the judgment on Rejchrt can indeed be universal. The incriminating statement thus comes from the mouth of: "Miloš Rejchrt, spokesman of Charter 77, and thus one of the leading representatives of the alleged 'parallel culture' in Socialist Bohemia," who "shares it with a number of other Chartists." Everything in the present tense! The only thing is, that Rejchrt wrote his letter back in 1977, and he was Charter spokesman in 1980, whereas Preisner's attack was published in 1983 (we don't learn any of these dates from his article, making it necessary to look up the relevant sources—a small but by no means insignificant silence). Incidentally, I myself nurse serious doubts as to whether Rejchrt was so well-acquainted with the work of Paul Ricoeur[14] or so influenced by it in 1977; nevertheless, we'll give Preisner the benefit of the doubt according to the basic *in dubio pro reo*[15]—however, he didn't have to invest so much Štollian[16] stubborn urgency just in trying to diabolize the influence this inspiration had on the otherwise "nice boy" Rejchrt.

The Pigeon Post

Whether the excessive pithiness of the concept of polarity and of discord between Christian and Gnostic culture that leads to Preisner's attitude (maybe this is the main weakness of what Preisner is really attempting, and where he undoubtedly says something new and important—in the end, a stubborn struggle to get to the root of things, to separate the wheat from

14 Paul Ricoeur (1930–2005) was a French philosopher of the school of phenomenology. His work has been translated into over 20 languages. Ricoeur had become close to Patočka during the latter's visits to Paris in the 1930s and actively promoted Patočka's work in the latter part of the twentieth century. See, for example, his preface to the English translation of Patočka's *Heretical Essays in the Philosophy of History*. (Ed.)

15 "In doubt, for the accused." (Ed.)

16 Ladislav Štoll (1902–1981) Stalinist author and de facto cultural commissar in the 1950s—notorious for his vile condemnations of everyone who did not slavishly follow the Party line of the time. (Ed.)

the chaff leads him into factual conformity with the Gnostic Manichaeism he is so keen to unmask) or whether other reasons are involved, it would be difficult to find a similar work in which so much space and energy would be devoted to pigeonholing—at least occasionally from the time of Adam's choice, and in the first centuries of the Christian era implemented quite systematically and with encyclopedic breadth of compass. It is not even pigeonholing in the traditional sense of classifying a butterfly collection. Preisner has one pigeonhole for "evil" and another for "good"; everyone belongs unproblematically and for ever and ever in one or the other— Socrates and Patočka alone presenting some kind of exception. However, an evil regime resourcefully rubbed out each of them when they tried to jump through the connecting doors from one pigeonhole to another (naturally, there is yet another pigeonhole for the "harmless" which, regrettably, gapes more than anything with emptiness or anonymity, for in truth neither author nor reader are much interested in such people). In the end that's a method too, one which undoubtedly brings many new perspectives and ideas. The reader would definitely be happier if some evaluation of the protagonists emerged from a sound explication of the relevant problems, rather than the existing situation, when in many cases he or she has to deduce Preisner's original opinions laboriously and inexactly (putting great demands on his or her education and ability—don't forget that although we may live in an allegedly humane age, it is under a government not overly inclined towards education) from the attached classification of appropriate personalities. The pigeonholing of contemporaries or quasi-contemporaries becomes a major stumbling block; on the one hand by its apodictic definitive quality, denying the possibility of salvation for sinners; on the other, by its simple lack of transparency, not admitting any interpretation other than the author's likes and dislikes (at random: why is "Patočka of the 1960s" evil, and "ancient Seifert" good, which even with the utmost effort cannot be deduced from the coordinates provided by Preisner?). Should someone subsequently (and with increasing interest) read another of Preisner's articles[17] published the same year, he learns with surprise that

17 "Dějepisné rozpravy o prvních předpokladech rozmluvy s více neznámými" [Historiographical debates about the first presuppositions of a conversation with more unknowns], *Studie* 85–86, Rome. (VB)

though the pigeonholing method continues, many personalities have inexplicably changed their place of residence; the philosopher Ladislav Klíma, evil enough to discredit the entire collection *Spektrum* and with it *eo ipso* the whole of Czech parallel philosophy, is now not only good but even has a downright promising pedigree, while professors Černý and Patočka have definitively returned amongst the good.[18] This sort of thing reveals Preisner's pigeonholing procedure as mere capriciousness, and proves it to be one of the polemical modes in the same category as those first two examined above—unfortunately, and to the detriment of the matter in hand, it seriously compromises the thoughts he expresses when using this approach.

But we can leave aside Preisner's irregular turnabouts; in the end all his complicated procedure derives from the fact that in his ingenious and challenging spiritual scheme he has tried to employ categories which don't belong here at all; in Czechoslovakia, "parallel" simply means a culture which defies regulations for gagging and liquidation, which realizes itself, and which develops from the efforts of responsible citizens for liberated self-help, nothing more and nothing less. To derive automatically some sort of artistic and academic values or spiritual orientation from this fact is to deceive oneself (one could at most speak of certain ethical values such as courage, fidelity or responsible service to one's calling; even here it would be appropriate to take great caution).

I want now to devote myself to a phenomenon which extends far beyond the framework of Preisner's study and which with increasing frequency and precariousness appears on the pages of the exile press; as a working title I inaccurately bestow on it the name "criticism"; in this case, condemnation from the right (of the parallel culture, "parallel" church activities, Charter 77, Christians in the Charter, Catholics in the Charter and everything else)— the treacherousness of the terms "right-wing" and "left-wing" and the way they come full circle is generally known. Nevertheless,

---

18 Ladislav Klíma (1878–1928) was a Czech philosopher and novelist, very much influenced by Nietzsche and existentialism. *Spektrum* was a samizdat journal published from 1977–1979—its editors were anonymous but close to the Charter 77 leadership. Václav Černý (1905–1987) was a prominent literary critic, essayist and professor of literature who translated Spanish, Italian, and French literature into Czech. (Ed.)

people of goodwill know exactly what they are talking about, and there's no point in addressing the others. I'm particularly pleased to hear such invective from people—and surprisingly they are the ones very ready in this direction—I've known for years (either personally or from their work) and to whom I've always had to define myself from exactly the opposite position; but that is perhaps too private a sigh to heave. It does not mean that I would deny someone the right to hold strong opinions, to criticize, and even, if necessary, to judge, or to change all of this; I would only affirm that exile (like everything else—it should not be necessary to explain to "right-wing-thinking" people) has its framework and order whose rules cannot be broken with impunity. Meaning that in theory the exile has roughly three ways to behave: a) assimilate with his new surroundings as quickly and thoroughly as possible; b) maintain a certain cultural autonomy and at the same time try to transfer to the new surroundings any of his human, political and other experience which could influence its functioning or raise its defensibility; c) carry on feeling like a part of home—involuntarily torn from the earth—and to a certain measure linked to his beginnings and his fate through this original mother earth. These three approaches can of course be combined; however, exile in the strict sense of the word is closely linked with the application of the third (and vice versa: if someone writes for émigré journals, particularly about domestic matters, *eo ipso* he works "for home" and professes the third principle). There is a dependency between this exile in the strict sense of the word and home (or whatever, in that graveyard of toxic fumes, attempts to maintain and substitute for home); it is a mutual dependency (I do not in any way want to undervalue the role of the exile—the devil knows that a house divided against itself cannot stand—and our task is to confront division) but at the same time hierarchical. Without you, we would perhaps succumb or at the very least become sterile; without us, however, you do not have any hope at all in this direction. The exile should then feel seriously bound at least to think over certain rules and, let us say, "strategic guidelines" as well, which I will try to explain (incidentally, this article itself goes beyond the framework of a "reasonable security risk": it does not have to be written, and if we all acted like brothers in Christ, it would not be written, but for my almost pathological faith in the possibility of understanding between the children of God)!

We who remain in Czechoslovakia are not infrequently chastised for being incapable of taking just one more step, for reeling half-heartedly somewhere between "yes, yes,",… "no, no." It seems we are not only insufficiently decisive in condemning Socialism and proclaiming this or that a crime, and him or her a "blood-stained dog," but even that some of us play around seriously—or at least with some sort of perverted pleasure—with direct contradictions of such declarations. At first sight this reproach appears self-evident and just. Why shouldn't our deeds be weighed and assessed with real critical rigor—all the more, since the deeds rely primarily on words, on testimony to a truth which has to be clear and unswerving—since an altered and clouded truth is worse than untruth? Why shouldn't our judge be precisely that exile, in the strict sense of the word, who has a convenient opportunity for dispassionate distance and direct insight into a wider context—while at the same time sharing sincerely and efficiently in our activities, his vital interests inherently linked with their results? Oddly enough, each of these "whys" has its own "because," which makes the whole matter enormously problematic. According to current criminal law, one of the constituent elements of subversion of the Republic is "hostility to Socialist society and to the state administration" and there are many provisions similar to those mentioned above. Well, decisions of this kind are above all a matter between God and myself; moreover, the question always poses itself anew: in a given situation, which is the most eloquent, a silent witness in prison or a "mealy-mouthed" speech in freedom? Even according to the Gospel (which should have priority over all the laws of mankind) those who come to preach the Kingdom of God and thus bear witness to the Truth are required "to be as wise as serpents, and harmless as doves."[19] And why not those in exile too? Everyone has an absolute right to leave any country, including his own, and it does not follow he should thereby lose the right to active participation in his country's affairs at a distance—this is part not only of the formulation of Pacts on Human Rights but of any of the suspect humanitarian ideals of the modern age—clearly following from the Gospel's separation of freedom and responsibility as far as the things of Caesar and the things of God are concerned. The only issue is that the Gospel always understands freedom as freedom *for* something,

---

19   Matthew 10:16. (Ed.)

the freedom of the Children of God; it sees rights and demands as a space for responsibility. In this sense the exile is in a special position; insofar as it is possible and appropriate to his position, he is duty-bound to publish his testimony (the more there are, and the more strident and urgent, the better for us, for the exile, and for the world); at the same time however, he has to impose certain limitations on himself in relation to his homeland, limitations which derive from the peculiarity of his position. I would like to draw your attention to some reflections from the article *"Etika anonyma"* (Ethics of an anonymous writer, 1983);[20] the émigré author experiences all the same advantages (to a much safer degree, naturally, as the Sword of Damocles of sudden disclosure is not hanging over him) inherent in anonymous writing published in samizdat, and I also see a far-reaching analogy between the relevant ethical requirements. We are duty-bound not to taunt the author with his exile, nor to envy him his advantages; not only from love for our neighbor and respect for the commandments, not only on the basis of an abstract recognition of his right to choose (and of the price he pays for these advantages), but also, and I would say above all, from the political awareness that the only community that can survive is one with a community spirit sensed as something unified and shared—that may be something we learned in recent years, and if not, I can at least promise that we are prepared to go about learning it resolutely and quickly. However, the exile is no less bound in his relationship to us; hasty, and above all sweeping, judgments should be avoided like the plague. He should use maximum restraint in the matter of judgments in general; it is part of his fate to get to know opinions well, but not the conditions under which the opinions were expressed, or the hidden reasons which led to their expression (when necessary, priority should be given to critical analysis and to the refutation of opinions, instead of making on the one hand a private attack on their origin—an attack on a specific person—or on the other, a global condemnation of all those bound to the given opinions by no more than participation in a joint effort). The émigré author, intoxicated and blinded by his freedom, is certainly not allowed to provoke and exacerbate discussion to the point where his counterpart at home has no other choice than to acknowledge his agreement, errors and inferiority through his silence—or

20   *Kritický sborník* 4/1983, pp. 42–45, samizdat, Prague. (VB)

alternatively to shoulder everything including the consequences of criminal justice, which can very easily happen to a citizen of this country. It is commendable to take Christ's Cross on oneself, but no one, not even if he himself is suited to be a shepherd, has the right to mete it out to another, especially if he does it from a comfortable distance—for it is written that the Good Shepherd protects his sheep. This command of restraint is valid not only when judging people, but very often cases as well. The conscientious émigré author should examine each statement about his homeland in advance from two angles: a) whether he is absolutely sure it is true, and whether there are not some facts known which contradict it (which is the general rule); b) whether insisting on evidence being provided of possible error could result in the case itself or those involved being critically threatened.[21] Any statement which does not fit only the second criterion, for example, should if possible be avoided—that is the specific commitment of the exile who really wants a right to share in our work. I could easily make these maxims more precise and distribute them; however, I think I have shown the basic aim clearly enough.

Nevertheless, I will always examine a very specific case of a technical or, let us say, at least situational nature; in fact I would like to close my reflections with some more fundamental questions and nobler themes—for example dialogue, tolerance and so on. Above all I want to say explicitly that I fully share the conviction of most "critics from the right" that it is impossible to have a real dialogue with evil (obviously, I also consider the teachings already discussed in this article as evil *par excellence*), that any

---

21 Because my formulation has to remain vague and even cryptic, I will try and help the reader's imagination with a highly fabricated example. I may be firmly convinced and even able to prove that some important document, which is not my property (and that is the case with the émigré author), is manufactured from non-flammable material. Because, however, my statement can be overturned only by destroying the document, I am acting unfairly towards the owner if I begin to broadcast it to the world—at the very least I do not leave him the possibility of defending the opposite conviction on a level playing field. And if the question of the inflammability or non-flammability is critical for the owner—for example, if some ethically relevant conclusions for his behavior derive from its solution—than I am behaving unfairly twice over; I am blackmailing him completely without mercy. (VB)

dialogue would be not only superfluous but even malignant—for the only apparent counterexample in the Gospels, the temptation of Christ in the desert, has its negative side and stark inner gradation, heading towards the definitively damning "*Apage!*", towards a truly distant dialogue. Likewise, I have my own opinions about the future prospects of "historical compromises," of "national unities and fronts." These and all other pacts with the devil, whether individual or collective, are naïve; what is gained from them is always only apparent, whilst the damage is guaranteed and usually irreparable. Moreover, I customarily employ a *reservatio mentalis* regarding the command "Love your enemies." I understand the validity of this command to have extremely narrow limits, insofar as it is not understood as living participation in God's plan of salvation. It's certainly appropriate to apply it to the defeated bearers of evil at the moment victory is safely assured; however, to apply it too narrowly or too literally in the face of a triumphant enemy can be understood as something very un-Christian and detrimental to my own immortal soul, as well as threatening God's case and the lives of many fellow men. The point is, the truth we serve is living and behaves as a living truth, not as some sort of always-the-same mechanical record, activated by pressing the appropriate button. It is also written that when we are not heeded (and how much more so in the various offices and similar places to which they drag us, where our speech, however compassionate, serves as a small stone in the mosaic of information and in completing the portrait of psychological manipulation), we have to shake the dust off our shoes—Jesus answers partially before the Sanhedrin and Pilate but is silent before Herod, for in human terms the truth could help Him, but would at the same time be exposed to ridicule, to being discredited, and to abuse.[22] Likewise, I am willing to oppose my overwhelmingly liberal friends by saying that fanaticism is in itself a debased form of announcing the truth; however, fanaticism must not be judged apart from its contents (and its values or anti-values). Fanaticism in the form of Stalinism is absolutely not the same thing as its precipitous conversion into the fanaticism of Bavarian Christian Social provenance. However, this is where my agreement with the "criticism from the right" ends; here ends also the realm of possible concessions to this criticism.

---

22 Compare Matthew 26:57–67, Mark 15:1–15 and Luke 23:8–11. (Ed.)

In what is perhaps the heart of the matter—and that heart will have to be cut back severely, or abridged—after all, I am only writing an open letter and appeal, not a learned book with subtle distinctions. The "criticism from the right" is essentially erroneous in its theory and unusually damaging in its practical impact, achieving in both cases the exact opposite of that for which it was *bona fide* striving. Theoretically it insists on the clear recognition and "non-forgetting" of guilt; it postulates the possibility of strict differentiation both between good and evil (a stance too much from the Old Testament; in the Gospels the only path to the Father is through the Son, who is Love) and between the good and the evil (plain Manichaeism and pride of spirit as it manifests itself from the *"non serviam"* of Satan through condemnation of Jesus for his contacts with sinners and customs officers, up to the contemporary theory of the class war—but this too we will leave to one side, as we are more interested in the unavoidable results). All of that is in sharp opposition to the Left-Liberal mind-set, which by taking social determinism into account tries to trivialize guilt or get rid of it completely, and which would like to reduce the possibility of distinguishing between good and evil to the purely formal criteria of completely arbitrary freedom (or of freedom as a recognized necessity, the same thing). It is however easy to show (even from the immanent point of view, although a Christian already knows it as dogma in advance) that everyone without exception bears blame for the given state, that it is not reasonably possible to draw a line beyond which not even complicity could come into consideration, that even those who suffered for many years (or who perished) are to blame at the very least in a double sense—i.e., that, like it or not, they worked and lived in this system and helped to maintain it, and that they lost their case (we hope provisionally and we hope not before the face of God), and thus bear responsibility for not having done what they should have done (slightly adapted, this also applies to the exile). And so it is with evil. Surely there are many who turn away from evil consistently and emphatically. Is it really possible, however, to sever such a subtle and fundamental fabric (which envelops evil) as is represented, for example, by language or the entirety of one's social ties? In fact, it is often the case that more elements of evil creep into the programs of the highly intransigent than anywhere else: to negate the disorder and dust of nothingness is still far from affirming the life and the order of creation. The principle of collective guilt is thus born from the theoretically thought-out "criticism from the right," and is conceived, in substance, in Manichaen terms, apportioning evil in a deterministic fashion. Such a principle therefore entails the virtual denial of guilt and the reduction of man to a mere bearer of good and evil, a passive substratum in the conflict of age-old principles. It is very difficult to find the subtle nuances by which the conclusions of this criticism differ from those Left-Liberal positions against which it was originally directed!

That is of course only a theoretical analysis of the given position; the tree of life is green and the Spirit bloweth where it listeth—the deciding fact for passing judgment will thus be the practical effect of the "criticism from the right." I am steadfastly convinced that thorough resistance to evil is fully compatible with a permanent struggle for the souls (and a struggle for souls without love and understanding is only an empty declaration) of those who from pride, lack of awareness or weakness gave themselves to its service; that this is the only suitable method of following Our Lord, who came to save sinners and reject the righteous, too certain of their salvation and preferring to observe the Sabbath rather than love their neighbor. I consider that this turning around, this conversion, is something essential for us *all* and for which we are in duty bound to strive for *together*, as the sole hope of this present time, so difficult and in need of missionizing. And the speed or strenuousness, the straightforward character or imperceptibility, of this conversion may not be a real measure of its authenticity. Evil is of its essence inanimate; but it definitely does not act unreasonably or without purpose—so it is certainly not mere accident that in the last decade it was Socialists of quite varied colors (Battěk, Šabata, Uhl[23]) who were mercilessly persecuted. The fact is, for more than one reason, such conviction and such

---

23 Rudolf Battěk (1924–2013) was a Charter 77 signatory and member of VONS. Jaroslav Šabata (1927–2012) left the Communist Party in 1969 and formed a group called Communists in Opposition. He signed Charter 77 and served as spokesman from April 6, 1978–October 1 1978 and from February 10, 1981 to January 2, 1982. Petr Uhl (b. 1941) served four years in prison after the Soviet invasion for his involvement in the Revolutionary Youth Movement. He is a Charter 77 signatory and member of VONS. He also served a prison term from 1979 to 1983 for his involvement in VONS. (Ed.)

awareness is not my own private matter but rather a dominant part of the whole domestic atmosphere; formally consummated or secret on-going conversions are evidently much more frequent than the inertia of staying put, while not even the most tenacious opponent would be able to lead me in the opposite direction, to conversion from Christian open-ness to ideological obstinacy and the service of evil. The "criticism from the right"— at least with the intolerance and sometimes even churlish-ness with which it has been led till now—instructs hardly anyone and de-cidedly does not spur anyone into conversion;[24] it is a mere slamming of the door, leaving the field free for all manner of erroneous opinions and stray deviances. It would be good to remember at this point that Catholic-ity will perhaps always lag behind various sects as to purity, authenticity and momentary effectiveness—its wit and its hope lies precisely in the fact that it is not intolerant, it is life-affirming, and it accepts creation as something positive, inviting us to joyful participation in it. Analogously, as the right-wing mind-set can never achieve the effectiveness and de-ceptiveness of the great ideological projects, the more it must cultivate that which it owns and that which is its truth all the more carefully: i.e., a sensitive respect for life with regard to values and traditions and a thor-ough understanding of the meaning and price of complexity (compared with delusions of revolutionary simplification and the cutting down of forests, in the course of which nothing much matters as far as the indi-vidual chips are concerned). Perhaps one can repeat with G. K. Chester-ton: that white pillars have to be whitewashed again and again, and to add to that, not even continuous whitewashing would be of any use with-out something like love and appreciation for the material and the sense of belonging; if it is missing, the foundations in the ground unnoticeably

24 Not long ago I was in conversation with one very left-wing friend—not with-out hope that I could in this way sow at least a tiny of seed of the apostolic message, both generally and especially politically—about openness and pre-paredness to accept the challenge. I was however caught out and silenced by her question whether I was able to name apart from myself some other "right winger" capable of real openness and practical tolerance? I certainly showed my unpreparedness as a debater; later on (and plainly already in vain) I put together a whole list of such, in spite of which however I saw something symptomatic in her objection and in my silence. (VB)

decay, paint flakes from the damp surface or rust corrodes the inside beneath the shiny coat, till in the end there is nothing left but a carefully whitewashed tomb.

I cannot avoid mentioning another, certainly unwanted and apparently accidental, but therefore even more sinister effect of the "criticism from the right." The large majority of the community of believers in Czechoslovakia (maybe I do not have to remind you that this community is by coincidence the only real social power in our country which is at least partially organized and at least partially independent of the state authorities) maintains restraint with regard to Charter 77 and any sort of civic engagement; in secret, it is incontestably sympathetic, but in practice it shows an almost uncomfortably distant restraint. It has good reasons; the experiences of the last forty years are truly bitter (an appropriate euphemism for damage and destruction which literally stopped at nothing) and too often the hopes of believers were disappointed and their best intentions vilely misused. It has bad reasons too: fear is a powerful mentor; it is very tempting to rely on hidden prayer and fidelity in the heart, but to carry out the required libation on the outside and to miss or disregard the testimony of the suffering. The "criticism from the right" which intends to be so uncompromising in distinguishing between good and evil, so activist and so rebellious, actually provides this majority, struggling in their conscience, with a very comfortable and substantial argument from the arsenal of bad reasons: they can now say, it is not my fear (for those who evidently have no reasons for fear are of the same opinion) but on the contrary, the intransigence and sincerity of my faith that lead me to have nothing in common with those questionable people and their efforts. I will try to adapt (i.e., I will go and vote in "elections" regularly, I will join various wretched organizations, I will teach myself and my children to lie, I will actively approve all kinds of sanctions against otherwise like-minded citizens—once let loose, logic of this sort hardly finds a limit) and survive so that I can maintain myself and maintain the church at least as an outer imitation of Christ's body (how much worse then is a Golden Calf?). And so one radical criticism paradoxically bears fruit which surpasses the wildest expectations of the authorities: simple passivity, surrender to evil, perceived as an almost heroic act. The dominating strategy of power is to shut every civic and spiritual activity behind the gates of the ghetto determined for gradual liquidation. Whether it is due to our own defense or to the arrogant excesses of a power which always goes a few steps further in persecution than is expedient for it and digestible for cautious consciences, this strategy so far has very problematic results and one could with some care speak rather of the opposite long-term trend. For example, the time chosen for the VONS trial[25] was extremely unpropitious, and the worst possible justification was given. In practice, such a justification prevented any sort of political or moral discredit of the accused and clearly revealed, in the course of the trial, that in legal terms the power could have been just as well served by any other justification. Similarly, last year's attack on the Order of St. Francis did no harm to much of anything, while it clarified much. At the very least it entered the civic consciousness that various independent cultural, and especially religious, activities (which the "criticism from the right" so much elevates and indicates as a positive antithesis to purely civic activities) were to a great measure indebted to Charter 77 for the relative expansion of the "space of the possible" and to the Charter's role as a kind of lightning conductor. It is still a very long road from this awareness of mutual dependence to genuine trust, solidarity and cooperation. This road simply has to be walked; the alternative is time without hope and the gradual destruction of an atomized society. Mostly in silence, and in any case with immeasurable effort and not without sacrifices, we have succeeded in travelling quite a distance down that road. The whole of this subtle texture of personal and material connections is built to be quite efficaciously immune against the interventions of power, but not against attacks of much less probable diseases; one single case of insensitive "criticism from the right" or unscrupulous and profit-seeking outpouring of fresh émigrés can often be enough on their own to spoil the work of many years—certainly only for the pleasure of the devil and other common enemies. Of course we will always begin again, our faith patiently dictates that to us, and we will accept with joy whatever at least somewhat resembles Christ's cross—however, from our brethren these things taste twice as bitter and one can never be certain whether the powers of Grace (when he has already long exhausted his own) will not suddenly let down. And as this is written in 1984, perhaps even the factor of time and its fatal shortage can come into play.

25 See Editor's introduction, p. xi–xiii.

Pro Deo, fratres, pro amore Dei: think about what it is you are playing with, and what is at stake! When Mehmed II besieged Constantinople the city was concerned much more with disputes about the *filioque*[26] than with a will to defend itself; and in our present time, a few days before the Khmer Rouge took Phnom Penh, the axis of public life (in cafes and at bazaars) was the recitation of mediaeval love poetry and disputes about its interpretation. Purity of faith is a matter of a fundamental importance, and dogmatic disputes or a correct grasp of literary expression may represent an important step in the history of salvation. But we also know that there is a time for everything; in the examples given, what followed was only the time of horse riders in the Church of Hagia Sophia, and a time of love in the form of thousands of involuntary, random marriages, and millions of dead. This world is the best of all possible worlds, admittedly some flaws (for example, original sin) have crept in; it also seems that at the present time this world is the most threatened of all possible worlds—and what would replace it (certainly only for a time, our hope is sure, however we too are only finite creatures and committed to act inside time) would quite likely not be "the next world" and the Kingdom of Christ, but rather the merciless rule of the lord of this world and his ally Death. There may be some sense in investigating whose fault it is, as long as this does not turn into mutual recriminations, but rather to finding the path to the salvation of the world and the righting of human affairs; for to search for this salvation and this putting to rights is a requirement of life and death and does not brook delay. We would very much like to see the expatriate community abandon permanent quarrels and rivalries and brace itself to face the impending moment of truth in true Catholicity. But that may well be an unjustified desire arising from a deep misunderstanding of the meaning and spiritual mission of being in exile. This mission must be "fulfilled" and in the long run unquestionably exceeds our capacity for just arbitration. Be finally reconciled, however, with the fact that from where you stand, not

---

26 Filioque ("from the son") refers to the theological dispute between the Eastern Orthodox Church and the Roman Catholic Church about whether the Holy Spirit proceeds only from the Father or from the Father and Son together. Mehmed II captured Constantinople on behalf of the Ottoman Empire in May of 1453. (Ed.)

even you can ever understand the deep origin of our reasons, and that it is not intellect but something higher and much more imperative that binds you to silence; stand reverently before this new experience of unity and solidarity. I would like to end this article (which I have been putting off for a long time, which I did not enjoy writing, which I feared writing, and in which, in spite of all my efforts, I understandably gave way in many places to purely human and intellectual passions) by expressing the hope that it will not evoke a new wave of indignant disputes and effervescing polemics but rather become an impulse for thought—at least for some.

January-February 1984

15

Letter to Roger Scruton

The following text is a reply to a letter from the British conservative thinker Roger Scruton to Czechoslovakia.[1] He is positive in his evaluation of Charter 77's efforts, but expresses serious reservations regarding its dialogue and cooperation with some unofficial peace movements (he draws attention especially to contentious parts of the United Declaration of East German and Czechoslovak Peace Activists of November 1984).[2] At the same time he warns against the dangers lurking when civic initiatives in the East get too close to this movement and to the whole context of the Western Left in general. The letter is informal and of a private nature, so unsuitable for publication. I have however used this opportunity to defend some of the standpoints of Charter 77 and to clarify in detail my own opinions on the given issue. At the same time I will express myself (at least implicitly) on other thoughts of the author published in his journal *The Salisbury Review* and in his book *The Meaning of Conservatism*. I have therefore decided, at least in this form, to make my reply available to my friends. I apologize to

1   Roger Scruton's letter, written on November 27, 1984, was addressed to Václav Havel, though Scruton knew that it would be circulated within the Charter community. Havel replied on January 16, 1985 (the actual letter has the date as 1984, but this must have been a mistake). We do not have the precise date of Benda's letter. However, Scruton replied to Havel, Benda, and Radim Palouš (who also replied to Scruton) on February 13, 1985, so Benda's letter can safely be dated as sometime in January. (Ed.)

2   *Informace o Chartě 77* 7, 1984, c. 11 (listopad), s. 15. *Informace o Chartě 77* [*Information about the Charter*] or *Infoch* was the newsletter published by Charter 77. All issues of *Infoch* are available on the website www.vons.cz under the "Documents" tab. (Ed.)

Mr. Scruton for capriciously quoting from his private letter. At the same time I expressly forbid this text or any parts of it to be circulated by "normal" reproduction techniques without specific permission from Roger Scruton.

***

Dear Mr. Scruton!

First, please forgive me for the particular discourtesy attendant at the cradle of this letter. I am replying to a letter from you which was neither sent to me nor indicated as being an open letter. However, I was—in view of the nature of your reproaches which chiefly concern Charter 77 and its attitudes to Western peace movements—acquainted with its contents. I feel duty bound to add some notes of explanation—if only because, as a spokesman of Charter 77 in the year of 1984, I carry the increased responsibility of its representation.

Charter 77 is a free association of people of quite varied ideological persuasions and political opinions and programs, bound together only by an awareness of shared responsibility for the fate of society, the inalienability of human and civil rights, and the indivisibility of freedom and the dignity of man. At the same time, the individual signatories of the Charter have markedly different opinions on fundamental questions. For example, they differ on whether human and civil rights are of natural or historic origin and the measure and the circumstances under which they could be legitimately suspended; on the question of the inevitable boundaries of freedom, whether dictated by responsibility for society as a whole or rooted in freedom itself; and on the actual source of the dignity of man and the inevitable threats to it. However, experience has convincingly demonstrated that, at least in Czechoslovak conditions, such a "minimal" and in many ways deliberately unexplained unity is unusually viable and effective; that it has become an important factor of social self-awareness and thus ultimately of politics. I'm taking this opportunity to refer to Charter 77 Document no. 2/1985, which contains a much more detailed and exact analysis of the given issue.[3]

3   See Blanka Císařovská and Vilém Prečan, *Charta 77: Dokumenty 1977–1989*, Svazek 2 (Praha: Ústav pro soudobé dějiny AV ČR, 2007), pp. 681–89. (Ed.)

Charter 77 does not in any way dispute its signatories' rights as individuals and as groups to defend much more far-reaching and radical political programs, insofar as they respect this "minimal space" of agreement; on the contrary, as far as it can it supports such efforts, for it sees in them a basic condition for the restoration of free political thought and later, political life in general. However, it cannot answer for its signatories in this respect, and should be judged by the documents signed by its spokesmen; only these express our common and committed standpoint. Now: in its documents of 1984 and of previous years, the Charter always emphasized that it is not a peace movement, and that it does not intend to identify with the aim of any of the existing Western peace movements. Whenever it has presented specific proposals for the abolition of nuclear weapons and for the withdrawal of American and Soviet troops from Europe (on the last occasion in a letter for the Peace Congress in Perugia), they have always been linked with the parallel elimination of conventional military superiority on either side.[4] Above all, it did not consider any step towards peace meaningful if it did not include greater respect for human rights, effective control by citizens over the actions of their governments and, last but not least, the right to self-determination of all European nations (including the nations of the Soviet Union; we could not mention them explicitly, but we were always careful to try not to exclude them in our formulations). I cannot recognize the legitimacy of your specific complaints in any of these respects. A step to disarmament, whatever it may be, was for us always a relatively secondary consequence—shall we rather say, an essential accompanying feature—of the promotion of conditions of real peace which, however, we regard as the heart of the matter.

Another problem is the way Charter 77's materials and contacts with other social forces have been publicized or exploited. Insofar as the materials are concerned the situation is relatively simple: on the one hand, our ability to correct what is said about us is negligible (with regard to the authorities at home, virtually nil); on the other, some of us think it is a misuse when, for example, President Reagan refers to our standpoints,

4   See Blanka Císařovská and Vilém Prečan, *Charta 77: Dokumenty 1977–1989*, Svazek 2, pp. 638–42. (Ed.)

while others feel the same way about the Western Left or the peace movements. However, we all roughly agree that consistent loyalty to truth and perseverance in the requisite limits, without regard to political calculation and possible momentary advantages, are our only guarantee against the abuse of our materials and provide us with the only real possibility of maintaining our identity vis-à-vis ourselves and the general awareness, at home or abroad. The second issue (the contacts) is obviously much more problematic. We have, however, unequivocally accepted the principle that we are willing to lead a dialogue with anyone who at least formally respects the conditions of real dialogue (that can even be, for example, a very unequal dialogue with the authorities insofar as the issues at hand themselves are concerned; not, however, a dialogue with the secret police whose open and unconcealed aim is the elimination of the partner). Many very serious reasons then lead to the outcome that outside this country we prefer to talk to various civic and unofficial social groups rather than to governments or institutions. The predominant political color of our partner depends not so much on us as on who is or is not interested in entering a dialogue.

That much is more or less the official position of Charter 77 presented on its behalf. On the contrary, the following notes are to be understood as purely personal and expressing exclusively my own political position. In defense of my friend Václav Havel (though I welcome your critical observations and your way of expressing them—it contributes to the cultivation of intellects and to the overall balance) I have to state the unalterable fact that for technical (and security!) reasons it is not possible for us to create a truly balanced and thoughtful text of a kind similar to your own. There is much, however, to suggest that the benefit of such joint declarations far outweighs their inevitable shortcomings. Besides, you yourself admit this fact. Therefore your criticisms of Václav Havel should be qualified with due regard to the circumstances. As for your criticism of the Charter, it is downright unjust, because, for whatever reasons, none of the three current spokesmen signed that particular declaration.[5]

5   There were thirteen East German signatories and sixteen Czech signatories to the Declaration. The three then-current spokespersons did not sign (Benda, Jiří Ruml, and Jana Sternová), though the sixteen included seven former

If I refused to attach my signature to this declaration, it was not only because I consider it badly written and sentence by sentence questionable; the truth is for me a living truth and we have no right to refuse the evidence just because it is expressed clumsily. I had however three essential objections. The first concerned the heading in which the signatories were described as members or adherents of peace movements. The other two are almost identical with your reservations. I am not in any way fully and without reservations in solidarity with Western peace movements as far as the explicit purposes for which they are striving (the equally authentic German variant of the text is still less acceptable on these grounds). As far as the sentence "Whoever tolerates social inequality or even increases it, is responsible for hunger and poverty" is concerned, it is completely inappropriate when inserted into the given context. The predominating Euro-centric orientation of this declaration is evidence that it is mendacious: in Europe, the countries where hunger and poverty are burning issues are Poland, Romania and maybe the USSR; that is, countries which vehemently proclaim and forcefully implement the requirements of social equality. Finally and principally, I am convinced (completely in the spirit of your argument) that denying social inequality always inevitably means also the denial of fundamental human and civil rights and freedoms. That is not an accident brought about by the imperfection of previous projects of social equality or those who realized them; social equality represents the liquidation of *societas*, the *polis*, its transformation into a shapeless, nonsensical and in the end permanently enslaved mass of individuals, dispossessed of their generally useful freedoms, of their human dignity and values and of their rights and privileges. Not even in the Kingdom of Christ (disregarding that any attempt to establish it by human force alone leads to destructive consequences) will there be equality in this sense: there will be places on the right and on the left, on the steps of the throne or nearby—

spokespersons. There had been a heated debate in the Charter community about its potential relations with various Western peace movements. It was sparked in the summer of 1983 when a peace congress was held in Prague. See Michael Žantovský, *Havel: A Life* (New York: Grove Press, 2014), pp. 257–58. (Ed.)

although their allocation will be directed by other than earthly criteria, and the last will be first.

I should however emphasize here that my attitude towards social justice is completely different (your sentence "what you defend has nothing in common with social equality or Socialist ideas of justice" is not, in a favorable interpretation, untrue; however, I consider it dangerously misguided, as it tries to reconcile the irreconcilable). The blessed are those who thirst after justice: *fiat iustitia, et pereat mundus!*[6] Guilt and punishment (or forgiveness!), merit and reward, the possibility of distinguishing between good and evil, these are evidently the most essential keystones of all human civilizations and religious and philosophical systems. Justice is absolutely inalienable; under exceptional circumstances it can be infringed, but this should never be done in the name of justice; rather, solely to the account of the personal guilt and responsibility of those who have, in a given moment, to choose between the lesser and the greater evil. There are certainly situations in which the end justifies the means (or at least pardons them); however, by raising this clause to a moral or legal principle, any sort of end is definitively shattered (which is, incidentally, one of many reasons discrediting contemporary Socialism in the majority of its forms). Justice can acquire countless, mostly incompatible, forms; every attempt to deny, force or limit it is, however, an attack on society as a whole. It turns the meaningful co-existence of autonomous beings—with their transcendence in an order, tradition or loyalty to institutions (I am here using your "conservative" terms as I consider them reasonable, although they are not the only conceivable terms)—into a mere war of disparate interests, devoid of any sort of value-distinguishing mark or historical aim. If the Church, Western states, or the spirit of modern civilization generally, have abnegated ideas of social justice, or at least neglected them (I personally hope that this was and is to a much smaller degree than our common enemy likes to reproach us with), they are together fully responsible for the evil that has come from it.

Through this we come to the problem of Socialism. To the disapproval of a number of my friends and close colleagues, on the whole I identify with your view that even "Socialism with a human face" is a

6   Let justice be done, though all else perish. (Ed.)

horrifying monster and that any contest here relates to something bad and long-discredited. I cannot see even a grain of good in Socialist ideas; the more they resemble some other reasonable and humanly justified ideas or feelings in some respects, the more they are unacceptable and destructive. The whole concept is so perverse that it completely spoils any elements of truth while it uses their appeal to deceive less experienced minds and less assured hearts. As a philosopher you are certainly right in diagnosing the term "social equality" as a mere empty slogan; as a *political* philosopher, however, you are completely mistaken when you thus trivialize its social effectiveness. It seduced and is still capable of seducing many to very effective and very unfortunate activity. If, for lack of space, I have to choose a slogan as well, I would formulate my position maybe thus: to oppose all Socialist ideas and fabrications untiringly and completely mercilessly; especially to unmask pre-emptively every camouflage which could enable it to rise again from the ashes (in this you draw attention to a truth whose importance we possibly undervalued). However, I would behave as considerately and tolerantly as possible towards all Socialists (I don't of course mean henchmen or guards of the Gulag), always be prepared to meet them more than half-way, and overlook a dozen of their unbearable habits and resentments for the single human moment which would perhaps enable them to recover from that fatal enchantment. You and I would certainly agree that the spirit of Socialism (though unfortunately for the time being not the weapons and power capabilities marked by this sign) is in inexorable retreat worldwide and that it may soon be possible to write off this erroneous step of human reason definitively. However, we must never write off the millions and hundreds of millions of fellow men who in one way or another succumbed to its error—the struggle for their souls will be less visible, but clearly a crucial part of our joint efforts. If we do not undertake it there would be nothing left for us but to impose the enemy's practices of discipline and order; who then is the victor and who the defeated becomes almost a matter of indifference. The outcome will be almost equally insupportable and it would be an illusion to hope that the superior origin of our values would protect them for long against degeneration brought about by the guilt of the means used. Again, to avoid misunderstandings: I do think that power should be exercised, and even that it is not necessarily bound in its performance by the standards of individual morality (I am, for example, inclined more towards the death penalty than against it). I see a grave danger for freedom in boundless and formally absolutized Liberalism, both in the sense of freedom being threatened by disintegrative tendencies and of it being impossible truly to pursue it without the existence of a background determined by a firm order. I decidedly do not reject fundamentally and *a priori* either the existence of weapons (including nuclear), nor their possible use (not only in the narrower sense of legitimate self-defense but also as a factor that, under certain circumstances, confirms and guarantees the dignity of man and can defend it effectively, and can oppose evil through force). Only that all these socially essential prerogatives (power, legal order in the widest sense of the word, force) have their strict limits, and after these have been crossed they become nothing else but despotism—unjustifiable, inexcusable and destructive. And in regard to what I just said, I would only note that good and evil are not equivalent and complementary, that totalitarian regimes cannot be eliminated by a mere change of directions in which its tools are used, and that to be against something (I consider myself a thorough anti-Communist) is important but far from being sufficient.

Few of us harbor any political ambitions and none of us at the present time could be labeled a professional politician (not even a professional revolutionary) in the usual sense of the word. It is just that for each of us a moment came when our conscience commanded us to say no to all the injustice, lies and maliciousness around us, when we were no longer willing to look on without doing anything as our society, with all its values, traditions and institutions, was gradually and deliberately transformed into a desert, into mere dust in the wind. Not even then did we want to get into politics. We allowed ourselves merely to appeal to generally accepted legal norms and valid laws (even keeping strictly within the boundaries of the hard and problematic legality under which we live). We voluntarily took upon ourselves our share of human and civic responsibilities for the unfortunate state of public affairs and their correction. We did this until the authorities declared us a public enemy and our appeal to morality a dangerous politicking. In the end it could have been expected: what kind of totalitarian state would allow someone to breathe freely even for a second, let alone to assume the right to an independent judgment of good and evil, and to politely draw attention to the fact that the government is breaking the laws it promulgated itself? Maybe we are politically inexperienced, but we are not naïve or blinded; we have come to terms with the fact that a political dimension forced us to do what we did, and we have learned to take into account the purely political impact which this or that action will have. But we have not subordinated our actions to political considerations even in part, not to speak about making them the absolute criterion.

However, I think myself that such a "politicization" of Charter 77 did not rest only in the mere recognition of the essential, that it was not only virtue from necessity; we soon understood that we had (maybe at first unwittingly) stumbled on something that has a much more universal meaning, that is closely connected with the hopes and fears of modern man (and mankind) as such. It seems that this conviction is shared by an ever wider circle of my friends, however different their "political" opinions are from each other (according to currently available information)— but to give you at least a suggestion of what I mean, I will have to make a small detour.

I must say first that I am immeasurably disgusted by every attempt (and the more sophisticated and pseudo-justified it is, the greater the measure of lies and danger it conceals) to put the American and Russians and their military presence wherever it might be on the same level, to see in the policies of the blocs the source of the evils of the world and to apportion responsibility equally between the two partners, and to infer that East and West have the same problems. This attitude argues that life is just as difficult and undignified there as here, that freedoms are restricted and rights violated there as here, that people can be jailed for their convictions there as here (it would be great if a couple of British women activists—better still if they acquired Czechoslovak citizenship—tried to camp in front of some Soviet rocket base in our country; there is a small quantitative difference between 14 days and 14 years imprisonment, during which they may come to understand that to disarm the West and rely on the good will of the East is not the best remedy. They would, however, first have to have the improbable good luck that someone would have betrayed to them the location of the base, and that priority would be given to their humane conviction over their permanent disappearance into the unknown). Such an attitude also labels your letter an expression of topsy-turvy Stalinism (I've come across such a judgment, even from otherwise sensible people). No, we live here and we know very well that the only things that function in the whole of the East are the consolidation and expansion of power; these, however, function with murderous efficiency. We therefore thank God for everything that tries to oppose this power and limit it, perhaps not very cleverly for ourselves. The meaningful existence of mankind will end on a planetary scale if we do not succeed in stopping this expansion—and thermonuclear destruction is only one of the possible consequences.

We are not however so mesmerized by this comparison as to confuse the symptoms of the illness with its real reasons and roots; in this respect there is on the contrary an extensive similarity of the error between anti-Communism and pacifism. The totalitarian systems of this century did not fall from heaven, nor did they enter history as some sort of irrational and unforeseeable factor. The ever more murderous wars and mass extinctions of whole nations are not accidental and isolated phenomena; nor are the dominance of amorphous crowds and, on the other hand, of militant groups, and the abandonment of most values, perspectives and beliefs. There is further the destruction of the environment and, for the first time in history, the real possibility of global destruction, "hot" or "cold"; and the growing misery of the Third World as well as its malevolent extravagances, which only an incurable optimist can call a childish malady, and in respect of which the rest of mankind not only relinquishes all humane and historical responsibility but also empowers their destructiveness by exporting terrible weapons and ideologies (in relatively recent times the warships of some European powers combated slavery on all seas without being restrained by problems of sovereignty—it was maybe arrogant but was at least honest; gunboat policy cannot be counted as one of the better policies, but if we have to fight against genocide, then we hail gunboats). Many more examples could be given; the world as a whole is in a difficult crisis which does not respect the frontiers between blocs. Mankind, liberally stimulated by slogans about automatic progress, evidently set off down this cul-de-sac several centuries ago, long before anything like blocs existed at all. This crisis requires fundamental healing which in all probability will come too late; life (and European life in an especially exalted form) has however this outstanding quality, that it does not surrender itself to the most hopeless circumstances. In your country, where democratic traditions really do go deep and which for some time was the essence of the Early Modern European spirit with all its virtues and vices, it is perhaps easier to overlook this crisis or to see it as a mere hiccup on an otherwise feasible path. If I am not mistaken however, European civilization made the world single and indivisible, so your institutions are being emptied one by one, and in particular your thinking today succumbs to that schizophrenia which inevitably leads to destruction. The Falklands War was a great eruption which did a lot to cultivate minds worldwide, and which broke the neck of the reigning assumption that the only effective policy and diplomacy is the permanent loss of honor and reason. Granted, that after decades of the disgraceful capitulation of large and small Western powers (among the most flagrant cases we remember the Pueblo incident[7] and the American Embassy in Iran; the only bright exception is the state of Israel, which unfortunately is not imitable for both historical and metaphysical reasons), the obvious bloody resistance of a handful of mariners and the no less obvious engagement of a national navy in regaining distant outposts was a remarkable testimony to the good state of preservation of your country, its people and its government and their mutual trust. Nevertheless, I don't really believe in the various Internationals; nation and state are actually so distinctive that a foreign solution rarely fits. I am therefore afraid that your country's world famous eruption is too simple an application of its classical and unrevised political traditions (and stereotypes) to be capable of offering such a permanent exit from the existing crisis as for example the American Moral Majority, Polish Solidarity or the French movement for the defense of the freedom of education; let time decide.

In this connection, however, I must very much oppose your statement "Messianic and (if I can put it this way) Fascist unity of common interest," addressed against the peace movement. This is a typical confusion of causes and effects, of the essential and the inessential. Certainly there is

---

7   On January 23, 1968, the USS Pueblo was captured by North Korean forces while on a mission to surveil the Soviet Navy as well as gather signal and electronic intelligence from North Korea. (Ed.)

only one true Messianism, which is to humans incomprehensible, un-chartable and unpredictable—all others are begotten of evil and beget evil. Certainly there is a Fascist, a Communist, and a Socialist "unity of common interest," false and malignant. However, one cannot infer the absence of disease from the finding that only inappropriate medication has been used till now. The human world has become a universe (maybe against our will, but what difference does that make) and its crisis has a universal nature; its healing has therefore to proceed according to certain common rules, some minimal code whose acceptance is a condition *sine qua non* for the restora-tion of reasonable diversity and variety. And another thing to which the label Messianism could also be very easily assigned: everyone has to begin at home, before his own threshold, according to his own specific conditions and possibilities, but it would be utterly foolish to rely on other than a global solution. Separated islands, though they be the size of half the world, may have a more lasting significance only as a starting point for an attack which will bring a final settlement and resolution. If we try to settle our-selves comfortably in our own truth and relative innocence, the flood of evil will simply engulf us. Seemingly the only chance is provided by mere defense, but for it to be effective in the long term it must, like it or not, copy the methods of evil and in the end become its mirror image; in place of one empire of evil there will simply be two and their rivalry will only make the field of future hopes smaller. Insofar as argumentation, details, and other connections and issues are concerned, let me refer with pleasure to *The Lord of the Rings* by Professor Tolkien; in this century it would be hard to find a specialist work which tables the essential questions of society with such urgency and thoroughness, analyses them so penetratingly and presents solutions so real, non-totalitarian and balanced (incidentally, this exceptionally conservative super-fairy-tale belies the conservatives' usual argument that the necessary tax for the accuracy of their analyses and the effectiveness of their practice is the weakness and vagueness of their the-ories).

The resurrection of civic responsibility for oneself, the community, and the human world in general undoubtedly belongs to the above-men-tioned "social rules." This means, among other things, to accept another human above all as someone close, a fellow citizen and a partner, not to reduce him to the bearer of a particular ideology, to his social, national or racial cipher, to a voter. Undoubtedly it carries a terrible risk; it may provide room for terrorism or for the overthrow of the state, it may leave us even more defenseless with regard to arbitrary and illegitimate power (the Greek cradle of democracy knew this problem already and unhappily tried to solve it by the institution of ostracism). Christianity teaches us that we have to undergo this risk unconditionally, albeit at the same time to define the threshold beyond which Jesus (and anyone who speaks in His name) plaits a whip and thoroughly cleanses His Father's house, which is also our only true home. In the terrible and extreme conditions of the modern age (I admit there were other more peaceful times when order reigned plainly enough, and at least outwardly one did not have to put absolutely everything on the line) it is thus demonstrated that a firm moral attitude which denounces pragmatism, simplification, and blind hatred is the ultimate weapon to remain effective against evil.

Now, specifically and specially on the current peace movements in the West: why, after all I've said, do I, who otherwise follows a crusade rather than the peace of capitulators and non-participators, not only want to appeal to them, but see in them an important ally and some sort of touchstone of our effort? Clearly I will not quarrel with you about the extent of Communist inspiration and control (even though I would recommend more careful differentiation); we are so much more deeply and remorselessly informed about these methods than you that we would never again undervalue them. A very important motif of these movements is a simple reluctance towards resistance and a highly sophisticated fear; a fear especially incomprehensible in those who call themselves Christians and otherwise tenaciously maintain that he who would save his own life will lose it, and that mankind as a whole has to fix its hopes in awaiting His coming and the end of time. The aims of most of the peace movements are simply unreal, they are empty or amoral slogans, and their language in general is the language of ideologues or crackpots. In spite of this, however, I put more than a little hope in these movements. Moscow cannot buy itself millions (and can manipulate them only up to a certain point), it cannot from mere fear germinate courage and decision in the victim, and even the fascination of bad slogans has its limits. I have the impression that with the simple majority of Western peace movements there is another factor in play, which simply eclipses the meaning of those mentioned up to now. I would call it a reaction to the crisis of civic identity which has engulfed the whole of modern society, the effort to assume again a unique responsibility, to make matters common to humanity comprehensible and meaningful. I am no historian, but tentatively I would want to draw attention to the analogy with the origins of the Socialist movement. At that time the sheer lack of understanding on the part of the secular and spiritual authorities substantially contributed to Socialism becoming the chief threat of our age. We cannot allow ourselves the luxury of repeating the same mistakes. This spontaneity is certainly very subconscious, badly articulated, and for the time being ruled by powers and slogans hostile to us. It is at a crossroads; so far it is not the sterile pacifism of the classic type, of extremist or terrorist movements, nor even an affiliated link of any sort of party or power—it can however soon become one of these. But it can also save itself from all these snares and become the beginning of something; the beginning of apolitical politics or, better, the restoration of politics as matters shared by responsible citizens loyal to the public interest, mutually respecting their own dignity, rights and privileges. I am afraid that if politics does not undergo such a renewal, they will soon be nothing like politics; only an inevitable power or no less inevitable death. The Western peace movement has two significant merits: a high degree of personal engagement on a large scale, and relative independence of established political mechanisms of every kind (many of these mechanisms have to be maintained, but their mere maintenance without substantial changes is no longer enough today to save the world from oppressive ruin). It is easy to criticize or condemn, but at this moment it is of vital concern to us all (especially those with a good understanding of their weak points and dangers) to take pains to ensure these movements understand their own nature and choose the only route which offers immanent hope for this world. We have invested a considerable part of our prestige in assuming that such a basis exists for the peace movements. Your opinions are closer to me than theirs; even so, if I'm answering your brief critical notes so extensively and controversially, I'm doing so because I really think politically —and I see the only real remedy for what is wrong in the world to be the possibility of communicating with at least some categories of idealists and ideologues.

January 1985

16

Not Only Moral Problems

It is wearisome and often painful to listen to comments from Christians and non-Christians about how the Vatican has once again maintained its untenably reactionary position with regard to matters of contraception—comments delivered with the matter-of-course conviction that it would never occur to anyone reasonable not to agree with them, and that it is a mere question of time before the Church too will renounce its fuddy-duddy opinions. It is wearisome and often painful to explain to the parties involved in a divorce that we do not agree with them, and condemn their act not because they have been unable to explain the reasons for their divorce in a sufficiently vivid way, but because they simply should not get divorced. It is wearisome and above all painful to listen to thoughtless reflections on the life or death of an unborn child; one does not regret the highly undignified circuitous routes and highly problematic compromise as long as one influences the decision in favor of life—what, however, can one feel for that vociferous sophistry which overlays the cloying stench of the crematorium with lofty slogans about freedom, the woman's right to choose, and human rights.

Weariness and pain are our inevitable guides; it is not appropriate to complain about them. On closer inspection it transpires that the large majority of our fellow citizens have a much more realistic and healthy attitude towards these deeds—i.e., contraception, divorce, abortion. Their attitude is that occasionally and quite commonly they do not manage to avoid them, but that this does not mean that they consider them harmless or perhaps even outright a virtue. Only it is that vociferous minority, for whom such behavior is almost a synonym of progress and modern liberation, that is heard and that sets the tone. It is not easy to speak out, to deviate from the general trend—who would want to draw attention to the limits of freedom, in situation when freedom as such is denied?; who has the right to doubt the absolute autonomy and self-determination of man, when man is at that moment being trampled on and humiliated?; who would be attracted to impose Puritan strictures on life, if life itself is threatened and at a crossroads, if joy from life ranks first on the list of what is proscribed? We are thus threatened with the danger that this fashion will become the norm, that face to face with these deeds no space remains for questions about good and evil. It would not be the first time; the loss of values is a characteristic feature of our age. Only, every further step on this road reaches more deeply into the flesh of our body and the marrow of our bones, so that the actual moment is looming when we are no longer able to be either free beings or God's creatures—while the scope of moral decisions mentioned above touches the very foundation of our being more seriously than might seem at first glance. This is where mere weariness or pain suddenly ceases to matter, much less considerations about the popularity of individual themes; for we bear responsibility not only for what we do, but for what we do not do—all the more so if our not-doing may become a stumbling block and initiator of harm for many. More and more, the silent come to share the guilt, and the argument that we should not judge, should not even cast a stone at another, when we ourselves are tangled up enough in our own iniquities, this is not in the least bit valid. To constantly forgive our neighbor, and to approve a sin actively or passively, are two completely different things which as a rule also have completely antithetical results. Double the amount of guilt then falls on those who—from whatsoever cause—feel obliged to bear witness to the misery and hopes of our time and to give testimony as to who is the Lord of the Times; one day they will find out that they lied and failed utterly when, with their minds on more immediate problems and serious tactical considerations, they failed to speak out on behalf of the smallest, the most defenseless and most miserable.

I should speak first to the brothers in Christ. However, he who wants to hear the words of Revelation can only with difficulty be in doubt over these questions, and he who wants deliberately to overturn them—well, for his own safety, he should perhaps not call on His name. So this is just a note for those who were called not long ago, and for the most part put the rest of us in the shade with their enthusiasm and sincerity: do not undervalue the seemingly small things, marked by the weight of carnality and by the drudgery of everyday service—the Christian cautiously leaves a too highly-strung fervor, too bewitching a liberation, to other spirits (Lucifer, for example). Otherwise it's maybe enough for me to say that I think contraception, divorce, and abortion are reprehensible practices and that in these matters I fully identify with the standpoints and with the arguments of the Magisterium— without, of course, being able to show myself unable to transgress against them; however human weakness is not and should not be a pretext for questioning moral standards. On the basis of God's promise concerning the lasting operation of the Holy Spirit in the Church, I cherish the firm hope that these standpoints will not fundamentally change, however great the outside pressure.

It is however much more urgent to reach those who do not know what they are doing, who are ostensibly acting in good faith, who pretend that preaching and Christ's words are something unknown to them, or something which lost their validity long ago. That is why I want in the following to limit myself strictly to arguments which appeal to generally shared standards and values, to tasks and aims considered to be unquestionably beneficial—and also to appeal to the indignation issuing from the "natural" essence of mankind.

However, there is another aspect in play, which in the end shows itself to be decisive. My former assertion about a "conspiracy of silence" seems in fact to have been overcome. In a number of countries these questions have become the subject of passionate political disputes and conflicts which can have a much more central meaning for the future shape of human society as a whole than we dare to hope for today. If such disputes do not occur in our country and passions seem to slumber, it is from a simple cause: that political totalitarianism, resting on a "scientific world view," excludes the official existence of two different opinions about anything at all, whether it be the length of your hair or how you crack your egg. It would, however, be highly pointless and irresponsible to assume that either these problems do not concern us, or that it would be better at least for once to use the advantages of totalitarianism and not to resist the non-problematic course of things in the current unfortunate direction. It would be no less unreasonable to team up—without the prior commitment of a thoroughly considered standpoint on the merit of the matter—with one side or another in the above-mentioned contests, just because we find it sympathetic for some other reason; in this way we would on the one hand expose ourselves to the danger that our integrity could be overturned by an inconspicuous smuggling in of very questionable slogans, and on the other we could so easily confer our unquestionable moral authority (unfortunately or fortunately, the only authority and power we have at our disposal) on something which is completely antithetical to our aims and from which we would, if we have direct experience with it, recoil with horror.

These questions therefore have to be answered as political questions too; and because today the political sphere—here thanks to its complete arbitrariness and over there to general deterioration—for the most part lacks the natural religious, moral or simply private corrective ("private" as in the independent order of household, dignity of the individual and absence of the need to be a member of the mass, devotee of fashion, or object of the paternalist care of the state), this part of the reply can have a crucial meaning. I will therefore in the following devote my most systematic attention to it. If it comes to that, I am in my own domain here: I try to testify above all as a citizen, and I assiduously and persistently take on myself my share of responsibility for civic and political matters. This, however, has far-reaching consequences. As a believer (and a layman!) I fully respect the authority of the Magisterium of the Church in matters of faith and morals; as a citizen and *cum grano salis* a politician, I am naturally bound to oppose this authority acquiring the attributes of secular power or stepping out of the field of faith and morals. For apart from the Kingdom of Christ—which is not of this world and in a sense not even of these times—all historical attempts at theocracy spring from evil and leave behind them only the question as to whether they caused more suffering to mankind or more damage to their God; the opposite would have been surprising. As a private person I have my strong opinions (by coincidence, in the given issue close to the official views of the Church), my moral standards and preferred values. However, I can only become a citizen and a politician (as the case may be, a political prisoner) at the moment when I take fully into account the existence of radically different opinions, standards, and preferred values, only if I am willing to create a community as a space (extremely uncomfortable, but the only human one) of their mutual dialogue, coexistence and mutual respect (this obligation is obviously reciprocal, only he or she who is willing to comply with it can be a fully-fledged partner and real fellow-citizen). It may be that my conclusions and "political counsel" will be quite different from my belief and from where the preceding argumentation has been heading. I ask my brothers and sisters not to suspect me of moral tepidity, but rather to accept it as my homage to the dignity of free moral decision-making, unsupported by any power. I ask my opponents not to consider my restraint weakness or a dishonorable trick, but to be all the more responsible in reviewing those opinions of mine which preclude any compromise.

Contraception

Contraception has been going on ever since the world began—indeed, every experienced married couple or pair of lovers confirm that the range of possibilities can never be exhausted even by the most meticulous list of licit or illicit means and that the volitional aspect plays a much more important role in conception than medicine or morality proclaims. However, that all moves in the field of probability theory, of reasonable essential procrastination or of various deviant fashions. Imagine now absolutely reliable contraception, not limiting mutual delight in any way and completely non-detrimental to one's health (nothing such exists, and there is a question as to whether for fundamental reasons it can ever exist at all—do not let yourselves be led astray by propaganda and advertisement). I admit that for me personally, such a possibility of "separating sex games from love" (Maritain) is not devoid of attractiveness, at least sometimes and at least on a certain level of looking at it—I do not want to be so skeptical, or to classify others according to the measure of my own sinfulness, but I have serious reasons to anticipate that a similar ambivalent position is, if not universal among mankind, then at least very widespread among people. The behavior of the guests at exclusive Roman banquets, who artificially induced vomiting so they could continue to consume another series of courses without interruption, nowadays evokes a general and spontaneous outrage which does not have to rely on some explicitly formulated ethical standard. But not only do we regularly practice analogical approaches in the field of sex, but are usually willing to tolerate them when practiced by our neighbor—and that is already saying something, and testifies to something serious, for our judgment of another is rarely marked by excessive leniency.

Most religious and moral systems resist and condemn contraception quite strictly, whether explicitly or with emphasis on the most numerous descendants being a direct measure of the value and "rank" of an individual's life; contraception, however, despite being banned, has flourished almost unimpeded in every age and in every form. That in itself is normal rather than strange (not to mention the fact that at this very moment this sphere is objectively uncontrollable and in the face of one's own conscience, often ambiguous). Only unusually misguided people, gods, or God, would ban something which is either completely impossible or which no one would ever think of doing. Nor do people, gods, or God, nurse any illusions that the ban would not be avoided—otherwise they would not supplement it with relevant sanctions or at least with an enumeration of negative moral consequences. And I am not sure whether people or gods or even God as a rule rescind their commandments just because they are momentarily more abundantly and obstinately broken—which ought to be understood as a subtle educational mission to the Magisterium (if a layman may hold to the concept of upbringing as a two-way process).

Everything said up to now indicates that the issue of contraception will accompany us for as long as this our troubled existence will last on earth. I will disappoint those who expect consistent argumentation and firm condemnation; I am not competent to the first, and with the second I would confound myself and do no one any good. I only know and understand, very unclearly, that contraception somehow always fundamentally threatens love as a synonym for God, and as the motive power of His creation—for the relatively extravagant theological assumption that sexual love is a rather special but nevertheless fully-fledged incarnation (for he who would understand, the whole omitted argumentation and the whole misery of contraception is indicated in this word) of that true love. If it comes to that, I am not thinking at all now about the age-old and minor sins of husbands and lovers (and maybe even mortal sins—for what else would forgiveness be for), who postpone something or cheat over something; but rather about that acrid and indigestible novelty of recent decades: vociferous and self-celebrating contraception which establishes pure pleasure and arrogant planning as the unmistakable priorities (it does not use the concepts of virtue and sin only because it long ago ceased to understand them); aggressive contraception, which disdainfully dismisses every objection as primitivism, obscurantism and reaction—if it is willing to tolerate them temporarily at all, if it does not directly apply the means of moral power and coercion.

There were certainly many causes for this. However, this rapid development and overturning of opinions took place and is taking place under the aegis of two basic mottos which at the present time serve as the main driving motifs. The first is the more modest, formulated according to the theory of the lesser evil: contraception has to be the main weapon against population explosion, and the means to achieve a planned demographic development. The only alternative is hunger and misery for millions, murderous warfare, the collapse of society in growing internal conflicts. The second motto is just another of those magic spells through which we still after several centuries, ruthlessly and without regrets, destroy ourselves: i.e., it was only with contraception that the gates of the sexual revolution opened, liberating us in our own bodies from dependence on nature or whatever it is that interferes with us; this will be another logical step on the path towards the emancipation of man and makes it possible in this important sphere of behavior too to establish an enlightened government of reason—or vice versa, the freedom of pure spontaneity (the revolutionaries have never been too clear about this, but—aside from the fact that in this connection they regularly beat each other's heads in—it is not generally interesting; both promises are equally unattractive and above all absolutely impossible to fulfill). Like fraudulent alchemists, enthusiasts will implement and propagate mottos; they will sometimes even be willing to discuss the suitability of individual means and in all seriousness revise the procedures used. They are after all reasonable and truthful people. Only they can never admit that the time has come (or could come at some controllable interval) to balance the sum of gold discovered and produced, to validate—or once and for all to reject—the magic formula.

Let us then on our own account try to put together some sort of balance. The first motto is, as I said already, more modest and down to earth; the corresponding benefit and damage can also be shown in a much less striking manner. In short, the results are quite unconvincing: the population explosion has definitely not been stopped, and it is not even evident that its redistribution between individual centers was somehow conditioned by implementing contraception. Paradoxically, miseries predicted as an alternative to promoting contraception are multiplying in places where an increase in the birth rate was limited. The impact of the mass implementation of contraception on the state of health and genetic quality of the population remains an unknown threat. On the other hand, it is undeniable that in a number of countries this method of fighting the population explosion has strengthened totalitarian tendencies and state control over the life of the individual and such primary social institutions as the family.

The sexual revolution ended up according to the immutable law of all its predecessors: it evaporated and only the mud of bureaucracy remained. I am not thinking only of the values and human meanings which this revolution deliberately denied or sacrificed—although we should perhaps be glad to retain each one of them, even at a much higher price than was optimistically offered. Let us try to evaluate the results of the revolution in its own domain, in what it intended and promised to introduce. The health consequences of general promiscuity and the extensive use of contraception practices (including abortion) and preparations are clearly catastrophic: the unexpected renaissance of sexually transmitted diseases; an increase of up to tens of percent of the infertile or sexually incapable parts of the population; the until now and into the future inestimable number of genetically damaged children; chronic disturbances and malignant, often previously unknown illnesses as a phenomenon which is almost obligatory for women in particular (certainly, other factors of modern civilization also play a role in most of these cases; it is however impossible to deny a direct connection with contraception and the sexual revolution). So the liberation of the body replaced peaceful and comprehensible dependency, in many cases by cruel slavery to its disturbed function. The number of unwanted children, the main argument of the adherents of contraception, has drastically increased with its general introduction and is still rising. In place of the richness of sexual life, its trivialization is in the ascendant, when the speed and purposeful directness of the act becomes the conventional commitment and eliminates most of the pleasures in advance, including the purely physical ones. Reasonable dominance and planned timetabling have yielded generally cruel disappointment and proved moreover to be a plaything in the hands of chance, of hysterical reactions and growing mutual aggression. In the best case, liberated spontaneity ended by recognizing the need to acquiesce passively to every sexual demand. In a fair number of cases, however, it became the victim of direct rape and sexual and human tyranny, before whose ruthlessness everything imaginable in the past, under the veil of valid orders, pales.

To summarize: I consider contraception to be morally flawed, something which seriously threatens love, the dignity of the human being and ultimately the fullness of sexual life as such. Moreover, I consider the results of experiments up to now with the mass introduction and glorification of contraception to be partly unconvincing, partly literally repugnant. However, there is no reason which would entitle me to deny my neighbor the right to a different opinion or different practices in this matter which would not touch the fundamental right of human freedom. This leads to the appropriate political conclusion: every modern state will probably be forced to think about its attitude to contraception (whether it be dictated by the anticipated advantages to the community or by the sum of individual moral attitudes). On its basis all the *indirect* means it has at its disposal for the support or limitation of contraception can and may be used (I would however recommend maximum restraint, for unlike divorce and family law, this matter is on the very limit of *raisons d'état*). Under no circumstances however does it have the right in any form (ranging from forced restraint to forcible sterilization) to order it; in this way the foundations of human dignity and freedom would be destroyed. Similarly (even if the state is founded on Christian principles, even if all its citizens count themselves as Christians and share the same moral convictions), it does not have the right to forbid contraception; here too the state would be crossing its boundaries, it would violate human freedom and usurp judgment in matters which by their nature belong solely to God.

Divorce

We shall be discussing these issues primarily with regard to a cultural and civilizational environment derived from Christian starting points. When we come to think of it, the inviolability of the particular "family" relationship is a universal feature of all human societies, except that in other cultures than the Christian, in place of the husband-wife relationship, its foundation stone may be the succession of ancestors and descendants, the bonds of lineage, the extended family, etc.

Again, there are a number of moral and religious reasons which speak against the possibility of divorce as such. Some of them draw attention to the essential degradation of human dignity and freedom; to permit divorce means that to interpret the finitude of man as an inability to make decisions which cannot be undone, as a kind of volatility and absolute submission to the course of time. There also exist counter-arguments of a logical and legal nature: it is confusing to formally invalidate any decision without dealing responsibly with the irrevocable consequences which that decision brought (children, changes of personality and of way of life). However, all these reasons have been formulated many times and by those more qualified; I will just leave them to echo in the subtext and context. I do so in addition to other reasons also because I do not intend to deny that there are marriages and life situations—far from exceptional but also not frequent, although that much more frequently popularized by divorce apologists—when divorce (or at the very least a complete separation from table and bed; people however have become unreceptive to the thought that they must at least pay some fine for their mistakes) is in all respects, including the moral and religious, the only solution and rescue for those involved and also for society. This does not of course stop it being wrong; all it can do is prevent much worse wrongs. I am even willing (in the spirit of my belief that love is more than law, but is not against the law) to allow that romantic, fateful love can sometimes be such a situation; on the condition that those involved do not excuse or even celebrate the resulting immoral step, that they are resolved to bear the gravity of their guilt without impatience, to accept adversity as just and to give out more of themselves than would be sufficient for the statutory fine. However, as I said, I do not intend to deal with marginal situations too much here or to focus on arguments valid absolutely and without exception.

What concerns me mostly is the social phenomenon, a kind of statistical prevailing attitude towards divorce. Let it be said that I consider marriage—at least in our cultural environment—as the basic model institution of mankind's time on earth, both in the sense of the fulfillment of individual existence, and in establishing our relationship to other human beings, in the possibility of the origin and continuation (far from just biological survival) of any sort of society or even community. Marriage should be the school of balance between liberty and order, the sanctity of love and the everydayness of living together and caring for offspring, individual self-realization and responsibility, commitment and obedience towards someone and something else, between the finitude of the individual in all its misery and hope and the possibility of transcendence in the orders of time, the fullness of being and the establishment of community (in all the horror and uncertainty that such an transcendence involves for the individual).[1] Yet marriage as the school of balance is, like all human institutions, very distant from any kind of ideal, and not even the mere glimpse of it in hope is easy and possible to guarantee

---

1   It may not be a coincidence that the alternative historical solutions (priests and monks and, in the relatively recent past, military and academic orders and castes) usually structured themselves in forms capable of imitating the basic functions of marriage. These forms include: the irrevocability of the commitment (more precisely, the permanent moral and professional disqualification should it not be maintained); the vow of purity (unconditional fidelity to the service of the church, to the heavenly bridegroom, to the beloved science or to the manu military [by force of arms] defended interests—analogies are in the end often derived from the marriage relationship); obedience (which surprisingly does not refer to absolute order and truth, for these are most appropriately revealed to us by our own conscience, but on the contrary means the acceptance of the yoke of chance and uncertainty with respect to the decision-making of others—as in every true interpersonal relationship, especially in marriage); and often poverty too (which is connected with the prevention of dependencies which could compete with the basic and sacred dependency—in marriage this dependency is so much connected with care for the partner and the children that on the contrary "material security" strengthens it; however, the effective principle remains essentially the same). (VB)

once and for all. Given the empirically observable and revealed character of human nature, I think it is virtually certain that even in the most perfect marriages (if we want to examine their sources, we should look beyond the romantic image of great love to the role of obedience and mutual devotion) there are necessarily moments of doubt and crisis, mutual guilt unpardonable from the human point of view, insurmountable conflicts and insoluble problems. And this is where, in my opinion, lies the mortal danger of the contemporary social trend which makes divorce a normal event, indeed, almost a fashion (after all, suicide presents an analogous problem except that in this case our natural biological mechanisms still provide more effective brake). Marital problems are almost always soluble if we understand we have no other possibility than to overcome them, or else to live to the end of our (or our partner's) days under their weight. However, as soon as we allow divorce to be a possible solution we will inevitably get into a situation in which it proves to be the most convenient solution, if not the only one. Marriage entered into "on a trial basis" or perhaps just with a provisional awareness that it is not an irremediable commitment, that if the original emotional motives pass away or if the difficulties significantly predominate over the benefits, you can always count on its abolition as the real starting point; such a marriage becomes the ground for tragic failures which can even be repeated without the participants understanding in the slightest what the stumbling block really is. Of course, even of those marriages closed in such an atmosphere and with such a predisposition, a number (whether we think it is a significant or a hopelessly inadequate number depends on our viewpoint) survive the onslaught of time; however, it forces us to ask whether mere human convenience does not have a significant share in this success (in fact, divorce only complicates one's life and leads to uncertain adventures) or simply the inability to establish a true partnership (in which case it doesn't really make much difference whom we formally live alongside, and only fateful events such as illness, long-term isolation and the like can stimulate thoughts of change). Again I summarize: I consider divorce to be morally intolerable and logically questionable. Especially dangerous, however, is the current fashion when it not only looks like something excusable, but becomes part of everyday calculations. This is not only about negative moral, social and other consequences, it is about the human being reduced and in its very essence deprived of its integrity; it is denied the freedom to build relationships not subject to the dictates of time and outside circumstances. If someone does promote such a relaxed form of marriage, he should be consistent, and advocate its complete abolition; at the same time however he should offer an alternative solution capable of taking on all the humanly enriching (and socially indispensable) functions which this institution fulfilled and fulfills in our cultural circle.

However, what sort of position should society and the state take up *vis-à-vis* divorce? It has to be said that—despite all the historical vulgarization and misuse—the statement that "the family is the foundation of the state" refers to a very serious and indisputable fact. The disintegration of the family does not concern only the two main participants; a number of other people are also involved, not least the children, and in this sense divorce is a direct burden on the whole of society. The state (society) thus has the right to intervene in this matter much more massively than in the case of contraception. It is in its very own interest to use this right on behalf of the protection of the family and the limitation of the divorce rate. I firmly believe the standing Czechoslovak norm—which provides divorced persons with a number of benefits (tax breaks, labor laws and other) unlike those who live in law-abiding and irrevocable matrimony— to be extremely unhealthy. Nevertheless, the duration or dissolution of the bond between two people is principally (despite all the social consequences) a matter for those two, their morality and conscience, and we know that every attempt at strict regimentation in this sphere not only fails to succeed but drives its author to lies, evil and futile violence. In addition, we stand, and maybe after all these times will still stand, face to face with the indubitable empirical fact that a certain percentage of marriages collapse irremediably and without hope, and that their further formal survival is a direct threat to the husband and wife, children, and immediate circle. I think therefore that the state does not have the right to outlaw divorce completely (again: not even if—especially if—the state is founded on Christian principles). It can certainly complicate it in every way, it can certainly use every opportunity to make the very thought of divorce extremely unpopular. However, the final decision in this sphere cannot (unfortunately?) be dictated by the law but by us, the feeble and the sinful—in the given case, the partners.

Abortion

It is with pain and shame that I speak on this topic at all, not to mention the fact that I treat it as a subject of impartial reasoning and cold weighing up of all the pros and cons. It is with pain and shame that I deal with it in one stride with the preceding topics: the incontestable logical and material connection could also mean the concealment of the ethical abyss. We stand here before the temptation of the pride of reason. It is with pain and shame that I realize how precarious is my own self-confident position and moral certainty. When, during our most recent pregnancy, my wife was invited to undergo various genetic tests, we unanimously refused them. The consequences of ultra-sound investigations in the early stages of pregnancy are examined quite inadequately at present and the probability of damaging the unborn or of spontaneous abortion when drawing off the amniotic fluid is, according to specialists, equivalent to the probability of a child being born with some genetic flaw. My wife, however, shamed me by pointing out that such a comparison of probabilities was in any case pointless, and that the tests would at best feed our inappropriate curiosity—because even the worst prognosis could not change her duty to bear the child, to love it, and to look after it with me. At first sight this might seem too extreme a standpoint; I think however that love and simple respect for life made itself heard here against the lofty niceties of unfettered reason— and in such cases not even truth is on the side of reason, not to mention other values. If it comes to it, past and present experiences emphatically warn us that we should not leave medicine more room than necessarily belongs to it, because as with every human factor it displays uncertainty as to its knowledge, but an inevitable tendency to lord over others, to manipulate them as mere objects; the bitter ends of all euthanasia projects is the most obvious of these experiences—but far from the only one.

In the fight for the legalization of abortion, two types of argument were used. The first referred to exceptionally unfavorable circumstances: health (see above) of the legal nature (for example, rape or a very young mother) and the social situation (inability to ensure the child at least minimum care). Secondly, it was pointed out that it had been impossible to prevent a rather large number of illegal, unprofessionally performed abortions which often seriously threatened the life of the mother or permanently affected her health. (This reason was apparently decisive in influencing the legislators, although it is an offence to elementary legal sentiment. For example, no society is capable of preventing a certain number of murders, and these usually take place in a very uncivilized and unprofessional manner. It would never, however, occur to anyone to solve this problem by a legal amendment which ensured, on the basis of proper registration and an application approved by the appropriate committee, the humane killing of the victim and the impunity of the culprit—sorry, applicant.) Even today we are capable of being deeply angered by, and feeling a moral superiority over, those barbarian nations of the past who hurled their less promising newly-born from the nearest cliff (health reasons), sacrificed a certain proportion of the infant population to Moloch or other gods (social reasons), or preventatively eradicated potential competitors for an inheritance or avengers of defeated enemies in their cradle (legal reasons). Despite this, our societies (it is difficult to ascertain whether it was originally due to a majority consensus or only thanks to a fanatical decision by our rulers) accepted the above arguments and abortion was universally legalized. Whatever the case, an attitude clearly predominates today which sees in this legislation, if not progress, then at least something normal.

At the same time however there was a qualitative leap analogous to the one we drew attention to in connection with contraception and divorce. The proportion of genetically damaged children worldwide is sharply increasing, but the proportion of socially or legally damaged has not in any way decreased. If even the most pessimistic estimates spoke about a certain percentage of illegally interrupted pregnancies, in "civilized" countries the percentage is large (in neighboring Austria, a predominantly Catholic country, about half, in our country more than a third); it is not possible to rule out, inasmuch as, even with the most expert care, the health risk to the woman (not to speak of the mental risks which are in general to be expected) increases at approximately the same rate.

In addition, however, it was shown almost immediately that all the arguments used are not only shortsighted and short-winded but false from the very start, purposefully intended. Nowadays women generally consider it intolerable and demeaning when their health, legal, or social reasons are to be scrutinized (even if purely formally) in order to get permission for an abortion. They organize themselves in vociferous campaigns, demanding to be allowed artificial interruption up to the sixth or the eighth month of pregnancy. So: what is stopping them from presenting a proposal tomorrow for permission to kill the child immediately after birth, or maybe up to one year old, if the mother is convinced that it does not suit her to keep the child, or that her maternal duties are too onerous? It would after all be logical and consistent. With regard to its defenselessness and inability to understand what to expect, the creature as-yet unborn and the one recently born are roughly on the same level. Where it comes to personality structure, they are undoubtedly closer to each other than, for example, a month-old child is to a grown-up (which should not be construed as saying that I attribute a greater measure of personality to an adult than to the smallest child). It is paradoxical that modern science, which attributes great weight to the natal and the prenatal psyche and which tries, not entirely without success, to penetrate their secrets, is so willing to become an accomplice in all these cruelties. That same science enables us to obtain film taken in the course of an abortion. The embryo looks very human and behaves in a very human way; it sucks its thumb. The technical operation of the murder takes place so efficiently that the child does not have time to react. But in the nuclear age this is not in the least bit exceptional, or even distinctive; the shadows of the adults evaporated at Hiroshima showed no sign of having had time to grasp their fate either.

If I have somewhat altered the wording of my objections, it is not any polemical trick but rather because the original arguments in favor of abortion were discarded like junk, intended at most to throw sand in the eyes of the opponent; now it all takes place and is being promoted in the name of the inalienable freedom of a woman to dispose of her own body. The beautiful Czech term *samadruhá* ("self and other") unmasks the falsity of this claim; what she has at her disposal is not just her own body but that of another.[2] I touched on some biological and anthropological

---

2   The Church's teaching on marriage is that "you will be one body." However, in spite of so much historical folly, it never occurred to anyone to infer from this teaching that the husband has the right freely to decide over the life or death of his wife. (VB)

considerations in the preceding paragraph. Where legal norms (and general legal feeling) are concerned, they express themselves with rare unanimity in favor of the human and legal existence of a child once conceived. In civilized countries a punishment may not be inflicted on a pregnant woman, particularly not the death penalty; for that would mean punishing the innocent. The legal relationship and obligations derived from fatherhood (even extramarital) often come into force long before the birth. In any case, it is usual in legislative and common law systems that a child once conceived becomes a fully-fledged entity with a claim to inheritance and other family rights (the actual exercise of these rights is of course delayed, in most cases until the coming of age); another nice Czech word is *pohrobek* (posthumous, for example, Ladislav the Posthumous), which confirms that this legal concept relies on ancient tradition. There is even special legal protection (for example in the field of labor law) pointing indirectly to this understanding, and the favoring of pregnant women which would otherwise be in conflict with the principle of the equality of citizens before the law. However, a direct laboratory demonstration of the fact that a child acquires a certain legal stature at the moment of conception is the incredible legal complications caused in connection with another contemporary problem, "test-tube babies."

It would be inappropriate to open here a detailed discussion about the origin, nature and reach of human rights. One thing however seems indisputable and common to all concepts, otherwise very varied; these laws have a universal and indivisible nature and hopelessly lose their meaning when they are instituted or implemented in a way which means the denial of these rights to our neighbor. I can agree to the common protection of human rights, to the fact that such unity should have priority over all divisions. I can also agree in practice with those from whom almost everything otherwise divides me; from the specific interpretation of these rights through political and social opinions as far as the whole personal experience and mentality. Nowhere in the world is the letter of the Universal Declaration of Human Rights and the relevant pacts fully maintained (perhaps fortunately), nor can it be—but it would be an unforgivable error to let this lead to skepticism, to give up trying to put things right. We humans are not perfect, we have our passions and our fears, our weaknesses, prejudices and pride; because of this our social institutions are less than perfect (if it comes to it, our ideals too are far from perfection, expressed for example, in the above-mentioned declarations and pacts). I must therefore come to terms with the fact that the matter and measure of rights is a highly delicate matter, that many impurities and serious failures will necessarily be admixed into my own practice and into the practice of my neighbors (not even to mention institutions)—but it should not become a reason to abandon them, or an excuse for discord. If someone forced their wife or girlfriend to have an abortion, I would consider it extremely tragic and wrong; principally, however, I would have to think seriously about the fact that even I could commit a similar step in the future, that here on earth there is no reliable inoculation against any sort of sin or doubt—and not to judge or to write off my neighbor and ally. If, however, someone postulated, in the name of freedom and a woman's self-fulfillment, that it was necessary to deny the basic human rights of still unborn children (or the rights of Jews or Blacks, Russians or Germans, believers or non-believers, Party members or non-Party members; it is all one whether some of these requirements sound sympathetic to our ears and can be supported by serious substantive arguments, the assassination of the essence of human rights is wreaked on them all severally and inseparably), then I not only cannot and do not want to come to terms with that, but such a person ceases to be a trustworthy partner for me. I have to consider their appeal to human rights to be a completely deliberate lie which can be suspended at any time to my disadvantage (even though several decades separate me from my prenatal state). The concept of human rights is not without rules: the more helpless the subject, the more dependent it is on truth, honor and consistency.

As far then as the state is concerned, unlike the preceding cases, decision-making about the admissibility or non-admissibility of abortions does not concern only moral (or religious) problems but the very roots of humanity and its social being; therefore, it cannot be the subject of political calculus nor even the outcome of pragmatic considerations. Perhaps I have shown clearly enough the incompatibility of the legalization of abortion with any sort of human rights. But even the state which does not formally subscribe to this concept would by such a step undermine one of the main justifications of its own existence: as a guarantor of the social and personal safety of its citizens; which means, principally to protect the weak from the strong, the powerless from the powerful—the latter are usually able to look after themselves and do not need any kind of state organization. I am therefore convinced that the state is not only justified but downright bound to prohibit abortion. I fear that this ban should be absolutely uncompromising and should not allow exceptions even for health reasons; on the one hand because of the above-mentioned threat presented by euthanasia, and the entrustment of too much power into the hands of the doctors, and on the other for formal and legal reasons: the law cannot well pronounce one life to be more valuable than another; it cannot guard against the (uncertain) threat to the life of the mother by the annihilation of the child. So much for the wording of the law; its practical application is naturally another matter and in my opinion it is only here that opportunities are provided to show moderation and humane considerations.

It may be that some supporters of abortion will return to the original arguments and complain that banning abortion would necessarily be accompanied by numerous human tragedies, an increase in specific criminal activities, would be a special burden on society and so on. I do not want to return to the comparison I already made here; I do not, however, want to downplay the significance of these facts and present the human lot in rosy colors. Instead of trying to answer I will therefore (loosely and from memory) quote from a parliamentary speech given at the beginning of the nineteenth century when the British parliament was discussing the draft of an Act to introduce an effective police system on the French model. "The British subject would rather have a few dozen corpses found on the banks of the Thames than suffer the police to enter his home and interfere in his life." The history of the last hundred and fifty years has emphatically confirmed the significance and direct prophetic vision of this attitude; it has taught us healthy mistrust with regard to those who cope with undoubtedly painful human problems (or with differing opinions) by shooting them (i.e., problems or proponents of these opinions) down in advance. In my reflection I have tried to show that abortion is a medicine exactly of this type; it cold-bloodedly brings death to millions of children, and in place of one misery offers women another misery that is more widespread and in the long term clearly more burdensome. For a man, incidentally, it means two kinds of shame: that as a citizen he consents to this evil, and that as a father he is excluded from decision-making over the life and death of his child.

Easter 1985

17

Back to Christianity and Politics:
How to Continue After Velehrad[1]

It's a historical milestone in two ways: partly because our numbers could finally be compared with Poland; and partly because the authorities decided to provoke a confrontation and
lost.
—Statement by one of the participants

1   I first wrote on this theme in 1978, by an accidental but significant coincidence
     with the election of a new Pope (the essay was published in the anthology
     Moc bezmocných [The Power of the Powerless] and later in various exile and
     samizdat journals, including the book *Charta 77 a křesťané* [Charter 77 and the
     Christians]). I used my letters from prison as an opportunity to develop and
     supplement my reflections, i.e., in a situation where an inadequate flow of in-
     formation was accompanied by continuous interventions by the censor. The
     article summing it all up fell into the hands of the secret police during a house
     search in 1984, and like other articles sits uselessly in its archives. This is there-
     fore my third attempt to express myself coherently on the given theme; if,
     with God's help, it succeeds in reaching the reader, it will, unlike the earlier
     essays, have the advantage of referring to facts where it was previously nec-
     essary to invoke eternal promises and realistically founded expectations, and
     that it can point to realistic promises and hopes where previously it had to
     rely on a miracle. Since, however, to those who knock it shall be opened and
     to those who have much it will be given, it would not be good to backpedal
     a little and waive requirements for other miracles—insofar as they flow from
     a desire for justice! (VB) [Benda is referring to his essay "Catholicism and Pol-
     itics" (ch. 12 of this volume) which first appeared in the volume *O svobodě a
     moci* [Freedom and Power]. This volume also contains Havel's essay called
     "The Power of the Powerless." (Ed.)]

What came before

What came before was certainly the mission of St. Cyril and St. Methodius and the thousand and one year activity of the Holy Ghost through the Church Militant.[2] Although I here affirm the fundamental spiritual meaning of the pilgrimage, I intend to examine primarily those aspects related to "social outreach," to politics, and to the involvement of Christians. I will therefore give just the facts from that field as economically and simply as possible; if I have to point to the wider context for their understanding, I will do so in another exposition.

The thousand and first anniversary of the death of St. Methodius, missionary to the Slavs and from ancient days one of the three patrons of Europe, was on April 6, 1985. This year it fell on Holy Saturday, a day unsuitable for church celebrations—a day of mourning, stillness and expectation. It was therefore a foregone conclusion that the celebrations would have to be moved to another date and that automatically gave rise to the danger of external interventions and manipulations. The first two events directly connected with the jubilee (better coordinated than participants later officially admitted) came at the beginning of 1984. Cardinal Archbishop František Tomášek,[3] Czech Primate—and as events show ever more plainly, *de facto* head of the Roman Catholic Church in the whole of Czechoslovakia—invited Pope John Paul II to participate in the celebrations; he received a positive answer in return. Twenty-two thousand believers, both clergy and lay people, addressed the Holy Father on the same matter; it was the biggest spontaneous collection of signatures in Czechoslovakia for the last fifteen

---

2   Cyril and Methodius were brothers from Thessalonica, where both Greek and Slavic were spoken. In the ninth century they were dispatched to the Great Moravian Empire as Christian missionaries. They trained and ordained a large number of priests and began using Old Slavonic as a liturgical language. Methodius became Archbishop of Moravia in 880 and was able to receive papal approval of the use of Old Slavonic for the liturgy. (Ed.)

3   František Tomášek (1899–1992) was consecrated secretly as a bishop in 1949. From 1950 to 1953 he was imprisoned in a labor camp and upon his release served as a parish priest in the village of Moravská Huzová. In 1977 Pope Paul VI appointed him Archbishop of Prague and also to the College of Cardinals. (Ed.)

years. The number of signatories was at least a magnitude higher than the most extensive civic activities. A reaction had to come from the authorities sooner or later. Cardinal Tomášek was informed—through Minister of Culture Klusák[4]—of the government's standpoint, i.e., that at the present time a visit from the Pope was undesirable and out of the question. A campaign of police repression was unleashed against those who had signed or distributed the invitation to the Pope, ranging from intimidation and discriminatory measures, through the confiscation of several sheets of signatures (hence the discrepancy between the reported number of 22,000 signatures and the 17,000 actually sent to Rome), reaching as far as the physical torture of several activists—torture intended to force these activists to reveal the "threads of the conspiratorial web." We can announce with joy and some envy that these young people withstood a painful trial of loyalty to Our Lord for many hours without breaking their silence.

Last year too, the Czechoslovak authorities devised a program for the consistent ideological, administrative and political disruption of the St. Methodius celebrations. Some Christians managed to obtain the text of these confidential instructions in time and published it in the Roman Catholic samizdat bulletin *Informace o církvi* [Information about the Church].

A specialized clergy pilgrimage was held over Easter 1985. More than a thousand clergy and several thousand lay people took part; it called, *inter alia*, for loyal clergy—meaning, those who will listen to the ecclesiastical authorities and will be true servants of the flock entrusted to them, instead of serving the atheist regime and organizations banned by the Church such as *Pacem in Terris*.[5] The state authorities reacted immediately and nervously, in the time-honored manner of carrot and stick. Two disloyal bishops received high awards and were (like some earlier disloyal priests) ostentatiously received by the President of the Republic (the carrot). Immediately after the clergy pilgrimage to Velehrad, many years of anti-Church repression culminated with a sudden blow against Roman Catholic samizdat (revenge on revenge—in addition to the inappropriate tone of the

4   Martin Klusák (1923–1992) served as Minister of Culture from 1973–1988. (Ed.)
5   *Pacem in Terris* (1971–1989) was a state-sponsored clerical organization dedicated to controlling the clergy. (Ed.)

pilgrimage, the publishing of those confidential instructions had to be properly "rewarded"). Several Christians were imprisoned and sentenced, hundreds were interrogated and intimidated, many house searches took place, and about ten duplicating machines and thousands of volumes of religious literature were confiscated (the stick).

The state authorities scheduled the general pilgrimage to Velehrad for July 7, the first Sunday after the Feast of St. Cyril and St. Methodius; this date naturally fell in the unsuitable holiday period and moreover coincided with the traditional Slovak Marian pilgrimage to Levoča, for which around 100,000 Christians gathered. All the media carefully kept the date of the pilgrimage secret; as far as we know, it was not divulged even by *Katolické noviny* [Catholic News]—this paradoxical weekly which had had the Church imprimatur removed, but to which the government liked to point as evidence (practically the only evidence of its kind) of religious freedom in Czechoslovakia. In other respects the authorities proceeded in the spirit of their directives, while none of their agents could be accused of a lack of passion and initiative—on the contrary. A joint state-church commission was created literally at the last moment, clearly intended by the authorities for one purpose: to take over the management of the celebrations (in part directly, in part through the collaborationist Bishop Vrana,[6] whose diocese includes Velehrad). In this way the impact of the mass nature of the pilgrimage—which was consolidating irreversibly—was as far as possible to be dulled by silencing its religious aspects and presenting it as a peace gathering of the usual type; that is, fully in the spirit of official policy (which has nothing to do with faith or peace, as can be seen from the speech given by Minister Klusák—which, however, departed considerably from the officially published version—where, in an effort to win the crowd at least by appealing to its chauvinism, a vicious anti-German tone came to the forefront). Perhaps this part of east Moravia had never before experienced such a cultural boom; there was not a single community far and wide in the locality—including Velehrad itself—where a firemen's or gamekeepers' ball was not organized for July 6 and 7, or an amateur performance, sporting event, flower show or pet show, or at least where there were no swings, roundabouts, shooting galleries or other fairground attractions, not to mention meetings of every kind

6   See ch. 7, note 1. (Ed.)

of society and organization with, as far as possible, compulsory attendance. Hand in hand with this more or less "positive" prevention, the authorities also deployed negative prevention. The evening before the celebration travel agencies throughout the republic had, without giving a reason, cancelled all reservations and prepaid coach excursions to Velehrad; this measure affected tens of thousands of people (around a thousand coaches were involved), while at a rough guess it can be estimated that maybe around one third of those disappointed in this way succeeded in reaching Velehrad by another method. Even some regular links were secretly diverted, to the great confusion of many travelers who knew nothing at all about the Velehrad pilgrimage and suddenly found themselves many miles away from their destination. Sports teams with their own buses were allegedly forced to give a promise not to take a route via Velehrad. At least twenty-four hours before the celebration itself, Velehrad was surrounded by several concentric circles of police barriers; we ourselves came on the first between Humpolec and Jihlava, around 150 kilometers from our destination (for those accustomed to think in different dimensions it is perhaps useful to know that a circle of "special measures" of this radius covers an area roughly half the size of Czechoslovakia). The technical condition of our car was checked (given the extent of the whole operation, this was normal), the drivers were examined (highly unusual and not really in accordance with the law) and their destination was carefully ascertained (unprecedented and illegal). This too succeeded in intimidating and dissuading a large proportion of potential participants. Access routes to Velehrad were closed to all private traffic and private buses three to ten kilometers before the village; a necessary measure, but carried out in an extremely tense atmosphere and in some cases handled with more than a little malevolence.

Allegedly, ten thousand policemen were assigned to Velehrad on the day of the celebration, predominantly plainclothes police; we definitely identified some of the StB "anti-religion" specialists from as far away as Prague and other distant places. This large presence avoided open confrontation but was all the more passionate about taking photographs and tried to upset the atmosphere and dignified course of the celebrations. The Church's original plan was that the "pilgrimage of youth" would begin in the early evening on Sunday, July 7 and continue with all-night worship; in fact, tens of thousands of predominantly young people were gathering on Velehrad as early as Saturday. Suddenly, however, the local clergy announced that for safety reasons the basilica had to be closed by eight in the evening and that the area in front of the church had to be empty overnight as well. Respecting the clergy's difficult service, and chiefly the House of God, the crowd cleared out of the basilica peacefully but just as peacefully remained in the area in front of it, where communal prayers, hymns, and the clamor of the crowd echoed throughout the night. No attempt was made to reverse this spontaneous manifestation of civil disobedience; thus, thanks to a stupid and unrealistic order, the state authorities lost face even before the main celebrations began (any attempt to enforce the order would—taking into consideration the context as a whole, the zeal of the crowd and the local topography—have been an open-ended game with a threat of tragic consequences for both sides; it would have been better not to give such an order). Safety measures went to such ridiculous detail that all loose stones and gravel had been removed from the whole of Velehrad, so the few handfuls of stones necessary to anchor the decorations on the altar could only be obtained by special permission from a strictly guarded garden which turned out to be the main rallying point for the police (the thinking is incomprehensible; Catholics do generally celebrate their victory through church worship, but worship is for them an opportunity for prayer, not for organizing the overthrow of the state). However, a riot of red banners with conventional peace slogans was also conspicuous. Even the positioning of a field altar, not in the logical place at the front of the main area but in a vacant lot behind the basilica, took its revenge on its instigators; thus the placement of the altar (positioned by the authorities such that the crowd surrounded it on all sides) probably made it difficult for state authorities to eliminate the background noise of the dissenters in the crowd and the official speeches of the state representatives could not be broadcast live.

What actually took place

The main thing is, that in spite of all the above-mentioned difficulties, around a quarter of a million Catholics took part in the Velehrad pilgrimage (as well as fifty or so foreign reporters and TV crews from Czechoslovakia, Japan, Austria, West Germany, etc.). Of the angry complaints addressed by Czechoslovak officials to the Western media, perhaps the only one that contained a grain of truth was that the media relied on a preconceived estimate of the number and composition of participants—but not that they had multiplied the real number (as they were reproached for doing), but on the contrary considerably underestimated it. By simply multiplying the density (relatively constant, because people were so tightly packed) by the surface measurements of the crowd, I myself reached a minimum estimate of 150,000 direct participants, and of course all the adjacent space and pathways were completely crowded. There are indirect ways to estimate it as well (I don't know at present how many people attended Eucharist that Sunday, but to get an idea of the situation as a whole you would have to multiply this important number by at least ten); 200,000 tickets (returns) were sold for the shuttle bus from Uherské Hradiště to Velehrad, which is one of the main approaches, but still only one of several. Moreover, most pilgrims covered the last part of the journey on foot. Incidentally, it might be worth mentioning the fact, not necessarily miraculous but nevertheless indicative, that a glorious summer sky without a single cloud arched over Velehrad the whole day, while most of the Republic, including not-so-distant Brno, was overcast with outbreaks of rain from early morning.

Most of those tens of thousands of participants in the vigil and night watch were young people, with a predominance of Slovaks (traditionally better prepared in the Christian faith). The prevailing mood was a mixture of pious arousal and militant dissatisfaction (this appeared not only during the chanting of slogans; in some of the numerous groups every reference to the freedom brought by Christ was acknowledged, repeated and applauded, while the common prayer and meditation emphasized that what this time requires is not quiet humility, but rather the decisive declaration of the Word of God and determination to give witness). However, the hundreds of thousands who attended the main celebrations were, with regard to age and nationality, much closer to a normal cross-section of the population (with a natural weighting in favor of "local" Moravians and the usual marked imbalance of Czechs with regard to Slovaks) and the atmosphere corresponded more to the traditional concept of a pilgrimage as an event both religious and social. The general mood was—at least at the beginning—unusually conciliatory; moreover, the very nature of the legacy of Cyril and Methodius strengthened the ecumenical atmosphere. Echoes of this can be seen in that the local collaborationist Bishop Vrana, willingly playing the part as the obedient servant of his lords and masters, was received, not exactly warmly, but at least without any hostile mass demonstrations, and that the Metropolitan of Minsk and Belarus Filaret was even applauded for his speech which, under a sweet frosting of frequent evangelical quotations, consisted only of much wickedness and yet more lies of the official peace propaganda. These, however, were anomalies to whose possible meaning we will return later. In other respects the authorities, with almost prophetic clairvoyance, tossed away one chance after another; in the course of a few hours each and every one of those quarter of a million believers received a striking lesson that you cannot serve God and Satan, and that the Communist regime is and intends to be the chief enemy of even the most humble, submissive, quietest Church community. They took the first step with the refusal to allow the Pope to visit, and the ban on the participation of West European and Polish bishops was clumsily compensated for by the numerically large All-Christian Peace Rally (composed of ecclesiastical dignitaries as quaint as they were exotic). Much however could still be camouflaged, and some people perhaps even had some understanding for the weakness of a government which simply does not understand the mentality of most of its subjects and therefore truly fears direct contact with real spiritual authority "as the devil fears the Cross."

Everything became clear at the moment when the ceremonies were introduced by, in place of a bishop or other consecrated person, the district functionary Lapčík; when, against all decency, in place of the Word of God, his words "We have come together at this Peace Celebration ..." sounded from the altar. The mental level of this unfortunate man was that of a local cop; it had clearly never entered his head that, as the mouthpiece of his lords and masters, he might be met with anything other than a timorous, bowed silence. Still less did it occur to him that anyone might actually be listening to his empty phrases, recycled for the thousandth time and undoubtedly uttered by him many times before—at the celebratory opening of a cowshed, at election meetings, and at the funeral of his deserving colleague and functionary. Ignoring the stormy explosions of protest that drowned most of his speech, he went on and on reading in a monotone, except that his voice faltered more and more; the only thing of interest about his presentation was whether he would get to the end before bursting into tears over the ingratitude of a world that thus repaid his devoted and unscrupulous service.

The Czech Minister of Culture Milan Klusák showed himself an experienced politician and skillful speaker; he waited for people to calm down, tactically deviated from the official text, turned to the crowd as jovially as he could, called on the authority of the bishops and national sentiment and later, at least for the sake of the media, pretended that the demonstrations of disagreement were really enthusiastic support (it was like a dialogue of madmen, but with a little bit of luck and technical skill on the part of the soundmen it could work). It was difficult, however, to repair the impression made by the first speaker, and even the Minister's Communist skill had its limits, typical of the constraints of God's enemies; for example, he was unable to utter the word "saint" in connection with Methodius, although it was the most frequent subject of confrontation with the crowd, which had gathered precisely to honor the memory of this great saint. So the Minister failed both on the spot and on television where, even though the clip was broadcast without sound while the newsreader recited the official text and then played applause (recorded somewhere else for someone else), his growing nervousness, confusion and rage were clear to viewers.

This intrusive management by the authorities had yet another unintended effect. The crowd was spontaneous and unanimous in calling for the Pope's visit, and enthusiastic in acknowledging its devotion to him and to the loyal bishops, especially Cardinal Tomášek. Nevertheless, there were at the beginning many who disapproved of the way the state representatives' speeches were whistled and drowned out; not that they agreed with what those speakers said, but they remained silent partly from natural politeness dictated by long-term habit, and partly from concern for the fate of the Church if it came to a direct confrontation with power. Eventually however, the endless dragging out of these very unholy speeches forced that "silent majority" to abandon their reticence and drown the speeches with stormy, rudimentary Christian chanting in Czech and Slovak: "We want Holy Mass!"

Cardinal Archbishop Tomášek, enthusiastically cheered long before the ceremonies started, had been assigned an inferior place and denied a speech of his own; he came some way down the list of speakers and was only to read a greeting from the Pope to the participants in the pilgrimage. Hardly, however, had the eighty-six-year-old primate opened his mouth than it was clear that, after all those ridiculous and creepy figures, here stood a true Prince of the Church, neither afraid of the throng nor having to pander to them, but confidently controlling them by the right of his pastoral authority and their loving obedience. It was the voice of this old man that really filled the environment, the mere change of his intonation determining rejoicing of many minutes duration, or alternatively the silence of the grave. It was the Archbishop's day of triumph, personal and spiritual—and political.

Cardinal Casaroli[7] was given a similar welcome—above all of course as the papal envoy and representative, for whose current faithful service to the Holy Father believers generously overlooked his personal share in the former unfortunate "Ostpolitik" of the Vatican, which did so much damage to our Church and whose legacy we are still forced to endure today, for example, in the form of collaborationist bishops.[8] He made an impression in his own person too; through his wit, clerical humility, statesmanlike skill and maybe even the fact that he gave his speech half in Czech, half in Slovak. Then he served mass, also in the two national languages alternately; it was a powerful confession of the faith of a Christian people and its hope in these evil times, founded on fellowship with Christ—and maybe best characterized in the words of the Eucharistic hymn "the mighty seat of Svatopluk fell, Velehrad of faith stands." Only the bishops were allowed to concelebrate; it was forbidden to the rest of the clergy—whether they had state approval or not. All the better; at least they could experience this great festival among the flock entrusted to them, could be encouraged by the flock's emotions and at the same time help them to articulate those emotions.

7   Agostino Casaroli (1914–1998) was an important Vatican diplomat, particularly with respect to his work with the Church in Communist bloc nations. He was an important figure in the implementation of Pope Paul VI's Ostpolitik (see following note) and then served under Pope John Paul II as Secretary of State for the Vatican from 1979–1990. (Ed.)

8   Ostpolitik was a geopolitical strategy implemented by the Vatican from the mid-1960s to the early 1970s. Pope Paul VI empasized a much less confrontational approach to the Communist bloc nations. He sought to avoid open criticisms and to create a dialogue with Communist Party leaders. In Czechoslovakia in 1973 the Vatican and the Communist regime struck a deal: the regime would allow the appointment of four residential bishops, but it insisted that two of the four candidates would be Josef Vrana and Josef Feranec (both collaborators). (Ed.)

It might be a good idea, to complete the picture, to mention two other very different details. During the mass, a few roving carnival workers who'd been granted space nearby tried using megaphones to lure people away to their attractions; against the background of singing and praying from the throats of hundreds of thousands, their attempt sounded like the last joke of the day, and of those in charge. They soon realized it themselves and waited for the end of the ceremonies. Then there was the Czechoslovak TV box, surrounded by a claque of several hundred that applauded in the "correct" places during the official speeches and kept quiet during the "incorrect" chants. In addition to this insignificant island there were, positioned through the whole vast crowd-filled acres like some sort of sparse (but more or less regular) network, persons barely capable of the appropriate responses during the mass but demonstrating fervent loyalty to the state; since these were almost exclusively men of working age there could be no doubt about who they were working for. In the light of my forty years' experience with the totalitarian powers and their practices, it is obvious that, in spite of their number and regular placing, they remained completely isolated in their behavior (whereas—in the biblical spirit—two or three voices should be enough to ferment tens of thousands). However, in the light of forty years of the proud and contemptuous arbitrariness of totalitarian power it is much more surprising that this network (apparently without any threats and certainly without any physical insults) thinned and melted away until it completely disappeared. At least for a while, the power of the community, or perhaps just the silent threat of the crowd, showed itself to be more powerful than the will of their paymasters, more powerful than years of the instilled feeling of their own superiority.

Direct impact or dice newly cast

I dare to venture that the Velehrad pilgrimage was an event of universal historical significance; that is, that none of the participating parties went through the experience unmarked (and those participating or interested were at the very least all citizens of this country—precisely as citizens, participants in the common affairs of the community), and that from now on he would be a blind or blinded man fatally prejudicing his own case who would be reluctant to understand it and draw from it the relevant conclusions.

The state authorities have long feared that the Church is an "old new" (or rather, newly resurrected) unknown, threatening to complicate their schemes of total destruction and of total control of society. Evidence of this appears in the ever more irritated declarations from official places, the various confidential instructions about the escalation of atheist propaganda and discrimination against believers, the intensification of the anti-religion police, and judicial repression, with an incommensurately high percentage of Christians among activists in independent civic initiatives who are particularly harshly punished.[9] Nevertheless, the state power was plainly relying on the tried and trusted method of the carrot and the stick (above all the stick—on the one hand it makes little sense to waste carrots on the weak and on the other, in a thoroughly corrupt society, it is almost impossible to distribute the carrots in the spheres that are completely resistant to corruption). The state has not taken too seriously the conclusions of various sociological research projects nor even the warning voices of some far-sighted or at least better informed representatives (former Minister of the Interior Obzina or the head of the State Secretariat for Church Affairs Janků). Increased expenditure on atheist propaganda and the anti-religious struggle does not automatically produce the desired effect, and the optimistic accounting of these expenses by interested (and paid) elements can significantly distort reality. In other words, the problem these Catholics pose is much worse and more dangerous than anyone had thought. The authorities seemed to sense that Velehrad could somehow become the incarnation of this mysterious threat and therefore did everything (including several attempts to hijack the event for their own purposes) to suppress it at its very birth;[10] according to a favorite saying of Ludvík Vaculík "she needed quiet so

---

9   I will illustrate this by a few details. No practising Christian was involved in the first anti-Charter 77 trial (Ornest & Co.) in 1977. In the trial of the Committee for the Defence of the Unjustly Prosecuted in 1979, half of them were. In subsequent individual trials of members of VONS, three quarters. (VB)

10   The regime expressed support for the event on a few occasions and tried to turn it into a kind cultural celebration—attempting to empty it of its religious content. They would have celebrated Cyril and Methodius as Slavic heroes rescuing local Christians from the rule of German/Latin Bishops. (Ed.)

she demonstrated disquiet."[11] It seems that Velehrad was a shock even for the most skeptical adherents of totalitarian manipulation (the first reactions from the "high places" confirm this; probably evidence of a panic which can express itself in all sorts of ways, beginning with spasmodic repression and ending with a sly attempt at apparently far-reaching compromises). Above all, it confirmed their suspicion that, in spite of all their efforts, the Church has at its disposal some immensely effective information systems independent of official channels and total official regimentation (for in our country even every cyclostyled parish magazine has to go through a complicated censorship procedure). They found it all the more mysterious in that two months before the pilgrimage, years of painstaking work had enabled the police to carry out a would-be mortal blow against Church samizdat periodicals when, in addition to a lot of already "printed" materials, they confiscated around ten duplicating machines—in Czechoslovakia an unprecedented number! The authorities were also clearly aware of the difficulties of getting together a quarter of a million people—especially in quite a remote locality—and knew that for an action of that size a powerful propaganda campaign would be needed, months or years of preparation, an enormous organizational apparatus, considerable financial means, and various other kinds of pressure. The fact and extent of the Velehrad pilgrimage, born in the silence of all the totalitarian media and brought about only by general enthusiasm, was therefore all the more of a shock for them.

The second and maybe most surprising lesson was the behavior of the crowd. Healthy instinct and years of experience suggested to the authorities that they were generally hated and that every anonymous gathering presented them with a direct threat; that was why they only liked such events as military parades, Spartakiads and carefully organized first of May processions,[12] and tried at least indirectly (for example, by using personnel

11 Ludvík Vaculík (1926–2015) was a prominent Czech essayist, novelist, and dissident. He penned the "Two Thousand Words" manifesto in 1968 and published a famous novel called the *The Czech Dreambook* in samizdat—it was a fictionalized diary of Vaculík's daily life as a writer and dissident under Communist rule. (Ed.)
12 Spartakiads were mass gymnastics displays held every five years in Strahov stadium in Prague. The first of May was celebrated as international workers' day in Communist countries. (Ed.)

files[13] to control the distribution of tickets) to extend their regimentation to the public attending large sporting and cultural venues. At the same time, however, the idea persisted[14] that Christians are some sort of naïve dupes, who—though they in some respects display a strange kind of stubbornness and endurance—completely lack any kind of civic consciousness and respect the secular authorities so scrupulously that they would not resist them, but let themselves be deceived and freely manipulated at the first "benign tap on the shoulder." The modus operandi was chosen completely in line with this idea and was meant to be that "benign tap on the shoulder." The modus operandi included the propagation of lies (using the magic little word Peace, which can surely leave no true Christian unmoved) meant to lead astray the amazing resurrection of the Catholic Church and at the same time strike at its roots.[15] It also included government representation at the ministerial level (unprecedented at any religious gathering of recent decades) and for good measure, the distinguished ecclesiastical honorifics of the permitted delegates from Cuba to India. However, the crowds of pilgrims did not get drunk on beguiling words and titles, nor did they react like a mob, blindly venting their despair and feelings of impotence—which would have been for the totalitarian regime a lesser and, most importantly, familiar evil. On the contrary, free and self-confident citizens made their religious, human, and political requests with

---

13 The Communist Party maintained personal files on each citizen which contained information about his family background (bourgeois, working class, etc.) and his own political profile. (Ed.)

14 An idea that was probably always erroneous in relationship to the Roman Catholic Church in the strict sense; however it undoubtedly once applied with regard to its formal "nominal majority," and to various Protestant denominations, marked by the frustrations of long-term persecution and second-class status. (VB)

15 I have been unable to determine whether the following story actually happened or whether it is merely an anecdote. Either way, however, it brilliantly illustrates the government's ideas about Christians, and the superstition that is the inevitable outcome of the pride of atheists. At one of the night gatherings at Velehrad the police demanded "In the name of the Law, disperse!" When there was no response, the same officials rephrased the demand as: "In the name of Jesus Christ, disperse!" However, the crowd still would not disperse. (VB)

dignity. As far as possible with a gathering of this size, it represented almost a return to free medieval disputation—every word was objectively weighed, and the lie condemned rather than drowned and booed. All at once, state power came face to face with a partner (and a real partner, not a more or less isolated handful of individuals) which, without fear or willingness to be bought, asserted its rights and its equal partnership (with, moreover, experience and discretion, rendering the usual tricks and guile of totalitarian policy impotent). This policy, this modus operandi, will for a long time to come still be looking out for dishonest and violent solutions. At Velehrad, however, it discerned the danger facing it; whether it will ever be able to recognize it and come to terms with it honestly is another matter. This points to a more fundamental problem that we will leave open—that is, whether this system can be reformed effectively or whether it can only be destroyed. For the time being, news from official corridors (which has however to be judged with great care, as disinformation gets into circulation as successfully as information) suggests that after Velehrad considerable tension is reigning; however, so far no agreement has yet been reached about how to confront the "crisis situation." One marginal but far from insignificant psychological effect should be noted; that is, the shock several senior representatives of the regime experienced from the direct confrontation (the first for one and half decades) with the disapproval of free citizens. A similar shock was experienced by several thousand masked attendants, who could not and did not try to terrify their neighbors by the usual methods, and even themselves suddenly felt something very similar to fear. This shock can however have ambiguous outcomes; doubts perhaps rise in some people's thoughts, opening a loophole for them to turn from evil; others will compensate for the moment of their hesitation by greater fury—in every case, however, the memory of the participants will be marked forever.

The authorities learned their third lesson incidentally and with due humiliation, that all their "transmission levers" in the Church are inconsequential froth, no matter how many medals and prebends they waste on them, no matter how important the ecclesiastical titles they secure for them. The explanation is childishly simple: while the Church is essentially a hierarchical organism, from the similarly essential conviction of believers, it is actually and effectively ruled by Christ, that is, by the Holy Spirit. Believers love their bishops and the Pope and because of this love can forgive them all sorts of things, almost any weakness; they really do listen to them, even in moments of disagreement. However, one cannot serve two masters, and Christ is Truth; if someone were to put himself at the service of lies, he would at one blow lose his educational and pastoral authority—even if he were a bishop, even if he were the Pope himself. It is clearly much more complicated both from the point of view of theology and Church law. From the historical point of view too, it would be possible to bring more than one credible objection. However, healthy Christian instinct sometimes surprisingly neglects subtle theological nuances. For the Holy Ghost blows where it wills, untrammeled even by the Codex of Canonical Law. Or, history is meaningful only in the form of the history of salvation, and following Christ and the Church has already gone so far along its Way of the Cross that it is immune to the errors of its more fortunate and vainglorious times. Whatever the cause may be, this fact of "insight" in the universal Church dominates our times. Indeed, our Polish brothers for example, to whom so much visibly points, managed in the last century to hang a collaborationist bishop, and in the last decade to throw rotten tomatoes at the papal envoy himself (who was incidentally applauded at Velehrad; both actions were in our opinion justified, but a more detailed explanation would distract us too much from our theme)—and these deeds strengthened rather than diminished the Polish reputation as a very Catholic nation.

The lesson the Church hierarchy took away from the Velehrad pilgrimage formed an independent chapter, important in several respects from the practical point of view. I have already spoken about the pitiful role of the collaborationist bishops and priests; here they felt very vividly their lack of unity with the universal Church in the most powerful sense of the word—let us hope that this experience will be for some of them at least the beginning of a conversion of their thought and deeds! Cardinal Tomášek—this shepherd who, in the midst of his persecuted flock and by an extremely indirect path, has grown into a great personality at an age when others would long have renounced any kind of work among men— was dominant in the human, clerical and political spheres. Above all, he filled to perfection the role of a powerful prince of the Church and primate of the land, so alien to his quiet, simple human disposition. He showed himself worthy of the office of the Servant of Our Lord and shepherd of the flock entrusted to him and, as a true servant, knew how to offer his natural and human humility as a sacrifice to the greater honor and glory of God. He thus achieved two major satisfactions, psychological and political. Systematically surrounded for years by disobedient and false servants, and defending the truth of his pastoral calling often with a feeling almost of isolation, all at once he stood face to face with enormous crowds full of the spirit of love and obedience and in the same spirit condemned the worldly folly of those of little or no faith. He—who for so long could protest only impotently against the curtailment of the last rights of the Church, and who had to be content that the authorities in their arrogance negotiated with him (or informed him of their decisions) as a matter of principle through the agency of inferior officials, censors and policemen— was thus suddenly witness to the failure of those authorities before a much greater authority, witness to the very moment of their embarrassment and fear when they flatteringly invoked his authority and at least implicitly relied on his protection. In the first place, however, it is similar to the fundamental Christian experience, a necessary consequence of faith in the One True and Living God, Creator and Lord of All. It would be folly to suppose that many servants of evil do not call in their last hour for a priest and forgiveness, and it would be even godless to assume that this forgiveness will be summarily denied them. Yet this was not just the experience of their last hour or of the Last Judgment and the invisible conquering power of God; in this moment the Church had triumphed visibly and on earth—or to say it with more precision and humility—their evil had failed and limits had been put on its claim to rule the world, to overpower the inherited destiny of the Lamb, to ruin it and turn it into a wasteland. We know that this was only for a moment, for the power is resilient and well fed by our sins and we need not underestimate the difficulties it still causes the Church both visibly and invisibly. Nevertheless we believe that this was a moment of truth, that next time we will be on the attack and they will be on the defense. Cardinal Tomášek saw it, and it strengthened his awareness that he is not the last of the faithful in a lost cause, but rather the head, nominal and actual, of powerful social forces that everyone in this country has to keep in mind; maybe these forces can still expect long intransigence and enmity, but nowadays they are already capable of truly exacting at least respect and courtesy.

It is no less important that the high curial representatives saw this too, in particular those who in person played an important role in creating the Vatican's Ostpolitik in the 1960s and 1970s—a policy which many Catholics here consider tragic, and almost every one of them as problematic. All the reports and analyses have been pointing in one direction for a long time now; it is, however, difficult for facts on paper to match direct experience. The Church is exposed to harsh persecution in this country, but it does not resemble the oppressed and perishing handfuls for whose survival, at least formal, almost any price has to be paid (the secular authorities here wanted to see it this way and behave toward it as if it were such, and even the Vatican once let itself be largely forced to this view, which was in harmony with the state of things, but not with Christian vision). To speak in the language of the Gospel: we must resemble the germinating mustard seed that is successful in spreading itself; birds will nest in its branches and exterminate harmful insects, and all kinds of maliciously sown weeds will helplessly atrophy in the shade of its crown. In such circumstances there is no reason to pay too high a price for insignificant and doubtful advantages (a further round of negotiations between Czechoslovakia and the Vatican foundered badly straight after the Velehrad pilgrimage, caused above all by flustered state authorities; but we hope that the curial negotiators will draw conclusions from this evidence). The question also arises as to whether the Church should even allow something that is obviously a religious right guaranteed by Czechoslovak law and by international pacts to be the subject of negotiation, of endless squabbling and of difficult compromises; whether the time has not come simply to demand the right, maybe to present the state with a clear choice in the form of an ultimatum. Either it wishes to retain its privileges and respect its commitments; thus to allow full, uninterrupted and free operation of the Church without delay, the appointment of bishops, and no impediments to novice priests and members of the Orders, free access to religious literature and the end of any kind of discrimination against believers. Or it considers all its commitments and laws as a mere functional scrap of paper, and is therefore completely unworthy of its privileges; then bishops and priests will be ordained, and all operations including teaching and the apostolate assured on the Church's own responsibility, determined to undergo further persecution and to remain disloyal with regard to the failed secular authorities. An

English king once threatened and saw to it that his bishop would not have a head on which to place any cardinal's hat sent from Rome; paradoxically everything testifies that a similar choice would be disastrous for the present totalitarian authorities, in other ways many times more powerful and concentrated. With the greatest probability, the Church's ultimate position would then be successful, although maybe only in part.

Velehrad put a definitive full stop[16] to one illusion that for many has determined speech and behavior over recent decades; the threat of a ban on the Roman Catholic Church in Czechoslovakia, or of a schism artificially induced by the state. In the 1950s there were wide-reaching attempts in both directions (the liquidation of the Orders and of all lay Christian organizations, the imprisonment or internment of almost all the Catholic hierarchy and of thousands of priests and laypeople—above all from the ranks of the intellectuals—and an attempt to create what was called the Catholic Action[17]). At that time, however, all these brought generally ambiguous results.[18] Since then, although the authorities have not stopped applying this threat covertly and even overtly from time to time, of all the interested parties, the current representatives of the state (rare exceptions only confirm the rule) probably consider it as the least realistic option. The argument is however vividly present in the views of the general majority of the priesthood, especially the hierarchy, and a considerable part of the laity, and this puts a harsh limit on more than one brave heart (for it concerns many others, besides those who derive dishonest conclusions from it and excuse in advance any measure of collaboration). The representatives

16 What follows is one of my key theses, which I have included here simply because it has to go somewhere; I would cheerfully repeat it ten times over, and then test everyone to make sure they had really understood, if this were not impolite toward my readers. (VB)

17 "Catholic Action" was a movement orchestrated by the regime to create the impression that the majority of Catholics supported the regime's approach to the Church. (Ed.)

18 See the remarkable study by Karel Kaplan about the relationship between Church and state from 1948 to 1956 in one of the recent issues of *Roman Studies* [magazine published in Rome by Czech expatriates], which derives predominantly from the views of the "other side" and considers the Church as much more resistant than when it was evaluated by sporadic Catholic sources. (VB)

of the Roman Curia probably acted in good faith when their hands were tied by decades of this "disastrous alternative" which forced them to accept the most dubious compromises (a certain fake conservatism probably played its part in the case of our hierarchy and that of the Curia, which in our own milieu I would call a mechanical adherence to the tradition of "Austro-Catholicism"[19] in its most infantile elements). I must first state that in the given case I consider every concession made under some threat or other as the most certain route for the threat to be fulfilled. It is not that I fundamentally oppose compromises nor is it that I fail to understand the extent to which the path of the visible Church, and its Catholicity, is connected with the ability to prioritize the Christian solution whenever at a crossroads between a militant attitude and a compromise (the Church has, by turns, chosen militancy and compromise, not in the name of the lesser evil, but of the greater good. It did not learn the art of such choices from the necessities of this world, but rather from the words of Christ and in a certain sense from the very fact of His Incarnation). Nor is it because I am a crack-brained radical, masochistically longing for martyrdom, whose creed is "the worse, the better" and who wants to drive the Church into the catacombs, into direct confrontation with the regime, at any price. I draw only from analyses of the concrete situation, from analyses of violent power in general and totalitarian power in particular. The bully executes all his evil intentions to the extent his strength allows; concessions or mild reaction on his opponent's part only spur him to the conviction of his own predominance and rouse him to still more far-reaching demands. Part of the essence of totalitarian power is the impossibility of reasonable fruits bearing compromise with anything that finds itself in its sphere of influence (indeed, the pitiful end of most contracts with totalitarian states in the last half century indicates that the problem extends beyond the boundaries of the given sphere of influence). It is just because of its totalitarian nature that it regards any compromise as absurd since it neither can nor wants to recognize any limit to itself, nor is it able to tolerate the existence

19 Recall that when the Czech lands were part of the Austro-Hungarian Empire, Catholicism was the state religion. Benda is suggesting that a legacy of that tradition is a willingness on the part of the church hierarchy to submit to the secular powers. (Ed.)

of any real partner. Nevertheless, it is happy to agree to such compromises and even make them one of the chief theoretical and practical weapons of its expansion (from Lenin's "they will sell us the rope with which we will hang them," through the policy of "national fronts" in East European countries, as far as the intricacies of "détente," disarmament negotiations, and resurrection of slogans of "national unity"). On the side of the totalitarian power, these contracts are absolutely non-binding, while three dangers immediately present themselves to the other side: it respects the restrictions adopted, it disintegrates internally under their unbearable pressure, and moreover, on their basis usually makes vitally important information available or even allows itself to be directly infiltrated and indoctrinated. Historical experience with totalitarian power confirms this rule, as does the experience of the Catholic Church in this country; unlike other denominations, it refused to compromise its principles even in the harshest of times. It is because of its suffering and loyalty that it enjoys today's resurrection and unprecedented expansion.

Many people do not agree with me on the impossibility of compromise with totalitarian power. Despite every bad experience they will always try again, considering it the only practical path to the reform of public affairs and even purely Church affairs. However, what I stated at the beginning of the preceding paragraph is important: next time, opponents and adherents of compromise alike can rule out any danger of an artificial schism in the church, or it being banned outright. Velehrad was an effective demonstration that the attempt at schism was doomed to failure and ridicule from the beginning. At the same time, it must be clear even to the "hardest" adherents to the power solution—since this pilgrimage at least (for its parameters, see the descriptive part of my essay)—that to forbid or radically limit Church operations would mean driving several million active believers underground (as we say, into the catacombs). This would be a highly organized underground which would not be threatened by any temporary loss of prospects (which Solidarity in Poland found difficult to avoid, for example), since its meaning would be drawn from eternal sources and its determination would soar directly in proportion to the extent of repression (the tradition of the martyrs is a living part of the Roman Catholic legacy, one of the bridges between the Church Militant and the Church Triumphant). In time the militant stance would prevail over quieter and more contemplative orientations

(Velehrad showed that the Church does not reject any of its fundamental experiences; the traditions of the great chivalrous and crusader saints is one of them). If today's totalitarian authorities have some bad dreams, then undoubtedly the one that dismays them most is the possibility of confrontation with such an underground. Not only would they guard against every step that could cause this "as the Devil against the cross," but they would probably be willing to make some concession, if only to avoid this alternative. Those who are guided by honest care for the fate of the Church in Czechoslovakia do not need to be afraid to throw out the threat of its forcible liquidation. Those for whom it served only as a cover to justify their bad intentions should start looking for a new and more convincing argument.

What experience did the believers themselves acquire on the pilgrimage, and what lessons did they carry away in addition to everything I described already, and which all the participants perceived for themselves in one way or another and acknowledged with pleasure? Of the latter we can recall in brief the joy of spreading God's Word, and that it successfully put down roots into this land, the larger part of which could until recently be considered almost a mission territory. Secondly, renewed self-confidence; the self-confidence however of the humble, whose source is the contribution of the suffering of recent generations and their own decision to give testimony. Thirdly, an awareness of their own strength; strength, however, that is derived from following Christ as the living, liberating and loving Truth. That is, strength capable in its own way of confronting the lie, but far distant from intending to replace it in the worldly way by a tyranny of truth, murdered and petrified, or the intention to exchange one totalitarianism for another (maybe an even worse version—because the violation of the best is always worst!). We will return to this distinction.

For several years now, there have been four great question marks, or four essential tasks (partial maybe, but nevertheless offering the only way out of all existing partiality and decomposition), ever more clearly confronting opposition initiatives, the Churches, and (when it comes down to it) every responsible citizen of this country. We could describe them as primarily political.

The first is how to restore a society which, through long decades of totalitarian power, has been intentionally atomized into a mere collection of manipulated individuals whose ties (between nations, generations, social groups, regions, communities, and enterprises, but also between acquaintances, friends and even family members) have been systematically destroyed—let alone restore it prospectively as a civil society, a *polis*.

Secondly, how to influence majority thinking in the Church toward true Catholicity, an essential part of which is a certain "social" and "civic" overlap (in the sense of service and responsibility—with a secular touch one could also call this "engagement"); how to contribute toward a general understanding that in conditions of totalitarian pressure and persecution such an overlap is even something primary that concerns the very foundations of faith and is the touchstone of its authenticity. There is nothing obvious in this, for a certain distance with regard to matters concerning the terrestrial Kingdom is an authentic part of the Christian tradition. At the same time, the Church is itself a militant organism that lives in this world and which therefore, up to a certain supernatural limit, displays all worldly traits, pressures and failings. For example, in conditions of long-term persecution and survival as a minority, it exhibits the typical mentality of the ghetto or sect: that is, isolationism with feelings of its own exclusivity, a defensive, distrusting attitude toward a hostile surrounding world, combined with an instinctive flight into "pure" spirituality with a search for justification in the mere act of faith without deeds (more usually—for guilt bears within itself its punishment— in some schizophrenia regarding deeds, in their consistent division into two categories: in the first category, the "sacred" and truly important, in an extreme case reduced only to the sphere of prayer, ritual acts and sexual life, in which the strictest zeal has to be preserved; in the second category, those that are only occasional, essential for contact with the external world and our existence in it, those which count so little that one can in this respect overlook any sort of wickedness—a Catholic of this sort will certainly not commit murder, larceny or false witness, not to mention blasphemy; he will however happily pretend that the things of this world are so alien to him that he does not see any connection between such ugly acts and, for example, his participation in elections or other pro-regime demonstrations, membership of a totalitarian organization, honest work for an immoral purpose, or perhaps jovial truthfulness during a police interrogation).[20] At the same time,

---

20 Most Christians can only envy the Jehovah's Witnesses the authenticity of their faith, the dedication of their deeds and the cohesion of their community;

however, the Church does not preach only the Good News to believers and non-believers, and does not mediate only the route to Eternal Life; it also provides the last purely earthly hope (the two are more closely connected than can be expounded in this context). In this country it remains the only serious social force which is organized and at the same time relatively independent of the totalitarian authorities, the only large community that has fundamentally resisted destruction and atomization. There is therefore no doubt that the defense of human rights and any attempt to reform political affairs must prospectively orient itself to the Church as its only natural ally (that is, precisely to the extent it is not to be merely an ineffective and exclusive protest, but rather contribute to the good of the *polis*); it must try to "mobilize" this power or, to put it in a more Christian way, must accept this yeast as its own and rest its building on this rock. Equally not in doubt—though much less obvious—is the opposite obligation. Directly: the Church gained a significant part of today's technical possibilities (an independent information system, for example) and real near freedoms (or at least the breaking of the silence which till now cloaked lack of

we should try to have an understanding smile for their sometimes too intrusive and decidedly too militant dogmatic intolerance, linked perhaps with a feeling of shame that it is sometimes difficult for us in an old world to be just as young and zealous as the gospel message; it makes us shudder only when in moments of testing we understand that they distinguish between "neighbors" and "closer neighbors," "our," "chosen," that the deed of the Good Samaritan would be condemned among them if it concerned their enemy or perhaps indirectly threatened the interests of their community—in short, when we come across the mentality of a sect which has a lot in common with the Church but is only its unsuccessful caricature, almost as the Devil is God's monkey. However, we ourselves are not spared the dangers of this mentality (I give a number of more or less academic examples here; in a text I wrote in 1978 I described one specific speech as "bun Catholicism" [see ch. 12 of this volume]). Insofar as the Church knew how to overcome it in its history, from conflicts over circumcision through to mysterious reversals of the Tridentine Council or the two Vatican Councils, it took place much more by the operation of the Holy Spirit than by the services of the frail human element. Only, the Holy Spirit respects the freedom for which we were created and only rarely awards it a lesson as thorough as that taught to the prophet Jonah; therefore we should always remind ourselves of what, with His help, we are to beware, and to what we should be open. (VB) freedom and repression, thus giving it almost unlimited possibilities) through occupying the space that the civic movement originally wrested from the totalitarian authorities and in whose defense it deploys itself as a kind of lightning conductor. Primarily however, indirectly: a secular Church operation exercised in cautious collaboration, or just in dignified sacred isolation, would perhaps offer some kind of escape and opium to the victim of totalitarian manipulation, but definitely not Christ with His Good News. Without the courage for a real "civic overlap," without the will to confront mounting evil actively (which does not mean to arrogate judgment over good and evil men, which should be left to God) the Church ceases to be the salt of the earth and becomes a mere piece of gold left at the mercy of the first impudent thief, a mere buried talent and white-washed tomb. This "path there and back" between civic initiatives and the Church is strewn with many obstacles, from historical resentments to communication and psychological barriers; at the same time, unfortunately, it is not only about *whether* the two sides will understand the necessity to overcome it, but whether they will understand *in time*. Oh Lord, remain with us, for it grows late. Personally, I am afraid that the other solution, that is, the secularization of the important Christian interest and the consequent politicization of a certain part of the civic movement in the form of some sort of Christian Democratic program and party cannot be realized in totalitarian conditions, and the Church and civic initiatives will be forced to drink to the dregs a cup in which the good wine is mixed with vinegar and gall, to consummate this marriage of convenience (or of necessity) and to justify it by the fruits that will ultimately testify to love.

Thirdly, how to get rid of the natural and artificial barriers between Czechs and Slovaks—and that without even setting out down the comfortable road leading to Hell, a road which sees the solution to problems in shooting them down in time, in getting rid of the differences at the price of the liquidation of national individualities. That certainly means finally bringing to an end recriminations which are equally justified and equally unnecessary on each side. With good will, accounts can otherwise be considered balanced. The First Republic denied the Slovaks an independent national identity in principle and inappropriately impinged on their Roman Catholic beliefs (*inter alia* by support for the Czechophile Protestant minority). The Slovaks thoroughly retaliated by disloyalty in moments of disintegration and the not very pretty wartime episode of the Slovak state.[21] (From the historical point of view the Czechoslovak state is also a mere episode; its permanency and value is yet to be decided). In 1945 to 1948 the Czech parties, including the democrats, betrayed or at least easily sacrificed the Slovaks, who consistently and successfully resisted the ascendant totalitarianism. They were then forced to suffer a double pressure for the next two decades: totalitarian pressure, and on top of that, pressure from the Czechs. In 1968 the Slovaks facilitated the defeat of the attempt to restore more humane political conditions—at the very least by their spontaneous preference for federalization over democratization.[22] In subsequent decades not even they hesitated to make use of the advantages their opportunistic step had earned. The Moravians had the most to shed tears about (they find themselves somewhere between two poles even where the extent and forms of religiosity are concerned). The Czechs consistently violated them regarding territorial autonomy, while the Slovaks, who flirted with them for a long time, betrayed them in the definitive moment of their success in the name of a narrowly and jealously understood national interest. They were right in that the Moravians are undoubtedly not a nation, but it was a graphic demonstration of how the abstractly understood principle of the self-determination of nations is untenable

21 After the Munich agreement in September of 1938, Slovak leaders declared their autonomy within Czecho-Slovakia. In March of 1939 Hitler invited Jozef Tito to Berlin and urged him to formally declare the independence of the Slovak state—Hitler added that if the Slovaks refused, he would take no interest in protecting the territorial integrity of Slovakia. On March 14 the Slovak parliament declared independence and quickly invited Nazi Germany to act as its ally and protector. On March 23 the Slovaks signed a treaty that formally subordinated its military and economic policy to Germany. (Ed.)

22 The so-called "Slovak Question" was bound up with the debates during the Prague Spring of 1968. Slovaks fought for more autonomy within the constitutional structure of Czechoslovakia. Gustáv Husák (a Slovak who would shortly replace Antonín Novotný as General Secretary of the Communist Party of Czechoslovakia) championed the slogan "Federalization first, democratization later" during the spring and summer of 1968. A more federal arrangement granting the Slovaks more power was eventually agreed to in October and went into affect on January 1, 1969. (Ed.)

in Central European conditions, and how essential it is for national linguistic sentiment to be combined with a certain territorial patriotism.
However, the mere silencing of recriminations, perhaps voluntary on
both sides, is only a first step and far from sufficient. The mutual psychological block, "for" the most part subconscious and thus all the more
dangerous, has to be patiently broken through. On one side, the haughty
instinct of the Czechs to see the Slovaks as some rather uncultured and
somewhat exotic appendage owing its independent national existence
purely to historical coincidences, and the Slovak language as a dialect
constituted into a literary language from irrational motive and somehow
"out of spite"; and on the Slovak side, a defensive instinct and some
"Minderwertigkeitskomplex"[23] which means they have to assert their national identity at every opportunity and with over-robust gestures, unnecessarily suspicious and peevish even where there are truly no evil or
ulterior motives. However, mainly it has to be understood that if we recognize the existence of two separate nations we must not in the same
breath reduce these only to linguistic or geographic boundaries, but
rather respect the deep differences in their cultural traditions, in their
mentality in general, and in their preferred aims; and to honestly confront
their consequences. That means we should see neither unwillingness to
cooperate nor evil intent when the other side is simply trying to be authentic in expressing a different historical meaning (be it at first glance
in very surprising spheres); hope for our fruitful coexistence in a dual
community lies only in the generality (catholicity) of these meanings, in
their harmony. One example of many, chosen from the political sphere,
is perhaps far from being the least important. Czechs have to come to
terms with the fact that for Slovaks the national aspect will play a much
more meaningful role; that (which is closely connected) human rights
and freedoms for them mean primarily, and sometimes exclusively, religious rights and religious freedom; Czechs have not only to come to
terms with this position but to acknowledge there are good reasons and
justifications for it. The Slovaks for their part must understand that in
the Czech lands reflections on the possibility of a Christian policy—
above all democratic but also founded on justice, on respect for the

23 Inferiority complex. (Ed.)

dignity of man and on the defense of recognized values—are subject to more constraints than just those of the ruling totalitarian power. The tragic religious conflict lasting for centuries which eventually (and Catholics bear no small blame for this) issued in an anti-Christian and especially anti-clerical mindset and in distrust, is our bitter but very real inheritance. Every offer of service conceals a danger that it will be not only a "stumbling block for many" (let's add unworthily), but especially a real obstacle for those who faithfully guard the inheritance of their fathers, who thirst for justice, or who sacrifice their life in service to their neighbor more consistently than most of us. We certainly do not know and, even in politics, may not offer a solution other than the Christian one, of whose truth and liberating power we are deeply convinced. It should be plain for Czech and Slovak Christians, and outside of any discussion, that they should never abuse their majority status (in Slovakia incontestable, in the Czech lands possibly a question today but a certainty tomorrow) to suppress minorities or to limit their rights. In the political field, I count among these rights the consistently lay nature of the state in which we live. However, in the Czech lands it is probably not enough to respect "normal" rights; a Christian policy must take into account more than one extravagant requirement, more than one turbulent emotion, more than one *a priori* aversion (already now, under the lash of totalitarian power, the art of Christian policy is connected with the ability to distinguish between real impulses and the purely purpose-made gestures that an anti-Church attitude makes use of only as camouflage for its fundamental antidemocratic nature). It will complicate our approach very much, including cooperation with the Christian-minded Slovaks; it would however be a thousand times worse if we repeatedly sowed the seeds of conflict, of a new tragic disunity of Czech society—a house divided against itself perishes—who sows the wind, reaps the whirlwind!

The fourth question is how to "internationalize" the struggle against a totalitarian power anchored in a single center and relying on a single imperial claim. Nation after nation invests its best forces and all its ingenuity, makes its most difficult sacrifices, in an effort to extricate itself from the bonds of totalitarianism or at least to interrupt and outwit the destructive process which involves not only politics but eventually interferes in every human sphere and value. Our world becomes "uninhabitable" and life "unlivable" in an incomparably more literal sense than in the fashionable phrases used by Western thinkers.[24] However, other affected nations look on these attempts as something that does not concern them directly, as something that is even suspect for them in its strangeness and timelessness, as something that could threaten their own interests and condemn their lack of faith (totalitarianism succeeded here in carrying out its long-term manipulation of suppressing every difference and individuality; when it is multiplied over time, even those who consciously resist it lose any sense of the meaning of dissimilarities, and the multifaceted quality of life becomes for them offensively complicated and lacking in potential). The other affected nations follow the inevitable defeat of these attempts with similar feelings, albeit with a certain gleeful satisfaction (after all, this confirms that their own defeat was fated and they are exonerated of any guilt for the failure of their own efforts at emancipation). They are often even willing to cooperate directly with their ruler in their own suppression, especially if it is connected with some momentary advantages (I would need to write a special reflection to shed light on the origin of this blindness, to explain why denying the principles of Christian solidarity, love and longing for peace in the name of universal hatred, envy and struggle—for example the class struggle—means a betrayal of the cause of the poor and oppressed, but that a throwing out the Sword of Christ and denying our strong God in the name of weakness with regard to this world and to the unjust peace of this world is an equal betrayal of the cause of the poor and oppressed). If the East European or Central European nations should

24 The universality of the current crisis is not in doubt. Humanity as whole is showing numerous symptoms of a mortally threatened organism, albeit manifested in various measures, in various ways, and in various places. Some put the predisposition to this disease down to the proud rebellion of modern times, others (maybe more logically) connect it with original sin. Alternatively, they see around them portents of the forthcoming end of days. The question, however, still remains unanswered (and taboo not only by those directly threatened but even by those who have *meanwhile* had the opportunity in free conditions to look for the answer) whether the militant totalitarianisms of the twentieth century are not a special infection, evoking most of the crisis symptoms even in parts of the organism of mankind not directly affected, or at least not by this factor, against whose virulence all previous attempts at therapy are hopelessly ineffective. (VB)

not go on relying on a miracle (which will not come, if only because God respects our freedom when performing His miracles and that therefore we must in a certain sense "deserve" it), then all their earthly and political hopes are subject to whether they are able, in their diverse aims and means, to recognize the basic unity of interest (and the same elemental threat), whether in the current hard times they will face danger by effective solidarity, and whether at the opportune moment they will pull together in a common liberating action (motives can be various, from almost nostalgically "conservative" to the insensitively "progressive"—if they know how to play their role, much will be forgiven them). We have to start creating all this already here and now; for, like death, the opportune moment can come at any time, and if it catches us unprepared it will be only the prologue to yet worse times. We have to keep in mind all the historical, psychological and other natural barriers but also the well-developed instinct of a totalitarian power which impedes any attempt to "internationalize" civil disagreement in its domain by every technical means and imposes extremely massive repressions. However, it is a matter of life and death for us to accomplish this task (the life and death of nations and individuals, just as, ultimately, life and death temporally and eternally). Christians are those who fundamentally side with life against death, who are prepared to sacrifice their own life in the struggle against it—thus following Jesus Christ who by His death overcame Death and who is both the Way and the Life.

We have examined these four main tasks (I am not saying they are the only ones) in greater detail, and with the appropriate argumentation for and against, not only in the light of their fundamental importance but also to demonstrate directly the lessons and changes in the situation that Velehrad brought into this field. I would prefer to remain skeptical over certain facts: that an active group of Polish youth took part in the vigils and their own pilgrimage; that hands raised in the "V for Victory" sign appeared here and there above the heads of the crowds (the reference to the well-known symbol of Solidarity adherents was unmistakable, though the old wartime tradition is not yet forgotten); and especially the fact that, in absolute loyalty to the Pope, his Polish origin was stressed in the sense of raising our awareness that not only is he our father *de jure* and spiritually, but he also experienced with us the same misery and hope. I am therefore not attributing an exaggerated meaning to these facts, and state that the "internationalization" of the struggle of the oppressed, the effectiveness of their solidarity in suffering and in success, remains an open task and that as far as fulfilling it is concerned, we have hardly got beyond the first small steps. Moreover many parts of this task present uncharted territory.

However, as far as the first three problems and tasks are concerned, everything has changed. Again I would prefer to begin with negative demarcations, primarily the fact that although the problems seem to be solved for a while, that does not in any way imply that we should allow them to slip from sight next time or that we at least know definitively "how to go about them." It should be clear enough to Catholics that the most noble momentary enthusiasms pave the path to the Kingdom of Heaven just as well as to Hell, that everything, or almost everything, depends on whether we are able to add order and shape and permanence to them, whether we are simply able to clothe them in words, deeds and later a body.[25] And to do that in a case like ours, when these enthusiasms were the logical result of a long-term and meaningful development, when some can see in them the fruits of their life-long efforts and sacrifices and others at least sense their fertility. What is far more important is an unambiguous answer to the problems and the universal good will (I hope it has been shown above that it should also be suitably representative) to solve these problems. Of course the answer is not at all

---

25   In the course of this we should not forget that:

a) Every incarnation entails many complications, evoking a deep distaste in any sort of Gnostic thinking (that longs to sterilize people, the world and later even the Creator; delight is welcome in all cases, it may not however bring with itself any fruits and commitments and continuation)—for even the Incarnation itself is essentially something itself unclean and offensive, at least for pure spirits of the Lucifer type.

b) True meaning to our motives is provided only by mercy and sanctification—which means in practice and *inter alia* that they are capable of becoming part of the order of sacred symbols.

c) The apotheosis of reason is certainly idolatry and shame from which, however, it does not follow that we may desecrate this gift of the Creator, one of the most fundamental—for whatsoever would be a permanent insult to our reason (there is of course a stumbling block here, for reason too is one of our impairable and impaired powers and a variety of forces struggle for dominion over it) is also a false motive and an infallible sign of an untrue faith. (VB) obvious, for a whole range of possibilities exist, from Pietism to Austro-Catholic Officialism which obscure or avoid them.[26] We certainly do not for the most part know "how?" and are very likely to commit many errors in the course of solving the problems; the salvific and liberating character of the solution were, however, already spotted, precisely at Velehrad.

There is an extra problem here, not irrelevant and not unconnected with previous doubts. To avoid betraying the logic and rules of effective communication, I will try to assign my separate statements to specific facts. I do so however with deep skepticism and really only for the sake of order. Everyone (or almost everyone) who was at Velehrad will consider my expositions superfluous, something which maybe helps to make his or her own experience more precise and articulate, but which also smacks dangerously of pedantry and the comminution of great things. On the other hand, for someone who was not at Velehrad, the provision of small and for the most part only anecdotal facts can serve at most as a guide, and definitely cannot be considered an incontrovertible argument; for almost everything stands or falls on the appropriate atmosphere. One can simply testify to moments of liberation and give weight to this evidence by subsequent deeds; one cannot, however, communicate it to those not present in the form of "instructions for use" or a methodical dictionary-style exposition.

Maybe what was most striking was that decades into the systematic destruction of society, a resurrected society arose "out of nowhere" (the only far-reaching parallel can be found in that tragic August week seventeen years ago; at that time, however, it was unfortunately only too plain that too much despair and hopelessness was mixed into the foundations of this fragile construction for it to survive). This was not an isolated sect of the elect, or expiring relics of better times, but a real countrywide representation, such as has no analogy. It was not unification brought about by a momentary interest which is disregarded (even the most noble) when this interest abates, or by natural centrifugal pressures, but

26 "Austro-Catholic Officialism" is similar to the "Austro-Catholicism" which Benda had mentioned earlier in this essay (see above note 19). Here, by the former, Benda means an empty, public preformance of the rituals of faith without substance, while pietism would be its opposite—a kind of otherwordly embrace of faith without any visible signs. (Ed.)

rather real fellowship with all that entails, from conscious human solidarity and shared responsibility, through a cultured and highly cultivated
system of connections, as far as commonly shared basic values and aspirations. The very number of participants is an eloquent and fundamental
fact; my lack of emphasis on its historical meaning was not accidental. It
is definitely important given the measure of representativeness; and it
definitely confirms to the totalitarian powers the existence of an independent information network and a general will contradictory to its intentions. But also (and chiefly) it testifies to the authenticity of this
society, to the stout roots of longing for a community in which "everyone
would be one"; for each participant had to arrange, and voluntarily sacrifice, more than one of his or her private arrangements for obtaining
some free days or holiday, and must undergo more than one risk— the
only reward for him or her being a just society in faith, hope and love
(and we can remind ourselves that on that day not only the Pope in Rome
but also millions of believers in all the churches of our Republic prayed
for the participants of the Velehrad pilgrimage and shared at a distance
in the community of sacrifice, thus multiplying the ranks of those who,
in a "statistical unit of the Czechoslovak population," create a truly
human community—whether despite or thanks to the fact they gave priority to the service of God). The spirit of Velehrad was thus unequivocally the spirit of the community; before God and before the world stood
one great family of brothers and sisters.[27] Let us content ourselves with
just two episodic albeit characteristic details. I enjoy wine and I'm a heavy

27   The last three words are not a decorative ornament, but a very important
     specification. In a normal family (and to a considerable measure in the Church
     too, just as in every viable society) there also legitimately figure relationships
     that are much more hierarchical and complicated than the simple equality of
     brothers. Testimony to the renewed and in truth evangelical (not however
     protestant, if that means through protest a permanent unwillingness to submit
     and bear fruits) nature of the Velehrad pilgrimage is precisely the fact that
     authority was eagerly sought, not just mechanically accepted; if the crowds
     demonstrated unconditional filial obedience to Cardinals Tomášek and
     Casaroli it was above all for their fidelity to the things of Christ—to another,
     their episcopal rank failed to provide even a feeling of personal security ("for
     they will in the end kill us here" was the naïve yet authentic statement of an
     eminent Church dignitary exceedingly honored by the state). (VB)

smoker; any sort of Puritan tendency is completely foreign to me and I consider any attempt at forcible regimentation in this direction, at the "extirpation of sins" in the sense of the Hussite Articles, to be deeply anti-Catholic.[28] In spite, or because, of this I was fascinated by a fact quite unprecedented in Czechoslovakia, that among hundreds of thousands of participants (and particularly towards morning after a sleepless night) not one drunk appeared, and there were hardly any cigarette butts in the main open space in front of the church (and by the cemetery)—and those there were undoubtedly belonged for the most part to the police watchers. At the same time it is important that no limitations were expressed, let alone enforced (as far as I know, for example, the offer of alcoholic drinks was on the contrary unusually generous), by real or at least moral sanctions; if this had been the case I would clearly have abided by the papal verdict in the well-known joke about whether one is allowed to smoke while praying or to pray while smoking. But it was not; the spirit of the community alone determined what was appropriate and what was not and everyone was glad to submit because this common spirit was the result of their own personal input as well. Another example: if there is any field in which the long-term efforts of totalitarian power to divide society can in some sphere claim an authentic and apparently permanent success, then it is in the creation of barriers between the generations. It is not even the result of some exceptional dexterity of official propaganda (in the end the meticulously cultivated seed of racial, national,

28 If Catholics enjoy a reputation for drinking, smoking, having sex and generally giving themselves up to the sins of the body, where many of them are concerned it is extremely unjust; it is however not nearly as unflattering as it might seem at first sight. Our Lord himself was called a glutton and drinker of wine and came to sinners, came to offer them salvation, not to punish them under the regulations in force. He did however curse as a "race of vipers" those who thank God that they are not as other men (I add that the Pharisees really did keep precisely to the letter of all the commandments and regulations)—and who thus begin and end with a judgment over others, an attempt to correct their moral and doctrinal profile maybe by force. It is not in any way a chance conflict of the historical Jesus with a no less historical group of Puritan preachers but rather the essential question whether people can in the name of God take things into their own hands and correct the Creator's "minor" blunders—for example, the fact that he gave man free will. (VB)

religious, social or anti-intellectual hatred either did not germinate at all or shamefully perished) but rather a natural psychological collapse of society in a blind alley where, moreover, guilt is not equally distributed. The complication of negative relationships and short-circuited reactions is almost incalculable. Some feel guilty and camouflage their guilt by aggressive self-confidence, pointing to inevitability or fierce nihilism. Others feel themselves to be defrauded victims and transcend their frustration by absolute irresponsibility, in a life consisting of constant reproaches, in a (would-be!) sophisticated choice of final wishes in the death cell. The middle generation carries something of both, as far as possible always the worse. All of them complain about their misery, often shifting their position and disguise and argument, but always consistently armored against any kind of possibility of understanding. It was therefore all the more of a shock when some elderly women sang some religious but very modern songs to a guitar and then quietly camped on the grass like regular hikers, while barely grown up children attached themselves to several fiercely patriarchal-looking fifty-year-olds and prayed with a rosary till daybreak; and when young people were generally accepted with love, and in their varied manifestations (from their hair to their preferred musical rhythms) was seen a reason for joy and hope, while they listened with trust and respect to those whose inheritance is also their task and to whom they were grateful for the mediation of the Good News. It was so terribly unlikely that it could all be solely the work of Christ. That was such a terrible defeat for the totalitarian authorities, it is almost better if at the given moment we can at most only speculate about its scale.

At Velehrad the will for "social outreach," for the shared responsibility of Christians for the problems and the government of the earthly community, was demonstrated so explicitly I do not need to add to or comment on the preceding description of events. Insofar as the form of determined, uncompromising protest this outreach took on itself at Velehrad is concerned, I already drew attention to why we consider it politically prudent and highly necessary for the whole nation—I will later try to outline my opinion as to why it is doctrinally flawless and essentially Christian, let alone why, here and now, it becomes a commitment of conscience. Two Church ceremonies figure here as two typical bolts between which arches more than a third of a century, an immeasurable gulf of suffering for Christians and everyone, but also the glorious, victorious testimony and conversion of many. Standing at the beginning of this period is the mass in St. Vitus's Cathedral when the Czech primate, Archbishop Beran, courteously refused in the name of the Church to consecrate the victorious totalitarian power;[29] whose storm troopers booed and hounded him into internal exile, which immediately turned into police internment and ten years later into real exile. At the end stands the Velehrad pilgrimage, a kind of countrywide referendum (for in the time in between, it changed from being arid mission territory to, if not the homeland of predominantly Christian people, then at least a place where the Christian message is generally regarded with great seriousness and hope). This is where uninterrupted loyalty to the Church was celebrated and at the same time the claim of the totalitarian power to dispose any longer of the fate of this country, of the bodies and souls of all its inhabitants, was rejected emphatically and with great shame (where the bodies are concerned, they can and for some time certainly will rule by sheer force, but only for a time). It depends of course on our point of view as to which event we call an end and which a new beginning.

The relationship of Czechs and Slovaks also acquired a new quality by the mere fact that so many of them and such a representative crowd came together at Velehrad—thanks above all to the Slovaks, who had to leave their native territory, miss their famous pilgrimage to Levoča, and even try to forget the nationalistic tilt of their own national tradition which links the mission of St. Cyril and St. Methodius primarily with Nitra.[30] It's difficult to guess what the Slovaks thought; on the Czech side admiration seemed to predominate: admiration for the courage and sincerity of their faith, for the internal

---

29 On June 14, 1948 Archbishop Beran held a Thanksgiving Mass on the occasion of the election of the first Communist president by the Czechoslovak Parliament after Communist takeover. However, on June 20, 1948 the Archbishop declared via a letter read in every church that this act did not in any way amount to approval of the regime. (Ed.)

30 Nitra is a town in Slovakia—the first in Slovakia to be mentioned in a written source (first half of the 9th century). It was also a residence of the first historical ruler on Slovak territory—Pribina. He built the first church there, consecrated by the Bishop of Salzburg Adalram around 830 A.D., i.e., thirty years before Cyril and Methodius came to Moravia. However, Methodius spent some time in Nitra too, and this gave rise to a specific Slovak tradition that "competes" with that of Moravia. (Ed.)

coherence of their community and (last but not least) for its perfect external organization. Fortunately and thanks to God, what emerged from this admiration were not feelings of alienation and envy, but rather joy from a success almost their own, a longing to be more closely associated and to learn, and a belief in the multiplication of gifts in a general unity. Maybe it would be immodest to suppose that there was something to be admired on the Czech side, something to learn, something to be enriched by—for in the end we know that Christ is the only true wealth, Christ who gives himself to us through our neighbor. Whatever the reasons, at Velehrad the spirit of love was dominant in the relationship of our two nations—not a contractual relationship in which each carefully calculates the advantages and disadvantages and is prepared to exploit every weakness of its partner for its own benefit. Nor was an "internationalism" present in the relationship, which results in the destruction of specific features, if not in outright "limited sovereignty." But rather a real, loving, brotherly relationship was dominant; it even seemed to me that for a while the age-old conflicts and resentments on the theme of birthright (Christian, cultural, national, political and I don't know what else) in which the two sides operate with many effective arguments and justified reproaches, shifted into the background—in the name of Christ's saying that in the Kingdom of Heaven the last will be first and the first last. This loving "openness to one another" of our nations was expressed in external ways as well; not only did the two languages alternate in the liturgy (from piety to the tradition of St. Cyril and St. Methodius there were even several sentences in Old Slavonic) but chants, hymns and prayers outside the mass could frequently also be heard with one voice, and I think the Czechs inclined to the Slovak version as spontaneously (and often artlessly) as the Slovaks to the Czech. So the only recorded manifestation of national rivalry was the contest between two disloyal pastors: Bishop Vrana of Olomouc lashed out at Bishop Feranec of Banská Bystrica with: "all of that was caused just the same by those Slovak Guardists of yours."[31] If the totalitarian authorities and their

31 "Slovak Guardists" is a reference to the Hlinka Guard. This was a militia set up by the Slovak People's Party—it operated from 1938 to 1945. This fascist party was committed to Slovak independence and its militia operated against Czechs, Jews, and Hungarians. It cooperated with Hitler after the Munich agreement of 1938. (Ed.)

minions themselves get entangled in the snares of nationalist discord that for years have been a useful weapon to them, all good people can only rejoice. For Slovak Christians these derogatory words are a badge of honor.

Elements of future strategy

Our reflections on the four main political tasks for today can be considered strategic. In many other areas it would be premature to map out a strategy; for on the one hand not even the basic principles are formulated, while on the other it is completely uncertain in what conditions and on what ground the struggle will take place. I therefore intend in this final chapter to comment just on two issues which underpin every strategy, or create its essential corrective. Whether and why Christians can, should, or even must develop what is usually meant by the words "political activity"? And if we do answer this question mainly or entirely in the affirmative, how to ensure fair conditions for such activity and how to provide effective guarantees against its misuse? Misuse either in the form of too much secularism and utilitarianism of traditional Christian parties, or in the much more tragic form of fundamentalist efforts to establish a theocracy, to having the earthly state absorbed by the Church in real time, before Our Lord's Second Coming.

Let us skip notoriously well-known biblical motifs and theological reflections on the theme of politics (making a virtue of necessity, as I could not squeeze even their very approximate recapitulation into this text; moreover, I provocatively assume a knowledge in the reader which I myself am far from having at my disposal); let us overlook extreme solutions on the two possible poles, and let us meanwhile be content with stating that generally for Christians, politics is only one of many worldly possibilities of how to achieve, or not achieve, one's calling, how to multiply or waste one's talents—it does not in any respect represent the preferred path, let alone one mandatory for all. It is just that, through the words of Christ and through the very fact of the Incarnation and its historical context, Christians were always very well aware of the meaning of the right moment and the right place. Now, *hic et nunc*, in this sorely tried country (as in similar countries) at the end of the twentieth century *anno domini*, when many see around themselves the last signs of the apocalypse and only a few remain blind to the symptoms of a deep crisis of *all* terrestrial institutions and values; *hic et nunc*, according to my deepest conviction, two aspects come onstage to dramatize the issue and radically limit the number of possible Christian responses. These aspects are legitimacy (or illegitimacy) and totalitarianism.

The existing state is essentially illegitimate. Not only was it established and maintained by force, against all written and natural law, but force and violence have been raised to its principle and have been made its permanent assets. That is not a trivial reference to the more or less justified definition of the state as organized violence which limits the freedom of some to preserve the freedom of others, or benefits the interests of the whole. What we are dealing with here (maybe for the first time in history developed with such consistency and precision) is force for the sake of force, force intoxicated by itself, which no longer has any other goals than its own multiplication and escalation. It is pure illegitimacy. One that makes a point of the fact that it neither serves nor is responsible to anything else (truth, human society, tradition, laws, not even to its own ideas) and that it can change everything—not just at the start with a revolutionary act but at any time and from day to day in complete arbitrariness, starting with the weather and ending with the souls of individuals.[32] I am not offering a hypothesis or hostile interpretation but only reproducing official doctrine; the thesis about the class war and how it will grow fiercer, about the dictatorship of the proletariat, the strengthening of the state, world revolution, the re-education of the masses and so on, these are the basis of the noetics, theory and practice of this power. I am afraid that the Church, on the other hand, lets itself be too fascinated (and that unfortunately and amazingly applies both to its previous caustic anticommunist opinions and to the excesses of liberation theology) by the apparent transparency of these declarations, forgetting that they are merely the ideological camouflage of a much more

---

32 In this sense, as was correctly noted not long ago, "Real Socialism" is the rightful heir of all Socialist attempts of a Marxist nature, their true consummation; for its predecessors and less successful contemporaries still had to prevaricate and coyly hide what it was really about by brandishing a dream of acquiring power to make a once-for-all improvement of the world—while "Real Socialism" can proudly announce and demonstrate its real nature: no reform, but rather sheer power, thoroughly secured in its permanence and arbitrariness (which in the context means the same thing as malevolence, the ability to produce only evil). (VB)

primary orientation to force and power. It often then happens that it enters a dialogue on completely unequal conditions, that it overvalues the meaning of ideological shifts and changes of emphasis, or that, from the possibility of Christian reinterpretation of individual theses, it even infers the possibility of coexistence with principles inherently hostile to God and to life.

The state authority existing in this country is totalitarian in the full sense of the word (otherwise remarkable reflections on post-totalitarian systems, etc., are of very small importance here as they deal solely with its technical management; the totalitarian claim remains untouched and can be implemented still more thoroughly[33]). That is something completely new. History knows many cruel and unjust states. Various military dictatorships and other solid despotisms and periods of unbridled terror existed and still exist; states sometimes emerge (not so exceptionally, and far from only in the dim and distant past) that betrayed their natural role so much that, for nationalist, racial, religious, political or other reasons, they set about systematically eradicating a substantial part of their own population. As far as Christians specifically are concerned, they never held any general illusions about the justice of most terrestrial empires. From the beginning up to today, they encountered those from whom they had to suffer countless humiliations and persecutions for their faith—the long lines of martyrs visibly testify to this (I can mention that more than one won their palm and crown in a country that externally ostentatiously declared itself to be Christian, or directly at its command—it is enough to go through the list of national saints). I do not want to compare the measure of horrors and sins crying to heaven; however, I contend that the totalitarian state is a phenomenon of quite a different order. The worst of the historical systems mentioned requires a certain amount of physical obedience whose rate may fluctuate but is essentially limited by the context of what the given culture considers the political sphere; as a rule it outlaws some external spiritual manifestations, or directly organizes some specific demonstration of loyalty (a cult). In these systems, "to be lord over life and death" is a mere euphemism that means nothing more nor less than that the state can execute anyone who defies

33 "Post-totalitarianism" was a term employed by Václav Havel. It is discussed most prominently in his essays "The Power of the Powerless" and "Stories and Totalitarianism." (Ed.)

such limited obedience or who otherwise causes displeasure. Compared with this, the totalitarian state (*ex definitione*) personifies absolute rule over the most fleeting tremor of our body, over the most hidden corner of our soul. In doing so it denies, with complete consistency, the existence of anything over which this type of government cannot be established. Totalitarian power is not atheist for a random historical reason, for example, because there was a moment when it petrified as "scientific worldview" some contemporary erroneous theory; it is atheist because it *must* be logically—until it succeeds in gaining secure control over religious enthusiasms with the help of chemical substances (the same reflection can however be used about the relationship of totalitarian power to culture and creative activity in general, to the individuality of human beings and to the particularity of nations, even in the field of love and sexuality where boundless generosity with regard to everything physical and well-arranged is combined with a puritan aversion to anything romantic and transcendent). The totalitarian state not only concentrates all *political* power in its hands but is also the only owner (including the rights to decide about the development and application of technology and about the distribution of national wealth, whether inherited, established and originating), the only employer, only teacher, only guarantor (and more frequently disruptor!) of all interpersonal relationships (beginning with the family and ending with national communities), and the only arbitrator of "thought crimes" (it is no coincidence that according to our legal code some deeds are punishable only when the reason for them is "hostility to the regime," and it is no coincidence that in legal practice this "thought crime" automatically and without further proof is assumed about anyone who in some way defies totalitarian manipulation and is not prepared to worship it). It therefore, unfortunately, has the ability in practice to implement its absolute entitlement, to have complete dominance over the body and soul of its subjects. It is thus "lord over life and death" in a much more literal and threatening sense.[34] There is, after all, only one Vanquisher of

---

34   And again: I do not, in saying this, subscribe to suspect Manichean-sounding opinions, according to which this century is the age of Satan's triumph. On the contrary, I think the ill will and appetite among the powerful of this world was always sufficient to require *everything*; however, they never had the technical means at their disposal, including special techniques of ruling over people that would enable them to realize this intention at least approximately. (VB)

death, Jesus Christ; totalitarian power can put its opponents to death but it cannot stop them being faithful to Our Lord, following Him in death and rejoicing with Him in the resurrection, in eternal life. It is, of course, unable to protect any of its adored leaders or devoted enforcers from death—one way or other it tries to avoid this unwelcome lapse; it is socially unacceptable to recall human mortality and even dangerous to recall how old the rulers are. When overthrown, the rulers leave only for a "well-earned rest"; otherwise they suffer at most "light influenza"—until the moment when (usually with a significant delay) the date and order of their state funeral is announced. However, totalitarian power really does rule over virtually every minute of our lives, over every gesture—even if only negatively, introducing the evil which is its essence and thus making life unlivable (or meaningless, which is the same thing). The life of everyone (both rulers and ruled) is transformed into a miserable existence of body and soul, into a sustained agony from which all flashes of joy and merriment are carefully eradicated (for they could rouse the most terrible enemy of totalitarianism, the will, or even hope, to live), an agony whose end is only empty darkness. Totalitarian power is also lord over the life of those who deny and defy, who become "dissidents" in whatever sense, or who just stubbornly defend the last foundations of their personal integrity. It is far from being merely the threat of death, imprisonment or torture (totalitarian power wisely does not renounce these means, but is post-totalitarian in this sense at least, that it is relatively moderate in its use of them, having at its disposal far more effective procedures that are at the same time less spectacular in the eyes of the world). In the end these things relate predominantly to the body.[35] The real danger

35 Prisons can however be quite different; and the effects on the human soul of, for example, "re-education" (linked with the possibility of prolonging punishment almost arbitrarily for one not recognized as re-educated, who one way or another continues in their "thought crime"), especially insofar as the soul's struggle is isolated and anonymous, would perhaps be worth independent treatment. I can maybe clarify the problem with the following analogy. Whereas regimes in both some traditional West European democracies and the worst Latin American dictatorships are the embodiment of the same concept of "politics" (qualitatively certainly very different), in a totalitarian state the word "politics" represents only a sequence of sounds whose meaning is, as a whole and in its singularities, nontransferable to any previous human ex-

maybe lies in the absolute dominion over everyday matters, in the unbearable pressure conceivable under this, and only this, regime. Numerous and very diverse witnesses (of whom many are still resisting and thus cannot be suspected just of trying to excuse their own weakness) testify that there is a time limit on the possibility of defying this pressure, that sooner or later the most powerful personality departs, breaks or perishes. I am afraid that these analyses contain a great deal of truth even while admitting they have been deliberately skewed; in the end, even the noblest motive, if it is purely human, has to succumb in the contest with totalitarian power, all the more if there is no reasonable worldly hope that this power will be defeated and destroyed. I am not talking about believers, whose ultimate hope is not of this world; yet the fulfillment of this hope *is* decided in this world and during this earthly life. They were promised that none of them would be tried above their strength. Jesus Christ did not prevail against the gates of hell for those gates to re-emerge, but for the faith of His Church to grow stronger in the repeated struggle against them. These believers should be (and are, according to many other no less credible testimonies) the exception and the salt of the earth, who are immune to the deadening pressure of totalitarian

perience with this concept. Similarly, imprisonment anywhere in the world, whether in places where drastic Early Modern Period practices survive or where the most recent educational and psychological theories apply (indeed, only God knows which is more humane!), is a more or less just, more or less reasonable, attempt to express the relationship between guilt and punishment. A corrective educational institute in a totalitarian state is something completely different—with a little malicious joy we could consider it rather the embodied ideal of this state as the prototype of a future Utopia. And let us add another element to our analogy which contributes little to understanding, but is an excellent aid for the almost mechanical distinction. State boundaries are sometimes only imaginary, or just lines drawn in open country; sometimes they are guarded more weakly or more strongly, and at other times again they bristle with massive fortifications. The point of them is however essentially the same; they are a clear demarcation, if need be a defensive barrier, against neighbors. One can be virtually sure of identifying a totalitarian state where the case is diametrically opposite: when all those fortifications face mainly *inwards*, towards its own population. The similarity to imprisonment is not accidental and therefore my note about prototypes of a future Utopia was not so malicious. (VB) power, and who moreover know with certainty (equal to other certainties of faith) that this power will be swept away in human, earthly and worldly time (in my opinion very foreseeable), and that the space demarcated for evil has an "educative" and not in any way ontological nature.

However, insofar as the political behavior of Christians is concerned, the aspect of illegitimacy and totalitarianism changes the situation in an unusually serious way. Many like to quote Jesus's famous saying in reply to the manifestly provocative question, "Render to Caesar the things that are Caesar's, and to God the things that are God's."[36] They comment on and misuse its first half, yet they remain silent concerning both the generally scornful tone of the second part of the sentence (in which Caesar's proud portrait and the worthless gold of this world are to be *returned* to him rather than recognized), and the extent of the commitment implied by this part (after all, if at first sight anything separates the jealous God of Israel who here speaks through His Son from the tangle of various gods and goddesses, then it is the uniqueness of His Divinity and His absolute entitlement to the entire person of man). Nevertheless, let us remain faithful to Jesus's words and not doubt the interpretations recognized by the Church; even if they are for the most part based on an anachronistic conflation of vastly different types of "state," we render to Caesar what is Caesar's! The catch is in the fact that as far as totalitarian power understands it here and now, what is "Caesar's" is not anything, precisely because it demands *everything* indivisibly, body and soul (an aspect of totalitarianism), and its claim arises exclusively from malicious intentions to the detriment of all mankind (an aspect of its illegitimacy—this is a government not only un-anointed, but also accursed by God and the visible Church). In my opinion, this means that Christians have no obligation toward a totalitarian power, and an implacable stand towards it is not in conflict with their respect for authority and the natural order of the world (they can hardly behave according to some former papal encyclicals, that are morally correct but nonetheless unrealistic and to some measure "otherworldly"; once their lives are subjected to this power, they cannot avoid contact with it, be it only the contact of a prisoner and his jailer, and they should not reject even the knowledge and discernment of its practices—albeit only for the purpose of combating it).

36   Mark 12:16–17; Matthew 22:20–21. (Ed.)

I see, however, much more weighty consequences than this negative demarcation alone. It is written that he who wants to save his life will lose it[37] (and this undoubtedly applies to the temporal life as well as to the eternal); a desire to reach fulfilment in earthly joys is just as unchristian as an exclusive orientation to one's own salvation. That is why, throughout history up to now, Christians have been able to endure more than one persecution, more than one arrogance, patiently and passively; believing that through their testimony and suffering they provide to others the light of hope, sow the peace of Our Lord. It is however also written (and these are the two greatest Commandments), that next to God we have to love our neighbor;[38] and that whatsoever we do to one of these little ones we do to Our Lord— and whatsoever we do not do and deny, we do not do and deny to Our Lord.[39] If someone turns the other cheek he is following Jesus Christ.[40] If someone turns away his face and his gaze when orphans and widows are bullied, when justice is denied, when a neighbor perishes, not only the perpetrator of these deeds will be accursed, but he too, who turned away—for in such a case he ought to have raised, not the peace of Christ, but His sword, he ought to have summoned the wrath of God and, according to human capacity, to have come to help. Totalitarian power destroys both body and soul, knowing neither exception nor pardon; it is not (like other historical governments), a mere inducement to sin and a test of human freedom, but rather a denial of this freedom and a reign of death. If, in the name of the identity of free creatures of God and for our own salvation, we are *allowed* to refuse all the claims of totalitarian power and to take a completely nonconformist attitude with regard to it, then, in the name of following Christ, in the name of love for our neighbor, we are *commanded* to lead an implacable contest against it. Our Church is certainly a catholic (= universal) church, and thus able to understand, tolerate and merge in a fruitful way the most distinctive forms of this contest, from the momentarily foolish intent to strike a blow under the sign of the Cross, through the strategically foolish intent to develop our strength in the routine of the cult

---

37 Matthew 16:24–26; Mark 8:34–36; Luke 9:23–25. (Ed.)
38 Matthew 22:37–40. (Ed.)
39 Matthew 25:40–45. (Ed.)
40 Matthew 5:39; Luke 6:29. (Ed.)

and the safety of the ghetto, as far as the universally foolish intent to rely on open dialogue and the power of the truth. I personally hope that as the Roman Catholic Church has always affirmed the refutation of heresies in the name of plurality and orientation toward life (we have to remember that, with rare exceptions, heresies express some justified element of sacred doctrine—their main fault is in the fact that they kill the truth, aggressively arrogating its ownership and reducing it to a definitive, rigid form), a formula will be found in relation to the political involvement of Christians in the contemporary world that will on the one hand become a *commitment* to face totalitarian power uncompromisingly, and not to succumb to its guile or deceptive ideas, and on the other (the help of the Holy Ghost will certainly be needed) be able to regulate the excessive zeal of all the above-mentioned follies and at an appropriate moment change them into the single act through which the wisdom of this world will be shamed. This will not, of course, establish paradise on earth (how many such promises already fell, beginning with the snake's "ye shall be as gods"[41] and the tempter's "command that these stones be made bread"[42]—and how much devilry was brought into the world by each acceptance) as this is reserved exclusively for the Second Coming of Christ; but it will mean the return of normal human conditions and the normal passage of the history of salvation, when the fruits of honest human work (in another context called "small works"[43]) and lasting service to God will have their rightful place alongside the extreme "heroic virtues." It should not be necessary to recall that the joy of the Christian is the peace of Christ and loving service to God and one's neighbor, not "holy wars" and Crusades (a desire for martyrdom may well turn out to be a mere suicidal despair and thus one of the worst sins)—it must however not be forgotten that historically, when Christians were driven to it, they fought and died exceedingly well and effectively, and anyone who sees in the contemporary people of God only an enfeebled and dying inheritance of the former glory of the Church is deceiving himself badly.[44]

41 Genesis 3:5. (Ed.)
42 Matthew 4:2–4. (Ed.)
43 See ch. 12, note 6. (Ed.)
44 Since we have made Velehrad the axis of our reflections, we will not deny ourselves one more quip, this time from the parallel Casaroli–Klusák discus-

I am convinced that the path to such a formula has been open, and that it was considerably advanced by the election of the present Pope and his early days in office; certainly thanks also to his experience with the suffering of the Church and people under a totalitarian regime and thanks to the merits of some of his famous predecessors (not only the immediate ones). I think that a possibility of the Church returning to its true calling is opening through this pontificate, hand in hand with an emphasis on an anti-totalitarian formula: both in the sense of reforming a centuries-long failure and inadequacy *vis-à-vis* the world, a reform for which the Second Vatican Council strove and for which it laid the foundations, and in the sense of overcoming the permanent destruction for which many mistook the reforms of the Council, and of the real *aggiornamento*,[45] that is, opening up to the world *as it is and as it is required by Christ*. This is not in any way the chimerical form once created (and for a long time harshly dictated) by left-wing intellectuals, and which some Council and post-Council theologians pessimistically embraced as their own, even as given for eternity. When the left-wing illusion collapsed at the turn of the 1970s and 1980s, when in place of the chanting of "God is dead!" in every square, the crowd's pleas (often, to be sure, confused, and thus easily abused) could be heard for the return of God and a return to God, for love and hope in Jesus Christ, for a return to the order of creation under the operation of the Church's wise Magisterium, pride so blinded some of these theologians that they saw the great divine gift of longing for a universal conversion as a personal insult and simply refused to take it into account. If theologians and priests of Western Europe and missionaries educated in their "universities" of the 1960s (here however the responsibility is much greater, for in the Third World the seed of the lie can bring unforeseen malignant fruits) behave so—it is perhaps a necessary consequence of the total confusion of ideas prevailing at the time. It is even a question as

sions. Two days before the pilgrimage Dr. Klusák (consciously or unconsciously paraphrasing Stalin's old question about how many divisions the Vatican had) ironically said to Cardinal Casaroli: "You're a general, but you don't have an army and therefore cannot ..." Casaroli returned to the comment at the gala lunch after the pilgrimage: "You got it wrong, Minister, I am not a general, only an ordinary cardinal—but as for the army, there is one!" (VB)

45   See ch. 13, note 8.

to whether, in individual cases, the stubborn defense of erroneous ideas is not more honest in the search for Christ than the opportunistic, too superficial acceptance of the changed atmosphere of the time. However, in our country too, and precisely in the ranks of those who suffered so much and who for decades rested all their hope in the renewed appearance of the glory of God, many can be found (amazingly, both "progressivists" and "conservatives" who once accepted the post-council changes only very grudgingly and now feel a little cheated, not wanting to be dragged out of their newfound certitudes and expose themselves to the risks of openness) who follow the upsurge and resurrection of the Church with mistrust (sometimes with almost sectarian jealousy), for whom it became "in" constantly to criticize every action of the Magisterium and for whom mass demonstrations of loyalty to the Pope are only an intellectual *faux pas*. After all, this Pope in fact turns to every sinner and alien; with little concern for tactics or sophistication he tries to return order and obedience to the Church; puts away his theological and philosophical erudition and offensively reiterates that good is good and evil is evil. We have certainly seen all this before (Jesus before the Pharisees, St. Paul to the Areopagites[46]). Let us not however be unjust to the men and women of this twentieth century (let us rather pray for them and whoever has the courage to blaspheme, let him ask God why he has tested them above their strength and when His mercy again outweighs His justice). Their case is indeed regrettable and tragic, for not only did they not receive any visible reward (it is a bad Christian who counts on that!) but for their steadfast fidelity and often immeasurable suffering had instead to pay three cruel taxes. In return for their fidelity—which, given the measure of suffering, had to be absolute and could not dare to let itself be rocked by cheap hope of this world—they often lost hope completely and the ability to enjoy earthly gifts; in their long-term resistance to the overwhelming pressure of totalitarianism they let themselves in the end be infected by its despair and nihilism. Because they had to fulfill their obedience to Christ not only in sharp confrontation with secular power but almost always abandoned, sometimes explicitly betrayed, by an improvident, or unworthy, ecclesiastical authority, disobedience and

46   Luke 11:37–44; Acts 17:19–34. (Ed.)

critical distance toward this authority became a condition of their Christian trustworthiness. Unfortunately, however, it later became a stumbling block as well, since denial of authority, even from very noble and humble motives, is, once realized, psychologically very difficult to reverse. Finally, very natural human (and Christian) motives led to a situation where the almost decimated Church here looked hopefully to all the real and imagined achievements of the formally free churches in the West without being able to distinguish the wheat from the chaff. Many therefore—even after the election of a Polish Pope through which the Roman Catholic Church visibly preferred the freedom to suffer for Christ and to defend divine creation over freedom without boundaries and limits—were unable to break free from feelings of provincialism, failed to understand that their focus remains fixed on a Church minority of little importance and little promise, that the chief sources of Catholic renewal were recognized in them, in the suffering, the poor (both literally and in the sense of visible spiritual possibilities—Christ, however, blesses the poor in spirit, blesses the reality of the heart in contrast to everything spectacular) and those who until then generally came last, that the labels metropolitan and provincial, the source and the stream that flows from it, underwent radical changes. I repeat, let us pray for these our brethren—for moreover, they bore their sacrifice for us too—that they may soon be brought to insight, that the dew of new hope may water their hearts. In the end, however, the Church is the Church of the living, not the dead, and must above all summon sinners and proclaim to them the Good News, not cure hardening hearts and attenuated reason. It is therefore good that the Pope does what he does, that he summons the unfortunate and offers the erring world order and a medicine—without asking too much whether it tastes bitter, or whether some polished intellectual noses will resent the smell (and if the learned theologians succeed in proving to us that this or that work of his breaks the Sabbath, so much the worse for the Sabbath and so much the better for man). We want to be unconditionally obedient to the Pope not only because of the authority of his office (there may even come, or come again, a moment when, at least in a few points, we shall have to resist the authority of this office; for the time of hard trials is not behind us by a long way) but because his efforts are our efforts too, because we want to recognize in him a servant who faithfully fulfils the new breath of the Holy Spirit; we want to be obedient even where we would not understand, and have to suppress our doubts in advance (that "even" would be superfluous if so much water had not flowed under the bridge since Abraham's sacrifice and the meaning of the word "obedience" had not become so muddled and obscured in the meantime).

Such obedience is an important strategic factor, which moreover can show amazing practical results already. Nevertheless, Rome is far and can be distanced from us still more by artificial barriers and moreover, the currently large measure of understanding for our problems there can change. We must therefore at the very least examine our own possibilities and strengths, if not rely on them literally (we certainly do not forget the help of God, only even this does not simply "fall from heaven," to some extent one has to deserve it and chiefly be capable of receiving it at all). Emancipation from the devastating influences of totalitarian power, defense of freedom of belief in the widest sense of the word (in secular jargon, "religious freedoms") is the essential task of the Church, even perhaps of the Church as understood before the Council as the "Church of the Clerics." On the other hand, the political struggle to eliminate totalitarian power, whose Christian necessity we repeatedly tried to show earlier on, should and must be won above all by lay people; it is not appropriate, and it is for just reasons forbidden for the "clerics" (in old-fashioned parlance "Men of the Church") to engage in disputes about the secular government at the expense of their service to God. Up to this point a clear and on the whole unmistakable scheme. The problem is that both of these struggles merge indistinguishably in a totalitarian state (it is certain that a temporary "coincidence of interests" can occur in any "normal" polis, but therein it is of quite a different nature); every freedom retained (thus the freedom of belief, too) means at the very least the beginning of the end of totalitarianism, while the eradication of the totalitarian regime (even if carried out by sworn atheists) is automatically a guarantee of the spread of religious freedoms.[47] The other side of the same coin is that in a totalitarian state every purely

47   The Vatican is very well aware of this problem, and has been responsible for more than one invective from Eastern propagandists because it allocates one measure to the diverse political associations of clergy anywhere in the world and another to the direct political consequences which inevitably flow from simple pastoral responsibility of the clergy in totalitarian states. (VB)

"political" aspiration of lay people (e.g., a Christian democratic party or movement) is swiftly crushed before it even begins to form, and usually already at the moment when two people dare to share a thought held in common. On the other hand, if it does not have the firm mass support of the laity, if it is unable to become a "political issue" serious enough for power to retreat before it at a given moment, every effort of the "clerics" to defend the rights and freedoms of the Church is condemned to defeat in advance (worse still: often condemned to ridicule and as a public nuisance). In practice therefore, in the foreseeable future (apparently identical with the duration of totalitarian power), I do not see any possibility of making or any reason for making a radical separation between attempts by the Church towards emancipation and the political striving of Christian lay people for changes in the system which would assure the world at least minimum habitability, including the possibility of living according to the commands of the Gospel.

However, if my reflections indeed have a *political* meaning, we should maintain a certain reasonable dose of realism: *inter alia*, we should not, on the one hand, undervalue the magnitude of earthly obstacles, nor, on the other, rest our hope and strategy primarily on earthly reasons. Now: from causes more serious than earthly ones (already because Christ is its head), the Catholic Church is not and never will be democratic, but rather inherently a hierarchical organism. That brings with it a number of advantages but also some risks that in our present situation acquire a special weight and which we should be prepared to confront. We have already said (and tried to document it) that as long as the flock will be at one with its pastor (and the pastor at one with his flock!), the Church will be a worthy opponent for totalitarian power and, with the help of God, the stone on which it will sometime stumble. At the same time we can virtually eliminate the possibility that the authorities intend to banish us to the catacombs, that they are prepared to surrender an important guarantee which is provided for them by at least partial control over the Church (in part usurped, in part more or less legitimately assumed from the complicated historical contest between secular and spiritual powers—it is not in the competence of our text to analyze the given issue, we can only indicate that the strict separation of state and Church is apparently the only exit point from excesses which as early as the Early Modern Period and to the detriment of both parties pile up in this area, above all in consequence of the radically changed concept of the "state"). This control however includes *inter alia* the investiture of bishops and other important dignitaries of national churches. It would be unwise to base our strategy on a belief in the physical immortality of faithful pastors (moreover aging and few in number) or on the assumption that totalitarian power will allow them to be replaced by pastors just as good (or by anyone who deserves the label "pastor" at all)—momentarily our hope can at the most be pinned on the Vatican not losing its head and preferring to leave the bishops' thrones unoccupied rather than entrust them to henchmen of quite a different power and interests. That, however, means that we must expect the ecclesiastical hierarchy in Czechoslovakia soon to be completely paralyzed and to exist only in name (if not something worse). I do not want to be mechanical in applying the old saying "A fish rots from the head" nor to state that a fish without a head is inevitably dead; I fear however that the Christian laity can, should and must bear the brunt of the struggle with totalitarian power, but that precisely as Catholics they will be defeated in advance (and it should be said that the clergy, the whole Church, the entire issue of God, will lose or win with them) if they are not sheltered and sustained by the appropriate spiritual authority.

Fortunately, for ages past the Roman Catholic Church has had at its disposal another safeguard against the risk of the local hierarchy falling in line with secular power, against the abuse of Christian obedience in the name of local and momentary interests (whoever the protagonist is, from a small feudal lord through the emperor to a pope pretending to secular power or enslaved to it). Whether they are aware of it and acknowledge it or not, this safeguard consists of the religious Orders and religious societies. Their central organization and the privileges provided guarantee them a considerable measure of independence from local secular and ecclesiastical powers, and their traditional and usually formally anchored type of spirituality makes them more resistant to the fashions and upheavals of the times; thanks to the adoption of evangelical counsels they are highly capable of action; they are less subject to secular temptations and intimidation (as a rule the effectiveness of both these instruments is given by targeting not the individual alone but primarily his human and material links with others), so it is more difficult to introduce disputes and splits among them from outside (all these assertions are only relative; monks too have their human weaknesses and not even the monastic life is free of numerous specific pitfalls). It was not always an accident that monks became the first target of any anti-Church attacks and it was not an accident that they often also became a last bastion which, through a long line of martyrs (in some periods warriors too, for there were also chivalric Orders) affirmed the faith of Jesus Christ and the Church He founded. In this respect not even the totalitarian power in our country was an exception to the rule; the religious Orders were forcibly liquidated soon after it came to power. They survived the last decades and subsequently live again somewhere on the fringes of the law, in principle not abolished but in practice forbidden and to a greater or lesser degree persecuted. This cross, long ago invested in the Orders, is however a powerful reinforcement to their evangelical operation. Whatever the *Codex iuris* canons say about this (indeed their privileges confirmed over and over again are evidence that not even ecclesiastical law can quite ignore this fact), religious Orders in fact always represented some sort of second, alternative, "parallel" spiritual authority in the Church. As to the importance of their evangelizing, modernizing and generally culture-shaping operation, they can often be considered the first authority. This state of things, in times of calm often criticized as an unnecessary luxury and a source of various disputes concerning competences, has in times of harsh trials shown itself to be that very safeguard of which I spoke above: that is, the last earthly hope for the unfortunate flock which has lost its pastor, or whose pastor voluntarily abandoned it.

I would like therefore to close these comments and reflections with an appeal to religious Orders and religious societies in Czechoslovakia, in particular with an appeal to their superiors (for I always thought it was immoral to appeal to the human responsibility of individual members of Orders in a way that could put them on a collision course with their obedience and other monastic commitments).[48] We are very well aware (at this moment I have to be specific; I certainly speak for myself, maybe for

48 If the monks who took part in the Velehrad and the subsequent Šaštín pilgrimage wearing the monastic habits so long forbidden to them did so with the agreement of their superiors, it indicates a radical break with their previous careful practice and thus essentially gives a positive answer to my later appeal. If they did so on their own account (without the intervention of a "third party"), it should at least give their monastic superiors cause for thought. (VB)

the vast majority of Christian lay people and also for a number of Christians and non-Christian activists in civic movements who have decided to defy totalitarian power in the name of justice, freedom and human dignity) of the almost immeasurable sacrifices and life-giving investment of suffering which monastic persons brought and still bring; we have expressed and will continue to express this awareness and solidarity with them. We understand that the monks long to rid their sacrifice of the impurities of earthly intentions and to consecrate it exclusively to Christ, to bring it for the redemption of their own guilt and that of the whole human race. We understand still better their justified mistrust in all kinds of deceptive words and promises, their effort to survive, to maintain their identity and to pass the Gospel on to future generations. If, however, totalitarian power triumphed completely and for a long time, the Church here would perish, and if the Church perished, all the religious Orders would also perish, for they are not an exclusive sect of Latter Day Saints but rather the body and blood of Christ, a limb of the Body of Christ. There is however a more serious argument than this "community of fate and interest." The moment can come and very probably will come when there will be no other authentic ecclesiastical authority in this country than that mediated by foreign broadcasting, by delayed messages, and by laboriously smuggled texts. We lay believers intend to bear the brunt of the struggle for the greater glory of God, to be faithful to Christ up to our necks—the unprecedented rise and resurrection of the Church in our country show that these words are not simply an empty declaration. At the same time, however, we know that, face to face with an overwhelming totalitarian power, we will necessarily succumb if we cease to be the Church; that is, a community steered by a single authority, a community endowed with appropriate charisms and justly relying on the direct cooperation of the Holy Spirit. Therefore with deep regret but nevertheless with all due urgency and for the Love of Christ we must ask the religious Orders to undertake another risk and sacrifice. And I fear that there are no respectable reasons for refusing this request (or rather, desperate cry)! The greatest commandment says that your neighbor in need has priority over all the Laws of Moses, rules of the Order, and every other human interest—and this is a call not from just an individual neighbor but from the whole Church and all its people.

For the preaching and school Orders or those focusing on defense and spreading the faith intact, the obligation to defy totalitarian ideology and all its power practices is already given of *"ex regula."* But not even the Orders focusing on social services should silently put up with the perversions produced in this sphere by the new totalitarian Utopia (everything can certainly be interpreted as divine punishment and offences are necessary; however woe to him through whom the offense comes—and woe also to him who explains away the offense as a manifestation of God's will!). In the same way the purely contemplative Orders whose importance for the smooth running of the world and the history of salvation we do not in any way underestimate, should hold to Jesus's "Whoever ... shall confess me before men, him will I also confess before my Father, which is in heaven"[49] and not conceal the intentions of their prayers only because they go against the intentions of the totalitarian power or concern their victims. We are not asking any of the brothers or sisters in the Orders to take the sword into their own hand (if it is necessary, and it will be necessary, we will do that ourselves), so they will not in any way be disloyal to their spirituality and vows. We do however need help; we need the spiritual authority which would unite us in resistance to totalitarian power and which would give our fight the consecration of Christian inevitability.

This fight will eventually be won, if mankind does not perish (which is possible) or if the main human instincts are not destroyed at their very foundations (which is very improbable); soon all that will remain of totalitarian power will be merely a grim and shameful episode of history. If, however, Christians are to be faithful to their calling, if they are to remain the salt of the earth, this process should not take place under their benevolent and defeatist neutrality, but rather it should be the fruit of their hearts and the work of their hands. Moreover, do not forget that the world was redeemed for now only in hope and freedom and that the history of salvation does not rule out even catastrophic failure and the rejection of God.

July–September 1985

---

49   Matthew 10:32 (Ed.)

18

Responsibility in Politics and for Politics

Dear Friends,[1]

I'm very pleased you have not allowed yourselves to be discouraged or deafened by adverse circumstances; that you are trying to search for Truth and "to put yourself entirely at its service"; that you feel a sense of responsibility for "the values which give shape and structure to our living" (moreover, I am understandably filled with deep gratitude that it is the Christian gospel which mobilizes and leads you on this path). I'm pleased that you do not doubt that a responsibility for politics is a priority for the Christian, and are at the same time fully aware of how many very different meanings the word "politics" can acquire, and how frequently evil and sinister actions can successfully hide behind this label. I'm very pleased too by the direct and decisive manner with which you turn to members of the older generation; you neither call them to judgment nor brandish their portraits above your heads,[2] but rather request an honest interview which would enable both you and them to meet on a common path and avoid repeating at least some past mistakes—I add the second part deliberately with embarrassment, for there is only one guide to the completely faultless life; and that is the one sharply condemned in the charming parable about

---

1 Benda is responding to a letter from a group of dissidents from the younger generation who sought information and advice from the Charter 77 leadership. Though their questions do not appear in Benda's original text, they have been placed here for purposes of clarity. A number of Charter members responded to the letter, and in 1986 the Charter issued an anthology in samizdat containing all of the responses. (Ed.)

2 By "brandish their portraits ...," Benda means using the reputations of members of this older generation as cover. (Ed.)

being entrusted with talents and then hiding them in the earth.[3] I agree in principle with a number of your other conclusions, above all as far as the Charter, politics, etc., are concerned. Charter 77 should not be "politicized" in any way, for that could have only two possible outcomes, the one worse than the other: either it would become a field for fruitless political squabbles and thus lose the ability to fulfill its original mission credibly; or else one clear-cut political trend would prevail, thereby totally betraying the Charter's mission. At the same time, it is clear theoretically and requested ever more urgently from almost every side that the Charter should open up a space for the development of purely political thinking and acting; this should necessarily take place outside the context of the Charter, but should be able to put full reliance on its support and solidarity (it would not be the first time; the independent culture, samizdat in the widest sense of the word, and various church activities owe a lot to the Charter for all sorts of things). Conversely, if this new political thinking and treatment succeeds in remaining faithful to the spirit of the Charter in its unquestioning respect for fundamental truths and freedoms, the long-term fate of our nation can be all the more hopeful. But you are more or less saying all that already. I would just perhaps like to correct the sequence in time: it is not true that it was politicians *par excellence* who became the most active people in Charter 77; it is true, rather, that the most active people in the Charter (who by profession and ambitions were in most cases completely indifferent to politics) in time became "politicians" *par excellence*. I will return later to this particular phenomenon, which on the one hand is typical for our totalitarian country; but on the other hand it is probably connected with the worldwide crisis in politics.

I am however afraid that the political inexperience you acknowledge, together with your otherwise commendable directness, has enticed you towards unreasonable demands. You expect us to "reveal to you clearly our political convictions (not generally civic, we know that), our political creed" with our "specific, clearly stated objectives, achievable by specific, clearly defined means." Even if I disregard the fact that your questions are better answered by a book than an article, by a work than a book, and by a life than a work, I am convinced that none of the answers you will get will be completely

3   Matthew 25:14–30. (Ed.)

truthful; not that any of those you question would consciously lie to you, just that when confronted with your naiveté all one can do is hurriedly begin to speak about something completely different, or withhold matters so essential that one's confession acquires a completely different meaning. There are essentially two reasons, or groups of reasons, for the necessary inadequacy of the reply (or rather, the decision not to reply). The first is narrowly linked with our actual situation and is binding on all; the second is absolutely basic, but only binds he who adheres to a certain concept of politics.

You yourselves use the phrases "perversity of society" and "an abnormal time." At such a time it is very rational for people to hide various cultural, academic and religious activities under the seal of anonymity, or pseudo-anonymity. I think, however, that in the case of politics, of the *res publica*, this approach is not feasible; you justly demand to know "who is who" and these impassioned political challenges justly provoke ridicule when there is no personal guarantee for them. However, among Christians there are relatively few who would underwrite their "political" standpoint with their own name—and not only from indifference to such "worldly" matters. Maybe it is rather because many Christians consider the given state of the community as fundamentally wrong; they do not see it as the mere result of a few chance errors that could be repaired by small reforms or a change of persons in authority. In the end, however, the same constraint applies to everyone, even the most enthusiastic adherents of Socialism. Anyone who would rather be directed by his conscience and reason than by the momentary directives of power automatically lays himself and his surroundings open to a repression whose extent one cannot sometimes even estimate. Moreover, if we take into account that although politics is unthinkable without morality and without certain theoretical foundations, it would be an error to confuse them with a mere moral posture (assumed as far as possible behind the carefully sealed doors of one's own privacy) or the mere presentation of Utopias and abstract considerations about the best state organization; if we take into account that the raison d´être of politics is action in coordination with others in the affairs of the community, then this argument gains importance. For on the one hand, it is clear that if simple adherence to some opinion or faith is persecuted, then any attempt to join with others to implement it effectively in the community will be brutally crushed before you ever cross the boundary of mere academic debates. On the other hand, however, this "perversity" and "non-normality" has the effect that the purely civic attitude you mentioned (from the traditional point of view it is more of a pre-civic attitude, common to humanity; for example, upholding the right to speak and defend one's opinion by non-violent means, and actively implementing the principle that the law has to give way to justice, and the arbitrariness of power give way to the law) paradoxically becomes supremely political and can (under favorable circumstances, but at least part of these conditions is in the power of each one of us) make an effective contribution to remedying conditions in the community. You will, therefore, have to tame your curiosity somewhat and judge "who is who" only from his "civic attitudes" and from the little additional information with which he eventually decides to cross limits set out— for each of us has to judge the risks and possibilities for ourselves. Indeed, our decision-making is not dictated only by the measure of our courage or cowardice, but above all by elementary political responsibility (if you cannot but regard us as politicians at any price); almost all of us are sincerely convinced that, in the given moment, our "civic attitudes" are as extreme and at the same time as effective as could be recommended for the good of the community—it is clear that maybe tomorrow already we will be able to go much further, and that our paths will crystallize, maybe even diverge in some things (we can only hope that none of us becomes so much of a "politician" as to get drunk on the new opportunities or even on power; that today's "civic attitudes" will remain a common foundation on which the varied architecture of the community will grow, but which cannot be upset or rejected with impunity).

The early classical thinkers defined man as a *zoon politikon*, a political creature.[4] Politics in the widest sense of the word is thus not simply one of many activities which we could abandon if necessary, but something in which one invests part of one's own life; according to some, it is part of the substance of man, something that distinguishes him from other beings (and from women, slaves, etc.). Christianity radically surmounted the unacceptable sides of this plan, including devotion to the material, earthly *polis*; in essence, however, the sense of having two homes was maintained, of man having two anchorages (it is already clear from the "greatest" Commandment, which is to love God above all else—"and the second is like

---

4   Aristotle, *Politics* I, 2. (Ed.)

unto it, thou shalt love thy neighbor as thyself"[5]). In a certain sense—at least by the concept of human freedom and at the same time by extending responsibility beyond the *polis* and the household to include whoever is one's neighbor—the importance of the "social" element in man is emphasized. Forgive me this abbreviated and necessarily inexact excursion into complicated problems, but I want to bring you round to the relatively obvious idea (*to prove it by its evidence*, in the relevant philosophical jargon) that the political or social dimension of human life is at least as rich and complicated as the private sphere.

Roughly from the beginning of the Modern Age a certain tendency has appeared in European thinking which we could on an ascending scale call a penchant for recipes or guides (for cooking, slimming, putting together or connecting appliances); experiments (taking place under controlled conditions and therefore repeatable at any time); standards (accurately defining the manufacturing process and "proper functioning" of anything); planning (education, economics and later the development of society in general); and, where appropriate, analogical advances (understood as something absolutely necessary and permanent, with regard to which a person has only one active role—that is, to recognize the patterns as accurately as possible). It doesn't really matter whether this penchant originated among the natural sciences, or whether the natural sciences of the Modern Age are its fruit; what we do know is that its achievements in science and technology have been so great that, in their blinding light, it has long been virtually impossible to discern any possible dark side (even today we automatically shrug our shoulders over the superstitious backwardness of the farmers who destroyed the first lightning conductor, while completely failing to make the connection with resistance to the building of a nuclear power station). Unfortunately, however, the penchant was very successful in another direction: the ability to swamp more and more fields and in the end to declare as non-existent those which in effect removed themselves from the possible impact of its domain. Now it was no longer good enough to overlook various disturbing phenomena: the crisis of religious faith (God is dead), morals (anything goes), culture (decadent, nihilist excesses and at the same time the chilling duplicity of "consumer"

5   Matthew 22:37–39. (Ed.)

products). In the end not even reason itself—which bears its share of the blame for the whole matter—is reprieved; there is no need to be surprised that in the environment of good old European rationalism the verb "to reason" became a term of abuse, and "common sense" at the very least some kind of eccentric inadequacy which has to be replaced by scientific thinking (one can clearly demonstrate that every irrational rebellion, from "innocent" spiritualist get-togethers to the murderous mystique of blood, soil, race and class, derive from the same family as this penchant—the same pride and desire for simplification lies at their root).

One could however confuse the disease and the cure to an even greater extent, affirm (and be sincerely convinced) that the symptoms of decline were only the consequence of insufficient doses of progress: "maybe something is dying away, but its importance for mankind was dubious at best and it will quickly be replaced by something newer and more valuable." It was only in our century that one could cross from theory to practice in fields with such a degree of complexity as economics, private life and politics. "Planning" successfully brought about economic difficulties and several great famines, even in what were at that time the world's granaries (Ukraine, Cuba, Indochina); as a prototype of the New Man, it presented the prisoner of the Gulag (don't be confused by the optical illusion that the Archipelago has disappeared; it is bit by bit turning itself into the mainland), or at best a semi-literate consumer of TV commercials; totalitarian states, which continue theoretically and practically to employ the idea that to achieve absolute perfection they have to spread throughout the world ("the revolution must triumph"), are offered as a model of the ideal order of society. Science and technology raise the stakes substantially, suddenly presenting us with the bill for everything which for centuries they appeared to offer so selflessly; complete control over the life of individuals would not be possible without them, nor the methodical efficiency of the extermination camps; it also had the effect that a partial economic error could threaten a whole group of states. This is what put the physical, biological and chemical means for worldwide annihilation into our hands; should we decide not to use them, we can choose the dry path of ecological catastrophes, generously supported by addictive drugs from heroin to cars. It is clear to almost everyone today that something somewhere went wrong, that events somehow got out of control. It is however difficult to surrender the illusions and ingrained ideas to which we sacrificed a considerable part of our life and in whose name we silenced our conscience so much; many of us therefore still try to reduce the problem to the correction of random errors which complicated the otherwise splendid and essentially unshakeable path of progress—or perhaps try to expel the devil by Beelzebub, and propose still more radical treatments.

Maybe the picture I've painted makes too dark an impression. I would like to emphasize that personally I cultivate the greatest faith and hope; not only eschatological— linked with the end of time and the Second Coming of Christ—but also a very ordinary earthly hope in the basic good direction of this world, created and redeemed by God, and in the human ability to learn from all these negative experiences and use them to our advantage. If I paint in dark colors, then it is with a purely didactic intention; we know (and do not necessarily have to be believers) that time and the right moment are immeasurably important and that all that may remain tomorrow of today's unused potential will be the requirement to pay the appropriate fine. Further: I don't want to look as though I'm promoting some sort of sentimental nostalgia, so I won't court drastic rejection by offering the spiritual, cultural, civilizational and social trends of past centuries—although my belief is that in these good by far predominated over evil. What does matter is the humility which brings a change of thinking and returns meaning to past deeds, rather than their desperate and suicidal negation, or attempt to throw the guilt on someone else (that is why the various "green" doctrines, which take something from both of these, combining disrespect towards inherited values with some sort of principled fatalism, are very foreign to me). The only thing that really needs to be radically set aside is man's overweening pride in himself and in his reason. In the name of this pride, two immeasurably valuable things, man and reason, were degraded to a mere means of achieving some sort of questionable higher aims and violated to the very edge of destruction.

Whoever agrees at least partially with the above must reject your formulation of the question about a "political creed" as inadequate (indeed, it is possible to come to the same conclusion from very different positions). The point is that in politics as in private life one can determine fairly accurately what has to be avoided (even that is relative—Jesus's words: "The Sabbath was made for man, and not man for the Sabbath" and "her sins, which are many, are forgiven, for she loved much" show that literal obedience of a ban can also be a sin[6]). On the other hand, "positive" political behavior can be defined solely by a context at best somewhat vague; which is not a drawback, but rather an expression of respect for human freedom and for the love which directs human choice when it faces the immense wealth and complexity of creation. I therefore think (and I'm certainly not alone) that every policy which boasts too much of its "specific, clearly stated objectives, achievable by specific, clearly defined means" and which is "the essence of previous (political) experiences" can be assumed in advance to be wrong, or at least suspicious, without us having to examine its objectives and means too closely. It is mere arbitrariness, a mere effort to reshape the community according to one's own ideas and one's own image (incidentally I observe that the validity of the principle "*corruptio optimi est pessima*"[7] is historically very well evidenced; the more aristocratic these ideas and their bearers, the worse the ends they came to—we think for example of theocratic states). The proper politics however means exclusively service to the community, service to a society of free citizens; the service does not consist of the imposition and enforcement of one's own ideas about what is good for another (one can perhaps raise small children by such a method; or better, keep watch on prisoners), but rather of attentive listening and deep respect towards that which the others consider good for them (of course, from time to time the perfect servant "mishears" something he considers damaging, or on the other hand, takes the initiative in correcting some sort of omission—however, these acts ennoble him only if he remains a faithful servant). Politics is not the distillation of previous experiences, but rather the will to go on learning; it is not a prepared program but rather the search for a path in complicated and rapidly changing conditions. In my opinion politics cannot, either today or tomorrow, do without humility (for the politician to be good and also successful, more of course will be needed—acumen, good fortune, the ability to catch the right moment), without humility with regard to reality, to the dignity of our neighbors (even the worst of them), and to their opinions (even the craziest).

That is the second reason I doubt the suitability of your questionnaire, or rather the formulations used. However, to prevent eventual

6   Mark 2:27 and Luke 7:47. (Ed.)
7   The corruption of the best is the worst. (Ed.)

misunderstanding, I think the following should be noted. Above all, I do not want what I have said to question in any respect the absolute subjugation of policy to fundamental ethical principles; if there are places that maybe allow for such a conclusion, let this be attributed exclusively to my clumsy expression. It is of course true (unfortunately? or thank God?) that, as in "private" life so in politics, the simple application of ethical rules which a computer could take care of is not enough. We still have to make up our minds between the greater and the lesser evil, or rather the lesser and the greater good. In short, however perfect our ethics, we are not rid of the problem of choice and responsibility given by our freedom; even if in this respect "political" morality does somewhat differ from "private," at least as to the nature of the most frequently occurring problems. I would also like to emphasize the fundamental radicalism of my concept; if I hold to the definition of politics as "the art of the possible," I see the only possible continuation of any sort of politics in the substantial elimination of the current state of affairs. It is not because I believe in the possibility of a definitive remedy, in the solving of every problem, in the realization of an earthly paradise by purely human powers. Politics, however—initially, thanks to certain unfortunate new-fangled concepts; later, thanks to their practical realisation as was experienced only by this century—somehow disengaged itself from its essential purpose: "went mad," one might say. Its only meaning lay in conquest and holding on to power; it lost its natural dignity, which consisted of service to something higher (the community, society, the value of the individual). Unfortunately, all the indications are that in this situation it will be the number of divisions rather than truth that will make the decision about returning to the normal order of things; armed resistance rather than a more self-resolute moral attitude (for the moment I consider these purely "moral" and "civic" attitudes to be far more effective preparation for a future armed encounter than some complicated conspiracy or impetuously desperate actions). I would like to quote the eminent Polish opposition thinker who until his recent arrest published under the pseudonym Maciej Poleski:[8] "It is possible to fight for the

---

8   Czesław Bielecki (b. 1948) was a Polish dissident and frequent contributor to Polish samizdat prior to 1989. He is an architect and served in the Sejm from 1997–2001. (Ed.)

freedom of the Christian *religion* through humility and mercy. But Christian *civilization* is always defended with fire and sword." In this sense a certain "black and white" vision is essential, in this sense we are bound to support and awaken the democratic forces of the West—although we should have great reservations as to their practice and to the seriousness of their own spiritual values—and all the same ultimately to rely on ourselves above all, on our own ability not only to survive somehow but also to triumph, to sweep the onslaught of evil back into that darkness whence it emerged. If we want to think and act politically, we must not surrender this emphasis on victory; defense against evil is the only thing that can justify politics and place the common interest above the interest and freedom of the individual. Let us remind ourselves of St. Augustine's statement that "Without justice, what else is the state but a great band of robbers?"[9] which played no small role in history and later—falsified to read that all states are only great bands of robbers—paradoxically became the ideological basis of one of the most terrible types of state ever known. If we want at the same time to think and act as Christians, for good measure we should not forget two things: that only God can bestow such a victory on us (and that the time and extent of the repulsion of evil remain His divine ordinance, before which our reason should fall silent); and that we often cannot and even should not avoid ("political") matters linked with the kingdoms of this world; however, we should not build exaggerated hopes on them (nor fears either, obviously).

I will try to answer your two questions rather more succinctly than this somewhat lengthy introduction:

1) "Please describe your political opinions, attitudes and activity in 1968."

My political opinions and attitudes in 1968 were roughly the same as today, although perhaps less articulate. I welcomed the developments and supported them with all my might, although I was from the beginning strongly pessimistic as to the outcome. In self-criticism, I must admit that

9   *City of God*, Book IV, chapter 4. (Ed.)

it was June 1968 before I seriously began to expect direct foreign intervention; until then I was only fearing an upheaval of the "Polish" type (I wrote something on that in May '68 and gave a paper at a Czech-German seminar in West Berlin; it seems however to be irretrievably lost). As I was a mere twenty-one-year-old college boy, there were of course major limitations on my political and civic activity (and thus responsibility). Despite this, I managed to arouse the displeasure of the authorities as early as 1967, but thanks to the accelerating changes, I didn't have to suffer for it. I even acquired a certain amount of credit, and was rewarded with the post of chairman of the student organization at the Philosophical Faculty of Charles University. In the spirit of my pessimism I left public appearances and excessive hope to others, and devoted myself instead to organization and "small works"[10] in general. It would certainly be unwise to go into details today about how far some of these organizational elements and work techniques may have survived the Russian occupation to become one way or another an impulse for the future. I confess penitently that soon after August 1968 I limited my political and civic activity to a minimum, mainly for family reasons (the birth of a first child is a more dramatic experience than that of the sixth— by that time I was spokesman for Charter 77 with all the duties and attendant inconveniences —although this fact should not be taken as measure of love and responsibility). I hope the spiritual foundations on which I try to rest my convictions and my whole life do not in any way differ from those I held then. For heaven and earth shall pass away, but His words shall not pass away. Any changes in my "political" personality can perhaps be limited to the following characteristic: at that time I probably would not have recoiled from the chance to perish gloriously in a street battle, whereas the idea of long years of imprisonment was manifestly beyond my strength and my patience; today I would be very hesitant as to whether this or that barricade is really worth it, but I think I'm much better prepared for long-term hardships. Simply, we grow old and yearn for our slippers! Because in theory it is clear that some sort of dramatic actions in the end can't be avoided, and in practice I fear further years in jail perhaps more than before.

10   See ch. 12, note 5. (Ed.)

2) "What makes politics distinctive and conceptually unique? What is for you fundamental in politics?"

I said a lot in the introduction, so I only have a few more or less partial notes. Politics is more than anything risk and uncertainty (just like faith, for example, or science, family, and in the end life itself); surrendering part of one's freedom, delegating control over certain aspects of one's own being to those in power is a step with many pitfalls, and by its very essence largely irreversible. It is not of course something we actually do—explanations about the social contract are only a myth to sweeten this bitter pill—rather, we are thrown into subjection to the state and politics simply by being born! Directly following from this are some basic demarcations to which every kind of politics which really wants to be worthy of its name must submit, in my opinion. On the one hand is strict respect for the difference between the private sphere and the public—indeed, the impossibility of crossing the boundary between them (there are of course exceptional situations, for example, war or other critical threats to the entire community, where one has to shift these boundaries or do away with them entirely; however, the point is that such measures must be perceived as an emergency and in principle pernicious; Greek communities quite often ungratefully banished the real "savior of the homeland" to forestall fears that his exceptional services and the position connected with them would overturn the democratic structure of the *polis*). In my opinion, the cloven hoof is kept hidden not only in the promise of paradise on earth (which I spoke about above), but in every paternalistic state which willingly and persistently removes from the shoulders of the individual the responsibility for this or that, and later for everything; human problems nevertheless remain in some form, but freedom very quickly vanishes. However, to a certain extent—and paradoxically—the other side of the coin is the liberal idea of the "minimal state," politics as a necessary evil confined to the bare minimum. The state should certainly not interfere in the private sphere; its precise definition depends on historical circumstances, but it should as the basic minimum at least hold that "thought crimes" do not exist, and that the mission of the state is not to "make people good" in any way—whether that means punishing his purely "private" sins, or forcing on him some system of values, faith, truth or something like that. On the other hand, the state should not and must not resign its responsibility (let's be direct: its authority) in the "public," "political," sphere. It should not and must not be a mere impotent observer lacking any system of values and blindly yielding to the game of chance forces. The existence (and necessity) of the state is justifiable only due to the fact that it brings some good into the sphere of social relationships; more precisely (and chiefly), it confronts various evils that still threaten them. As soon as the too liberally understood state surrenders the possibility to compare effectively (and also powerfully) the value of different political opinions, programs and discussions (for example, the election of another deputy instead of an attack on the polling station; the requirement to get rid of unemployment, instead of the requirement to get rid of the Jews); in this way in theory it loses the reason for its existence and in practice has a good chance of being quickly replaced by an administration in which someone can irreversibly disappear into a camp of one kind or another for merely uttering the world "freedom."

I do not in the least undervalue the depth of the crisis in which politics is mired throughout the contemporary world, including the Western democracies. I recognize this crisis mainly in the "emptying of content" and "loss of meaning" in politics, in the lack of hope or on the other hand, in the excessive hope invested in it. In Czechoslovakia the only thing one can recommend is a return to the traditional structures of parliamentary democracy (this was not always the case, and cannot be mechanically applied outside the Euro-American sphere even at the present time; hence the many stupid acts of American foreign policy, as well as fears aroused by the Russian nationalist-Orthodox opposition). In addition to the fact that these structures themselves provide quite a wide variety of choice, one can still consider various ways of improving them (though personally I think that what matters is for content and meaning to be returned to politics, that—with an adequate amount of civic responsibility and independence—"classic" democracies can function just as well in heavily populated states as in the former tiny communities, and that in overcoming the crisis, it is precisely in those lands which experienced totalitarianism that conditions are exceptionally favorable), for example, elements of self-administering organizations, self-administering republics (*res publica* = public affairs). I insist however that this return to the starting point of traditional democratic forms is essential, that every attempt to jump over or get round it risks the multiplication of existing evil—and since not much room remains for secular "political" rescue, we cannot allow too much experiment.

In conclusion, a couple of more or less disparate notes: first, illumination as to what I mean by these "traditional democratic forms," and what I prefer among them, or consider simply essential. I would like to point out that even a democracy following all the rules can be a very ugly dictatorship, especially with regard to ethnic, religious, social, political and other minorities (when it comes to it, the Hitler regime came to power by relatively democratic paths, and the Communists came very close to it in this country in 1946); the "government of the people" has much better prerequisites for totalitarianism than any other kind of government,[11] and it is therefore immeasurably important for its scope to be firmly limited in advance (the "will of the people" must not under any circumstances be the supreme law) and that there should exist some kind of "democratic culture," some sort of permanent respect for plurality, for human dignity and freedom, for the accepted principles of an open society. It is clear that once the democratic culture (as referred to collectively) is betrayed, the very best formal guarantees cannot be of much help; they can perhaps delay the passage from democracy to a totalitarian society, but they can't provide any protection against it. It is however clear at the same time that any politician can appeal morally (in words and by his own political behavior) to the democratic feeling of his fellow citizens; in practice, however, he can chiefly contribute to the maintenance of democracy (that is, to those of its Janus faces which became the inheritance and hope of the West) by creating and respecting its formal guarantees and limits. Of these I would want to emphasize as essential the principle of the simple separation of legislative, executive and judicial powers (in recent times the last-named is

---

11 The few can certainly force the many in a very unpleasant measure; however, that far from compares with the slavery to which the many can submit the few (for example a minority cannot really exterminate a subjugated majority, while we have experienced the opposite more than once). Instead of this double-edged word "democracy," I prefer to use the word "parliamentarianism," which both etymologically and in historical tradition is connected with a plurality of opinions as something essential and permanently present. However, a more detailed discussion of this issue goes beyond the context of my reflections. (VB)

frequently neglected, to the great detriment of the matter—let us be reminded that parliaments in north-west Europe were originally law courts above all, and that in France in the end they were even degraded to mere law courts). It seems to be better if at least (and also at most!) one of those powers is indirectly derived from the "people" (i.e., from elections)— that, however, is a matter of individual political opinion and local traditions. I would also prefer delegates elected for a limited period of time in whose ability to make right decisions the electorate invests its trust, over the possibility of direct interventions into government (for example, the use of referenda or some form of corporative system), the recall of deputies or their strict obligation to follow some previously given program (e.g., the party line). Connected to that, I would prefer a majority system with individual electoral districts over countrywide proportional representation, which virtually excludes independent candidates in favor of party machines. It is of course true that if political life acquires an expressly party nature, this system can actually deepen it and invoke numerous disproportions (from a purely mathematical point of view an overall majority in parliament could thus be obtained on the basis of a mere 25.1 percent of votes cast). The presidential system is probably a better guarantee than mandating the premier on the basis of a parliamentary majority (in pre-war Czechoslovakia, the powers of the president were formally meager but the role was determined by the exceptional authority of Tomáš Masaryk). Etc., etc. One could recount many themes of this kind, all of which, the requirement for the separation of powers excepted, are equally as contentious.

Two objections are usually made to similar concepts. In our present condition, isn't it all just idle speculation, and shouldn't we be setting up more modest, more realistic goals? Well, I believe that any sort of half-hearted aim, any sort of reliance on various transformations of existing forms of power is nothing other than unconditional capitulation to this power (and cannot end in anything other than a new tragedy). Naturally, we do not know when we will succeed, and whether the turning point will come in a few days, or the process will last for years: but we cannot for a moment take our eyes off what we are really striving for and what once and for all we reject. The second objection concerns the fact that the resulting emptiness could bring much worse things than before. There are many signs that the majority population could be inclined to redeem decades of humiliation and forced complicity by orgies of revenge (this phenomenon naturally has a positive aspect: it unsettles the existing rulers). This has to be avoided at all costs, not only for moral reasons but also for utilitarian and political ones: victors who are not capable of showing sufficient magnanimity are already preparing their next defeat. As far as future development is concerned, the opportunity to begin again and better, I have so much great confidence in the "people" (unlike those theoreticians who brandish that term always and everywhere) and its legitimate interests that I do not hold any major fears that some serious danger might threaten democratic development once we have got rid of totalitarian power.

November 1985

19

The Meaning, Context and
Legacy of the Parallel Polis[1]

I shall begin with a personal reminiscence. None of my essays has been so frequently quoted, both approvingly and polemically, and none has been the source of so many inspired slogans, as the one entitled "The Parallel Polis." At the same time, none of my essays was more improvised. When the "second crisis" of Charter 77[2] took place (the first, in the spring of 1977, was related to Patočka's death and other events, and the rest, from the third to the nth, happen with iron regularity almost every year without arousing much attention), I was given the honor of taking part in a meeting of the Charter 77 "brain trust" which met to

---

1   Translation by Paul Wilson. This essay was written in response to an inquiry from the Canadian scholar Gordon Skilling. Skilling asked Benda and numerous Charter signatories to reflect on themes raised in the original essay "The Parallel Polis." His questions included: Do you think the term "independent society" is relevant and meaningful under present conditions in your country? If so, what would you include as being essential features of independent society? What are the immediate purposes of the independent activities and organizations thus conceived? What are the implications and possible consequences of such an independent society? Benda's and seventeen additional responses can be found in *Civic Freedom in Central Europe: Voices from Czechoslovakia*, edited by H. Gordon Skilling and Paul Wilson. (Ed.)

2   This second crisis would have occurred in the winter of 1977–78. The first was caused by the death of Professor Patočka and the vicious anti-Charter campaign unleashed by the regime in the spring of 1977. By the close of 1977, the initial sense of exhilaration and achievement had waned among Charter members. There was uncertainty regarding how to make sure the Charter movement would endure and how to develop a long-term program which would preserve a sphere of action outside of totalitarian control. (Ed.)

study further opportunities and outlooks for the movement. With the zeal of a newcomer, I complied with the general instructions (I was the only one who did, as it turned out) and prepared a discussion paper, which was essentially the text now known as "The Parallel Polis." At the same time the need to face up to a real crisis and real doubts led me to adopt an unambiguously optimistic outlook. Because my contribution to Charter 77 at the time was largely technical and only incidentally intellectual, my paper was by and large a report on very down-to-earth possibilities.

In the years since then, even my most audacious expectations have been considerably surpassed. Thank God for that, although it is also true that for the most part we are only limping far behind the far more impressive developments in Poland. Today it is perhaps no longer necessary to show that the parallel polis is possible: time has shown that even in the spheres of "parallel foreign policy" (which most of my critics considered an arbitrary hypothesis introduced more for the sake of logical completeness) and of "parallel economics" (which even I conceived in a largely negative sense, in terms of the black market, theft, bribery and other phenomena that go along with a centrally directed economy) many things are realizable that neither we nor the Poles even dared dream about ten years ago.

I don't want to turn this essentially positive answer to the question: "Is it possible?" into a celebration of my own foresight and our mutual merits. There have been successes and failures; there was progress and regression. We wasted our energies almost everywhere, naively allowing ourselves to be outflanked by repressions or to be bogged down in internal controversies. In almost every sphere, we remained far behind what was possible, even considering all the unfavorable conditions that prevailed. In one area we failed catastrophically: independent education. There were and still are different attempts to do something about it, but all of them have been marred by an excessive exclusivity (not only regarding the circle of participants, but chiefly in the form and content of the course of study), considerable vulnerability to repressions and lack of clear-sighted, responsible generosity.

Perhaps this last failure was inevitable. Young people are caught in the tough totalitarian network of predetermined possibilities, obligations to work from a tender age and compulsory military service (for men). Given the total destruction of the family, there is not really a great deal of space for maneuvering here. Let us take a closer look at our school system—and at the educational system in general, where systematic regression is taking place far more rapidly than in any other sphere of social life, and where even the basic totalitarian principle of dispensing advantages and discrimination is becoming largely imaginary, because there are hardly any real advantages left to dispense, and where discrimination is beginning to function as a defense against infection by stupidity. (Here is a persuasive proof of the interdependence of education and tradition: as soon as fools are artificially included in the chain of tradition, nothing but stupidity can any longer be passed down.) This failure may prove to be a fateful one both for citizens or oppositional movements, and for our whole national community.

Even today bitter problems related to the changing generations are arising in the Charter, in the Church, and in independent culture. Unfortunately these problems differ from the ancient generational conflicts in that the rising generation is not marked by a healthy, or even an unhealthy self-confidence, a desire to rebel and take its proper place, but rather by a tendency to declare itself inadequate and place all the blame for that inadequacy on the preceding generation (a conclusion that in a practical respect is just, but in its rejection of the human condition and shared responsibility, deeply godless).

Then, of course, the future presents us with the threat of absolute destruction in a nuclear catastrophe, in economic or ecological collapse, in the perfect and ultimate triumph of totalitarianism. I personally think that a no less effective, exceptionally painful and in the short term practically irreparable way of eliminating the human race or of individual nations would be a decline into barbarism, the abandonment of reason and learning, the loss of traditions and memory. The ruling regime—partly intentionally, partly thanks to its essentially nihilistic nature—has done everything it can to achieve that goal. The aim of independent citizens' movements that try to create a parallel polis must be precisely the opposite: we must not be discouraged by previous failures, and we must consider the area of schooling and education as one of our main priorities.

And now some terminological clarifications, and concretely, an explanation of why I used the term parallel polis and why I consider this term even today as much more appropriate that "the underground," "the second culture," "independent culture," "alternative culture" or whatever other terms have been suggested. My arguments are directly related to both elements of the phrase. The program I once sketched out consisted neither in some sectarian or elitist exclusivity of a group or ghetto of people who "live in truth," nor in a one-sided attempt to preserve some preferred values, whether they be literary, musical, philosophical, or religious. If this program gave unequivocal priority to something, it was the preservation or the renewal of the national community in the widest sense of the word—along with the defense of all the values, institutions, and material conditions to which the existence of such a community is bound. This, then, is where the word "polis" comes in, or perhaps "structures." It is also where doubts come in about whether terms like "underground" or "culture" represent an excessive narrowing of the intellectual, social, or thematic perspective.

As far as the appropriate adjective is concerned, it is obvious that a community created with such universal claims cannot completely ignore the official structures and systematically remain separate from them (this is reflected in the more extreme aspects of the ideology of the underground) nor can it merely reject them and be their negative image (as the words "opposition," "second" and to a certain extent "alternative" and "independent" suggest). The adjective "parallel" seemed, and still seems, more appropriate than other, more categorical solutions. It stresses variety, but not absolute independence, for a parallel course can be maintained only with a certain mutual respect and consideration. Furthermore it does not rule out the possibility that parallel courses may sometimes converge or cross each other (in geometry only at infinity, in practical life, however, much more frequently). Finally, it is a global characteristic, not merely local. For example, there is obviously no relevant official counterweight to parallel philosophy or theology, just as in the foreseeable future there is not likely to be a parallel counterweight to military power. The global nature of "parallelness," in my opinion, bridges over these disproportions and opens the door to a merging of both communities, and even more, to the peaceful dominance of the community anchored in truth over the community based on the mere manipulation of power.

As I have already said, all concrete tactical tasks, all "small-scale work" involved in creating the "parallel polis" are, for me, connected with the renewal of the national community in the widest sense of the word. For the main principle of totalitarian control is the utter destruction, the atomization of this and every other community—replacing them with a paramilitary pseudo-party or, more probably, with a perfectly subordinated, perfectly sterile life-threatening party apparatus. The Iron Curtain does not just exist between the East and the West: it also separates individual nations in the East, individual regions, individual towns and villages, individual factories, individual families, and even the individuals within those entities, from each other. Psychologists might even study the extent to which such an Iron Curtain has artificially divided various spheres of consciousness within each individual. In any case, it is clear that we have far more precise and up-to-date information available about Australia than we do about events in a neighboring part of the city.

To tear down or corrode these miniature iron curtains, to break through the communications and social blockade, to return to truth and justice, to a meaningful order of values, to value once more the inalienability of human dignity and the necessity for a sense of human community in mutual love and responsibility—these, in my opinion, are the present goals of the parallel polis. In concrete terms this means taking over for the use of the parallel polis every space that the state has temporarily abandoned or which it has never occurred to it to occupy in the first place. It means winning over for the support of common aims (taking great care, however, to ensure that the usual proscriptions of state power are not only not brought down on it prematurely, but that they are held off for as long as possible) everything alive in society and its culture in the broadest sense of the word. It means winning over anything that has managed somehow to survive the disfavor of the times (e.g., the Church) or that was able, despite unfavorable times, to come into being (e.g., various youth movements, of which the most articulate is the "underground").

The point is that the totalitarian regime is subject to a strange dialectic. On the one hand, its claim is total—i.e., it absolutely denies freedom and tries systematically to eliminate every sphere where freedom exists. On the other hand, it has proved incapable, in practical terms, of realizing this claim (those who believe in divine creation, or who at least give precedence to the richness of life as against the poverty of ideology, consider this incapacity to be intrinsic and irremediable)—that is, of permanently preventing the constant creation of new centers of freedom.

There is, however, a fundamental difference between the natural resistance of life to totalitarianism and the deliberate expansion of the space in which the parallel polis can exist. The former is a cluster of flowers that has grown in a place accidentally sheltered from the killing winds of totalitarianism and easily destroyed when those winds change direction. The latter is a trench whose elimination depends strictly on a calculated move by the state power to destroy it. Given the time and the means available, only a certain number of trenches can be eliminated. If, at the same time, the parallel polis is able to produce more such trenches than it loses, a situation arises that is mortally dangerous for the regime: it is a blow at the very heart of its power—that is, the possibility of intervening anywhere, without limitations. The mission of the parallel polis is constantly to conquer new territory, to make its parallelness constantly more substantial and more present. Politically, this means to stake out clear limits for totalitarian power, to make it more difficult for it to maneuver.

Even in the apparent non-historicity of the Czechoslovak situation, much has changed [since 1978]. State power has not lost any of its will to totality and the repressions have certainly not become milder, but their psychological effect has essentially changed. In the mid-1970s the persecution of a handful of people was enough to frighten and warn off thousands of others. Today every political trial is a moral challenge for dozens of other citizens who feel a responsibility for taking the place of those who are temporarily silenced. As soon as this reaches a certain level, the parallel polis can obviously be eliminated only by totally destroying it, or at least by decimating the entire nation: a perfect example of this is the evolution of the Polish situation after the declaration of the state of war.

At the same time, however, we come to the first paradox here, connected with the basic and, so far, little-understood mysteries of totality. From the other side, it is probably impossible for the parallel polis to destroy, replace, or peacefully transform (humanize, democratize, reform, or whatever the other terms for it are) totalitarian power. I have no intention here of analyzing the obvious theological aspects of the problem. I would emphasize most strongly that this has nothing to do with the fact that we are unanimous in preferring non-violent forms of struggle. Every anti-totalitarian tendency worthy of that name (that is, that offers more than just another version of totalitarianism) is, in essence, aiming at the good of the polis, at genuine community, at justice and freedom.

Totalitarianism devotes all its strength, all its technical know-how, towards a single goal: the unimpeded exercise of absolute power. It is capable of the most bizarre tactical somersaults imaginable, but it can never, under any circumstances, admit that anything is more important, more sacrosanct, than "the leading role of the party." In August 1968, after the enemy invasion, there was a great deal of radicalism inside the Communist Party of Czechoslovakia, and a lot of heresy, but on one question an almost pathetic agreement prevailed: no matter what happened, and no matter if all the previous values were suddenly turned inside out, the party must under no circumstances go underground, become an opposition, give up its position of power.

Looking merely at the completely different set of values each side prefers, anti-totalitarianism and totalitarianism are not equal adversaries in the struggle for power. Totalitarianism, concentrating all its efforts on this struggle, must always win. The more headway the threats to it make, the more drastic means it chooses from its repertoire, which knows no limitations, to suppress that threat. There is no systematic doctrine capable of liquidating totalitarian power from within, or replacing it. That power, however, works consciously at the outer limits of its own possibilities: a single loose pebble can cause an avalanche, an accidental outburst of discontent in a factory, at a football match, in a village pub, is capable of shaking the foundations of the state. The important thing is the chance factor: totalitarian power can successfully block any apparent adversary, but it is almost helpless against its own subjects who foolishly and infectiously start working to bring about in practice the notion that they need not go on being mere subjects.

Even more important, however, is the social situation, the level to which the parallel polis has built itself up, in which these accidental (chance) events take place. Neither the Committee for Social Self-Defense (KOR) nor the Catholic Church brought the Polish Solidarity into being, but to a significant degree they shared in the formation of that movement. Regarding Charter 77, I doubt that anyone thinks we are capable of starting a revolution. I suspect, however, that everyone realizes that should a revolutionary (or shall we merely say dramatic) situation arise, our voice—"where do we go from here and how?"—will not be insignificant and that we will have to discharge our responsibility (which we, after all, voluntarily assumed) in something more than mere idle chatter and vague declarations.

Which brings me to what I consider the long-range or strategic mission of the parallel polis, the one genuine way of evaluating and justifying this type of "small-scale work." My conclusion is based on several loosely related assumptions. Totalitarian power has extended the sphere of politics to include everything, including the faith, the thinking and the conscience of the individual. The first responsibility of a Christian and a human being is therefore to oppose such an inappropriate demand of the political sphere, *ergo* to resist totalitarian power.

Turning to local conditions, the greatest amount of ingenuity, courage, or willingness to make sacrifices has so far not been enough to emancipate us from the sphere of totalitarian power. Afghanistan might become a turning point, yet precisely because of this infectious example, it is highly unlikely that the occupation armies will soon withdraw from that country. I am aware, and all of us here in Central and Eastern Europe are more or less aware, that the possibilities of a parallel polis and of any other kind of opposition are strictly limited, and that successfully overcoming those limits is conditional upon the world situation. Totalitarian power is a part of our fate (and perhaps God's punishment for our sins) and not just a mere parasite that can be eliminated by divisive action on our part.

At the same time, however, history teaches us that irregularly, but with iron necessity, those "favorable global constellations" come about, in which even small nations cease to be mere vassals of their fate and have the opportunity to become its active captains. In this century such an opportunity has presented itself to Czechoslovakia at least three times: in 1938, 1948, and 1968. Each of these historical opportunities were different, but in each case they were lost or squandered in the most painful and lamentable ways. Despite the situational differences, I observe a common factor in all of them: not once could the failure be blamed on our peoples who, on the contrary, demonstrated an exceptional amount of civic responsibility and willingness to sacrifice themselves. The failure was always that of their political (and military) leadership. We can be certain that we will find ourselves in similar suspicious situations in the future, and it is only a guess whether this will be tomorrow or in twenty years. Given the profound deterioration of our political leadership and of civic culture in general, we may with some reason predict that the next chance will be missed and lost as well. My private opinion is that the cardinal, strategic, or long-term task of the parallel polis is to prove this gloomy prediction wrong.

In the direction of our opponents, this task will consist in the "formation of cadres": people who are sufficiently well-known and who enjoy sufficient authority to be able, in a crisis, to take the place of the degenerate political leadership and who will be capable of presenting and consistently defending a program that will liquidate the principles of totality. This last statement, which is perhaps too simplified and declarative, requires more detailed commentary. It is in no way to be interpreted as a scheme, either hidden or overt, for seizing power. From what I have said before, it should be clear enough why the parallel polis would be incapable of carrying out anything like that, and why it would not even try.

As for the changes in personnel suggested by my references to "cadres," I see a far greater likelihood of difficulties than success. If by some miracle my good friend Václav Havel were to become General Secretary of the Central Committee of the Communist Party, I would immediately become his toughest opponent. Ontologically, because freedom granted on the installment plan, and as a favor by the totalitarian regime, would have little to do with real freedom; practically, because miracles are a mere exception to the orderly course of things in the world. Hence Václav Havel would either very quickly lose his position as general secretary, or he would equally quickly adapt to the *modus operandi* of the totalitarian system, even though he might introduce many interesting and dramatic new features. Given his human decency, I have no doubt that his would be the former case. I shall, however, let this remark stand as an answer to the constant speculations about Gorbachev and the tiresome, often capricious questions on that theme.

As I see it, the strategic aim of the parallel polis should be rather the growth, or the renewal, of civic and political culture—and along with it, an identical structuring of society, creating bonds of responsibility and fellow-feeling. The issue is no more and no less that this: when the next crisis comes, the next moment of decision about the future of our nations, the good will of most of society (and I repeat: this has so far been incredibly good and always brutally disappointed) will find a sufficiently clear and a sufficiently authoritative articulation. In other words our political leadership should be at the same level of thinking as society, and if it is not, so much the worse for the leadership.

Let me give an example that is now ancient and has ceased to be painful. The proclamation: "Give us arms, we paid for them!" from 1938 is mere propaganda if it is not followed up with a concrete plan as to where these arms are to be distributed and under whose command they are to be used. If there is any justification for the existence of an army, then their leadership, at a moment when the civilian politicians have betrayed their trust and the nation is in mortal danger, will not resort to theatrical suicides, but to a military coup—which is my answer to the question regarding *what* arms and under *whose* leadership.

Modern totalitarianism is held in check by two great limitations: it is intrinsically suspicious of, and even hostile to, any genuine authority, and it is capable of decisive action only in defense of its own power prerogatives. It is this that gives the parallel polis its strategic location and its long-range task: at a moment of crisis, it is our clear, unequivocal words that will be heard, not the confused and defensive stammerings of the government. For the sake of completeness, I should add that the appropriate clarity, courage and authority is not something automatic, or a gift from heaven; it must be earned in hard, "small-scale work" and also with the appropriate sacrifices. And if in the next moment of potential choice we should fail, this would be far more at the expense of Charter 77 and the parallel polis than it would be at the expense of our miserable government. We have taken up arms; now we shall have to fight!

June 1987

20

The Family and the Totalitarian State

The following article is not based on any methodologically relevant research and correctly acquired data, since—taking into consideration our domestic circumstances—it cannot be so. It derives primarily from personal experience and from lengthy, frequently perplexed discussions between us on this theme. It is a topic in all respects provisional and hurriedly improvised: the author therefore (of necessity) avoids references to the appropriate literature and tries to maintain a distance from all pre-packaged ideological schemes— including Christian principles, regardless of how close these are to him. At the same time, however, he intends to formulate some of his ideas very critically and peremptorily. He believes this to be essential when holding a material polemic which concerns both their feasibility and their acceptability, a step which can only contribute to the refinement of opinions on this theme. From the methodological point of view it should perhaps be noted that although the author does not underestimate the influence of material and social attitudes, nor of actual or officially valid moral principles, he does however apply a very special meaning to that vague factor called "fashion," "common sense" or "the prevailing social atmosphere."

The Communist state, from the very beginning and in the name of its totalitarian demands, attacked all the institutions of society. It completely harnessed some of them—the army, the police, the political-power apparatus—to its service. Others it virtually annihilated—the economy, education, science, culture—or deformed to its own image. It was really only the Church and the family which showed remarkable resistance with regard to totalitarianism and which remain an unresolved problem for it today.

The family was always a thorn in the eye for Communist totalitarianism. The most striking proof is the principle of "origin" and the

hostage-taking of all close relations as a guarantee of their "proper" behavior, a principle which survives with racist stubbornness all the variations
in Communist tactics. Nevertheless, the family proved to be a problem of
a particular kind; for purely biological considerations it cannot simply be
abolished, banned or infiltrated in a totalitarian way like other more complicated formations of society. At the same time, however, it is not so easy
to switch the terrorist practices regularly used for the liquidation or isolation
of inconvenient individuals over to the family factor. Primary radical tendencies do not last long, i.e., those which have as their aim the liquidation
of the family in the name of some sort of sexual or emancipatory revolution—a tendency characteristic of the Soviet Union in the 1920s and
echoed in other countries in their first years of Communist rule. Totalitarian power soon realized that the issue of the family touches the roots of
human nature, and that with the relaxation of ties in this sphere it would
be faced with the threat of alternative bonds even more difficult to bring
under control. From that time, it held steadfastly to a very rigid model of
the family. It naturally tried to drain this form of all significance and to rid
it of all its vitality—social, moral, and even, if it came to it, purely reproductive.

Even if totalitarian power has not yet succeeded in bringing the family
to an end entirely, it does not mean that this institution has not suffered
critical injuries. Married couples, parents and children, as well as other relations and close friends, are joint hostages. In the better case they are all
forced into lying and dishonourable behaviour; in the worse, they renounce those closest to them, or inform on them. In some cases at least,
such extreme pressures can turn out to have the opposite effect;[1] yet the
less drastic but still difficult pressures of everyday reality continue to exert
themselves.

In cases of families with a lot of children it is also crucially essential
that mothers with children of a tender age go back to work. If the family
wants not just to survive but to maintain at least an average standard of
living, two breadwinners are forced to work much more than eight hours

1   That is, the effect of bringing families even closer together and in effect steel-
    ing them to endure further pressures (as was the case with the Benda family).
    (Ed.)

a day since, particularly in the case of blue-collar workers, overtime is an essential part of their wages. The countrywide housing shortage has in real terms been getting worse over the last forty years. It seems that this is not only a product of the general inability of a totalitarian power to solve any sort of social problem, but also part of an intentional political aim to weaken the institution of the family, to prevent an apartment from becoming a true home, an asylum, and providing at least temporary shelter against outside manipulation. One can find evidence of this intention in the current laws concerning the housing sphere, which do not allow anyone other than a narrow layer of prominent people to occupy more than twelve square meters of living space per person (or, with certain restrictions and higher dues, up to eighteen square meters). This means that by law (and disregarding the actual possibilities, which are infinitesimal) not even young couples with the most promising reproductive potential are able to obtain an apartment which would correspond to the anticipated size of their family. The legislators put all young families in an impossible dilemma; either they accept in silence the fact that their living conditions will deteriorate to a point beyond endurance; or with the birth of each new child they try, at great expense and effort, to exchange their apartment (with small hope of success) for something bigger. The same severe limits apply to small houses built with a family's own money and often with their own hands (the law simply doesn't allow for the existence of larger families, so that where at least partially acceptable accommodation is concerned, these families are completely dependent on the benevolence of the authorities). The state finds this situation so acceptable that it tolerates in its own name an extensive black market in accommodation, as well as tens of thousands of unused apartments held by means of "dead souls" and other legal tricks for the needs of as yet unborn sons and grandsons, and the actual "double-ownership" of a large part of the population which, in habitations described as "holiday homes," find compensation for the less than desirable conditions of their apartments (an extreme but far from exceptional case is a holiday cottage two kilometres from the village where the owner has his registered home—since the law does not allow him to build a house equal to his needs and wishes, he is forced to commute schizophrenically between his two homes). However, the whole construction industry, which produces exclusively apartments of an inappropriate size (up to sixty square meters) intended primarily for sleeping and maybe watching television, testifies to this political intention. All these newly-built apartments are constructed around what is called a core facility (WC, bathroom, kitchen), providing for the elementary physiological functions. Because the public has not yet got used to having intercourse on the toilet, sleeping in the bathtub, and watching television in the kitchen, there is a temporary necessity to create some sort of hinterland. This could be the place to examine in detail some more factors tending towards the deliberate destruction of the family; from dysfunctional service to the completely intentional overtaxing of children, who have to face demands for schoolwork and extracurricular activities far exceeding the legal eight-hour working day for adults. Also worth mentioning is the systematic abolition of small local schools, the only "gain" from such centralization being the hours children spend every day commuting on foot or by public transport—from the point of view of weakening family relations, the gain is of course considerable. However, it is time to proceed to the positive side of this exposition.

I consider marriage and the family to be so essential that I am unwilling to accept the regular clichés about liberation from these obligations. So, in the Christian version as we know it, which for centuries dominated the Western world, the family was, as well as many other good things, a visible embodiment of the three most fundamental gifts or dignities that a person could receive (I do not mean by this that the family and equivalent models in other cultures are not just as productive—come to that, they are generally even more rigorous). The first gift illustrated here is the fruitful fellowship of love, in which we are bound together with our neighbour without pardon by virtue simply of our closeness; not on the basis of merit, rights and entitlements, but by virtue of mutual need and its affectionate reciprocation— incidentally, although completely unmotivated by notions of equality and permanent conflict between the sexes, Christian culture cultivated respect towards a woman in ways for which we cannot at the present time find any parallel. The second gift is freedom, given to us so absolutely that even as finite and, in the course of the conditions of the world, seemingly rooted beings, we are able to make permanent, eternal decisions; every marriage promise that is kept, every fidelity in defiance of adversity, is a radical defiance of our finitude, something that elevates us—and with us all created corporeally—higher than the angels. The third and final gift demonstrated in family fellowship is the dignity and unique role of the individual. In practically all other social roles we are replaceable and can be relieved of them, whether rightly or wrongly. However, such a cold calculation of justice does not reign between husband and wife, between children and parents, but rather the law of love. Even where love fails completely (which is surprisingly difficult in the family and rarer than one might think from first impressions or from the family's portrayal in romantic poetry and in supposedly realistic ideologies), and with all that accompanies that failure, the appeal of shared responsibility for mutual salvation remains, preventing us from giving up on unworthy sons, cheating wives, and doddering fathers.

Like every visible embodiment—with the exception of Jesus Christ—the family demonstrates every possible human weakness, inadequacy, and sin. Nevertheless—or precisely for that reason—it was for thousands of years favoured by the powers of this world; it was a dependable foundation of their government, although at the same time it declared the limits and boundaries of those powers. That was so until a government emerged with utterly unbridled power (as to sexual libertinism, more than one preceding regime has surpassed it, including the Renaissance popes), until a government with totalitarian aspirations decided to declare war on the very idea of the family. After a minimum of two decades, even in countries where, to its regret, the government could not put its opponents up against the wall or send them to the Gulag, but at the most silence and discredit them, a left-wing intellectual terror achieved what it wanted: marriage and the family became extremely problematic institutions.

I agree with those—ever more numerous—young people from Western Europe who refuse to have their marriages officially sanctioned. If the affirmation is to be a mere legal act that has to ensure a young couple certain advantages (in Czechoslovakia, even disadvantages) in the form of state contributions, tax relief, and conventional moral satisfaction, then it is truly a mere formality, non-binding and moreover not very dignified. Thanks to a sequence of seemingly small steps justified by, at first sight, irrefutable arguments which always have generalized some extreme situation, modern marriage is not a mere developmental form of marriage proper, devoid of excessive strictness and other ballast, but rather something fundamentally different and in many respects even contradictory to it. If the marital relationship is indeed an experiment from which one can retreat during the first serious collision, if one is allowed to follow one's own discretion in eradicating unborn children and rejecting children already born; if fashion dictates rebellion against one's parents as the only method of affirming one's own identity, then it is indeed humiliating to look for state confirmation of such peculiar family conditions and in this way to expand the field of possible interventions by the state (incidentally, we can remind ourselves that marriage is the only Christian sacrament the bride and bridegroom grant each other—God and the people of the Church are assigned only to the role of witnesses who give their blessing). No human life and no human reciprocity is free of heavy moments of despair. A marriage made with the prospect of dissolution the moment the disadvantages outweigh the advantages can survive only thanks to well-established customs and inertia regarding change—and these are not usually the best life mentors. It is difficult to act in your life with gratitude for the fact that you were not murdered in your mother's womb or later abandoned, and it is no less difficult to play your life's role with the awareness that your very own witnesses, blood of your blood and flesh of your flesh, can, according to the prevailing fashion, find their identity only in mockery of your role—not of its imperfections and misuse, but of its most truthful core, which you succeeded in embodying.

One should at the same time give ear to those who want to resurrect the original concept of marriage and family. For example, in Czechoslovakia young people—and young people in particular—like to swear they would never divorce, that their own rebellion against the morality of previous generations does not take the form of general amorality, but will be a new beginning. Unfortunately, the opposite is usually true: sexual extravagance, promiscuity, relationships easily entered into and broken off, disrespect for life. The question here, however, is whether this is a failure of the individual and his or her desires which are unmistakeable and visibly demonstrable, or whether what is operating is that deposited poison, those artificially and deliberately created external conditions.

What do the inhabitants of this country instinctively long for? In my opinion, they long for a family of dependable equilibrium, enabling affectionate mutual relationships and ensuring a permanent and indestructible share of responsibility; and for a home which would be a real, intimate space for living and at the same time provide a shelter from all external infelicities and attacks. The reality of these longings is naturally bound up with a whole host of conditions, some of which are in our power and others not. We have therefore to be fearless in implementing those which are in our power, and strive as much as we can for all the others to come within our power.

We have above all to renew or to search for such family conditions as would provide hope (not a guarantee, for in this world, fortunately and unfortunately, we have no absolute guarantees) of some sort of reach into eternity which would enrich all the participants. That definitely means neither patriarchal tyranny nor crazy feminist excesses, but equally neither any form of comradely uncommitted pseudo-equality, nor even the worshiping of children and the subjecting of everything to their mainly fabricated interests. (In connection with the modern idea that whatever is new is automatically "progressive" and positive, there is a strong subconscious attraction to this last concept. It is all the more dangerous in that it denies in advance one of the main purposes of the family, that is, to be a guarantee in time of the continuity of the human line). The family cannot survive as a community if the head and center is one of its own members. The Christian statement is simple; it has to be Christ who is the true center and in His service the individual members of this community share in the work of their salvation. One hopes that the well-grounded family can exist even without this distinctively religious affiliation; however, the focus of service to something "beyond," whether we call it love, truth or anything else, seems essential. Let us, however, return to that idea of mutual service and mutual subjugation directly connected with it. I incline to the radical Christian transformation of Plato's model of the social orders, in which rigid subordination based on ancestry, proprietorship, or intellect is replaced by the differentiated roles of the individual limbs and parts of the same Body of Christ. What is essential is that each of these limbs and parts can exist meaningfully only in service to the others; that the measure of their privileges is or should be weighed by the measure of their duties and obligations. This is true extremely clearly in the sphere of the family. Equality is virtually unrealizable for purely biological reasons. An inequality which does not respect personal irreplaceability and is far more generous in the allocation of obligations than of privileges is immoral and finally destructive. Psychologists know very well the tragedy that results from attempts to stand in for the male or the female role, that is, to merge them in one, and what a burden it is to be the only child. The author considers the ideal to be the conditionally hierarchical relationships in the "normal" (or "natural," that is, more numerous) family. The wife should be formally obedient to her husband and unconditionally loyal to him; with the reservation, naturally, that certain spheres of family life are her exclusive domain and that thanks to her specifically female processes (inscrutable to the author, as evidently to the majority of men) she shows herself able to transform her formally proclaimed obedience and loyalty into an exceptionally effective source of power. The hierarchy among children is natural and useful. The older autocratically rule over the younger, at the same time however accepting responsibility for their upbringing and protection. The younger children learn obedience, at the same time bask in love, and the example of their siblings leads them to trust in the meaningfulness of the world (for when it comes to it, their older brothers are prepared to renew it physically) and to an effort to outdo their older siblings.

Unfortunately, the material conditions for the existence of a family of this type are for the most part illusory. At least three conditions must be fulfilled. One is the adequate social welfare of the family on the basis of the husband's salary; that has long been the dream of Czech wives, willing to sacrifice to it all sorts of emancipatory and feminist fancies. In passing: should the husband not be in the position of the one who provides for the family materially, who provides it with protection (even though he need not as of old keep intruders from the cave with a cudgel) and ensures its social prestige, his duties are not equal to his claims, and his whole authority remains in some way very doubtful and contestable. Analogously, the woman who returns exhausted from her paid employment to her domestic duties can maybe cope satisfactorily with the hygienic, trouble-free running of the household and marital life, but can only with difficulty provide anything more for any of the family; for example, anything like love, which essentially needs enough mutually devoted time, patience and real interest. Also for example, something as trivial and at the same time didactically very significant as the gradual introduction of the children to individual household tasks which form the very basis of their approach to nature, to the human lot and to fundamental values; naturally, the mother can allow such initiation (not to be confused with the awarding of partial tasks which the child "just about" manages—that "just about" clearly tells us they are boring for him or her, non-innovative, merely an unpleasant obligation) only when the deciding criterion is not pressure of time and the maximum efficiency of domestic works (a cook can break an egg in a second whereas a child under guidance can—but may not—succeed in roughly five minutes; and although those five minutes have greater value for the child than the subsequent eating of the eggs, the employed wife simply cannot afford them)— notwithstanding the obfuscation of their inherent nature by too large a share of various ready-to-cook goods and services (if only those at least functioned in our country!).

The second requirement is that the apartment be a real home: that is, a place which is liveable and set apart, sheltered from the outer world; a place which is a starting-out point for adventures and experiences with the assurance of a safe return (in today's world of high-rise prefabricated apartments, the prodigal son would have to wait for someone to die before getting an empty bed, never mind his penitence and the good will of his parents); a place to which any member of the family can invite his or her guests even for purpose other than always watching television together (according to the slogan, we feel safer in a crowd); and from which any uninvited guests can be evicted. I would have to devote a lengthier treatise to this whole issue, which exceeds the scope and possibilities of this article ... let it be said that the solution is more dependent on its functional concept and on the completely non-architectural guarantees of family life rather than the mere size of the apartment. Finally, I would like at least to outline my private Utopia. Approximately two centuries ago the industrial revolution wrested mankind's work away from the area of the home, first gathering workmen and clerks, later agricultural workers, women and children, in gigantic barrack-like mills of a kind whose development brought only trouble and stress and fully conformed to Parkinson's Law. All the continuity of the work of one's fathers, all the meaning of mankind's labor, all the social prestige of the individual and the family, everything was reduced to the financial value realized; we have to recognise with bitterness that in spite of his insane conclusions, Karl Marx's premises about the "alienation of labour" are very shrewd. However, does not the current computer and communication revolution together with the transfer of most workers to the "tertiary" sphere, i.e., the sphere of services, provide an opportunity to reverse this unfortunate trend? Could not the gates of a number of expensively supported manufacturing, administrative, health and educational institutions be closed and their output shared by individual homes? This looks promising to the author from many angles, and in any case he knows that the shoe mender next door mends his shoes better and more cheaply than the state footwear enterprise—and even if the shoe mender's children go to university or become politicians, something of that shoe mender's honesty will remain with them.

In the third place, education must be education, and not a programmed denial of personality and the destruction of all moral qualities. That obviously concerns all state (there is no other) pre-school, primary, secondary and tertiary education. It is a scandal that such immeasurable demands in time and intellect are placed on children, manifestly not with the aim of achieving some educational results but to subvert and control the personality of the child as much as possible. It is a scandal that a child's access to education is dependent on the "class profile" of its parents. Another scandal—last but not least—is represented by the fact that, in defiance of international treaties signed by Czechoslovakia, parents are unable to decide freely about the orientation of the education of their children, who are subjected exclusively to the atheist and Socialist model.

Unfortunately however, that concerns the internal possibilities of the family itself as well. It is the right of infants to be suckled and to wee into their nappies. To pose a million questions. To wear out their trousers and to break the occasional window. To react with pubertal hypersensitivity and post-pubertal self-confidence. To have, in spite of all of this, their own safe and guaranteed place in the family circle. For it is only from such a place that appropriate authority and hierarchy can be respected. If the family does not provide children with their rights, it cannot reasonably expect them to fulfill their commitments and duties.

Winter 1987–1988

21
Prospects for Political Development in Czechoslovakia and the Potential Role of Charter 77[1]

I will begin with a brief outline of the present situation. What is loudly proclaimed to be the "progress" of the last two years, linked with so many hopes, is limited in every field that matters to mere words with no practical effect. In the field of politics in the narrower sense of the word—that is, how we are ruled and who rules us—there have been only insignificant cosmetic alterations and shifts whose meaning is at the most debatable—in political anecdotes, popular wisdom interprets them as unequivocally negative (with such comments as, for example, "at least there was enough snow under Husák").[2]

As far as human and civil rights and freedoms are concerned, not a single new guarantee has accrued, nor have repressive practices diminished in intensity, though they may have changed in form (and in the field of religious rights and freedoms even deteriorated). To ordinary members of the public, economic reform looks like a monstrosity whose main purpose is to prevent any sort of regeneration of anything at all—and the experts,

1   A meeting known as the Third Forum of Charter 77 was forcibly interrupted by the StB on January 17, 1988. In lieu of this meeting, Benda was one of three prominent Charter signatories to be asked to submit their reflections in writing for circulation in order to prompt further discussion amongst the Charter community more broadly. (Ed.)
2   Gustáv Husák (1913–1991) replaced Alexander Dubček as First Secretary of the Central Committee of the Communist Party of Czechoslovakia in April 1969 and served in that position until November 1987. He is closely associated with the so-called "normalization" era of the 1970s and 1980s. (Ed.)

in their learned expositions, essentially confirm this impression. In the ecological sphere a strange direct proportionality applies: the more it is acknowledged that the natural environment has been damaged by man and
is quickly deteriorating, the further any possible rectification is postponed
into the third millennium. In the field of the official culture and of cultural
policy, any sort of changes were emphatically ruled out in advance. And
finally, in the sphere of *"glasnost,"* of the public's access to information,
which is the most sensitive because it is the province proper of the word
and therefore does not allow strict distinction between the verbal and the
actual, there were substantial changes whose impact is, in my opinion, open
to debate if not downright negative: systematic lying (which enables everyone to arrive at relatively reliable—albeit incomplete—truths merely by
changing the signs) and the suppression of any sort of criticism (which
provided an open field for spontaneous, relatively targeted general discontent) have been replaced by the production of semi-truths and pseudo-
criticism incapable of contributing to the correction of anything at all,
whilst very effectively spreading general insecurity and disorientation.

Nevertheless, for justice and completeness I do have to admit the existence of at least two positive features of the present development. It
would seem that even the repressive components of the apparatus of
power are submitting to the general tendency to mere verbalization: attacks
in *Rudé právo* which, in the 1950s, would have meant the hangman´s rope
or life imprisonment for those under attack, and still in the 1970s many
years in jail, pass almost unnoticed and with "moderate" consequences (I
must quickly add that even these "moderate" consequences are not inof-
fensive; even nowadays people can be sent to prison for their convictions
and, in particular, there are political prisoners still imprisoned for many
years to come without hope of reprieve, for acts which, in the worst case
nowadays, would now be dealt with by a reprimand or a fine). Closely connected with this is the (paradoxical?) fact that the stagnation of real life is
tied up with rapid changes in the psychological atmosphere. We're finding
that the barrier of fear, for decades constantly maintained by the totalitarian
regime, is pulverized and removed from below, and that it's happening
spontaneously; see for example the number of initiatives (however debatable), see the hundreds of thousands of signatures under very militant
Roman Catholic petition (when not long ago we counted it a success when

far more "innocuous" appeals were supported by tens of thousands of Christians).

Personally, I am extremely skeptical as to both Mr. Gorbachev's intentions and his actual possibilities—and even more skeptical regarding the current rulers of Czechoslovakia. On this point I break ranks with many of my friends and colleagues in Charter 77: most of them are ex-Communists, but even people I could not remotely suspect of a Socialist orientation are optimistic. I believe this difference is a matter of subjective inclinations and opinions which in the end are not so very important. However, there is the thesis about the "leading role of the Party" which is objectively demonstrable and specifies the limits of every reform. The Communist Party is not a political party in the classic sense of the word but a paramilitary organization with one aim: to grasp power and to hold on to it. If this intention and this determination are surrendered, then it means the liquidation of the Party as a party, and that has nothing to do with reform. Nagy[3] tried this (possibly!) in Hungary in 1956 and ended up on the execution block. Dubček[4] decidedly did not try it, and in this regard he was telling Brezhnev the truth: the Action Program of the Czechoslovak Communist Party in the spring of 1968 was an absurd attempt to square the circle, that is, to wear the human face of Socialism beneath the dogma of the leading role of the Party. Dubček was possibly more honorable in his intentions than Jaruzelski;[5] nevertheless, things turned out worse for him. He not only failed as a politician, but in the Moscow Protocol surrendered his proclaimed ideals and the chance to become a martyr; he then sacrificed

3   Imre Nagy (1896–1958), leader of the Hungarian Communist Party during the 1956 Hungarian Uprising. (Ed.)
4   Alexander Dubček (1921–1992) replaced Antonín Novotný as First Secretary of the Central Committee of the Communist Party of Czechoslovakia in 1968. He quickly became the symbol of the reform movement within the party that had been developing during the previous years. After the Soviet invasion he was abducted, along with other members of the Czechoslovak government, and taken to the USSR. (Ed.)
5   General Wojciech Jaruzelski (1923–2014) became First Secretary of the Central Committee of the Communist Party of Poland in October 1981. In December of 1981 he introduced martial law in Poland to quell the movement led by Solidarity. (Ed.)

his supporters by putting his signature to the extraordinary laws of 1969,[6] and at the present time has announced publicly that what concerns him is the restoration of his Communist honor, and that the concentration camps he helped to plan in 1968 were not intended for the Stalinist or pro-Soviet fifth column but rather for "counter-revolutionary elements"—which means anyone who allows himself to think democratically and does not acknowledge the divinity of the Communist Party.

From the practical point of view, it is a great step forward not to be hanged for one's opinion, merely thrown out of one's job. From the political point of view, however, the advantage is debatable; even the worst regime prefers to have the loyalty of its citizens and resorts to terror only when it is unable to win that loyalty. As long as the Party does not decide to share its power with anyone or even, should its citizens make a free decision, to surrender it, until then all liberalizing, democratizing and similar steps (which can be expected, even if a sharp turn for the worse is not ruled out) will only be gracious gifts bestowed by an autocrat, which can be revoked in the event of any sort of "misuse," that is, any sort of questioning of the absolute prerogatives of its autocracy. It is in this sense that I speak of the present regime as being unreformable. It is of course unreformable in another sense too: a successful reform (which is usually thought of today as a streamlining of all spheres of state, economic, and social life) is unthinkable without the real activity and initiative of those ruled—however, activity and initiative are among those few things that cannot be enforced "the hard way;" after numerous bad experiences, one can hardly expect that Czechs and Slovaks will go into "cooperative mode" once again without guarantees that the authorities would find unacceptable.

Now let us turn to the possible political role of Charter 77, which amazingly merges almost perfectly with the most effective anti-totalitarian tactics and strategies I could imagine at the given moment. We live in a totalitarian state which, however, even in its "best" times could not manage to be completely totalitarian, and now it is becoming ever more

6   Dubček signed the Moscow Protocol which officially welcomed the Soviet invasion and the laws of 1969 which authorized crackdowns on "anti-socialist forces." (Ed.)

aware of this (in my opinion, only in this aspect is it reasonable to speak about "post-totalitarianism"). That is, it showed itself capable of implementing its total demands in practically every area of life of society and the individual; technically, however, it is unable to manage *all* these fields at the same time and to ensure at least some sort of their functioning. Through this, relatively large tactical possibilities open up for Charter 77: it can occupy every space the state leaves empty, or where it lowers its guard a little; it can uncover new spaces, for life is always richer than even the most thorough records record. It is in its way a dialogue with Power, even if a little different from what some of us were imagining eleven years ago: let us say a dialogue with a cane. Only, a cane cannot be everywhere, and one can even accustom oneself to its blows, or at least to withdraw a shorter distance than would be wished. We do not underestimate Power: if it once decides, it is capable of liquidating or perverting almost anything. But not quite everything! We should continue to surround their totalitarianism with our reality. For to assert itself, totalitarianism needs complete emptiness, nothingness. If it comes up against solid reality in any direction, it can ultimately be forced to hesitate, to prevaricate, to lead a real (even though insincere) dialogue. (Ten years ago I sketched this concept in a thesis about the parallel polis—incompletely, and in many respects naively. For emphasis, I repeat that the Charter cannot and must not become an opposition, a political party, a religious movement or an independent association of pigeon fanciers—even if all the signatories suddenly agreed to this. On the other hand, it can be the initiator of all sorts of independent movements and can provide them with a shelter against the malevolence of Power.) Nevertheless, I am afraid (see for example the Polish experience) that even when forced to such a dialogue, totalitarian power will leave an escape hatch open and later be capable of confronting the threat of even the most compact "parallel polis" with the reality of tanks and machine guns to which it has exclusive access (even if it's clear that these measures don't dispose of the threat, only postpone it!). I therefore attribute only tactical significance to the building of the parallel polis.

My idea for a long-term political strategy is based on two findings:

The first is that internal conditions in Czechoslovakia are now dependent on the constellation of global—or at the very least European—forces to the extent that no strategy exists which would lead to major success as long as the unfavorable constellation of external powers lasts. We have had at least three opportunities in the recent past (1938, 1948, 1968— historians can shift these data in various ways but nothing changes the nub of the issue) to intervene in our own fates and to take matters into our own hands. All these opportunities were hopelessly wasted. I would state that in none of those cases did the nation fail to act with adequate enthusiasm or resolve or willingness to make sacrifices; rather, it was always a case of catastrophic failure of political representation. History teaches us that sooner or later a similar opportunity will inevitably arise (but again, that there are not so many of them that we can afford to squander it). Any reasonable strategy must therefore be focused so that at the earliest occasion we can avoid the errors of the past.

Secondly, it seems to be empirically verified that the destruction of totalitarian power cannot be realized programmatically, that even in its most difficult crises this power is so strong it can nip in the bud direct attempts at resistance, whether open or conspiratorial. More or less random causes and extremely unforeseeable events can unleash an avalanche capable of shaking the very foundations of totalitarianism. Such an avalanche is like an element of nature: it is blind, it can cause much suffering, and it can ultimately be completely unsuccessful. Ultimately, however, it is just the sum of popular will and thinking; although it cannot be deliberately triggered, in its early stages it can be channeled (and it itself looks for such direction and for firm orientation points) and later transformed from a mere explosion of discontent into purposeful and effective action.

I think that Charter 77 has exceptionally favorable prerequisites for it substantially to influence a solution to both these problems. Under no circumstances should it politicize itself, that is, become an opposition with a defined political program; by doing so it would lose its very special identity, and if it were to collapse into internal disputes it would undoubtedly be vigorously suppressed by the authorities. On the other hand, if the Charter maintains its own moral authority, its unswerving and non-negotiable vigil over certain basic truths (concisely labeled "human rights") accepted by a consistent consensus of otherwise politically very variously minded signatories, insofar as it is capable of being the bad conscience of the current leadership, of influencing any political representation that really cares about something, conceivably of contributing to the origin of a parallel and alternative representation (however, the Charter cannot and must not identify even with this); also insofar as it can seriously intervene in the course of that avalanche of which I spoke (for various reasons I object to the term revolution).

I would end by saying that Charter 77 is today—even in the purely political sense—more important than most of us would allow (we started so innocently with our Humanism, with our individual liberating gesture in the middle of the general marasmus). We must learn to live with this fact: not to indulge in priding ourselves on it, but with an awareness of the increased responsibility that comes with it.

In this outline I have tried to capture what I intended to present as an introductory paper for the Charter 77 forum, broken up by the secret police. It was designed as a polemical proposition whose definitive form would be fixed in the course of discussion. I therefore ask potential opponents to polemicize with anything that is unacceptable in my statements, and not with the fact that they are inadequately argued; since with a view to the breadth of the theme and the permitted length of the submission, I have hardly been able to expound anything exactly enough to satisfy myself, let alone my honorable opponents.

February 24, 1988

22

The Spiritual Renewal of the Nation:
A Way Out of the Crisis?

"Arise, and go into the city, and it shall be told thee what thou must do."
Acts 9:6

Hardly anyone today doubts that our society is going through a serious crisis. A crisis of values, a moral crisis, an economic and ecological, a social and political crisis. There are various diagnoses of its origins and various prognoses of its future course; however, everyone on the whole concurs that if "nothing is done about it" it could soon be the end of us. Christians have always understood that their mission, their share in God's creative and redemptive work, is to heal and restore, both themselves and everything around them. Therefore they understand more than anyone the urgency of this task in today's evil and—in many ways—apocalyptic times. They are at the same time aware that any true renewal must begin from within, through the renewal of their own selves; however, it must not end there— true inner restoration must be accompanied by effective love for one's neighbor and responsible service to the world as the work of the Creator. An important condition for the effectiveness of restoration is for none of us to stand alone, but rather as a community, as a church; and Christians want to share in the renewal so desperately needed today as a community and as a church. This common will requires an external framework and so the Roman Catholic Church in the Czech Lands has announced a contextual program: the Decade of the Spiritual Renewal of the Nation.[1]

1   Two priests who studied theology secretly and were ordained abroad were instrumental in developing this program: Petr Piťha and Tomaš Halík. (Ed.)

This program, instigated "from below" and specifically Czech, albeit inspired by the nine-year Marian cycle successfully realized by the Polish church in the 1950s, presupposes a thorough decade of preparation for the millennium of the martyrdom of St. Adalbert,[2] the first Prague bishop of Czech blood. At the same time it should be a harbinger of the gateway to the third millennium of the Christian era. If things go well, it should be something more than mere preparation and anticipation; it should be the central point from which the life of Christians and non-Christians of this country should develop over the next decade, as well as a signpost providing a common orientation point. We could say that only Christ can be the real central point and signpost; however, His Gospel has to be proclaimed to all nations and His mystic body, the Church, has to increase in growth by new flesh and blood. Christians have to be the salt and yeast of the world and, with the help of the Holy Ghost, *everything* in them has to be transformed and sanctified—it is precisely this striving in Christ which is the aim of the Decade of Renewal program.

Each of the ten years is devoted to one of our Czech saints, and at the same time based on a theme common to Christians and all mankind (the choice of these themes was inspired by a "positive" interpretation of the Ten Commandments). The coordination of the individual saints and themes is not random; an effort has always been made for the theme to correspond with the primary charism of the saint in question, to evoke the heart of his or her testimony about Christ. For example, the theme of the first year, consecrated to the Blessed Agnes of Bohemia, was service to life and the defense of life. The Bohemian princess did so much in this field that she shames us still today as much by her practical performance as by her faith.

The Decade of the Spiritual Renewal of the Nation was officially announced at the beginning of Advent 1987 in a pastoral letter from all the bishops and ordinaries (including the now deceased Bishop Vrana[3]) as a spiritual program for the Roman Catholics of Bohemia and Moravia. Cardinal Tomášek[4] and the Catholics turned to all the Christian churches in

2   Or St. Vojtěch, as St. Adalbert is known in Czech. (Ed.)
3   See ch. 7, note 19. (Ed.)
4   See ch. 17, note 2. (Ed.)

the Ecumenical Appeal and especially the Easter Ecumenical Message (1988), appealing for their cooperation in this shared work—cooperation which would not merely be a copy of the Catholic initiative but rather an expression of their own traditions in the name of Christ, which binds us all. We have heard some formal objections from Protestant circles and especially their official representatives about the preparation of the program having been monopolized (I personally suspect them of, if not expediency, then a deficit of realism and wisdom—but I'm happy to allow I'm being unjust in this respect). As a whole, however, the response was positive and it can be hoped that many things have been set in motion in the right direction with regard to ecumenism. The Catholics' largest mass action of recent years (more than 600,000 signatures), Augustin Navrátil's petition for the renewal of religious freedoms,[5] explicitly affiliates itself with the program of the Decade of Renewal. Many of the first year's activities (the Blessed Agnes pilgrimage, the Novena, the St. Adalbert pilgrimage, and so on) were exceptionally successful with many thousands of believers taking part.

The program of the Decade of Renewal has been blessed by Pope John Paul II and is supported by many leading personalities of the Christian world. The Roman Catholic Church of Slovakia and of most of our neighbors (especially those whose spiritual tradition is marked by the activity of St. Adalbert) were unequivocally positive in their welcome, ranging from solidarity in general to direct participation in individual actions (for the most part, certainly in spirit or in prayer).

But how should we understand this program; or rather, how do I propose we understand it?

It is definitely a program of "spiritual renewal," that is, a search for "conversion" in the biblical sense of the word, for realization, for the deepening and intensifying of the Christian position. Some of the participants and initiators of this program burn with impatience for us at last to be settled down in prayer and on our knees before God, as it seems this is "the only essential." Prayer is certainly something we cannot manage without (chiefly, without the faith in God's assistance that is the basis of prayer). However, allow me to doubt whether prayer remains essential

5   See ch. 9, note 25. (Ed.)

when proclaimed the *only essential*. The one thing Czech Catholicism, for centuries at least threatened by sickness, is definitely not suffering from is a lack of prayer, fervor, and humility before God. It suffers rather from a lack of truth (which means moving away from Christ) and from its inability to carry out the second part of the first and most important commandment—that is, love for one's neighbor, and hence a thirst for justice and responsibility in a world which was good when God created it and entrusted it to man. I thank God for all the monks, pilgrims and other good people who pray for the salvation of the world and of my wretched soul, which would be lost without their intercessions. I thank too these people themselves, for without their intercessions God's patience with His unfaithful world could come to an end. However, those who seek above all their own salvation (for whosoever will save his life shall lose it), those who concentrate on the care of their *own* soul, who think of prayer as a symbolic washing of hands and an escape from the disloyal and sinful mass of people, they might as well be pietistic heretics rather than Catholics and Western Buddhist obscurantists rather than Christians.

Perhaps then my interpretation may be acceptable, that this program should have a "selfless" orientation and rise above the context of individual salvation, that it should be oriented towards "the people" rather than towards an exclusive intellectual society. According to this interpretation, the program should be vigilant with regard to the severity and optimism of the current age—indeed, without this vigilance every program beyond the message of the Gospel is mere audacity. Like it or not—for the word nation is already in the title—it has to be accepted that the Decade of Renewal is a program of re-evangelization of the Czech Lands and must have first and foremost the nature of a mission. It has to turn to the masses, where one part of the vast majority never heard the joyful tidings of the Gospel, while the other (larger) part has been successfully immunized against it. Remember, moreover, that this program is not about the re-evangelization of Albania, or of France, but of the Czech Lands with their—at best—ambivalent experience with Christianity and its historical forms. Perhaps we are on the best path to overcoming this ambivalence; but it would be ruinous if we wanted to get there by denying and forgetting our own historical experience.

Without wanting to involve myself in the craft of mission experts, I think that traditional mission fields can be divided into roughly three categories. In the first, the missionary encounters a culture in which a natural religious sense is predominant, expressed only to a limited extent and also deformed only to a limited extent (i.e., "pagan" in the proper sense of the word). The main task here is to proclaim God and God's truth, available only through revelation. In the second, the missionary encounters a highly developed and cultivated religious sensibility which is at the same time deformed and sometimes quite treacherous and hostile towards God. Here he has to proclaim the true God as a replacement for the false gods, and his chief argument should be the joyful and liberating tidings of the Gospel of Christ. In the third, the missionary encounters a highly cultivated religious sense rooted in the true revelation and the acknowledgment of the true God—but nevertheless incomplete and not in agreement with church doctrine. The question mark hanging over what the missionary should do in this case becomes ever more pronounced. After the Second Vatican Council, which replaced the prayer for the conversion of the Jews with a prayer for them to maintain their loyalty to their acknowledged (Old Testament) form of God, and which speaks of an ecumenical dialogue rather than missions to our "separated brethren," and of the shared efforts of all Christians for unity, it seems as though this will no longer be a field for classic mission activity. I would just mention, by the way, that traditional militant atheism can fit quite satisfactorily into the second category.

The task of mission today is seen quite differently in our country—in a way until now unusual in history. This way provides extraordinary opportunities, but also dangers and difficulties until now unprecedented. The issue is not only that the religious sensibilities grounded in human nature have been abused, deceived and deformed. It is true that people continue to bow to a variety of gods and idols: television, sport, the building of solitary castles in high-rise apartments, luxurious cottages and in venom-producing gardens, and power in itself (containing neither meaning nor aim). However, unlike the Old Testament backsliders who took refuge in these gods and idols from lack of faith, dissatisfaction over the severity, jealousy and absolute demands of the Lord God and at the same time from mere expediency (at first sight well-calculated), the inhabitants of this land in our day and age bow down before their idols bereft of all hope; television is ever more idiotic, sport ever more corrupt, the privacy of apartments and cottages falls victim to ecological catastrophe, power is ever more powerless with regard to anything other than cruelty and injustice. People use a variety of opiates which cure nothing; all they do is ease the pain for a moment, which they know very well. The old Marxist and atheist motto, that religion is the opium of the people, has had its paradoxical fulfillment; without religion, even imperfect, opium is all that remains to mankind —a somewhat camouflaged but all the more definitive death.

Any program of renewal in our conditions, whether for an individual or a group, is faced with a cruel and inevitable choice whose consequences cannot be avoided: one chooses either the pursuit of one's own salvation, retreating into the mentality of the ghetto and its confinement; or, in accepting the broadest and most absolute mission obligation connected with risking one's own salvation and share in the Kingdom of God, the pursuit of salvation for one's loved ones and fellow believers—but also for one's neighbors (and enemies) in all their corporeality, discomfort and hopelessness. I hope my presentation of the choice is so tendentious a Christian will find it virtually impossible to subscribe to the first option. If it comes to that, the Decade of Renewal program, proclaimed for the idea of the renewal of the *nation*, has already made its Christian choice. The only thing is, that theoretical choice and general declaration is merely the first and smallest difficulty. I am writing this essay with the intention of showing the logical outcomes to which such a choice leads, and the number of serious difficulties and risks it will inevitably beget.

It is better to speak of the re-Christianization of Czechoslovakia rather than its re-evangelization. A necessary condition for its effective and above all permanent re-Christianization is cultural renewal in the broadest sense of the word (incidentally, the monks of times of yore did not see anything strange in beginning with the cultivation of the land, social conditions and agricultural techniques; according to legend, St. Procopius, to whom one of the years of the Decade of Renewal is dedicated, ploughed a stony valley before he began to plough the fallow land of the human soul). Such cultural renewal can only be accomplished with a renewal of the community and society, with the rehabilitation of civil (which is merely the Czech translation of the word "political") life in the full sense of the word. I will therefore try to disprove the objection that for many people the Decade of Renewal is only a dignified pretext for expressing their political discontent and that it loses its inner quality and even (so important and desirable!) controllability wherever it deviates from mass appeals and is let loose on previously unchartered territory. I will try therefore to establish that without this "political" and mass dimension the Decade of Renewal would only be a hopeless folly—not foolish enough to become a stumbling block to the wisdom of this world, yet too cautious and opportunist to intervene seriously in the course of this world.

Let us disregard—yet just mention in passing—the truism that renewal is change (and by definition a not unimportant change) and that in a state with totalitarian aspirations even the slightest change, when not dictated from the center of the totalitarian power, becomes a political action *par excellence* which threatens the very essence of totalitarian power and provokes the whole range of its defensive reactions. This is so whether we like it or not, and even if we naively assured the authorities a thousand times over that we had no intention of making the slightest change to existing power conditions. One has either to submit oneself unconditionally to the violent and totalitarian power which sees a threat in every shadow and every free breath, or to confront it and to pit real strength against it (even if this is "mere" moral strength, for even that has shown many times in the history of Christian civilization how effective it can be). What is without any sense at all is to try to persuade the power that we mean well, and that we intend to limit its monopoly (its very essence!) only in its very own interest.

Let us look in more detail at the principle on which the power relied for decades and by which it ensures its smooth operation in this country (in this country especially; as in this tactical respect, totalitarianism displays plenty of significant nuances in the lands of "Real Socialism").[6] This decisive *modus operandi* of Czechoslovak totalitarianism is the atomization of society, the mutual isolation of individuals and the destruction of all bonds and facts which might overcome the isolation and manipulability of the individuals, which might enable them to relate to some sort

6   See ch. 6, note 8. (Ed.)

of higher whole and meaning and thus determine their behavior in spheres beyond pure self-preservation and selfishness. I like to use the image of an "iron curtain" lowered not only between East and West, but also between the separate countries of the East (it is very noticeable that our contacts with the West increasingly take the form of an absolute idyll in comparison with the difficulties and adversity we encounter in establishing direct relationships with people from other Eastern countries), between separate social classes and groups, between separate communities, regions and enterprises. But iron curtains were and are lowered inside communities and enterprises too, and—when it comes down to it—even within families (we'll leave aside curtains around individuals and in their inner selves, whose functioning would require a more subtle analysis). The magic formula "democratic centralism" rules out horizontal ties on any level (Vasil Bil'ak's political autobiography[7] demonstrates almost anecdotally how strictly these ties were always forbidden, even at the level of that supreme and allegedly collective organ of power, the Presidium of the Central Committee of the Czechoslovak Communist Party—incidentally, if I am not mistaken, the ban on "factional activity" dates from Lenin's time). Hand in hand and in simple logical connection with the destruction of all social bonds is also the denial of any sort of truth which would be just somewhat impersonal and beyond current practical utility (not long ago I was shocked by young students' simple unfamiliarity with orthodox Marxist terminology—even in *their own* schools they no longer try to *pretend* they are presenting some truths), the collapse and reduction of all values to nothing, the denial of any sort of order, morality and responsibility and eventually the particular perversion of freedom (that supreme gift of God), which is tolerated or even preferred only as mere license and arbitrariness. Many other things whose preservation and repair I consider essential in the context of renewal have of course been destroyed completely or partially. However, I cannot enlarge on specific issues here. Over the forty years of its operation there is nothing the

---

7 Vasil Bil'ak (1920–2014) was a Stalinist member of the Politburo of the Czechoslovak Communist Party and one of the signatories of the letter to the Soviet Politburo that asked the Soviet Union to invade Czechoslovakia in 1968. (Ed.)

Communist totalitarian regime in Czechoslovakia can point to that could be considered to be its incontestable and specific contribution—even an improvement in the quality of spaghetti, for example. There is no sphere—be it, let us say, the incidence of bats—which has not been negatively affected by this regime (many of my friends with a Marxist anamnesis will find this hard to listen to—but they have not yet been able to demonstrate a convincing antithesis one way or the other). If there are any undoubted facts in this world, one of them is certainly the conviction of the overwhelming majority of the population of this country that Communism is the gift of the devil. Unfortunately, no answer to "what next" emerges from this conviction, no answer to how to crush or at least outwit this devil. It is doubly unfortunate that not even a resolution that something has to be done emerges from it (for where a resolution emerges, an answer is always found—with the help of God, or from simple common sense).

It has in the end been demonstrated (to the ridicule of all those Enlightenment and Socialist schemes based on a profound contempt for the masses who—without a universal education and a vanguard with revolutionary awareness (i.e., the Communist Party)—are materialistic purely in an earthly way) that in fact we are all, to the very last one of us, created in the image of God rather than in the image of the Socialists, and that man does not live by bread alone. From time to time he would even prefer to accustom himself to do without bread rather than without other, equally good, gifts: his freedom, dignity, responsibility, sense of being and his love-based community. The Catholic Church is practically the only structure left in this society which has been able to survive the destructive pressure of totalitarian power (albeit with numerous scars and compromises and at the price of innumerable victims) without being destroyed, or becoming the more or less compliant instrument of that power. Catholics remain the only significant strength that is relatively well-organized and relatively independent of the totalitarian state.

That has brought with it amazing advantages and a kind of boom: conversion to, or at least flirting with, Christianity, has become almost a social requirement and fashion statement, especially among young people. However, it carries its own responsibility and problems, and in many respects unease too. If we, as Catholics, have defined the program

Decade of the Spiritual Renewal of the Nation in a time of national crisis and simultaneously during a "Catholic boom," we have in so doing taken full responsibility on ourselves; we have announced that we want to solve problems and to overcome perplexity. If some believers come to us just because we are the last consistent opponents of totalitarianism we should not stop being that; we should however assure our brothers that following Christ is something that goes considerably and forever beyond mere resistance and opposition. If young believers come to us (just as frequently) affirming that knowing Christ and meeting Christ has solved all their practical problems, that is, made them less significant, we have to object that Christ came not to abolish the law but to fulfill it, and that love for God and love for one's neighbor form one indivisible commandment. If the Church is to accomplish her mission successfully in this country, in a situation of general collapse and confusion of natural morality, she has not only to preach the Gospel but also to carry out tasks to which in other circumstances she would ascribe only a secondary meaning, or not even concern herself with at all.

Included here are traditional problems of morality at work and in the family and of sexual morality, although their labeling has changed considerably; for example, one cannot elevate as a Christian virtue the zeal of a clerk at the Ministry of the Interior, of workers on projects damaging to the environment or the community, or students spending the summer in a variety of meaningless activities (work practice and brigades which only distract them from their true calling). In such circumstances one cannot pillory even pure laziness as a sin, for often, albeit somewhat unheroically, it prevents much greater sin. It is just as important (still a stumbling block, especially for traditional Catholics) for the sinfulness of a low-cut dress, the conception of a child out of wedlock, and the abortion of this child before it is born, to be judged by completely different yardsticks. Christ teaches that whosoever looks on a woman with lust has committed adultery. However, He also says that "her sins, which were many, are forgiven; for she loved much."[8] And He addresses an unprecedentedly harsh curse to whosoever "shall offend one of these little ones."[9] How can you imagine

8   Luke 7:47–50. (Ed.)
9   Matthew 18:5–6; Mark 9:42. (Ed.)

a worse way of offending them than aborting a small unborn child before it can accept its own free responsibility for its fate and before it receives the fullness of the hope of a Child of God through baptism (these innocent ones, of course, receive the baptism of blood, for they can do nothing other than deliver painful testimony before their Creator, and are thus transported immediately to stand by His throne—that does not, however, exculpate their murderers in any way)? It should be made abundantly clear that a sinful sexual life and scorn for the sanctity of marriage are indeed wrong; but that to carry an illegitimate child to full term and to give it an orderly upbringing represents repentance and sacrifice, in the light of which the most pitiful penance for the murder of an unborn child merely represents a reckless reliance on God's mercy. (I have written somewhat extensively on the subject of abortion because I always consider it crucial both theologically and politically; a subject on which both good and evil spirits will define themselves and which will eventually decide the nature and ends of our civilization.)

Traditional charitable and social works also belong here; here too, however, we have to be vigilant to ensure that the Church does not sanctify another intensification of repression camouflaged by social interest (see for example sins against the property of a neighbor, or the immoral and still more immorally abused law about parasitism[10]—immoral in itself and still more immoral when abused). Nor should it accept (not even as the lesser evil) those forms of charity which are highly ineffective, whilst the regime carries them on in a pronounced anti-Christian and anti-humanist spirit: from the utterly tragic children's homes, through the completely inadequate care for the sick and handicapped (based on a deep contempt for everyone who cannot be quickly healed and "fit for work") as far as the old folks' homes which begrudge access to a priest in every possible way and where the personnel (financially dependent on their "success") are capable of bullying miserable old women with hunger, just to dissuade them from taking the sacrament.

The issue of education and art belongs here too, one in which the Church has traditionally involved itself; however, in our times and conditions of civilization, more just in the form of some sort of

10   See ch. 5, note 3. (Ed.)

"superstructure" on "secular" education and art whose autonomy has had to be respected for several centuries, and therefore in the form mainly of religious education and art directly connected with divine worship. However, the educational system in Czechoslovakia, from primary level to university, is in deep crisis and its state is deteriorating day by day. It is difficult to say what share the instinctive effort of the regime to block its citizens' access to the truth and the free use of reason has in that, and what share its profound inability to organize anything at all, as well as its lack of foresight, manifested as scorn of everything which does not have a direct impact in the current year of the presently running Five-Year-Plan (which will not be fulfilled anyhow). Despite my cynicism with regard to the absurd possibility of "Real Socialism," I was a bit shaken when I read in the daily and specialist press recently that the newest (and very radical) education reform has virtually collapsed, and yet apparently we may not "make a scapegoat" of them (i.e., the well-meaning originators of the reform). Moreover, among those judging the extent of this disaster and proposing yet another educational reform in this unending line, will be eighty percent of the very same representatives who initiated the disaster—a great recommendation, both for the objectivity of their analysis and for the quality of the new solution! When an architect's badly designed house falls down, he may be sentenced, but at least he will certainly be struck off the architects' register. Here, however, we are not allowed to "make a scapegoat" of those who have condemned a whole generation to a substandard education. In this century especially it has been convincingly shown that while, with the help of God and thanks to human skill, what seemed to be irreparable damage by war, economic failure or ecological disaster can be erased in an inconceivably short time. On the contrary, where human skills, education and cultural traditions are lacking, not only God's help fails to come, but even billions of petrodollars cannot help. Well, maybe our children will be able to cope with the prefabricated high-rise blocks which are going to collapse after a few decades (more exactly, they will become uninhabitable and undemolishable) and with the other atrocities we grandly bequeath to them. But they can hardly cope with the fact that we have not only sinfully squandered the treasures of knowledge accumulated over hundreds of generations, but that we have arrogantly and illegally disinherited our children with regard to the reduced remainder which survived our disastrous management. When it comes to art, we will content ourselves with saying that if it is not concerned with truth and freedom (two different and frequently antithetical things, for whose balance artists for the most part fight bitterly), it ceases to be worthy of its name. Even here the church cannot remain merely a generous and non-puritanical supporter of art directly connected with divine worship, or at least in the wider sense of the word declaring glory to God (that was always in its history). The Church should be the protector of every true art against the prohibitions imposed by power and manipulation (as has happened in neighboring Poland in many cases); we know very well that it is not only human dignity, freedom and the desire for truth that are substantially interfered with by the suppression of art, but also our "creation in the image of God"—that is, the possibly of sharing in His work of creation at least to a modest extent (this possibility can emerge in a fuller form in parenting—physical and spiritual—but apparently nowhere else). The Church in her wisdom (endowed by the Holy Ghost, and—just a wee bit—by thousands of years of experience) knows that every human destiny and every human possibility is marked by the burden of inherited sin, but it knows at the same time—and at its greatest festival sings of the "fortunate fall (*felix culpa*)"—that it would be folly and the sin of sins to reject this destiny and these possibilities for their sinful potential, and to fall into despair.

Many other tasks, often no less important, are included here. I cannot lay claim to have mapped them completely, since I consider the ignition of the first lights in the darkness to be a more hopeful step towards its removal than even the best public lighting project planned for the future.

There are however tasks which are completely new for the Church which belong here and have become a persistent stumbling block. Above all, the duty to contribute somehow to society itself: not simply in some special tasks (care for the poor and abandoned, for the sick and the powerless, for morality and justice) which society in its sinfulness does not fulfill, or fulfills only inadequately, but also in its very essence, in care for the mere existence of civil and secular society as such. Society itself, and its most fundamental functions and support (for example, the family), were in part deliberately destroyed by the totalitarian regime, in part deformed to the point of being unrecognizable. I once described this task in a different context as building a "parallel polis." A flight into the ghetto will certainly not enable it to be realized, nor will joining an exclusive society of the "enlightened," "converted" or "just," whether in a Christian or in a civic sense. This society can, and clearly must, become an important first step on the path to the true renewal of society—insofar as it shows itself able to deny itself, to take up Christ's Cross and to follow Him. Let me be clear: Christ's Cross is above all *our cross today*—He did not suffer on the Cross for His own sins but for ours; to follow Him means to go where he leads us, now to Mount Tabor[11] and another time to Golgotha. On the one hand, it is true that without true conversion, without peace in one's heart and among one's loved ones, no real peace is possible either among citizens or among nations. On the other hand, salt which is not sprinkled has no flavor, and the seed must die to give rise to new life; and if I understand the program of the Decade of Renewal correctly, it expresses the resolution of our Christians not to be salt sprinkled in vain, or infertile seed (nor even safely buried talents), but to take the risk of sharing in Christ's sacrifice. I think uncertainty and risk are things that belong to the most fundamental instances of Christianity. In that I oppose both the highly sophisticated atheists who reject faith as a mere crutch to avoid human responsibility, and the naïve young converts who, in accepting Christ, see an end to all their problems rather than the beginning of a journey on which they must face much more serious problems and undertake risks going beyond the context of their earlier existence. If one of the last words from Our Lord on the Cross ("My God, my God, why hast Thou forsaken me?") is filled with doubts, where can we sinners, if we want to follow Him in the end even into that suffering, gain assurance that we will be spared from doubt? The experiences of the martyrs who, beginning with Peter, fell so many times at the start, and the experiences of the profoundest Christian mystics, their "dark night of the soul" are evidence of something quite different.

---

11 Mount Tabor (the Mount of Transfiguration) is a hill in Galilee, Israel, on the summit of which Christ revealed His Glory to three apostles (Matthew 17:1–9, Mark 9:2–8, Luke 9:28–36). (Ed.)

A somewhat dual form of this task is that which is often spoken of as the "civic transcendence" of Christians and, in the end (though with some limitations), the Church as well. At first sight this "civic transcendence" does not appear to be a serious problem, since predominantly it concerns matters to which in olden days the Church devoted a large part of its attention and activity. However, two circumstances render this problem non-trivial.

On the one hand, whatever this activity may be, whatever expression of love for one's neighbor reaching beyond the sacral space and mutual courtesy in the queue for the Eucharist, in the conditions of the totalitarian state it is *de jure* and *de facto* forbidden as something subversive or at the very least suspicious. If I may, however, paraphrase the New Testament saying: If Caesar claims everything, including the things of God, then he is not entitled to anything. The second—and in my opinion more serious—amending circumstance comes from the fundamental obligation of individual Christians and the Church as a whole to make sure that both their words and deeds proclaim Christ's truth, that is, the living, complete and free of sin. It is the sure duty of the Magisterium of the Church to lead believers in matters of faith and morals (that is, in virtually all matters mentioned above) and admonish them where they falter and sin. However, it would be hypocrisy, and would make a mockery of the Magisterium, if the Church called believers to Christ's truth, and at the same time were to kowtow in devotion to a regime established fundamentally on lies, and if it approved the regime's enforcement practices (or simply kept quiet about them) with whose help it tries to turn all its subjects into fellow participants and fellow culprits in its great lie. Maybe the fact (power naturally uses even much more subtle and far-reaching methods) that by participating in so-called elections and other manifestations, believers give *carte blanche* to all subsequent evils including their own discrimination and persecution, should be a reason for their pastor to warn believers against such pacts with the devil—or if they lack heroic virtue, at least keep a dignified silence and not confuse the conscience of their flock with mistaken casuistry. It applies no less to a number of other commandments as well (Thou shalt not kill! Thou shalt not commit adultery! Thou shalt not steal! Thou shalt not bear false witness!), whether understood purely as a prohibition, or positively (as the themes of the

Decade of Renewal try to do). The Church cannot harshly require believers to fulfill these basic postulates of God's Law and Natural Law and at the same time remain blind with regard to her own ostentatious and offensive infringement by the state (and we know from the Gospels that offence is more serious and much less forgivable than mere sin)—let alone accept this breach with enthusiasm as a step forward on the path of the history of salvation.

The situation is such that the Church—especially in the context of the Decade of the Spiritual Renewal—cannot stay silent about the fact that the roots of many evils stem directly from the intentions and practices of the totalitarian power, and it cannot exhort believers to display traditional obedience towards the secular authorities nor rebuke them for disobedience; at least not in matters in which the orders or intentions of the authorities are quite clearly aimed against both divine and natural law. An inseparable part of renewal is the emancipation of the Church from totalitarian power (if not direct antagonism), as is symbolized rather than specified in the requirement for the separation of Church and state. It would be sad if that emancipation—that is, "separation"—should turn into a compromise based on the formula: If you don't meddle in our affairs, we won't meddle in yours. Sad and unreal on both sides: for the Church is the community of the people of God living its earthly destiny, and though it testifies mainly to a different kingdom, it cannot deny shared responsibility for matters of this world, including political matters—while totalitarian power would cease to be totalitarian if it renounced its claim to some part of society or to some area (even a purely spiritual area) of life. In my opinion then, not only is a gulf between Christianity and any kind of totalitarianism inevitable, but every attempt to bridge it amicably seems like something immoral. That does not mean that the Church as an institution could and should play the role of the political opposition *vis-à-vis* the totalitarian state; it must maintain its own identity with regard to the state and must emphatically and persistently reject totalitarianism's sinful claim to things that belong only to God (and, of course, I do not mean only sacrifice and divine worship, but every inappropriate expropriation of God's creation, whether it concerns nature or man in his dignity, freedom and moral order regardless of whether the person involved is a Christian or a pagan). The Church, however, must not demand for itself secular power nor bind its believers to the realization of any specific political model.

In times of need the Roman Catholic Church, if it is not to betray its own mission, must take on itself responsibility for the fate of society and the possibility of its reform, even if this reaches far beyond its normal remit. In this sense the Decade of the Spiritual Renewal of the Nation must not to be construed as some narrowly conceived pastoral task of a hierarchical Church and its Magisterium, but rather as a general program of *renewal*, in which every Christian has the apostolic right and duty to participate and which concerns the whole nation; a program whose integral component is the struggle against all obstacles which prevent full development of a Christian and thus a truly human life.

The present situation is, and apparently will remain for some time to come, strange and unnatural. The Church as a hierarchical church and Magisterium, which should keep itself apart from matters too secular and at the same time be a passionate fault-finder of all sins and excesses of the world and a bearer of tranquility, unity and meaningful hope and which should be some sort of third force, not neutral in any way but standing above particular party positions, and inclining to the greatest justice—such a Church does not exist in this country at present. On the one hand, the state in its totalitarian claims refuses to recognize any sort of independent partner (even though its kingdom is not of this world); on the other, the hierarchical structure of the Church has been deliberately destroyed and today too much is piled on the shoulders of one man, the ninety-year-old Cardinal Tomášek.[12] Even the Church as the people of God—whose every member is connected with the earthly destinies of their nation and their homeland (although not only with those) and bears the appropriate share of responsibility for them, cannot fully function in our country today—for the totalitarian state harshly suppresses every expression of this civic responsibility, and especially every attempt by independently thinking Christians at a shared, and thus socially relevant, activity. That is why it is for the time being essential that the strange and, in many respects, onerous alliance between the Church hierarchy and civic or politically involved Christians remains; if one of these

12 The original text speaks only of the "primate." (Ed.)

partners breaks this alliance—whether in the hope of more favorable treatment or in an attempt to express their own position more clearly— they surrender themselves in the end to looting and bondage. This is my protest against political clericalism and against shepherd-clerics who, for the supposed advantage for the Church, expose the flock entrusted to them, or even just any of their neighbors, to the mercy of a still fundamentally hostile power. As long as external pressure is no less of a threat than our own sinfulness, it is necessary to confront it hand in hand. The more successful the process of renewal becomes and the further it advances, the more the totalitarian claim on the individual and society will be shaken, and the larger will be the space for clear differentiation between the positions of the Church and the position of the politically engaged Christians, between purely spiritual renewal and the renewal of civic, national and patriotic virtues. If, with the help of God and through our own efforts we arrive at that period, a sharp dividing line will have to be drawn between the Church and (let us say) the Christian Democratic Party. In our country, however, at this moment, not even the Church, not even the civic "opposition," engages in anything resembling politics in the usual (and unfortunately extremely profaned) sense: the mere defense of fundamental human rights, including the natural right to life in a decently ordered society respecting the moral principles and dignity of each individual. In recent days John Paul II clearly proclaimed (in a speech to the European Commission for Human Rights) that the defense of human rights is an indivisible and essential part of the Church's mission on earth.

A postscript on the earthly importance of pilgrimages

An important feature of the first year of the Decade of Renewal was the effort to renew the tradition of the great pilgrimages in Bohemia and Moravia (after the good Slovak example). I would very much like this endeavor, faced with the usual teething problems and under the pressure of increasing antagonism, not to weaken, but rather that in future years pilgrimages will become a cornerstone of the program of renewal. It is written that wherever two or three are gathered in His name, there is He in the midst of us—if a thousand or hundreds of thousands are gathered, then we can safely hope in His presence. It is written that whosoever shall confess Him before men, him will He confess also before His Father—for a large part of those hundreds of thousands, the pilgrimage is the best and often the only opportunity they have publicly to confess the things of Christ.

There is something deeply Catholic about a pilgrimage and thus inherently multifaceted: stalls with aids to devotion, shooting galleries and carousels are part of it just as much as a precise liturgy; individual confession and the deep spiritual experiences of small related communities just as much as the somewhat exuberant anonymity of crowds; miraculous pictures and actual miracles just as much as a public manifestation. And so on and so forth. It is not being over-prudent to want to get rid of some of the dimensions of the pilgrimage forcibly; more dangerous and directly anti-Catholic, however, is the effort to reduce the pilgrimage only to one of them. For the pilgrimage is by definition an open-ended journey; we should not find at its conclusion only carousels, without even one universal guide on how to come closer to God and find the way into His Kingdom. The pilgrimage (*pout*) as a journey means above all breaking away (*odpoutání se*) from the confining designation of place, property, social order and, last but not least, fear. However, this is not the same as mindless thrashing out, mere negation and opposition; the pilgrimage means above all following, a steadfast orientation towards that gate where we are advised to plead and knock—maybe even roughly and violently— for it to be opened to us. The pilgrimage is something in that new order of the Redeemer who comes "to fulfill the Law" but in the end "has not where to lay His head."

Christianity is fundamentally an offensive religion: in spite of all its nonviolence and humility, it rejects every kind of aloofness and passivity, and it requires the Gospel to be preached to all nations, witness to be given under every circumstance, and the whole world to be transformed through it. Jesus' entry into Jerusalem at Easter is not only voluntary but even triumphal—the last drop in the politico-opportunist speculation of the Sanhedrin. In this sense pilgrimages, a demonstrative method of following Christ as a mass, are one of the most striking manifestations of Christian offensiveness (and I emphasize, not only Roman Catholic —the Czech tradition is marked by the Hussite pilgrimage). I therefore close this reflection with reference to the traditional Marxist axiom: that the Revolution is defeated the moment it limits itself to defense and puts up barricades around itself. We Christians are in our essence professional revolutionaries, if by revolution we mean a radical turning to Christ, described of old as *metanoia*. And so we wish pilgrimages all the best!

August–October 1988

23

Inherent Risk

The more foolish part of the world falls victim to Gorbymania—a symptom of an advanced stage of the disease known as fear and lack of hope, whether in God or in its own strength. The apparently less foolish part of the world is talking about the twilight and demise of Communism, which will apparently occur inevitably and automatically (if, for example, on Tiananmen Square the Chinese elders proved that their teeth had been impeccably renovated by Western dentists, then that little incident should be as far as possible isolated and forgotten so as not to interfere with the continued development of cordial economic relations accompanied by hopes that Communism will voluntarily deconstruct itself). Finally, the least foolish—again apparently—experts and creators of public opinion occupy themselves chiefly with the problem of whether and how they can protect themselves against the apparent economic bankruptcy of the Communist states on the thorny path from capitalism to capitalism (as Communism was defined in a popular joke). Incidentally, this problem has been made a central argument of the current Communist anti-reform propaganda; it no longer tries to parade any existing or future positives whilst, however, vehemently emphasizing that after the fall of Communism things would be still worse, that there is no way out of the impasse into which it dragged the nations of a certain part of Europe.

I believe that all these predictions rely on completely erroneous assessments of the actual forces and opportunities in play. On the one hand, they fail to realize that the essence of Communism is not dependence on pseudo-rational projections of mankind's future, let alone on rigid ideological dogmas, but that it is purely a matter of power. Only on the basis of this error could anyone make the optimistic assumption that manifest ideological impotence and a practical inability to stand up to international competition would lead to the automatic peaceful abdication of Communism. Lenin once stated that the capitalists willingly sold to him (that is, to the "revolutionary proletariat") the ropes on which they would eventually be hanged. If I were today's Western capitalist, I would include in market research the question as to whether Lenin's less solvent heirs aren't by any chance toying with the idea of obtaining the aforementioned ropes on favorable development credits. I fear the Communists still have certain trump cards up their sleeve in the field of pure execution of power, and that they will not resign themselves as simply as their utter failure in other areas could suggest. On the other hand—partly with ideological intent conditioned by acceptance of, or alternatively through the mere inversion of, Marxist theories—economic difficulties are overrated both in the literal sense of the word and in their impacts in other spheres of the life of society. Historical experience teaches us that not even virtually unlimited injections of petrodollars and development loans are capable of enabling any country of leapfrogging states with a developed (industrial) civilization; indeed, the monetary infusions are often counterproductive (it would be too much of a detour to explain why some East Asian countries manifestly avoid this scheme—we can at least mention that these countries are generally the inheritors of ancient productive civilizations, albeit of a non-European type). However, historical experience also teaches us that a mature civilization cannot be liquidated merely by the destruction of its material wealth (after the Thirty Years' War, Europe rose from the ashes immeasurably stronger than before; after World War II Western Europe was resurrected, maybe with foreign aid, but still within the incredibly short time span of a few years). In the case of Czechoslovakia especially, a country ranked in the past among the foremost of the cultural, civilizational and industrial powers, I think it completely wrong to doubt that there is still a way out of the impasse of Communist economic bankruptcy (which is truly profound) or that there is any possibility of returning to the family of developed nations. Further, we should not think that this possibility is conditional on so many painful concomitant phenomena that it would be more humane to choose a quick death in the smog of power generators and metallurgical conglomerates (which ceased to produce useful outputs a long time ago) than to try to improve conditions.

As a Christian I have to defend the thesis that the acceptance of pain and suffering is the only path through which the world can truly be consecrated and approach the Kingdom of God. However, as a practical politician (certainly not of my own free will), I am convinced that every possibility of fleeing the impasse of Communism brings directly with it illumination and benefit for the majority: even the worst possible choice has to be better than this rule of lies and darkness. In the case of Czechoslovakia I do not doubt that *today* we would still be able to return quickly to the living standard and productivity of developed countries (even without foreign assistance)—I emphasize "today," for the irreversible processes of economic, ecological, political and cultural decline continue at a fast rate and this return (by our own strength) to the family of civilized countries becomes more difficult to realize every year.

Two basic strategic tasks stand before us, more closely linked than might seem at first sight: how to get rid of the totalitarian regime, and how to renew civic society with all its fundamental features from economic prosperity through democratic political life to Christian civilizational and cultural tradition.

Future prospects for the fight against totalitarianism

At first sight these prospects do not seem too hopeful. The crisis is in itself not so acute and perceptible as to drive our nations to spontaneous outbursts of resistance. Although the opposition does have absolute passive support, however, as far as a mass base and organizational maturity is concerned, it can put into play only a fragment of those forces which in neighboring Poland forced the radical questioning of totalitarian policy. The ruling clique is, on the contrary, so enchanted with its twenty-year-old policies of inaction and stagnation, executed under the slogan "after us the deluge," that it is incapable of taking any radical steps even when faced with the threatening catastrophe; it fortifies itself in its luxurious bunkers and its meaningless rhetoric, in the hope that another day may bring some miracle which will return to totalitarian power its undermined certainty and future prospects. Conservative Soviet circles openly encourage our governing comrades in this policy, while Gorbachev remains silent and "does not interfere with internal matters." The extreme Stalinist part of governing circles even dream and speak of some sort of "mini-Peking" which would allegedly solve the problems of declining power—and part of the security and propaganda apparatus is doing everything it can to dramatize the situation and provoke open confrontation. And what is worse: even though, in spite of all the above-mentioned reservations and possible bloody dreams of some holders of power, it is more or less plain that the fall of our present rulers is a question of months rather than years, there is no reasonable reformist alternative in high places, nor even any possible symbolic reformists (in this our situation differs tragically both from the Hungarians and from the Poles). A real danger therefore threatens that even very radical changes in personnel at the summit of power will not only not lead to essential reforms, but on the contrary delay them, since for some time the changes will confuse and weaken pressure from the discontented public. However, the very worst outlooks often conceal a manifest positive. If the leadership is lacking a reform faction —however timid—it is because for the last twenty years at least the Communist Party has consistently built itself up as an association of opportunists based on the principle "you scratch my back and I'll scratch yours," seeing the main danger (which, with its bearer, it liquidates quickly and uncompromisingly) in any sort of policies or crystalised politico-ideological positions at all, without regard to provenance from "left" or "right." However, this also means that our country lacks a part of the party and its apparatuses that would be relevant both sociologically and in terms of power while at the same time so ideologically firm or so desperate that it would be willing to risk a real struggle to maintain totalitarianism. The "Chinese solution" remains an open possibility—naturally, only in the event that the other side will not defend itself and that victory is guaranteed in advance by, in the worst case, the intervention of Soviet tanks. Since neither of these conditions can be reliably fulfilled, this type of solution is extremely improbable. And although the opportunism of today's Communist Party provides small hope for effective reform "from above," it offers that much more hope for reform "from below"; any signals that the current power positions are shaken and that the chances of victory incline towards the "opposition" forces (and such signals are heard ever more clearly) will probably lead to a realignment of forces within the Party and to a hurried attempt to move their bet to the potential favorite. It does have its drawbacks; the opposition is not an opposition in the sense that it would just like to take over the rudder of totalitarian power from the present crew—it is about the human dimension and the definitive abandonment of the totalitarian claim. Similarly, it is not going to be the sort of combatant which, if victorious, would take the role of God upon itself and punish with a merciless hand all the wrongs and injustices of the last forty years. There are quite a few injustices, to be sure; however, revenge—let alone thoroughgoing justice with no trace of mercy—cannot be the starting point and cannot renew the hopes of the nation. Essentially, it is a stalemate: the rulers do not believe they could be forgiven all the horrors they have committed and all the catastrophes for which they bear direct responsibility, and would rather trap themselves bit by bit in still greater horrors and catastrophes just to postpone their downfall from one day to the next. Meanwhile our two nations,[1] face to face with that totally irresponsible clinging to power for power's sake, are ceasing to believe in the possibility of a constructive solution and fix their hopes on an extreme possibility, beginning with complete social and economic collapse and ending with armed resistance.

The next few days (I'm writing these lines in the week before the anniversary of the invasion of 21 August 1968, when the tension in civil society—incited and directly provoked by official propaganda, which is apparently betting on a confrontation and openly threatens bloodshed and terror—is close to exploding) can bring various unexpected denouements. I am however persuaded that neither terror and a state of emergency nor even a pseudo-reformist solution (even if backed up by the still operative symbol of the "Dubček" type) can bring a real denouement. The possibilities of terror are limited by the geographic position of our country; if it is unleashed (which is not completely ruled out), it will be the very accomplices in it who—desirous of an alibi—will quickly and bloodily liquidate the leading players.

The August days passed without any sort of evident denouement.[2] It seems that all the interested parties committed serious tactical errors which only complicated the existing problems. As far as we—the independent representatives of human and civil rights who have gradually and inevitably

1 Benda here speaks of the Czechs and the Slovaks: Czechoslovakia was a federal state consisting of the Czech Republic and the Slovak Republic. (Ed.)
2 This part of the essay was apparently written in September 1989. (Ed.)

become the "opposition" (those quotation marks becoming ever more superfluous)—were concerned, almost all of us were aware of a tragic dilemma in connection with the August anniversary: we could not sit back and do nothing and leave the spontaneous civic discontent to its fate—at the same time, any of our appeals for civic action could become a pretext for terror in the streets and subsequent widespread reprisals with regard to the civic initiatives. We solved this dilemma in an unsatisfactory way: by cautious and half-hearted appeals to peaceful civic protest. Some of us, moreover, often the most prominent, lost our nerve under the pressure of the bloodthirsty official propaganda and at the last moment publicized a point of view which sounded like a repeal of even such minimal protests as we had previously considered essential. The third side, not in any way negligible—that is, Western broadcasters in Czechoslovakia—provided a disservice by, on the eve of the August anniversary, giving completely disproportionate publicity to these capitulating voices as well as to the bloody forecast of various Western commentators. The second mistake made by these stations—which they shared with most Western reporters and commentators but not, fortunately, with either the official or the unofficial commentators from the East—was a notorious distortion of numbers. I explain it this way: when a Western reporter sees 1,000 demonstrators, he judges (rightly) that the official Czechoslovak media will report a hundred eccentrics—yet not wanting his figures to appear exaggerated, he allows for merely 200 demonstrators. However, the "ruling" party failed to take as much advantage from our mistakes as we offered them. On the contrary, it failed to maintain the face of a worthy and credible participant in the European humanitarian process—being involved too much in threatening, prohibiting, arresting, beating and imprisoning people (foreign visitors not excepted). However, it did not succeed in unleashing any really drastic and systematic repression which would—perhaps—have been able to freeze civil society for a while. Instead, out of two possible positions it unerringly chose the one least advantageous for itself; in the eyes of the world it behaved shamefully, emphasizing this by attacks both physical and propagandist on foreigners and reporters, and unloosed serious judicial reprisals against almost the only target it should have avoided hunting down— prominent figures of the Slovak opposition, especially Roman Catholic. I am furious about the imprisonment of my friends Ján Čarnogurský and

Miro Kusý[3] and will strive with all my power for their release and vindication. To be honest, however, I almost envy them at the moment; they are far more likely to experience the glory and authority of victorious symbols of resistance than long years of imprisonment. All serious crises in our two republics turn into catastrophes for the existing regimes at the moment when the fragile balance of ethnic and religious affiliations is inappropriately affected. If we focus on the end of the 1960s, Novotný's regime[4] would maybe not have fallen apart so quickly, in spite of all the discontent, if it had not exacerbated Slovak national feeling; on the other hand, "normalization" in 1969 and the following years would not have had such deep and tragic consequences if it had not relied, at least to start with, on the latent consensus of most Slovaks, obtained through the appealing and utterly deceitful slogan "first federalization, then democratization"—"then" being quickly forgotten, and "first" being a pure formality, for truly equal coexistence between two nations is not possible under totalitarian control. Nevertheless, I repeat: if the arrest and subsequent forced release of Havel[5] could still be interpreted as the existing regime's deliberate—albeit unsuccessful—strategy, the arrest of the prominent Slovaks should be understood as a totally suicidal act through which the regime reduces its political acumen to pure nihilism, to a desire to be destroyed absolutely and without remainder. Today it will seem more like a tragi-comedy if the allegations against these people can be so skillfully prepared that they are sentenced

---

3   Ján Čarnogurský (b. 1944) was a lawyer who defended dissidents put on trial. Consequently he was barred from practicing law. As a Catholic he was also involved in the underground church. After his arrest on August 14, 1989, he was released through a presidential amnesty on November 25. After 1989 he became a leading figure in the Christian Democratic Movement and served in a variety of governmental positions in the Slovak Republic including Minister of Justice. Miroslav Kusý (b. 1931) was also a Slovak dissident who served as Chairman of the Federal Press and Information Office of Czechoslovakia after 1989. (Ed.)

4   Antonín Novotný (1904–1975) served as First Secretary of the Central Committee of the Communist Party from 1953 to 1968 and as President from 1957 to 1968. (Ed.)

5   Václav Havel was incarcerated from January 17 to May 17, 1989. He was arrested for "incitement" for his participation in a memorial demonstration for Jan Palach. (Ed.)

to ten years' punishment instead of five; for they will leave prison in great glory, and leave it not in judicial time but political—and *that* will run out for their opponents very quickly.

Prospects of renewal

In spite of all my initial doubts, the description of the prospects of the struggle with totalitarianism sounded in the end relatively optimistic; totalitarianism itself has degenerated so much that in spite of all our inadequacies and errors it leads us step by step to inevitable victory. Only our task is different and more far-reaching; it is not only anti-Communism, although I consider that to be a worthy and, in our conditions, a morally obligatory position. Our duty is to establish (and establish quickly) a dignified and viable replacement for the previous general morass. Something like that cannot be done quickly, yet nevertheless it must be done quickly and radically, indeed, with a surgical precision if it is to have at least the slightest hope of success. A major role can be played here by the Decade of National Spiritual Renewal announced by the Roman Catholic Church and accompanied by an ecumenical appeal to the minority churches and to non-Christians—as long as it does not become too much of a spiritual matter, so that in the name of private improvement and salvation we ignore the desperate state of society and renounce serious efforts to change it (with a somewhat unchristian, but definitely not unjustified acknowledgement of the disproportionate risks). It will be no less important for help from the West not to be premature and hasty, and to show itself at the right moment to be sufficiently generous (not in the interest of humanity in general but in the interest of the West, for whom such a development is a far more trustworthy security guarantee than SDI[6]—not that I want my statement to be interpreted as a criticism of this defense initiative).

The following statement may appear trivial to many, and at the same time ungrounded, but I think all the same it is essential to repeat it. In our

6   The Strategic Defense Initiative (SDI) was a program initiated by President Reagan in 1983. The program was responsible for developing an anti-ballistic missile system to defend the United States from attacks by the Soviet Union. (Ed.)

country it is inevitably necessary (and a vital matter not only to the Communists but also those so far conformist masses who are willing to poison their spirit with lies and their body with horrible poisons, destroying nature and man) to renew civil society and eventually the democratic state with all their virtues and vices: human rights and freedoms and human responsibilities and duties, the chaos of plurality and indispensable order, striving for general prosperity and its real moral limitations. That cannot be done without sacrifices, not only social, and—after the fifty-year-long destruction of all traditions and democratic experiences—it cannot be done without mistakes either. These sacrifices must be born with an awareness that the only alternative is a society-wide catastrophe; we must risk even mistakes with the good hope that it cannot be any worse. Unfortunately it can. And therefore it is a matter of our moral responsibility and civic maturity whether we are able to face up to the evermore brutal deadly spasms of a collapsing totalitarian regime and at the same time not to fall into the temptation of replacing one totalitarianism by another, however well-meant. We have to strive for victory; to be victorious, however, our victory must not be the triumph of new ideologists. Its characteristic must be sobriety and renewal which will take the wind out of the sails of those who will strive for the dominance of their own personalities or their Utopias.

July-September 1989

Part III:
Reports and Defenses

Reports and Notes

24
The Prosecution of Two Roman Catholic Clergymen in Slovakia

I can report the following, based on verified information:

On February 28, 1978, Róbert Gombík (b. July 30, 1949), Roman Catholic priest in Senec, and Marián Zajíček (b. January 23, 1951), Roman Catholic priest in Pezinok, signatory of Charter 77, were held by the StB. At the same time their temporary and permanent residences were searched. House searches also took place at the homes of Marián Zajíček's brother and parents. Both the accused were charged with the criminal act of subversion of the Republic (Art. 98, para. 1 of the criminal code) in the context of criminal proceedings against an unknown offender issued on January 6, 1977, in connection with Charter 77. (That is—as far as I know—a new aspect, among other things contradicting the statement by the official representatives of the Czechoslovak Socialist Republic. The criminal proceedings against that unknown offender initiated on January 6 have, until now, been used to justify interrogations and house searches of signatories of Charter 77, but never for the individual prosecution and sentencing of signatories.) The two priests were released on March 3, 1978; however, criminal proceedings against them have not been dropped and they are being investigated while at liberty.

The two priests committed the criminal act of subversion of the Republic by circulating the original declarations of Charter 77 and the reflections on it by the late philosopher Jan Patočka, spokesman of Charter 77. No written materials connected with Charter 77 were found during the house searches (the StB obtained the materials on which the prosecution is based by unlawful monitoring of correspondence); a typewriter was confiscated, and a large amount of religious materials and other pastoral aids. A curious phenomenon by Czechoslovak standards is the fact that the accused were not deprived of their state license[1] and are allowed to continue in their priestly office.

Each of the accused was subjected to four more interrogations after his release; a number of other people were also interrogated in connection with their "case." The interrogation of the witness Zajíčková (sister-in-law of the accused Marián Zajíček) breached both the Czechoslovak criminal code and elementary humane requirements. Throughout the interrogation the interrogator used a desk lamp to disorient the witness, who is pregnant, and tried to upset and influence her with offensive remarks about her marital life and her husband's possible infidelity.

Among those interrogated in Prague by the Bratislava StB in connection with the case of Róbert Gombík and Marián Zajíček include the singer and poet Jaroslav Hutka, the psychologist Jiří Němec, and probably (the interrogation is scheduled for today) the writer Pavel Kohout.

April 20, 1978

---

1   For any performance of religious office—including confessions—a priest needed state consent. The consent was valid exclusively for a given church building. To perform a mass in a different church or, say, meet with groups of believers elsewhere, was to be guilty of "thwarting state supervision of churches" (Art. 178 of the Criminal Code), a crime punishable by up to two years in prison. (Ed.)

25

Poland and Us

An Interview with Václav Benda, spokesman of Charter 77

How satisfied are you with the present development of cooperation between Charter 77 and the Polish opposition movement represented mainly by the Committee for Social Self-Defense (KSS-KOR)?[1]

Very satisfied. I had counted in advance that corrections would have to be made to the original plans, resulting from too much generosity from one party, too much caution and uneasiness from the other, and the agility of the two police apparatuses involved. I would nevertheless welcome it if permanent working groups were better stabilized from both sides: the current state, founded predominantly on general willingness and good will, provides many interesting impulses but unfortunately gives rise to quite a lot of confusion which, with communication already difficult, we cannot allow.

How do you see the future prospects of this cooperation and what tendency do you think would be decisive?

One possible prospect: supranational unity during food distribution in a Siberian labor camp. Preferred tendency: a decrease in the likelihood of this prospect.

I think the agreements already achieved are an outstanding success, in that our cooperation does not increase the likelihood of the prospect

---

1   The KOR (Komitet Obrony Robotników—Committee for the Defense of Workers) was founded in 1976. In 1977 this organization was renamed as Komitet Samoobrony Społecznej-KOR (Committee for Social Self-Defense). There was some inconsistency in the use of the acronyms referring to this organization in the original Czech—we have altered the text for the sake of clarity. (Ed.)

mentioned above but, on the contrary, lowers it. It seems to me that becoming aware of how our fates and aims are interconnected is a fact (or tendency) of such fundamental importance that the content and form of specific cooperation is secondary and derivative with regard to it. In this spirit, I see the expansion of our work to the civic movements of other countries to be a crucial tendency (and some hopeful initiatives recently appeared in this direction).

Do you see any possibility of cooperation between Charter 77 and KSS-KOR in the preparation of specific documents? What issues should such documents be concerned with?

No. Currently they represent, on the one hand, common aspects and acts of solidarity, and on the other, a theoretical exchange of opinion on the limits of our possibilities. The differences of the social situation in our two countries and its historical roots are so deep that any possible common document would inevitably become bogged down in ineffective and opportune generalities (and I leave out of account the technical difficulties in their creation). Maybe there are two exceptions: a document on the Communist Party and the formal power structure of its operations, and a document on the issue of emigration and relationships towards it. Even these exceptions are not without substantial snags: on the Czech side, the first theme is considered enormously "fiery" and "risky," especially by those who could contribute to its clarification; while on the Polish side the treatment of the second theme would perhaps—I am of course only guessing—evoke complications.

It's known there were several meetings of representatives of Charter 77 and KSS-KOR in the Krkonoše Mountains last year, where further possibilities of cooperation were debated. A discussion arose among signatories of Charter 77 regarding these meetings. Some said that this sort of contact is impractical and too risky. They pointed out what had happened to a spokesman for Charter 77, Dr. Jaroslav Šabata,[2] on one of these occasions. What do you think?

2   Jaroslav Šabata (1927–2012) was a Czech dissident and political scientist. He was a signatory of Charter 77 with the first group and served as a spokesman from April 6, 1978 to October 1, 1978. On October 1, 1978, when attending one of these meetings in the mountains, Šabata was taken to the police station

Because of the doubts expressed, I am going to speak more broadly and very openly on the question. In its early phase at least, this form of contact has been essential and very much worth the risk. Meanwhile, the truth is that the latest (failed) meeting was more the fruit of friendly enthusiasm than urgent working necessity. We knew in time that Czechoslovak security had carried out an extensive preliminary raid in the border mountains and that Polish security probably even had specific information about our plans. Moreover, the Czechoslovak participants to a man failed to maintain some of the previously agreed security precautions. Judged from the purely conspiratorial point of view, the meeting was thus dangerous and pointless.

However, if we apply such a yardstick, Charter 77 is just as pointless; what sort of conspiracy publishes the names of its participants and conscientiously provides the authorities with the results of its work? I'm therefore emphasizing that our actions—including contacts with the Polish KOR—were and are legal, that Charter 77 emphasizes its insistence on the maintenance of and respect for the law. The fact that the state power is not interested in observing its own laws is of course another story, one which in itself carries a certain risk for our work (indeed, at the very least those seventy-five percent of the signatories who signed Charter 77 subsequent to its public launch were clearly aware of these risks). The failed meeting acquired greater importance than all the others, for it demonstrated that the police forces of two states have to be mobilized to prevent a friendly meeting between a few citizens on the path of Czechoslovak-Polish Friendship, and that an embarrassing and illegal farce has to be staged to trap the spokesman of a civic initiative for upholding human and civil rights—a farce with a scenario in which a fifty-year-old university professor

on the Czech-Polish border village of Velká Úpa for the formal reason that his identity card had to be checked. When he attempted to destroy a document that he and his fellow dissidents had been drafting, he was forced to strip naked and was beaten by the police. He retaliated by slapping one of the officers across the face. Šabata was then charged under the criminal provision of "gross insult of a public servant." He was sentenced to nine months plus seventeen more from a previous sentence and was imprisoned from the end of 1978 until 1980. (Ed.)

and experienced politician makes a symbolic slap at the trained staff of a police station; any witnesses present who are not already under official subordination are—just to be on the safe side—accused of various criminal acts; and a defense attorney slow to understand what is going on is banned from the legal profession.[3] I'm not saying that its importance is altogether positive: it is undoubtedly difficult to replace even temporarily a personality of the standing of Dr. Jaroslav Šabata.

I envy those who think they know a safer and more effective way to transform society; however, none of them yet have demonstrated the practical effectiveness of their approaches. By signing Charter 77 we have voluntarily set out a path which is definitely not easily passable and secure, and on which we are striving to rectify the worst social ailments, often at the price of testing them on our own skin. Naturally, respect for individual temperament and capability is part of the pursuit of freedom and dignity. I think none of us has the right to reproach those for whom, in the given moment, continuing in the fight is beyond their strength for some reason or other and who, consequently, made an honorable retreat. We don't even have the right to determine for others what a "reasonable" level of risk might be (which already becomes a note to the Vaculík-Pithart debate).[4]

---

3   The "illegal farce" involving Šabata—see previous note. Persons under state employ were under "official subordination" and incapable of being independent witnesses. (Ed.)

4   This debate between Ludvík Vaculík and Petr Pithart (with Václav Havel a participant) was launched with Vaculík's essay "Notes on Courage." Pithart responded with an essay called "The Shoulders of the Few." Vaculík had suggested that young people often did not have a full understanding of the risks involved in dissident activity, so one should be more wary of encouraging people to take risks for which they might not be prepared to endure the consequences. This essay can be found in *A Cup of Coffee with My Interrogator*, George Theiner trans. (London: Readers International, 1987). On the debate, see Jonathan Bolton's *Worlds of Dissent: Charter 77, The Plastic People of the Universe, and Czech Culture Under Communism* (Cambridge: Harvard University Press, 2012), pp. 231–38 (Ed.)

In Poland 4000 signatures were gathered in defense of Kazimierz Świtoń[5] Would Charter 77 be capable of such an action?

Essentially yes, undoubtedly, only it would be at the price of several months' concentration of all our energy. For the Poles, meanwhile, it was just one action among many. There are, indeed, qualitative differences here—but what is not possible today, might be in the future (and further, there are some points in our favor as well).

You are Roman Catholic. In your view, what sort of reception should the choice of the new pope have among Czechoslovak Catholics?

Enormously positive. I think it was universally considered to be a direct and highly improbable manifestation of God's will—or, in our "churchy" terminology, a miracle. Like every miracle, the choice (and ergo its reception) is difficult to evaluate and apprehend if we use only basic arithmetic. Nonetheless most Catholics—from lay people to the upper hierarchy—clearly understand that they are facing a completely new situation and must react to it in a new way. I have tried to estimate the course of this reaction in two extended essays whose contents I cannot do sufficient justice to here.[6] I am however definitely expecting great things (and soundings in appropriate quarters only confirm this for me), including radical transformations of the attitudes of many Catholics towards the Charter 77 initiative and a fundamental strengthening of their role in this civic movement.

As spokesman of Charter 77, do you welcome the journal "Poland and Us"?

I welcome the journal with eagerness and gratitude, both as spokesman and as a private person. In my private capacity, I had serious reservations regarding the content of the introductory informative text. As spokesman,

5   On October 14, 1978 Kazimierz Świtoń was beaten and arrested by plain-clothes police. He was sentenced to a year in prison, but after much publicity by opposition groups and international attention, he was released on March 3, 1979. (Ed.)

6   See chapter 12 of this volume. The other essay to which Benda refers is "Pope Karol Wojtyła, the Catholic Church and the World." Though this essay appeared under Benda's name, its real author was Zdeněk Kratochvíl. (Ed.)

I wish the journal all the best and I hope that through future issues it will soon achieve such variety that even I as a private person will get something out of it.

March 1979

26

Information on the Activities
of Charter 77 Spokespersons
and Forthcoming Materials

The three new spokespersons of Charter 77 (we cannot here speak for the fourth, Dr. Jaroslav Šabata, as he is still held in prison) resolve to stick strictly to the following two principles in their work:

1) In harmony with the calling of Charter 77, to provide information without delay and as effectively as possible about every activity they undertake in its name, both to signatories of Charter 77 and to the general public;
2) To be in permanent working contact with as wide a circle as possible of signatories and supporters of Charter 77; to receive and coordinate their initiatives and as far as possible consult with them on all further working aims.

1) We have held to this principle with all materials published up to now (document no. 24 about freedom of movement;[1] communication about the trial of Jaroslav Šabata and the setting up of the Fund for Civic Assistance;[2] letter to the federal parliament and the federal government on an absolute right of way;[3] telegram to the IKS congress with a request for solidarity with Jaroslav Šabata, who is threatened with 18 months in

---

1   See Blanka Císařovská and Vilém Prečan, *Charta 77: Dokumenty 1977–1989*, Svazek 1 (Praha: Ústav pro soudobé dějiny AV ČR, 2007), pp. 225–40. (Ed.)
2   See Císařovská and Prečan, Svazek 1, p. 223. (Ed.)
3   Ibid., p. 224. (Ed.)

prison[4]). If in some cases, as an exception, we hold back some information on the request of another party, we want always to do it on the basis of a firm, preliminary agreement about the term and form of its publication. We try to ensure that, within the limits of our technical means, we acquaint all those in the circles of both signatories and sympathizers and in the media with the materials of Charter 77 completely and rapidly. We have provided several interviews both jointly and individually; interested parties at home will have an interview available with Václav Benda in the journal *Poland and Us* and with Jiří Dienstbier in *Information about the Charter*. We have decided to publish regular information about our activities in the latter journal. In fact, in the future we want to devote maximum attention to the problem (superficially only a technical one) of how to distribute information. We take this opportunity to ask all signatories who are able and willing to ensure the flow of information to offer their cooperation. We ask all signatories (at home and in emigration) who have the opportunity to influence the work of foreign media to commit themselves to the greater authenticity of published information about Charter 77 (see for example the extremely imprecise news service of the radio station Voice of America). Finally, I ask everyone who provides any sort of information to the foreign media to anticipate the possibility of misinterpretation and to express themselves very advisedly (see for example the article full of disinformation by David Andelman in the *International Herald Tribune*, allegedly based on the opinions of a "former member" of Charter 77). An important role of the spokespersons is to confirm the authenticity of documents; only those signed by the spokespersons can be considered Charter 77 materials. This principle should be maintained by everyone who cooperates with us or passes on information about our activities. We can in this way protect ourselves from confusion or direct abuse (not only by the domestic propaganda, but even by some foreign media), such as recently happened with an article about the deportations of Germans which was completely unjust and not connected with the activity of Charter 77.

2) In the context of this intention, the spokespersons jointly and individually have arranged several meetings with groups of signatories in

4   Ibid., p. 241. IKS is the Italská komunistická strana or the Italian Communist Party. (Ed.)

Prague and elsewhere (Brno, the Ústí region) and are preparing more meetings. We are supporting the emergence of working groups within Charter 77 and want to maintain close contact with already existing groups (VONS, FOP,[5] and groups dealing with Czechoslovak-Polish relations, with conditions at the workplace and other trade unions issues, ecology, and child protection) and to share the preparation of documents and of other activities with them. The same applies to relationships with various samizdat journals, publications and other expressions of the unofficial culture. Insofar as the concept of the actual documents of Charter 77 and the method of their preparation is concerned, we want to revive discussion on this theme and to summarize their conclusions in writing in connection with document no. 21.[6] Meanwhile we intend to apply individual approaches based on the nature of the document in question. When serious discussion contributions are written concerning "controversial" documents (currently a document about nuclear power stations is available), we will publish them promptly under the number of the original document. We are preparing to publish fundamental points on the issue of consumer protection that should become the starting point for a broad public discussion. We would like to reach the point where a standing working group would be formed for each serious issue. The groups would prepare and register materials on the given field, stimulate discussion among both experts and the general public, and keep them informed about how the situation is developing.

March–April 1979

---

5   *Fond občanské pomoci*—Fund for Civic Assistance. It was intended to provide aid for the families of those imprisoned. (Ed.)
6   See Císařovská and Prečan, Svazek 1, pp. 176–78. (Ed.)

27

I Do Not Share Your Conviction …

Reply to the revocation of a signature to Charter 77

Mr. Benda!

I turn to you as spokesman of Charter 77 and at the same time to inform you that by this letter I revoke my signature to Charter 77, the reason being that I do not agree with the concepts of your activity, which are in conflict with my personal conviction. I signed the Charter on impulse and in ignorance of the political connections in today's divided world. For these reasons I would not like my name to be misused by the Charter. I have had the occasion to be convinced that your activity and that of your friends is in conflict with the interests of the Czechoslovak Republic. For these reasons I emphatically request that my name is no longer connected with the activities of the Charter.[1]

Dear Sir!

I am in receipt of your letter of March 26, 1984, in which you inform me, in my capacity as spokesman of Charter 77, that you are revoking your signature to Charter 77. I do not share your conviction that the activity of Charter 77 is in conflict with the interests of the Czechoslovak Republic; nevertheless I fully respect any sort of conviction, as I do the right to change one's conviction on the basis of new information and experience. Since one of your new pieces of information—that is, my district house number—could only have been obtained from the Ministry of the Interior, I fear that the rest of your knowledge of my activities and those of my friends must have come from the same source, which renders any further discussion pointless.

1   A carbon copy of the letter to Benda was found among his papers and is printed here along with Benda's response. (Ed.)

I emphatically object to the claim that your name was misused by the Charter in the past; all our activity strictly maintains the principles of the introductory declaration of Charter 77 of January 1, 1977, to which you once freely attached your signature and from which you distanced yourself only now—we hope, just as freely. I assure you, however, that your name will no longer be linked with the activities of Charter 77 and that the widest circle of my friends will be informed of your standpoint—unfortunately, it is my only available possibility of publication.

I sincerely hope your new decision will be to your advantage and that of your whole circle. Peace be with you.

P.S. It unfortunately often happens that someone who sends me a letter receives a reply in my name without my being in the least aware of any of this correspondence. I am therefore sending this letter by registered post and will ask one of my friends, when the opportunity occurs, to visit you and endorse the authenticity of your letter—providing you do not come to Prague yourself and seek me out in the meantime. Please do not look on my conscientiousness as a form of harassment or any sort of coercion.

April 1, 1984

28

I Turn to You with an Urgent Appeal

Letter to the German Peace Conference

Dear Ladies and Gentlemen, participants in the conference "*Wege zu einer europäischen Friedensordnung*[1]"!

I want above all to thank you most cordially for the generous invitation to your Peace Congress. I apologize for my late reply, but our postal service delivered your letter only after substantial delays.

Unfortunately I will be unable to attend in person, since even if the Czechoslovak authorities did allow me to travel, I would face the very real danger that at the end of the conference I would not be allowed to return to my native land. I am therefore using this method at least to declare my solidarity with the endeavors and quest expressed in the title of your congress. As far as I and my friends are concerned, I can refer you to our attitudes to the peace movement and to the possibility and aims of further dialogue set out in detail in the relevant documents of Charter 77, in particular the letter from Charter 77 to the World Peace Congress ... in Prague in June 1983;[2] the open letter from Charter 77 of November 14, 1983, to the peace movement;[3] and the open letter from Charter 77 of May 1, 1984, to the British peace movement CND/END;[4] as well as to the joint standpoint of several of my colleagues addressed directly to your congress.

---

1 The Way to a State of Peace in Europe. (Ed.)
2 See Blanka Císařovská and Vilém Prečan, *Charta 77: Dokumenty 1977–1989* (Praha: Ústav pro soudobé dějiny AV ČR, 2007), Svazek 1, pp. 520–21. (Ed.)
3 See Císařovská and Prečan, Svazek 1, pp. 557–58. (Ed.)
4 See Císařovská and Prečan, Svazek 2, pp. 619–22. (Ed.)

However, I turn to you with one very urgent appeal, asking you as far as possible to inform participants about the following matter: it is the case of Dr. Ladislav Lis [1926–2000], a courageous member of the anti-Fascist resistance, for many years a leading functionary of the Czechoslovak Youth Union and the Communist Party of Czechoslovakia, later spokesperson for Charter 77 and one of the most active supporters of the idea of the struggle for peace and cooperation with the peace movements in the West—indeed, his activity in this field is not unknown to you, as you invited him to your congress. Last year, on the basis of trumped-up charges that he had tried to spread these opinions among people he knows, he was sentenced to fourteen months' imprisonment (he served the full term in spite of protests from us and the international community). This was followed by another three years of "protective supervision," a kind of internal exile with substantial restriction of basic civil rights, and under strict police supervision.[5] Dr. Ladislav Lis subjected himself in a disciplined way to all these restrictions, even though they were applied to him in a much harsher form than to the most dangerous criminal; even though, for example, the repeated checks at night on his apartment threatened his family life and the mental wellbeing of his children. However, as a consistent advocate of civil rights he flatly refused to comply with commands that have no basis in law and are a mere expression of police arbitrariness and vengeance; for example, the ban on travelling to his country cottage and looking after the animals which are one of the sources of his livelihood.

Not long ago therefore, two months after his release from prison, he was again taken into custody and charged with "obstructing justice"; he is threatened with a trial and renewed imprisonment. He was aware of the danger of persecution and announced in advance that in that case, he would immediately start a hunger strike; however, he is already in prison for his beliefs for the fourth time, his health is undermined, and in the given situation, his life may be directly threatened.

I therefore appeal to all participants in the peace congress: don't allow this honorable man, who for most of his life has selflessly sacrificed himself to the ideals which you yourselves embrace, to be unjustly sentenced and imprisoned yet again. Make use of the importance that the

5   On "protective" or "preventive" supervision, see ch. 5 of this volume. (Ed.)

Eastern powers attach to the peace movement and emphatically demand his immediate release. Try to use your influence on active individuals, various organizations, political parties, or even the governments of your countries and ask them to stand up for Dr. Ladislav Lis.

I thank you in advance for any kind of action you can use to try and prevent this shameful process, and I send my greetings to your congress.

May 20, 1984

29

Notification of Criminal Activity

Letter to the Procurator General of the Czechoslovak Social-ist Republic JUDr. Ján Feješ

Mr. Procurator General!

For the second time this calendar year some men in civilian clothes have visited me in my apartment, identified themselves as employees of the Ministry of the Interior and told me that they have been sent to provide me with protection. This protection consisted of the following: over the next days and nights three men sat in a car in front of my house; should I venture out, they accompanied my every step and anyone I met or who came to visit me was required to produce their identity card. These two occasions coincided with the state visits of the British and French Ministers of Foreign Affairs.

I never asked for any police protection and it seems to me highly unlikely that the Czechoslovak government would invite official guests who would pose a threat to individual Czechoslovak citizens. It is true that the above actions of the members of the security forces did not on the whole exceed the scope of their statutory authority. Nevertheless, I propose you investigate, at least from the point of view of possible economic crime, those who gave the order for this operation—many fellow citizens were outraged by such a patently meaningless waste of state funds which, in the end, comes out of our own pockets.

However, on May 24, 1985 (the second day of the visit of the French Minister) SNB[1] officers stopped any visitors from entering my

---

1   *Sbor Národní Bezpečnosti*: National Security Corps, the uniformed police (distinct from the Státní bezpečnost or StB). (Ed.)

apartment, and not even my wife's brother was allowed to enter. At the same time they refused to give any explanation and answered the polite protests of the visitors by threatening to take them to some unspecified department. I believe such behavior constitutes the offence of unlawful restraint of personal freedom, that is, abuse of office by a public servant, and you can consider this letter as the appropriate notification of criminal acts.

***

At the same time I take this opportunity to turn to you with a request linked to a matter that has not yet been dealt with. In connection with a search of my apartment by members of the StB on August 16, 1984 (and with my subsequent 48-hour detention), I submitted a complaint to you on September 12, 1984, a notification of criminal acts and at the same time a request for the immediate return of the confiscated items. Not only have I not yet received a reply to my letter—which is in conflict with the law on the procurators' office and government regulation no. 130 Ú. 1./1958—but your office has not even confirmed receipt (I cannot consider as an answer the rejection of the complaint I submitted directly to the protocol on house searches; that affects only my assertion, that is, my requirement for the immediate return of items illegally confiscated without objective examination). The StB investigator Cpt. Blaho, who by order returned to me on December 7, 1984, two empty envelopes and two pieces of paper (many thousands of manuscript pages, documents, publications, an address list, typewriter, etc., had been confiscated), took the opportunity to inform me orally that all the other confiscated items were being examined by the Procurator General and that only he (you) could decide about their return. Quite apart from the fact that the majority of these writings could not be connected with the criminal prosecution initiated at that time (because of the distance in time and theme), nine months is perhaps long enough (your office in particular should not ignore one of the basic principles of Czechoslovak criminal law) to review all the connections, and for the singling out of those materials which could be important for further criminal proceedings.

I therefore request that you immediately issue an order for the return of the confiscated items (or that the StB investigator does it, should his oral information have been inexact or false), or else refer the decision in this matter to the appropriate court.

May 30, 1985

30
A Besieged Culture

First question: How does the situation briefly described here affect you personally, from the standpoint of someone (artist, etc.) whose work achieves fulfillment only at the moment when it comes into contact with the public?

Second question: How does this situation affect you as a member of the national cultural community? How do you come to terms with it?

Third question: What practical steps on the part of the state power and its official institutions could provide the beginning of a way out from the existing oppressive and critical situation? Is it within your powers to influence the cultural policy of the state, or to contribute in other ways to overcoming the present situation?

Fourth question: A feature of the intellectual situation in Czechoslovakia is the endeavor by the state institutions to prevent the free flow of intellectual impulses, ideas and information from the rest of the world. What do you miss most of all in this artificially-created isolation? Do you expect any concrete steps by the European Cultural Forum towards overcoming this isolation?

Fifth question: What positive steps by foreign cultural institutions and personalities could, in your view, contribute to overcoming the stagnation in Czeckoslovak culture?[1]

---

1   In the spring of 1985 an introductory text and the above questions were sent to a group of writers, artists, journalists and scholars in Czechoslovakia. The responses were published in English translation in the volume *A Besieged Culture: Czechoslovakia Ten Years after Helsinki*, edited by A. Heneka, František Janouch, Vílem Prečan, and Jan Vladislav. (Ed.)

Let me first of all add two points to your introductory note. The "exceptionally difficult time of crisis" you mention has not afflicted Czechoslovak culture merely in the past 15 years but for no less than 46. The two brief periods when conditions were relatively good are unfortunately only exceptional episodes in a long story of unremitting cultural genocide. For an entire productive life-span scientific and artistic truth has now been stifled and distorted in Czeckoslovakia, artists and scientists imprisoned, executed, exiled, or at the very least forced to do menial labor instead of working in their professions, while the heritage of the past has been filtered through the mesh of rapidly changing ideologies. The only lasting value, and at the same time the most effective argument, has been fear. Let me quote a case in point, much more controversial and less outrageous than many others, but for that very reason perhaps applicable elsewhere and not just in our part of Europe: while working on a certain anti-fascist study (I refrain from giving any details about it, since our political police considers the retyping of a text of Lenin's by one of us to be no less incriminating than the retyping of something by Solzhenitsyn), we badly need to read the actual writings of Nazi ideologues, in particular Hitler, Streicher,[2] and Rosenberg.[3] We discovered, however, that these sources were not accessible in the official libraries, while those specialists who had possessed them had long ago destroyed them out of fears whose intensity (and relevance!) has not diminished with the passage of years. We live in times when monuments are torn down, streets renamed, and convictions changed *en masse*—rarely is this in any way admirable, but it is deeply human. And, who knows, perhaps society does have the right (not very sensible and, as Herostratus' example shows,[4] very difficult to implement) to set the seal of forgetfulness on certain facts. But if an artist or scientist is to praise or condemn something, as they are asked to do, they have first to know what it is they are

2   Julius Streicher (1885–1946) was a German politician and publisher of anti-Semitic propaganda. (Ed.)
3   Alfred Rosenberg (1893–1946) was an important and influential Nazi intellectual whose chief work was *The Myth of the Twentieth Century*. (Ed.)
4   In the fourth century B.C. Herostratus burned down the Temple of Artemis in the Greek town of Ephesus and loudly and proudly took responsibility for the deed in hope of achieving fame. The Ephesians responded by forbidding the mentioning of his name upon penalty of death. (Ed.)

lauding or denouncing, otherwise they are nothing but liars and lackeys, no matter how worthy the cause. Alas, one can rarely discern, in the "cultural policy" practiced in our country for well-nigh half a century, any other intention than that of deliberately turning creative people into liars and lackeys.

My second point concerns the hundreds (no, thousands, as has been documented) of artists, journalists and scientists whom the powers-that-be have ostracized, both as individuals and as artists, journalists or scientists—and whenever anyone is persecuted, the persecution *invariably* extends to his family and friends. This is not just an arbitrary extra sanction but the usual practice of a well-run totalitarian system. All these people really were lucky in their misfortune: by the time they were expelled from our culture and banished to the fringes of our society they were already mature personalities and their work had given them a certain amount of experience and a certain reputation. Many have indeed been able to continue working, though this has proved difficult for all and impossible for some (such as actors, film directors, and some of the scientists). Some have actually produced their very best work only in these unnatural conditions. But we should not forget that the purges were not just a one-off act of retribution by our rulers—they are part of a systematic program, so that this destructive pressure has not lost any of its intensity in the sixteen years since 1968, and in fact the situation in all areas of our culture is deteriorating still further. During that time, under normal circumstances, two new generations consisting of thousands of artists, scientists and journalists would have made their debut yet some have been denied access to the necessary qualifications and to work in the profession, while others have received training which gets increasingly more threadbare and dubious. With the exception of a few doubtful and isolated cases, there is no cultural life in this country (I use the world "cultural" throughout in its widest sense, taking in art and science, politics, the media, human and civic ethics as well as religion), our cultural heritage has been badly distorted and access to it made difficult. And if some young people, despite all these obstacles, do manage to make their laborious way to the beginnings of a creative career, they soon discover that the first (and then all other) step depends on their willingness to lie, to allow themselves to be humiliated and corrupted, that honest toil will forever remain profitless, bringing them nothing but suspicion and strife. Those who happen to be well-known can either proudly keep their good name or use it to obtain certain, often highly dubious, advantages; but what of all those unknown ones who have nothing to offer and on whom the powers-that-be do not have to waste too many carrots, for they are duty-bound to express gratitude even for the stick that is used on their backs. It is in these people, who have never been given the opportunity of working creatively, who may not even realize that this is their true vocation, that I see the chief and the most tragic victims: sharing the unhappy fate of the whole nation, they have had the additional misfortune of being born at the wrong time.

No doubt, given certain propitious circumstances, there are individuals who, being particularly talented and single-minded, occasionally succeed in making something of themselves in this cultural graveyard. The fast-growing "parallel" culture has doubtless given a number of beginners—artists as well as scientists, politicians, and journalists—a certain space in which to develop their creative personalities and even a kind of "public" exposure, though only very rarely could it offer them a proper education or any firm guidelines for their life and art. But unfortunately it is not just a few exceptional individuals who can provide a yardstick for the standards of a culture and guarantee its continuity; rather this yardstick and guarantee are to be found in the frequently despised "average" which might appear grey and uninspiring but which gives the culture its continuity and its ability to blossom. I shudder to think what will happen when those generations who still had this kind of background die out. To say this is not for a moment to forget the injustices perpetrated against individuals, but I want here to warn most emphatically against the physical and spiritual liquidation of the nation, for a nation deprived of its culture ceases to exist.

Now to the questions themselves. Not wishing to repeat well-known facts and proposals, I have linked them together and will concentrate on a particular, and seemingly secondary, problem: any significant improvement in this area (as, for that matter, in any other) would signify a radical change in our situation. Taken from a historical perspective, it is the rule

rather than an exception that various artistic and scientific works should
be banned and their authors persecuted—only in our case this rule has
exceeded the customary measure. But I can find no historical parallel for
one aspect of the situation: the police arbitrarily confiscate manuscripts
that have scarcely been begun, personal diaries and correspondence, documents, archive materials and notes, etc. The confiscation of Karl Kosík's[5] voluminous manuscript of his philosophical work is well-known,
thanks to the international outcry it caused. The Evangelical priest Jan
Simsa was sentenced to eight months' imprisonment because he refused
to surrender to the police a personal letter send to him by his friend and
teacher, the late Professor Jan Patočka. The historian Jozef Jablonický has
regularly had the manuscripts of his studies, notes, card indexes, and scientific literature which he needs for his work taken away by the police.
(With nine house searches each, he and I probably hold the Czechoslovak
record in this respect.) Last autumn, the security people confiscated the
entire *oeuvre* of the Moravian poet, Iva Kotrlá. And just the other day a
court ordered the confiscation of Jiří Dienstbier's writings, which had
been seized during the time he was imprisoned, including all his notes
from the time when he was a foreign correspondent in Vietnam and the
United States in the 1960s. These are just a few examples, and I could add
many more like them.

As to 1): I personally consider this kind of preventative action against
creative people to be far worse and more monstrous than the impossibility of communicating in a normal fashion with the public. Yes, even
than the threat—and the reality—of reprisal by the authorities. I myself
last year lost a manuscript of an essay on the commitment of Christians;
and while I learned to admire those who are able to reconstruct works
destroyed by the police, despite all my efforts I found myself unable to
emulate them.

As to 2): Also from the point of view of the entire cultural community
this eternal uncertainty is extremely damaging. It causes some people not
even to attempt undertaking more extensive work or work that depends

5   Karel Kosík (1926–2003) was a prominent neo-Marxist philosopher. His ad-
     vocacy for democratic change during the Prague spring led to his dismissal
     from Charles University in 1970. (Ed.)

on a great deal of research; instead, they fritter away their talent or their expertise on the occasional undemanding effort. Others hide irreplaceable material which they use to research their project in the apartments of their less endangered friends, to whom they also immediately take each page as it gets written. This is psychologically extremely dispiriting, with moments of creative inspiration effectively marred by dint of technical difficulties. Their working tempo and in the end the quality of the finished work cannot but be unfavorably affected. Not to speak of the irreparable damage which the nation's culture suffers when these manuscripts or personal archives vanish inside offices of the secret police.

As to 3): Without wishing for a moment to suggest that everything (or indeed *anything*) is fine where our state policy is concerned, or that it is in order to send artists and scientists to jail because they are trying to go on working as artists and scientists, I'd like to put forward one or two modest proposals, the adoption of which would help solve this particular problem.

a) The police should simply obey the law which states that when a warrant is issued for the purposes of a house search, the incriminating articles should be described as accurately as possible. For example, "the murder weapon, probably a 7.65 revolver," "jewelry taken from the flat of Mrs Novák," or again, "such-and-such a book or periodical," "correspondence with Jiří Pelikán," "documents relating to the conditions in Czechoslovak prisons," "a pamphlet on the occasion of 21 August"—but not "anti-state written and printed materials" as invariably happens in all political cases. The citizen is thus, among other things, debarred from recourse to the letter of the law, according to which a house search is only to be undertaken if the person concerned refuses voluntarily to give up the objects the police are seeking; neither he nor the police have the slightest idea what exactly it is that is being sought. For this reason the policemen take away everything they consider unsuitable or suspicious (frequently for no better reason than that it is in a foreign language, whether it happens to be a detective story or a typed thesis in mathematics), and that despite the fact that these materials have nothing whatever to do with the investigation. All that is needed to improve this situation is for the Supreme Court to rule that no house search may be undertaken without the objects the police are interested in being described in the warrant.

b) The law should be changed to prevent the security agents confiscating any original written material or document—if necessary, they should have copies made and then could order them to be produced in court.

c) The law should be amended by setting a legally binding date by which the confiscated material must be returned, unless the court has in the meantime ordered its forfeiture. At the same time it should not be possible for the court to confiscate written material and other objects which have no bearing on the case before it.

d) The rules and regulations governing imprisonment and detention should likewise be amended. Insofar as a political prisoner is allowed to write anything at all (apart from censored letters to his family), such writings are taken from him and, in all probability, destroyed. In keeping with time-honored European traditions, and out of mere respect for human beings, a prisoner ought to have his writings returned to him when he is released on expiration of his sentence.

e) Lists should be published, or some clearcut definition arrived at, of literature which, for example, it is prohibited to import from abroad, to own, or to lend to others. (Or let the Czechoslovak delegation officially deny the existence of such lists and the sanctions Czechoslovak authorities implement where literary works are concerned.) Even though this itself, *nolens volens,*[6] is to accept a situation which is immoral and which goes against both the letter and the spirit of the Helsinki Accords and the later agreements reached in Madrid, I base my request on the fact that citizens can defend their freedom and dignity much better under laws, no matter how strict, rather than a situation of complete arbitrariness.

As to 4 and 5): We find all expressions of solidarity extremely valuable. Every instance of pressure upon the Czechoslovak government urging it to behave in a more humane fashion and to show greater re-

6   Literally willing or unwilling, or "like it or not." (Ed.)

spect for culture is helpful to us. It would therefore be good if, at the European Cultural Forum, it was emphatically pointed out that in a number of cases (and perhaps most glaringly in the area of religious freedom and in connection with the cultural activities of the faithful, many Czechoslovak citizens have been imprisoned for importing, duplicating and distributing—or even just possessing—religious literature, for independent educational efforts, for cultural and educational work with young people, for producing works of art, etc.) Czechoslovakia has infringed the agreements concluded in Madrid. Those who show their solidarity should not allow themselves to be put off by the seeming indifference of the Czechoslovak government to their complaints: in fact, whenever there is a determined protest by the international public, the Czechoslovak authorities almost invariably ease up, and for every instance of exemplary repression there are at least ten others which are not resorted to for fear of the effect this would have on Czechoslovakia's image abroad. As regards positive steps taken by foreign cultural institutions or individuals, I do not believe in various boycotts or in preconditions being placed on mutual relations. On the contrary, there should be extensive official contacts, but it should be seen as a matter of course (and insistence should be made on reciprocity, because Czechoslovak delegations in the West do so automatically) that the official guests have a right to meet whomever they choose, as well as to point out to their hosts that such-and-such an individual ought perhaps to have been invited to an official banquet rather than languish in prison. It is equally beneficial for cultural agreements to be signed, but they should never be phrased in such a way that the Western partners are then forced to accept persons or topics chosen by the other side, while the Czechoslovak state is in a position to select according to its own ideological (and police) criteria, to keep secret from its citizens names and events which come up at this international forum on the exchange of information and culture if it finds them not to its liking. It would be ideal if Czechoslovakia could be accorded some kind of cultural "most favoured nation status" removing various bureaucratic complications as regards authors' fees, taxes, students and scientific grants, employment of artists and others (paid and properly secured by written agreement) across state borders, etc. This would not mean any great sacrifice for the West, but it would serve to do away with an important factor which contributes to the discrimination practiced against independent culture in our country.

June 1985

31

Concerning the Imprisonment of Juveniles

The following reflections and findings concern exclusively male juveniles imprisoned in the Czechoslovak Socialist Republic. They rely above all on my experience from my involuntary stay of over two years (from April 1981 to May 1983) in the Reformatory (NVÚ) in Libkovice near Most.[1] Since, on orders from above, I had to be isolated from fellow prisoners, I was kept for almost the whole time in the reception facility.[2] Thanks to this I became personally acquainted with everyone who at that time entered the prison (which means the entire population of the camp, for the day I was released I had, I think, the third lowest number[3]). I also had access to their basic personnel files.[4] The liquidation of the stricter Reformatory in Opava was completed

---

1   NVÚ is the acronym for Nápravně výchovný ústav which can refer to a particular prison facility or complex of buildings—in this essay it usually refers to the juvenile prison or reformatory in Libkovice. In these instances it is translated as *reformatory*. However, it can also refer to the prison system in general—in those instances the acronym appears in the text. (Ed.)
2   Benda was transferred to this juvenile prison in April of 1981 because the state wanted to keep him away from both his fellow dissidents (e.g., Václav Havel, Jiří Dienstbier, and Petr Uhl) and from adult prisoners more generally. They also wanted to isolate him at this facility in particular (and thus prevent him from exerting any influence on these inmates), so they housed him in the "entry" section where newcomers were held for a short, provisional time and only thereafter housed with the rest of the inmates. (Ed.)
3   Each prisoner was assigned a number upon arrival. Benda having the third lowest number upon his release means that he had been at the prison longer than everyone save two other inmates. (Ed.)
4   Conditions in this section of the prison were better as were the prison staff. A psychologist employed in this "entry" section befriended Benda and even grew to depend on him for advice about where to place (with which class of

during 1981 and the remaining prisoners were transferred to Libkovice, which became the main camp for juveniles in Czechoslovakia. With some other eyewitnesses, I had the opportunity to consult the earlier conditions both in Libkovice and in Opava, whereas I have "no" information at my disposal on the situation after May 1983.

All the numbers given below are only of a general and illustrative nature, due not so much to a lack of precise statistical data as to their rapid fluctuations at imperceptible time intervals. Factors such as the short average period of punishment, transfers to I.NVS[5] after reaching the age of eighteen, moves from Opava after its closure, and the major impact of individual amnesties and so on, played a role here. Apart from around 400 juveniles, there are around 100–150 adult prisoners in the Libkovice Reformatory (auxiliary camp personnel, heads of crews, skilled workmen) whose issues I completely leave aside here. Around 1,500 juveniles passed through during my stay; I will try to relate my conclusions to the whole of this group. I rely on my interlocutors (both during my confinement there and after), and rather than treating in detail the general problems of imprisonment in Czechoslovakia (the mindless drilling; the vacillation between the repressive concept and the educational one, which leads to pure formalism; the totally false image of social reality which virtually prevents the re-socialization of prisoners; illegality and cruel treatment; and exploitation at work), I will focus on the differences from the adult situation.

Relatively positive points

I have been unable to ascertain any case of undoubtedly political persecution, and even exceptionally hard or clearly unjust punishments were rare.

 inmate) juveniles at the facility. This is why Benda would have had access to the files. (Ed.)

5 NVS is the acronym for Nápravně výchovná skupina. This refers to the category of the correctional regime employed at a particular prison. "I" was the mildest and "III" the harshest from the standpoint of such things as letters, parcels, visits, etc.—thus an III.NVS institution would have been for the most hardened criminals. Juvenile prisons or reformatories stood outside of this classification system, hence upon reaching the age of eighteen a juvenile would have been transferred to an I.NVS facility. (Ed.)

It can be estimated, on the contrary, that where the wording of the law lays down a sentence of half the adult rate for juveniles, the measure actually used is approximately one-third. One peculiarity is that, provided the crime involved is not one of the worst,[6] the courts often, even repeatedly, give only a suspended sentence, even if the offense took place within the previous probationary period. That creates a completely chaotic situation (both for the person concerned and for possible statistics), as the juvenile usually comes to the Reformatory with a relatively minor punishment which, with the gradual accumulation of suspended sentences, can grow to become a multiple of the original sentence.

As far as the quality and quantity of food is concerned, it is immeasurably better in the Reformatory than in adult prisons. The selective principle (in itself immoral) is applied, but in a much more acceptable form; large portions are not a reward and a privilege but a basic right which can be reduced only as a punishment.[7] Work standards are also visibly lighter and approach those in civilian life.

The juveniles are not treated gently (with the best will in the world it is often not possible), nevertheless, that blind brutality well-known from other camps hardly ever occurs. If in other institutions there is a predominance of highly mentally disturbed people among warders, with a lax minority which finds itself temporarily in this profession due to some external advantages, in Libkovice the former occur only occasionally (unfortunately sometimes in high positions), while the latter predominate. In addition, the group of persons who consider their work to be meaningful and want to achieve something is not insignificant here. It is true that this group does

---

6   Naturally, theft is very frequent and problematic: the law does not discriminate between someone who forcibly divests his neighbor of a packet of cigarettes and someone who deprives him of all his property. The criminal act of sexual abuse can also cause a problem with the gypsy element of the population, with its different cultural paradigm; two people (by our standards underage) can live together more or less as a couple from the age of thirteen, but as soon as one of them reaches the age of fifteen, he or she becomes a serious offender. (VB)

7   The selective principle was the practice of providing different quantities of food rations for different prisoners. In adult prisons the size of one's rations was often tied to the fulfilment of work norms. (Ed.)

not have a very long lifespan; however, unlike their "lax" colleagues at other NVÚ institutions, they do not leave because their moderate methods have compromised them in the eyes of their superiors, but rather because a series of failures has convinced them that their actions are in vain, and they either become indifferent or leave for another career. The cultural level of the warders in Libkovice appears to me pronouncedly higher than in other NVÚ institutions (without regard to the nominal educational level which I am unable to compare and which can often be exceedingly misleading); many of them have a secondary and tertiary education.

Relatively negative points

In cases of juveniles especially, the investigating authorities often do not bother about finding proof, but rather immediately, in the first days, force a confession which they subsequently and formally garnish with some material evidence. In the case of virtually all juveniles there is a sheer lack of awareness of the law connected with this; they don't have even that natural instinct of wily criminals who know at least that "silence is golden" and that one has to use every possible means of defense and delay. Whatever a juvenile does (even after thorough and repeated instructions about how to defend themselves) is always to the detriment of their status; utterly helpless when face to face with the judicial system, they find their only way out in giving the nod to every leading question and vague promise—which the investigators and the judge blatantly misuse. Unfortunately the defense counsel (in these cases defense is always mandatory and almost always *ex officio*) often follows the line of least resistance in preference to their professional honor (and to be honest, it is almost impossible to get a juvenile to subject himself to the defense strategy adopted) and contents himself with purely formal, indifferent participation. Attention also has to be drawn to the fact that the juveniles' perception of time (future and past) is as a rule reduced to a few short hours or at most days. Their reliable motivations include a proffered cigarette or threatening slap; imprisonment prolonged or shortened by a year, however certain, is simply a chimera without interest if it's not going to be decided for several months. That plays an essential role not only in the investigation but also in the "re-education process" in the camp. In the absence of a radical transformation of the way the juveniles' time is spent (I don't know how such a transformation would occur) and as long as their re-education is based on a system of rewards and punishments (every other system anticipates an individual approach which is impossible under existing conditions), it will necessarily be ineffective. To be effective, the formulae "an increase in pocket money or solitary confinement[8] next month" and "release on parole or an additional punishment next year" must be replaced by the formulae "more food or a ban on smoking this evening" and "a film screening or duty on Sunday." As I have already indicated, the same applies in relation to the past; as a rule, juveniles have only very vague awareness of what criminal offense they committed and for how long they were actually sentenced. If the letter of the law, which provides impunity for those who "are not capable of understanding the point of the prosecution" were strictly followed, a large number would have to be released immediately. And that is without regard to some isolated cases where it is clear to the layperson that the person concerned belongs in a psychiatric facility or an institution for the mentally handicapped, not in prison.

In the years in question the chronic overcrowding of the camp was an exceptionally burning problem; capacity constantly hovered around the minimum cubic meters per person laid down by the Code of Sentencing. Due partly to this and partly to the unofficial hierarchy among of minors (valid even in the shower), combined with a lack of basic cultural habits among many, the level of hygiene is deplorable and the number of dermal and ulcerous infections (often with secondary septic complications) is alarming and always on the increase. I cannot deny that the medical service was professional in its endeavors; it was more humane and not so subservient to pressures of various interests "from above" as at other camps. However, its effectiveness was to a large measure limited by the fact that it had to face an enormous onslaught from both faked and deliberately induced injuries and illnesses (unfortunately, young people are both unusually resourceful and extremely hardened in this direction). Moreover, the prescribing of a large number drugs is ruled out in advance because of their possible abuse (more on this later). Juvenile apparel is shockingly

8   The Czech word "díra," here translated as "solitary confinement," literally means "hole." (Ed.)

inadequate; they receive hardly any winter clothing and are forced to spend long periods in bitter frosts being counted ("roll calls") and then working for days in unheated workplaces in only shirtsleeves and light canvas overalls. That means a choice between bare-faced disobedience of the rules (wearing track suits, pajamas or some other stolen or illegally obtained item of clothing beneath the overalls) or half-freezing to death every day.

The working arrangements for juveniles form a separate chapter. All their workplaces have to be within the guarded area of the camp. Given these circumstances, together with their inadequate qualifications, low output and absolute indifference to the quality of work forcibly performed, companies' interest in cooperation is negligible (which is very different compared with the situation of adult prisoners; entire branches of the economy are dependent on their work, and moreover profit from it). If businesses do assign their outlying workplace to the Libkovice Reformatory, it generally involves the least popular share of production. Deliveries are irregular, frequently "there is nothing to do," while at other times the young people are literally flooded with work and material—if this method has any success at all in instilling some kind of working morale, then it is its most debased form. Machinery is minimal, outdated and unreliable, and there is a chronic shortage of work and safety aids. I consider the situation to be at its most shocking where safety at work standards are concerned. Businesses try to economize in this sphere, and the generally cramped working space plays a role in addition to the circumstances mentioned. Almost every day there is a slight or more serious work injury (most frequently the amputation of fingers or part of a limb). Even fatalities have been recorded in the past. Much of it can be attributed to deliberate self-harm or gross negligence but there is a disproportionate amount even of the doubtlessly unintentional injuries. Moreover, in some workplaces, chronically flooded with materials and hermetically sealed because of the danger of escapes (of which there are many, although for the most part merely demonstrative without the least hope of success), a fire or other accident would almost inevitably turn into a tragedy, possibly with dozens of fatalities.

A reformatory should provide juveniles with the opportunity to acquire or complete a basic or middle school education, an apprenticeship in various fields, or success in various vocational courses to the broadest extent possible. However, two obstacles, virtually impossible to overcome, mean this remains only a paper ideal: first, the young person would have to have an exceptionally long sentence to complete an entire cycle of school or apprenticeship; secondly, participation in such interesting and, for their future life, useful vocational courses (such as welding, forklift driving, machining, etc.) depend on them being over eighteen. There are however other, much less innocent, obstacles. Above all, nothing must interfere with the exploitation of the youngsters, and therefore study and professional training have to take place outside working hours and without any kind of respite—that obviously limits the interest and quality of the results achieved. Further, not only is funding unavailable—neither is there any willingness or organizational ability to create a system enabling juveniles to complete an education they had started, and in which they were often quite advanced (whether middle school or in various vocational fields). When it comes down to it, the whole system of continuing education and vocational training is extremely unpopular, limiting itself exclusively to the completion of basic school[9] and a few courses (for example, separating ferrous metals for Kovošrot[10]) whose value is completely spurious beyond the camp gates. Unfortunately, I don't know how the extension of compulsory schooling to ten years in 1984 was reflected in this situation.

Actual state: the juveniles' own guilt

In spite of the above-mentioned advantages, life for the average juvenile in Libkovice is much harder to bear than the life of a prisoner in any other camp. This is not directly the fault of the camp authorities, maybe not even indirectly, but the fault of the fellow-prisoners. The brutality among them is unbelievable; no one even stops to look at a bloody nose—it has to be a broken jaw or fractured skull to be investigated more widely. Homosexual relationships are common; it belongs almost to "good manners" that they are forced by brutal violence and humiliating conditions in every respect.

9   Basic school encompassed first through eighth grade (children 6–15 years old) and was compulsory. (Ed.)
10   Literally "Metalscrap"—a company collecting metal scrap. (Ed.)

The juvenile is usually "relieved" of his modest personal property (parcels from home, purchases out of his pocket money) the moment he gets it. So a large part of his work production for the most part benefits someone else.

In every other camp, alongside the officially imposed hierarchy, there exists a spontaneous hierarchy and organization of the prison community (self-administration), often also in some sort of symbiosis with the former. We should not be under any illusions regarding it; it is an unjust system, cruel and completely indiscriminate in its means, especially in encounters between individual clans. Ultimately, however, it is a system which serves for everyone's survival under inhumane conditions. The survival may be very uneven; nevertheless, acceptance of even the most inferior place in the unofficial hierarchy brings not just slavery and various humiliating services but also the right to a reward or at least protection. It is, in its way, a kind of feudal relationship: the "seigneur" has his first night rights and definitely exploits his "clients"; if, however, he does not want to jeopardize his own position, he has to leave them a fair reward or share ("wet their beaks" as the mafia saying goes) and above all has to make sure that his own protection (with regard to other "lords" and "kings," but also to the warders) does not turn out to be ineffective. The "lord" mustn't have too sensitive a conscience and undoubtedly lives more luxuriously than others; however, his position does not allow him to just "to laze around" (that possibility is reserved for some prisoners in a more inferior position)—not only because he is always under threat from the competition but also because he is weighed down by a real responsibility for the whole of his "clientele." Among juveniles, all that remains of this somewhat abnormal and immoral but nevertheless functional hierarchy is a mere horrible remnant. Without any selectivity, without any sort of rules, and often from mere arbitrariness, packs of juveniles terrorize the whole of their surroundings and each other as well. Compared with adult camps (eternal pariahs exist even there, mostly people handicapped in body or mind, some of the "buggers"[11] and also some political prisoners cunningly proscribed by the prison administration—but those are mere exceptions proving the rule), the principal difference is that brutality is not used merely to achieve conformity and respect for the unofficial hierarchical layering, but rather as an aim in itself—anger and despair wreaking themselves directly on objects in easy reach—on fellow prisoners. Conformity here is just as small a help as non-conformity; perhaps only strong fists and a gang of friends from outside can provide some sort of protection. If a sociologist or an ethnologist wanted to study a truly primitive, barbaric community he should look at Libkovice first, rather than the Amazonian jungle. If someone doubts the existence of hell, he should have himself locked up as a juvenile.

Actual state: society's guilt and that of the political power

The worst criminal offenses can be committed by juveniles too: murders (sometimes serial murders or exceptionally cruel ones), brutal rape (sometimes with injury to health and lifelong disability) and so on. In many cases (surprisingly, not all) and a not insignificant percentage of others it is absolutely plain that the offenders' depravity has reached such a level that even a partial correction cannot be reasonably expected—with all probability their future life will be spent going from one prison to another, until they land permanently in Valdice.[12] I do not dare to try to settle the question whether such a fate among people so young has always been unavoidable or whether the failure of society and the relevant state authorities has sometimes made a decisive contribution. I am, however, relatively competent to judge the conditions under which they are punished (I was for some time assigned to them as a team member, so this is not secondhand information). These juveniles are placed in a special division (set up in Libkovice after the closure of Opava, where it had existed from time immemorial) which is deliberately isolated from the rest of the camp and has a very

11 This slang term (in Czech, *prcačkář*) is generally used for sexual delinquents. However, in the prison community the automatic degradation connoted by the term does not relate to common rape (justly so, since with most of them guilt is extremely doubtful and a not insignificant number are simply the unjust victims of the idiosyncratic "Czechoslovak divorce"), but rather only to those committing criminal sex acts with relatives or children and to homosexuals. (VB) [By "Czechoslovak divorce" Benda refers to a tactic of Czech wives accusing their husbands of rape, which would speed up divorce proceedings. (Ed.)]

12 A prison housing the very worst offenders. (Ed.)

tough internal regime, essentially identical with imprisonment. It is a debatable solution, nevertheless I am not at the moment able to propose anything better—maybe only that the criteria for inclusion in this section, such
as the seriousness of the criminal act and the length of punishment, should
be applied in a less formal and automatic way. The first serious error made
by the prison administration is to include in this special division juveniles
who have repeatedly or to a serious extent breached the camp regime elsewhere (in practice mainly the "runaways"). As I mentioned already, those
who resort to flight (mostly just hiding somewhere inside the camp with a
completely vague idea of what to do next—or alternatively making a spectacular attempt to climb the barrier fence under the eyes of the guards and,
from fear of the dogs or of being shot, give up immediately) and similar
demonstrative acts are exclusively the mentally or physically weaker individuals incapable of bearing the pressure of conditions in the camp. They
try to draw attention to their predicament in this way (the frequency of
these attempts is inversely proportional to the length of the punishment;
not infrequently they carry it out a few weeks or days before being released,
which of course lengthens the sentence by months or years). They thus
automatically find themselves in a much more aggressive and ruthless environment. Another serious error of the prison administration is that the
whole regime of the special section and its method of intervention (or
rather nonintervention) in its internal conditions is dictated above all by
fear. The fear is not entirely irrational: some of the youths who have received the maximum sentence (ten years or close to that) like to boast that
knifing some prison warder is hardly likely to make their situation worse.
The recent tragedy in Opava, which I cannot describe here in detail, as well
as serious incidents in Libkovice, are evidence that as far as these threats
are concerned, it is not a long step from words to deeds. A man for whom
all hope is gone and whose actions are dictated purely by hate can be a burden on society and very difficult to manage. And if the law does not allow
his permanent solitary confinement, he becomes a burden on those who
are forced temporarily to share his earthly damnation. The outcome of the
two errors of prison administration mentioned above is that inside the
Libkovice hell there is a sort of super-hell where those who still nourished
a spark of hope and in their own naïve way sought a different remedy from
beating and sexual abuse often find themselves. It is exactly the beating

and sexual abuse that remain to them—this time guaranteed and on the daily program.

The prison administration does not bear the blame for the other problems I try to touch on here, nor do the imprisoned juveniles themselves: responsibility here falls unequivocally on society, and since this means society administered under a totalitarian system ("the dictatorship of the proletariat," "the leading role of the party") and with a claim to the guise of science, then above all on the political powers.

Despite the fluctuation of other indicators, the proportion of more than half the juveniles in Libkovice being of gypsy nationality does not change. Even in camps for adults, the number of imprisoned Gypsies (ten to fifteen percent) greatly exceeds their indicated share (about three percent) of the population as a whole; for it to be fifteen to twenty times higher among juveniles is appalling and allows only two explanations. One is that Gypsies are by nature rogues and all of them deserve to be locked up (or exterminated straight-off). I indignantly reject this racist explanation, not only for ideological reasons, but also on the basis of the considerable experience I gained from over four years locked up with my gypsy brothers—those experiences were sometimes excellent, sometimes terrible, maybe not better, but decidedly not worse, than with my white-skinned neighbors. Or (*tertium non datur*[13]) all the attempts of our political authorities to assimilate the gypsy element of our population or to create an independent cultural environment for it have completely failed. In that case almost all Gypsies are imprisoned unjustly, their alleged criminal acts not based on the specific facts of the case, but in that the cultural pattern of their behavior has not succeeded in being fitted into the paradigms required by the established power. To trivialize: in a certain cultural context, vagrancy (termed "parasitism" in law), theft or breach of customs regulations can be serious criminal acts; with regard to a *nomadic* nation which considers freely ranging hens as natural prey and smuggling horses as one of the main sources of livelihood, the application of these paragraphs is not so much an act of justice as genocide, or at least cultural hostility.

Seventy to eighty percent of young "white" delinquents (with Gypsies this number is apparently considerably lower) have spent years (or even

13   A Latin idiom meaning there is no other alternative. (Ed.)

most) of their lives in children's homes of various types. This proportion is alarming and evidence of a deep problem, if not of the absolute failure of the social care of those children for whom parental care is lacking or inadequate. Unfortunately, I do not have the statistics available on the basis of which one could convincingly overturn the claim that blame should not be attached to the system of social care but rather to the children being predisposed to crime (whether genetically or through erroneous family up-bringing at a tender age). Thereby they necessarily find themselves first in a "reform school" and later, at the age of legal responsibility, end in prison. However, indicators speak against this hypothesis; it seems that the distri-bution of ages in which juvenile delinquents first find themselves in social care institutions is relatively even across the scale, beginning with nurseries. I am personally convinced that statistics could demonstrate that the level of depravity of juveniles and the seriousness of their criminal acts are di-rectly proportional to the length of their stay in children's homes and sim-ilar institutions (that is, inversely proportional to the age when they were first admitted). I can state with absolute certainty that a considerable part of the brutal and immoral practices I indicated as being characteristic of the cohabitation of the Libkovice juveniles were actually imported from the children's homes. Mainly just from a few of them; maybe there are even those from which no future delinquents are recruited and which therefore escape our scrutiny—I would like to hope so. I do not think I would de-scribe conditions in Libkovice in too rosy a light; nevertheless, I know sev-eral cases when juveniles, "released" from prison and escorted straight back to children's homes, immediately committed otherwise pointless criminal acts with the simple aim of avoiding having to live in the home and to stay in Libkovice till they reached their maturity. It is evidence of the sad truth about what society can offer abandoned or problem children—having proudly liquidated the care provided by the Church and by private chari-ties!

Approximately one-fifth of the juveniles are officially registered with (non-alcoholic!) drug dependence at various levels. More than half the ju-veniles admit previous experience with various drugs—with classic hard drugs only exceptionally, far more frequent is the abuse of some medicines and their combination, or inhaling intoxicating substances. Even in prison conditions (and with the threat of hard disciplinary punishment), at least ninety percent of juveniles look for, and make use of, every opportunity to take drugs. All these frequencies are so high that they cannot be explained by mere natural inclination or misplaced curiosity. These too are an indictment of a society that is not able to offer the rising generation any other solace or hope than inhaling the vapor of some chemical substance.

July 1986

32
A Critique of "The Idea of a Christian State"

It is very difficult to be precise in defining the pertinent objections, as the text is itself extremely imprecise and amorphous.[1] The situation is further complicated by the fact that the version published in *Rozmluvy* (7/87), which is all I have at my disposal, has abbreviated the essay precisely in the most contestable passages. One example is the extensive passage about contemporary fundamentalist Islamic states which, for all its formal distance, does not deny a certain sympathy for similar theocratic solutions; then there are details of a future "Christian" regime involving the obligation to work, including workbooks and strict penalties for "parasites" (I should note here that even the harsh rule of the medieval feudal states fully respected the existence of those who were "unclassifiable and unwilling to be classified"—Gypsies and Jews, actors, comedians and troubadours, wandering students, mendicants and beggars; although these people had virtually no rights, privileges or prerogatives and corresponding social prestige, they were nevertheless free of obligations and enjoyed various freedoms going far beyond the capabilities of modern liberalism).

Nevertheless, I will try to make a critique, arranged as far as possible in ascending seriousness:

1) As a layman, I do not feel competent to correct the historical references of a professional historian. (Nevertheless: is the number of victims of the Jacobin reign of terror in one year really the same as the number of victims of the Spanish Inquisition over 300 years? Such an equation of numbers is very questionable when it is not clear what is included. The number of victims of the Jacobins' judicial terror is given

1   The text is Karel Bor, "Idea státu křeťanského" [The Idea of a Christian State], *Rozmluvy*, No. 7 (1987), pp. 73–99. (Ed.)

as 4000—are these victims of the terrorist practices of the civil war, or war casualties as a whole? It is the same with the Spanish Inquisition: are the difficult centuries of the *Reconquista*—when the nature of the Inquisition's terror was national and cultural much more than religious—included or omitted? Is the cruel and unsuccessful pacification of Protestant currents in the Netherlands included or omitted? And is the Conquista of the Americas—about which I do not want to express an unequivocal judgment but which nevertheless undoubtedly had resulted in millions of victims —also taken into consideration?)

2) It is extremely unconvincing to see proof of ancient Christian tolerance in the fact that, after Constantine initially recognized and subsequently established the Church, it still took several decades before pagan cults were definitively forbidden (and I consider it completely unfair to refer to the fact that these cults were marked by ritual prostitution, or that for some time they were still tolerated in remote regions).

3) I consider the author's concept of the essence and origin of human rights and democratic principles to be on the one hand superficial, on the other protestant and tendentious (especially in his admiration for the American constitution with its "right to happiness" which is extremely tricky and, thought out thoroughly, godless).

4) Unfortunately the author contradicts himself almost routinely. There are moments when he categorically rules out of the Christian repertoire all violence, blood-spilling or even just artifice, but in the next paragraph he countenances the military and police terror of a (Christian) government and nostalgically extols the virtues of the Christian warriors of Vienna and Lepanto.

5) I consider one of the most serious inadequacies of this text to be the subconscious ignoring of the Word, or perhaps more precisely, the overvaluation of concrete reality. Bor's vision of a Christian and democratic state in fact proclaims in advance its vulnerability and helplessness with regard to all anti-democratic, destructive and nihilist proposals, whilst however permitting and requiring very totalitarian attitudes towards pornography, promiscuity and other common sins of loyal Catholic citizens.

6) However, I consider the following point to be the root of the misunderstanding and the only serious political (and not only political!) heresy.

Bor quite rightly returns to the "requirement of a Christian state whose laws would correspond to both mediaeval Christian morality and the Christian world view." Personally, I would be more cautious about canonizing the Middle Ages and I would especially recommend more careful distinction between what the laws (infrequent, incomplete and frequently barbaric) actually stated and the corrective role played by the independent spiritual power with regard to the arbitrariness of the secular powers. Never mind; Bor's interpretation is on the whole sustainable and the Middle Ages not the worst mirror we can set to the current unfortunate realities. It is similarly possible to agree that a democratic and just state respecting human rights and freedoms (which are not necessarily synonymous; under certain circumstances these conditions may be more or less irreconcilable—take, for example, the relatively democratic establishment of the Hitler regime and on the other hand the formally very problematic abolition of slavery in the USA) does not have to be, and should not be, a weak state surrendering to the arbitrariness of anyone who decides to do away with these sentimental political principles. Yes, a state founded on these universal principles (which we believe can be fully expressed only through the Christian message) certainly has the right and the duty to defend these principles and to use its power to take harsh steps against its opponents (for this and subsequent observations I emphasize that it is irrelevant whether every single citizen is a Christian and whether Christians form the majority in the state or are only a minority).

Bor, however, immediately makes a poor and inexcusable shift: from a state which firmly defends its humanist principles to a state which is the guarantor of good and some sort of superintendent over the morality of its citizens. This state is allowed to suppress pornography and prostitution, implement thorough censorship and work obligation, and not permit any sort of doubt or debate about basic, unchangeable moral foundations (censorship would undoubtedly suppress the morally questionable casuistry through which Jesus saved the adulteress from stoning, not to mention His frivolous statement that "she will be forgiven much because she loved much"). Moreno's statement[2] is approvingly quoted and commented on: "Freedom for all except those who are evil and those who do not know self-discipline, because they would abuse it."

2   Gabriel García Moreno, President of Ecuador 1869–1875. (Ed.)

Theologically this is utter nonsense. God created us free, including the freedom to sin and to refuse His gift. The New Testament emphasizes that the tares have to grow among the grain up to the end and that it is the role of a judge not of this world to separate them—in addition, it is said many times that even the best of us has more than a few tares within and that, after all, granting mercy belongs to only to God.

Politically it is an extremely dangerous idea that opens the gates wide to arbitrariness and totalitarianism, albeit this time Christian and Catholic (although *corruptio optimi est pessimi*). Who will judge what is evil, and what is not entitled to freedom? God judges our heart; humans are capable of judging deeds only at most, and the state will always be inclined to think that any lack of loyalty to the politics of the ruling party is an evil. Who will decide what is pornography and what is a celebration of the Creator's work?

One cannot approve an antisocial and nihilist ideology whereby the state is simply "organized violence" and hence must be removed as quickly as possible (indeed, without exception these ideologies lead to the pure hypertrophy of the state, to the postulating of its totalitarian claim on man). One cannot approve the liberal minimalist concept of the state as a "necessary evil" (indeed, this concept leads amazingly quickly to the deification and abuse of a state so zealous in implementing very obscure freedoms and rights that in the end it easily succumbs to any kind of malevolence—or, in the best case, denies most of its citizens the right to reason and to distinguish between good and evil). The state is a good and useful institution which we cannot not do without, as long as we do not become completely depraved or as long as it is not replaced by the Kingdom of God. However, like all human institutions (including the visible Church, for that institution is human too), its reason and justification last only as long as it does not fall subject to satanic pride, as long as it respects the measure and order of its operations. There are times when Christians do not realize that the idea of the forced establishment of paradise on earth and the emancipation of man with regard to any kind of higher authority comes from the same crucible as the idea of the improvement of sinners (or elimination of their occurrence) with the help of draconian laws, the idea of Christian dictatorship (totalitarianism): rebellion against the Creator stands at the root of all this, the same longing arbitrarily to correct imperfections in His work of creation. I fear that even Bor is quite unaware of this.

In conclusion I will quote freely the thoughts of one of our Polish contemporaries: "The Christian religion, if it wants to remain faithful to itself, has to preach non-violence. Christian civilization, on the other hand, has to defend itself by fire and by sword."[3] I consider these insights to be very pertinent, and at the same time as a serious reminder for us not to confuse religions and civilization; that is, the Church and the state.

1987

3   See ch. 18, note 8. (Ed.)

33

The Unlawful Practices of State Security

A Letter to the Federal Parliament of the Czechoslovak Socialist Republic, the Justice and Legislative Affairs Committee

Dear Sirs!

My acquaintances have in recent months informed me of at least four attempts at a plot to compromise me, fomented by members of the StB and aimed at the moral or even criminal compromising of my family members and myself. I feel extremely threatened, because I fear that those acquaintances who informed me about these attempts in spite of the threats and promises of the StB, represent only the tip of the iceberg and that I must always anticipate completely unexpected provocations from completely unexpected quarters.

At the start of the school year at the high school attended by my eldest son, supposed criminals gained access to the headmaster and some of the teachers and told them that my son belongs to a gang of drug abusers and alcoholics—it is obviously a dirty slander, but one against which I cannot defend myself well enough, and you are in a much better position to identify and punish the originator.

I do not have enough faith in the legal guarantees of this state to be prepared to expose my informants to the possible vengeance of the StB. Nevertheless, I can state that the secret police have won over a number of my friends and acquaintances, both close and more distant, through threats, promises, or even financial rewards, to provide information about me and my family or to organize a provocation concerning us. Without committing any dangerous indiscretion, I can describe at least one instance—the case of a man who emigrated a few months ago, was maybe even influenced to do so by this pressure from the StB. I'm speaking of the mathematician

Dr. Dan Pokorný, my fellow student from the beginning of the 1970s who until now was occasionally in touch professionally with my wife. He was repeatedly interrogated about my family, for the last time in September of this year, when members of the StB again tempted him with cooperation and proposed that he should offer me a safe illegal channel for correspondence abroad—managed by the StB.

I will allow that I am involved in something that could be described as oppositional political activity. I was even, for my pains, sentenced to many years imprisonment, and completed that punishment. However, like any other citizen I have the right to be protected from intrigues and machinations, whatever their source—so I now appeal to you to guarantee that right, in the name of your official obligations and in the name of your conscience. I am of course aware that the StB is such a powerful institution that more than one obligation fades into the background and more than one conscience falls silent.

In the light of this, I would prefer this letter to be considered an open one.

December 29, 1987

34

A Pilgrimage to the
Blessed Agnes of Bohemia

I would like first to say what preceded the pilgrimage—that is, a meeting with Cardinal Tomášek and the Bohemian and Moravian bishops and ordinaries: last December, a ten-year program of national revival was announced, connected with the millennium of St. Adalbert which will take place in 1997; every year is consecrated to one saint and to one motto or concept from the Ten Commandments, in the course of which 1988 is consecrated to the blessed Agnes and the defense of life.[1] In the context of this plan or program, a countrywide pilgrimage was announced for March 6 with a celebratory Holy Mass in honor of the Blessed Agnes and with prayers for her canonization which should take place in the Cathedral of St. Vitus and be served by Father Cardinal Tomášek. All these facts were then announced (in advance of the event) in pastoral letters, foreign media and so on. The state power regards this matter with extreme displeasure. Furthermore, after initial hesitation, this initiative of the Roman Catholic Church was linked with an extensive petition, probably the biggest petition in Eastern Europe in recent decades, whereby Czech, Moravian and Slovak Catholics as well as many Protestants and even non-Christians call on the authorities for the restoration or fulfilment of religious freedoms, in 31 points. This petition has so far been supported by roughly 400,000 Czechoslovak citizens, and the action is still continuing.[2]

In the last few weeks a number of articles and items have appeared in the press and been shown on television which basically consist of

---

1   On this program see ch. 22 of this volume. (Ed.)
2   See ch. 8, note 1. (Ed.)

attacks against the Catholic Church in general, against individual activists (both lay people and clergy), and especially against the Slovak church. Two weeks ago on Saturday there was an attack mainly on Czech Catholic activists. The authorities then carried out various precautions before this celebratory Holy Mass and countrywide pilgrimage that are remarkable precisely in the way they demonstrate the functioning of totalitarianism.

On the one hand, several hundred uniformed and plain-clothes police attended the mass itself or were present in the vicinity of St. Vitus Cathedral and the Castle; their behavior —including the filming of participants— was nevertheless proper. It seems that the whole celebration ran quite peacefully in a spirit of tolerance and could have given the uninformed foreign visitor an impression of the generosity of the government with regard to this church occasion. On the other hand, the whole mechanism of the totalitarian state's possibilities went into motion several days beforehand. It started with a change in the television schedule so that, completely out of the blue, that morning Czechoslovak Television broadcast an extremely popular feature film. Then they closed the nearest metro station (Malostranská) for the day and rerouted the tram that normally runs closest to the Castle. Finally, they announced an official traffic safety weekend, which meant that checkpoints were set up on all the approaches to Prague, at which not only the roadworthiness of the car and the behavior of the driver were checked, but also the crew of private vehicles and public transport alike (whoever was inside)—and not once, but repeatedly. For example, on Lenin Avenue between the airport and Dejvice roundabout there were four such checkpoints. Thus extensive intimidation and deterrence made it difficult for anyone to take part in the pilgrimage, while all bus excursions were cancelled and the regular bus routes from Bohemia and Moravia reduced to a minimum; and this minimum either never set out or went round various detours. The result was that probably, I can't tell, of the 100,000 or 150,000 pilgrims who would have taken part in the pilgrimage, about 12,000 to 15,000 actually got there.

In spite of everything, the ceremonies took place in a very dignified way. I draw special attention to the fact that Cardinal Tomášek began the celebratory mass with a prayer for those who could not take part in the mass because they had been prevented from doing so. This was understood as a clear allusion to those whom the Communist regime had prevented from attending: for example, a few dozen imprisoned Catholic and civic activists who could not attend the mass because they were on pre-trial detention or under house arrest. On to the ceremonies themselves: after the Holy Mass the Cardinal went into his palace on Hradčany Square; several hundred pilgrims gathered in front of the palace, chanting, and cheering the Cardinal, cheering the Holy Father, demanding a visit from the pope, demanding religious freedom, calling for the need for loyal bishops, and so on. The Cardinal appeared on the balcony several times, even though the authorities had more or less forbidden it, and blessed the crowd. Later he asked them to move away from the palace, a request observed by the believers in a disciplined way, as they held hands and moved away from the palace to form a big circle all round Hradčany Square, singing religious songs, all of them later kneeling on the pavement to end with a closing prayer for the Cardinal.

March 6, 1988

35

The Prague Demonstration
of August 21, 1988

A Reply to a Questionnaire

A demonstration took place in Prague on August 21, 1988, in which, according to es-
timates, around 10,000 people took part. The relative size and assertiveness of the
event surprised not only the security organs but also—which is very interesting—the
representatives of independent civic activities and even the demonstrators themselves. It
has to be admitted that after twenty years of apathy and (clearly apparent) indifference
no one ever hoped for such resolute dissent on the part of the Czechoslovak public. With-
out overestimating the importance of the given events, we think it illustrates a certain
movement in society on which we should reflect.

1) On the anniversary of the invasion,[1] were you expecting Czechoslovak citizens
to express their disagreement with the presence of Soviet troops on our territory and
with the situation created in this country after their arrival?

2) What method of possible protest seemed appropriate to you, that is, adequate
to the state of society?

3) How and when did you come to know about the event in Prague and how im-
portant do you consider it (if you think it was important at all)?[2]

Most of all, I have to confess that I think the way you have formulated the questions in your survey is unfortunate; it tempts one to pride
oneself on one's own foresight, or maybe heap ashes on one's head for
one's cowardly absence, or construct various "what ifs" rather than make

1   The twentieth anniversary of the invasion of the Soviet and other Warsaw
     Pact troops, crushing the "Prague Spring." (Ed.)
2   This preamble and questionnaire were signed by the editors of the samizdat
     journal *Revolver Revue*, where Benda's response appeared. (Ed.)

a sober evaluation of the events and above all outline an approach for the future. Moreover, I think the preamble to the survey is downright unjust and viewed only from your own sectarian turf. For three years now we have been witness to "such resolute dissent on the part of the Czechoslovak public"—for example, the Catholic part of the public— and often much bigger than this event (in 1985 at Velehrad, 150,000 people whistled the Minister and called for religious freedom; 20,000 people took an active part in the Bratislava demonstration; more than 600,000 signed the petition for religious and civic rights)—and I haven't even mentioned the more modest events which prepared the ground for this change in the social situation.

Re 1): after the publication of the flier by the Czech Children[3] I was expecting more serious expressions of dissent; nevertheless, I was surprised by their extent and especially their civilized course. On the other hand, my forecast that the incompetence of the police in prevention and in action would significantly contribute to the success of the demonstration was completely fulfilled.

Re 2): This method of protest was the best and the only one adequate to the state of society.

Re 3): I heard about events only through listening to foreign broadcasts at my country cottage (in July I received an official [police] warning against travelling to Prague [for the anniversary] and I was again monitored [by the police] on August 20—so on Sunday the twenty-first I preferred to go on a day outing rather than have any more contact with the police).

I consider the demonstration to be of exceptional importance because of the spontaneous appearance of forces outside any kind of specific context. Only such forces can eventually free us from totalitarian powers. However, they can also cause a great misfortune if they let themselves be drawn into a battle they will not be willing to fight!

September 1988

---

3   One of the dissident movements that declared itself in May 1988 with a manifesto "The Return of the King." It had a monarchic flavour while declaring itself non-political. (Ed.)

<h1 align="center">36</h1>

Do Not Create a False Image of Us

Letter to the editor of the *Information Bulletin* of *Czechoslovak-Polish Solidarity*

Friends!

I have been receiving the Information Bulletin of Czechoslovak-Polish Solidarity as an active participant since the "historical" meeting of 1978, and I follow it with interest. Right from the early days of the periodical I have noted with some disquiet the Marxist and left-wing orientation in whose spirit your reports are conceived, and the selectivity of your information about independent movements in Czechoslovakia. I am distressed by this left-wing dominance which reigned after the promising beginnings of Czechoslovak-Polish relationships in the late 1970s; I do, however, appreciate the valuable work of Anna Šabatová[1] and her husband Petr Uhl,[2] and that of Petr Pospíchal,[3] and I respect the right of every journal to have its own profile and angle. Nevertheless, I am not prepared to remain quiet about information carried and obscured in the thirteenth number of the Information Bulletin dated February 7, 1989.

I mention more or less in passing that in his interview, Alexandr Vondra[4]—clearly without any evil intention—makes a number of factually in-

---

1   Anna Šabatová (b. 1951) was a Charter 77 signatory, serving as a spokesperson from January 7, 1986 to January 6, 1987. She was also a co-founder of VONS. (Ed.)
2   See ch. 14, note 23. (Ed.)
3   Petr Pospíchal (b. 1960) was a dissident based in Brno and signatory of Charter 77. He was imprisoned on several occasions and was active in public life after 1989. (Ed.)
4   Alexandr Vondra (b. 1961) was a Charter 77 signatory involved in samizdat

correct statements: Ivan Polanský[5] was not sentenced to half a year but to four years in prison, the trial with VONS did not take place at the end of 1978 but in 1979, and the sentences he gives are inaccurate (Benda received not three but four years, Dienstbier[6] not three and a half but three years, Bednářová[7] three years, and Němcová[8] two years—the last two suspended sentences). There are more imprecisions about people.

Nonetheless, the real reason for my protest is the tendentious "Overview of independent initiatives in Czechoslovakia" on pages 18–20 of your bulletin. It mainly concerns two utterly unfair disparagements.

1) It is untrue to say that Catholic initiatives have not been strongly demonstrated until the last two years. Catholic groups played an important role from the very beginning of Charter 77 and other initiatives (for example, of the ten imprisoned members of VONS in 1979, five were decidedly Catholic in orientation). Charter 77 presented an undoubted inspiration for Catholic initiatives; however, these initiatives had already been developing autonomously for ten years. They far exceed the purely civic activity in their social impact and outnumber it in their achievements. The monthly journal *Informace o církvi* (Information about

activities. He helped organize the demonstrations during Jan Palach week in January of 1989 and was imprisoned on two occasions that year. Since 1989 he has served in a number of governmental posts, including Ambassador to the United States, Minister for Foreign Affairs and Minister of Defense. (Ed.)

5   Ivan Polanský (b. 1936) was a Catholic dissident who was a very active as an underground publisher. In 1988 he was sentenced to 4 years in prison for subversion of the Republic. (Ed.)

6   Jiří Dienstbier (1937–2011) was a Charter 77 signatory, serving as a spokesman from February 8, 1979 to May 29, 1979 and from January 6, 1985 to January 7, 1986. He was also a founding member of VONS and was imprisoned from May 29, 1979 to May 28, 1982. He served as Minister for Foreign Affairs after 1989. (Ed.)

7   See ch. 3, note 4. (Ed.)

8   Dana Němcová (b. 1934) was an organizer and signatory of Charter 77. She had also worked to publicize the fate of the members of the rock band The Plastic People of the Universe, connecting them with many prominent members of the scientific and literary community in Prague. She was also a founding member of VONS and was put on trial in October of 1979 with Havel, Dienstbier, Uhl, Benda, and Bednářová. (Ed.)

the Church, from 1980) is the second oldest and probably the most widely distributed *samizdat* periodical (several thousand copies). No less than half the *samizdat* periodicals (in Slovakia ninety percent) are of Catholic origin and if one reckons the number of copies, this share is much higher (incidentally, *Křesťanské obzory* [Christian Horizons] is a fortnightly not a monthly, as is incorrectly stated). After timid beginnings (1977), Catholic petitions have gathered many signatures (1985: inviting the Pope to visit Czechoslovakia, 27,000; 1986: protest against the liberalization of the abortion law, 16,000; 1988: petition in support of religious and civic rights, 600,000). These initiatives surpass the parallel actions of purely civic initiatives by several orders of magnitude. In the matter of public demonstrations too, the Catholic environment is well ahead: even if we ignore the pilgrimages to Slovakia, which are a permanent source of nervousness to the regime, 150–200,000 pilgrims demonstrated their disagreement with official policy at Velehrad in 1985. The wave of street demonstrations in 1988 which culminated in the events in Wenceslas Square in January 1989 was set off by purely Catholic actions: the national pilgrimage in honor of the Blessed Agnes of Bohemia in Prague Cathedral and the Bratislava demonstration for the appointment of faithful bishops and for human rights (both in March 1988; many thousands took part in these actions in spite of the drastic repressive treatment).

2) The Movement for Civic Freedom (HOS), which you frequently quote in the notes, is, unlike many described ephemeral movements, the first enterprise with an explicitly political articulation (an attempt to link all democratically thinking powers from the moderate left to the moderate right), supported by more than 300 declared activists and a far larger number of agile sympathizers. It was no accident that criminal proceedings were initiated against HOS less than two weeks ago after the publication of its introductory manifesto "Democracy for All"; that nearly all the declared members of HOS were persecuted by the police; and that six leading activists received a prosecutorial warning against further HOS activity (one of them was Václav Havel and this warning was abundantly used in a defamation campaign against him and in the course of his trial). Even so, HOS continues its activities; it was an initiator or co-organizer of a number of occasions of civil disobedience and protest. It began to issue the independent political journal *Alternativa* and for its members the bulletin

Zpravodaj HOS (HOS Newsletter). Numerous regional or specialized HOS political groups and clubs are also emerging.

Please publish these factual corrections to your notes on independent Czechoslovak movements. The vast majority are movements which claim no relationship with socialism and want to have nothing to do with it; only very isolated individuals defend Socialism as something more than a necessary evil which we must accept under the unfavorable real-political and geopolitical situation. Maybe this skepticism regarding Socialism of any kind is an extremity of its own and you intend to polemicize vehemently with it. That is your right; nevertheless, it is not appropriate for the Bulletin of Czechoslovak-Polish Solidarity, with whom we have a shared interest and shared experience, to create an absurd and false image of us.

1989

Notes on Individual Texts

These notes are based on the more extensive ones prepared by Patrik Benda for the Czech edition of this volume. They specify the provenance of the texts and their publication history. An "independent samizdat text" indicates that the essay was circulated as a single text. The essays were often first published in samizdat in Czech journals (domestic or émigré). The notes also include information about relevant circumstances surrounding the origin of a text and indicate when different versions of a text exist. I have also noted when the title of an essay was added by Patrik Benda.

A Small Lesson in Democracy
Independent short samizdat text, Prague 1977. A later copy with handwritten corrections has survived among the author's papers.

From My Personnel File
Independent short samizdat text, Prague 1978. Also in *Svědectví* [Testimony] XV, 1979, no. 58, pp. 273–76. A later undated copy has survived among the author's papers.

They Did Not Pass!
Independent short samizdat text, Prague 1978. Also in *Informace o Chartě 77* [Information about Charter 77] 1, no. 2 (January 15 – February 6, 1978).

Why Hesitate Over a Final Solution?
Independent short samizdat text, Prague 1978.

One Year After Orwell
Independent short samizdat text, Prague 1985. Also in *Informace o Chartě 77* 8, no. 2 (January 11–February 10, 1985), pp. 11–13, where a note is

added at the end: "After this feuilleton had been written there were further changes in the conditions of Jiří Gruntorád's preventive surveillance. A police officer carrying out the surveillance acknowledged that the previous conditions had been against the law and new ones were being set in conformity with the law on preventive surveillance."

Concerning Politically Motivated Repressions

Informace o Chartě 77 9, special number (May 1986), pp. 10–13. Also in *Proměny* [Changes] 24, no. 2 (April 1987), pp. 17–21; Vilém Prečan (ed.), *Charta 77 1977–1989. Od morální k demokratické revoluci* (Scheinfeld-Schwarzenberg and Bratislava 1990), pp. 140–45. Title added by Patrik Benda. The recording of an *Infoch* discussion with Václav Havel, Ladislav Hejdánek, Jiří Hájek and Václav Benda from the end of April 1986 was preceded by four essays which became the subject of the subsequent discussion.

The Church Militant

Lidové noviny 1, no. 4 (April 1988). This volume reprints the typescript version with the author's handwritten corrections found among his papers. The version printed in *Lidové noviny* contains numerous omissions and changes.

Three Important Memoranda from the Czech Primate

Informace o Chartě 77 11, no. 11 (1988), pp. 16–17. Also in *Studie*, IV–V/1988, no. 118–19, pp. 375–76. A typescript with handwritten corrections survives among the author's papers.

A Call from Bratislava

Informace o Chartě 77 11, no. 12 (1988), pp. 10–11. Also in *Informace o církvi* [Information about the Church], no. 7 (1988), pp. 21–22. A typescript with handwritten corrections was found among the author's papers.

The People's Party: Problems and Hopes

Lidové noviny 2, no. 11 (November 1989). A manuscript and a typescript with handwritten corrections were found among the author's papers. The differences between these and the version published in *Lidové noviny* are minimal—the latter appears in this volume.

The Parallel Polis

Independent samizdat text, Prague 1978 (with the heading: "For the spokesmen and signatories of Charter 77"). Also in *Informace o Chartě 77* 1, no. 9 (June 20–30, 1978), pp. 15–20; *O svobodě a moci. 1* [Concerning Freedom and Power] (Cologne and Rome 1980), pp. 101–10; Blanka Císařovská and Vilém Prečan (eds.), *Charta 77. Dokumenty 1977–1989*, vol. 3, (Prague 2007), pp. 260–65. Typescript among the author's papers.

Catholicism and Politics: The Situation Today, its Roots and Future Possibilities

Independent samizdat text, Prague 1979. Also in *O svobodě a moci. 1*. (Cologne and Rome 1980), pp. 111–26; Vilém Prečan (ed.), *Křesťané a Charta '77. Výběr dokumentů a textů*. (Cologne and Munich 1980), pp. 265–79; *Studie*, III/1980, no. 69, pp. 209–23; Václav Benda, *Křesťanství a konzervativismus* [Christianity and conservatism] (Prague 2002), pp. 13–24. An English translation by Paul Wilson is included in John Keane (ed.), *The Power of the Powerless. Citizens Against the State in Central-Eastern Europe* (London 1985), pp. 110–24.

Comments on Some Frequently Heard Comments

Polis a religio. Gratulační septet k sedmdesátinám Josefa Zvěřiny [The polis and religion: a congratulatory septet on Josef Zvěřina's 70th birthday] (Prague 1983), pp. 122–35. Also in *Studie*, II/1984, no. 92, pp. 154–59; Eva Kantůrková, and Josef Zvěřina, *Dialog o víře* [Dialogue about faith] (Munich 1984), pp. 62–68; A typescript survives among Benda's papers.

The Ethics of Polemics and the Necessary Measure of Tolerance

Independent samizdat text, Prague 1984. Also in *Rozmluvy*, no. 2 (1984), pp. 197–209. A typescript with handwritten corrections survives among the author's papers.

A Letter to Roger Scruton

Setkání. Panu profesorovi Václavu Černému k osmdesátým narozeninám [Meeting. For Professor Václav Černý on his eightieth birthday], Prague 1985, pp. 36–55 (as "Odpověď na dopis britského konzervativního myslitele Rogera Scrutona do Československa" [Reply to a letter from the British conservative thinker Roger Scruton to Czechoslovakia]). Also in *Střední Evropa*, no. 2 (1985), pp. 65–76; *Rozmluvy*, no. 7 (1987), pp. 31–41. The letter from Roger Scruton to Václav Havel to which Benda is reacting is published in the same number of *Rozmluvy* on pp. 28–30. Two typescript versions of the letter exist among Benda's papers.

Not Only Moral Problems
Independent samizdat text, Prague 1985. Also in *Kritický sborník* [Anthology of criticism] 5, no. 2 (1985), pp. 25–41 (shortened); *Studie*, IV–V/1985, no. 100–01, pp. 384–97; Václav Benda, *Křesťanství a konzervativismus* (Prague 2002), pp. 39–52.

Back to Christianity and Politics: How to Continue after Velehrad?
Independent samizdat text, Prague 1985. Also in *Střední Evropa*, no. 4 (November 1985), pp. 5–32 (considerably shortened); *Rozmluvy*, no. 6 (1986), pp. 7–37 (shortened with a simplified title: "How to continue after Velehrad?").

Concerning Responsibility in Politics and for Politics
The title comes from the name of an anthology of Charter 77, Prague 1986. The actual letter from "Your young friends" to which the individual contributions react appears on pp. 11–14. A typescript with the author's corrections is preserved among his papers.

The Meaning, Context and Legacy of the Parallel Polis
Independent samizdat text, Prague 1987. Also in Václav Benda, *Křesťanství a konzervativismus* (Prague 2002), pp. 5–11. Translated into English in Gordon Skilling and Paul Wilson, *Civic Freedom in Central Europe. Voices from Czechoslovak* (London 1991), pp. 48–56. Part of a manuscript survives among the author's papers.

The Family and the Totalitarian State
Vokno, no. 13 (Winter 1987/1988), *VV1. Nezávislá revue pro výchovu a vzdělávání* [Independent review for upbringing and education], Prague 1988, pp. 52–61. Two different typescript versions survived among Benda's papers which apparently circulated as independent samizdat texts.

Prospects for Political Development in Czechoslovakia and the Potential Role of Charter 77
Informace o Chartě 77 11, 1988, no. 4, pp. 12–15. Also in *Svědectví* XXI, 1988, no. 83/84, pp. 626–30 (shortened); Blanka Císařovská and Vilém Prečan (eds.), *Charta 77. Dokumenty 1977–1989*, vol. 3 (Prague 2007), pp. 299–302. An independent samizdat text has survived among Benda's papers (with the date "January 1988" added by hand), where however two and a half paragraphs are missing from the conclusion. The longer version appears here.

The Spiritual Renewal of the Nation: A Way Out of the Crisis?
Independent samizdat text, Prague 1988. Also in *Křesťanské obzory* [Christian horizons], no. 12 (December 1988), pp. 14–24; *Střední Evropa* [Central Europe], no. 12 (January1989), pp. 56–71; *PARAF (PARalelní Akta Filozofie)*, no. 10 (1989), pp. 4–20. An earlier version survives among Benda's papers with the title *"Desetiletí duchovní obnovy národa – východisko z výročí jeho katastrof?"* [The ten-year spiritual renewal of the nation – a way out of the anniversary of its catastrophes?] which differs mainly from the later version in its introduction.

Inherent Risk
Independent samizdat text, Prague 1989 (with handwritten corrections by the author). The typescript was apparently prepared for circulation, but it is not clear whether this actually took place. The manuscript also survives among the author's papers.

The Prosecution of Two Roman Catholic Clergymen in Slovakia
Informace o Chartě 77 1, no. 6 (April 22–May 17, 1978), pp. 8–9. Also in *Křesťané a Charta '77. Výběr dokumentů a textů* (Cologne and Munich 1980), pp. 185–86; Milan Kubes and Ivana Šustrová, *Charta 77 k situaci církví a věřících v ČSSR* [Charter 77 on the situation of the Church and believers in the CSSR] (Munich 1987), pp. 137–38. The names of the two clergymen have been corrected.

Poland and Us
Polsko a my (March 1979), pp. 4–6. The title of the essay is the name of the journal itself.

Information on the Activity of Charter 77 Spokespersons and on Forthcoming Materials

Informace o Chartě 77 2, no. 5 (March 23 – April 10, 1979), pp. 2–3. Also in *Křesťané a Charta '77. Výběr dokumentů a textů* (Cologne and Munich 1980), pp. 95–97; Blanka Císařovská and Vilém Prečan (eds.), *Charta 77. Dokumenty 1977–1989*, vol. 3, (Prague 2007), pp. 269–71.

I Do Not Share Your Conviction...

Informace o Chartě 77 7, no. 4 (April 1984), pp. 17–18. Appearing here is evidently the original letter's carbon copy, found among the author's papers. The title was added by Patrik Benda. The letter announcing the cancellation of a signature to Charter 77 is signed (including the address) and dated March 26, 1984.

I Turn to You with an Urgent Appeal

Informace o Chartě 77 7, no. 5 (May 1984), pp. 12–13 (without heading). Also in *Studie*, III–IV, nos. 93–94 (1984), pp. 335–36 (as *"Dopis Václava Bendy mírovému kongresu"* [A Letter from Václav Benda to the peace congress] in the section *"Mírové iniciativy Charty 77"* [Peace initiatives of Charter 77]). The title was added by Patrik Benda.

Notification of Criminal Activity

Informace o Chartě 77 8, no. 7 (May 11–June 3, 1985), pp. 14–15 (as *"Dopis generálnímu prokurátorovi ČSSR JUDr. Jánu Feješovi"* [Letter to the Procurator General of the CSSR JUDr. Ján Feješ]). The title was added by Patrik Benda.

A Besieged Culture

Typescript, Prague 1985 (with handwritten corrections probably by the author). We have taken the title from the book of the same name (see footnote). The introductory questions were sent in English and in Czech, signed with the initials F. J. (= František Janouch) and V. P. (= Vilém Prečan). According to the notes at the beginning and the end of the text, Benda's reply was sent on June 4, 1985 for translation by George Theiner, with the author's postscript: "I note with regret that I have only very loosely kept to the rules of your questionnaire and have hopelessly overrun the stated formats. I therefore leave it completely up to you whether: a) you throw my entire contribution into the wastepaper basket; b) you use only the first part – or, alternatively, the second part; c) you cut it at your own discretion; d) you use my text as an 'individual contribution outside the questionnaire' (perhaps 210 lines would pass muster, with a wink of both eyes simultaneously). Sincerely yours, wishing you all peace and much success, V. B." In the end the entire contribution was published.

Concerning the Imprisonment of Juveniles
O československém vězeňství. Sborník [On Czechoslovak prisons. Anthology.], Prague 1987, pp. 83–94. A typescript with handwritten corrections survived among Benda's papers. After 1989 it was published officially by the publishing house Orbis: *O československém vězeňství. Sborník Charty 77*, Prague 1990 (Benda's contribution is on pp. 92–103).

A Critique of "The idea of a Christian state"
Independent short samizdat text, Prague 1987. Benda's essay is a reaction to Karel Bor (= Radomír Malý), *"Idea státu křesťanského"* [The idea of a Christian state], *Rozmluvy*, no. 7, 1987, pp. 73–99. The text may have "circulated" at least partially in samizdat as Karel Bor reacted with the comment (preserved among Václav Benda's papers): "Nevertheless I regret I must reject the typewritten "Critical thesis for 'The idea of a Christian state'."

The Unlawful Practices of State Security
Informace o Chartě 77 11, no. 1 (1988), pp. 7–8. A carbon copy of the original letter survives among the author's papers.

A Pilgrimage to the Blessed Agnes of Bohemia
Studie, II–III, no. 116–17 (1988), pp. 224–25. The title was added by Patrik Benda. Transcript of a telephone recording arranged by Radio Free Europe on March 6, 1988 and published as part of *"Z pouti k blahoslavené Anežce České v Praze 6. března 1988"* [From the pilgrimage of the Blessed Agnes of Bohemia in Prague 6 March 1988], in the section *"Dojmy přímých a nepřímých účastníků* (2)" [Impressions of direct and indirect participants (2)].

The Prague Demonstration of August 21, 1988
Revolver Revue, no. 11, (1988). The title was added by Patrik Benda. The preamble, "*Ankety RR*" [Questionnaire R.R.], signed by the editors, has been shortened.

Do Not Create a False Image of Us
Typescript, Prague 1989. There is also a manuscript that survives among Benda's papers, but in some places it diverges from the typescript. The typescript version appears here. The title was added by Patrik Benda.

Index

remarkable achievements of, 49
reply to revocation of signature to,
282–283
role of as lightning conductor, 102
second crisis of, 211
signatories of, x, 3, 4, 5–6, 7, 8,
15n4, 18, 21n1, 21n2, 36–37n1,
41n2, 69, 84n5, 87n9, 99n23,
108–109n5, 271, 274–275n2,
275, 276, 324–325n4, 324n1,
324n3, 325n6, 325n8
spokespersons for, ix–x, 10n4,
90, 205, 271, 273, 279–281,
280, 282, 285
subgroups of, ix, 281
ten-year existence of, 26
VONS as supplementary organization
to, xiii, 281
Chartists, 9, 12, 13, 14, 15, 16, 90
Christian and Democratic Union-Czech
People's Party (KDU-ČSL), 44n2
Christian Horizons (Křesťanské obzory), 326
Christianity
"Back to Christianity and Politics:
How to Continue After Velehrad"
(Benda), 140–194
and Communism, xviii
in Czechoslovakia, 29
as having deeply civic dimension,
according to Benda, xix
as offensive religion, 258
Christians and Charter 77 (Křesťané a charta
77), 85
Church Militant, 141
"The Church Militant" (Benda), 32–35
Churchill, Winston, xvi
"Comments on Some Frequently Heard
Comments" (Benda), 75–82
Committee for Social Self-Defense (KOR)
(Komitet Obrony Robotników), 218,
273, 273n1, 274, 275
The Committee to Defend the Unjustly
Persecuted (VONS), ix, xiii, xxiii, 27,
31, 151n9, 281, 325
Communism/communism, xiv, xvi, xviii,
xx, 12, 65, 248, 260–261, 262

Communist Party
Czechoslovak Communist Party, 6,
41, 43, 217, 235, 247
membership in as condition for
employment as philosopher, 9
"Concerning Responsibility in Politics and
for Politics" (Benda), xxi
"Concerning the Imprisonment of
Juveniles" (Benda), 299–311
conservative radical, Benda as, xxi
contraception, 120, 122, 124–128, 132, 134
criticism from the right, 97, 98, 99, 100,
101, 102
"A Critique of 'The Idea of a Christian
State'" (Benda), 312–316
Czech Catholicism, xix, 33, 57–74, 243
Czech Catholics, 62, 64, 74, 277
The Czech Question (Masaryk), 68n6
Czechoslovak Catholic Church, 59, 160
Czechoslovak Communist Party, 6, 41, 43,
217, 235, 247
Czechoslovak divorce, 307n11
Czechoslovak People's Party, 43–45
Czechoslovak Socialist Republic, 39, 44,
271, 287, 299, 317
Czechoslovakia
contemporary political stratification
in, 67–68
fight for freedom, ix
"Prospects for Political Development
in Czechoslovakia and the
Potential Role of Charter 77"
(Benda), 233–239
Roman Catholic faith in, 29
"The Spiritual Renewal of the Nation:
A Way Out of the Crisis?"
(Benda), 240–259

Decade of the Spiritual Renewal of the
Nation, 32, 34, 36, 240, 241, 242, 243,
245, 246, 249, 253, 255, 256, 257, 267
Declaration of Charter 77, xi
democracy, small lesson in, 3–7
democratic forms, according to Benda,
xxii, 207, 208
Dienstbier, Jiří, 280, 294, 299n2, 325